Queer Masculinities, 1550–1800

Also edited by Katherine O'Donnell and Michael O'Rourke
LOVE, SEX, INTIMACY AND FRIENDSHIP BETWEEN MEN, 1550–1800

Queer Masculinities, 1550–1800

Siting Same-Sex Desire in the Early Modern World

Edited by
Katherine O'Donnell

and
Michael O'Rourke

With a Preface by George Rousseau

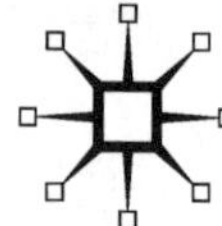

First published 2006 by
PALGRAVE MACMILLAN
Houndmills, Basingstoke, Hampshire RG21 6XS and
175 Fifth Avenue, New York, N. Y. 10010
Companies and representatives throughout the world

PALGRAVE MACMILLAN is the global academic imprint of the Palgrave Macmillan division of St. Martin's Press, LLC and of Palgrave Macmillan Ltd. Macmillan® is a registered trademark in the United States, United Kingdom and other countries. Palgrave is a registered trademark in the European Union and other countries.

ISBN-13: 978–1–4039–2044–7 hardback
ISBN-10: 1–4039–2044–3 hardback

This book is printed on paper suitable for recycling and made from fully managed and sustained forest sources.

A catalogue record for this book is available from the British Library.

Library of Congress Cataloging-in-Publication Data
Queer masculinities, 1550–1800: siting same-sex desire in the early modern world / edited by Katherine O'Donnell and Michael O'Rourke; with a preface by George Rousseau.
p. cm.
Includes bibliographical references and index.
ISBN 1–4039–2044–3 (cloth)
1. Homosexuality, Male–History. 2. Homosexuality, Male–Historiography. I. O'Donnell, Katherine, 1966- II. O'Rourke, Michael, 1976-

HQ76.Q427 2005
306.76'62'0903–dc22 2005047598

10 9 8 7 6 5 4 3 2 1
14 13 12 11 10 09 08 07 07 06

Printed and bound in Great Britain by
Antony Rowe Ltd, Chippenham and Eastbourne

This book is dedicated to the memory of Philip Brett (1937–2002)

Contents

List of Illustrations

Notes on Contributors

Richard Godbeer is Professor of History at the University of Miami, Florida. He is the author of *Escaping Salem: The Other Witch Hunt of 1692* (2004). *The Devil's Dominion: Magic and Religion in Early New England* (1992) and *Sexual Revolution in Early America* (2002). He is currently working on a book: *'The Overflowing of Friendship': Love Between Men in Eighteenth Century America.*

Dan Healey is Senior Lecturer in Russian history in the Department of History, at the University of Wales Swansea. He is the author of *Homosexual Desire in Revolutionary Russia: The Regulation of Sexual and Gender Dissent* (Chicago: University of Chicago Press, 2001), and co-editor (with Barbara Evans Clements and Rebecca Friedman) *of Russian Masculinities in History and Culture* (Basingstoke: Palgrave, 2002).

David Higgs, a Professor of History at University College at the University of Toronto, Canada, has published on aspects of French, Portugese and Brazilian social history and edited the collection, *Queer Sites: Gay Urban Histories since 1600.*

Gary P. Leupp is Professor of History, and Adjunct Professor of Comparative Religion, at Tufts University, where he coordinates the Asian Studies Program. He has taught at the University of Hawaii, University of Michigan and Yale University. His works include *Servants, Shophands, and Laborers in the Cities of Tokugawa Japan* (1992), *Male Colors: the Construction of Homosexuality in Tokugawa Japan* (1996), *and Interracial Intimacy: Japanese Women and Western Men, 1543–1900* (2003), and many articles on ethnicity, gender and sexuality, criminality, urban life and labor in early modern Japan.

Chris Mounsey is senior lecturer in English literature at King Alfred's College, Winchester. Author of *Christopher Smart: Clown of God* (Lewisburg: Bucknell, 2001), a further biography is in progress on Daniel Defoe. Work on gender and sexuality has been published in various journals and the collection of essays *Presenting Gender* (Lewisburg: Bucknell, 2001) and *Queer People* (Lewisburg: Bucknell, forthcoming).

Martin Nesvig holds a Ph.D. in Latin American history from Yale University (2004) and was a Fulbright fellow in Mexico City, where he resides. He is editor of the forthcoming two-volume project*: Local Religion in Colonial Mexico* (University of New Mexico) and *Religious Culture in Modern Mexico* (Scholarly Resources Press).

Katherine O'Donnell lectures at the Women's Education, Research & Resource Centre (WERRC) in University College Dublin. She has published a number of articles on the Gaelic dimension to Edmund Burke's speeches and politics and is currently editing (with Leeann Lane and Mary McAuliffe) *The Palgrave Guide to Irish History*.

Michael O'Rourke is a Faculty of Arts Fellow in the School of English at University College Dublin. He is the co-editor (with Katherine O'Donnell) of *Love, Sex, Intimacy and Friendship between* Men, *1550–1800* (Palgrave, 2003).

Walter D. Penrose, Jr., M. Phil., is an Adjunct Lecturer of History at Baruch College and of Classics at Hunter College. He is a Ph.D. Candidate in History at the City University of New York Graduate Center. Walter is the author of 'Hidden in History: Female Homoeroticism and Women of a "Third Nature" in the South Asian Past.' *Journal of the History of Sexuality* 10:1 (2001): 3–39. He is currently writing a dissertation entitled *Bold with the Bow and Arrow: Amazons and the Ethnic Gendering of Martial Prowess in Ancient Greek and Asian Cultures*. Walter is currently serving a three-year term on the Board of Directors for the Center for Lesbian and Gay Studies in New York City.

Helmut Puff, Associate Professor at the Department of History and the Department of Germanic Languages at the University of Michigan, Ann Arbor, works and publishes on culture, gender, and sexuality in the late medieval and early modern periods, primarily in German-speaking Europe. His latest publications include *Sodomy in Reformation Germany and Switzerland, 1400–1600* (2003) and *Zwischen den Disziplinen? Perspektiven der Frühneuzeitforschung* (co-edited with Christopher Wild, 2003).

George Rousseau was the Regius Professor of English at King's College Aberdeen and is now a member of the Faculty of Modern History in Oxford University. His primary interest lies in the interface of literature and medicine, for which his work has recently been awarded a three-year Leverhulme Trust Fellowship. The author of studies dealing with medicine and the humanities, his most recent books are *Gout: The Patrician Malady* (Yale University Press, 1998), written with the late Roy Porter, *Framing and Imagining Disease in Cultural History* (Palgrave Macmillan, 2003) *Nervous Acts: Essays in Literature, Culture and*

Sensibility (Palgrave Macmillan, 2004), and *Yourcenar: A Biography* (Haus, 2004).

Michael Sibalis is Associate Professor of History at Wilfrid Laurier University in Waterloo, Ontario, Canada. He has published articles on The nineteenth-century French labour movement, the police state of Napoleon I (1799–1815), and the history of homosexuality in France. Most recently he has co-edited a collection of essays with Jeffrey Merrick: *Homosexuality in French History and Culture* (Binghamton, NY: Harrington Park Press, 2001).

Goran V. Stanivukovic is Associate Professor of English at Saint Mary's University, Halifax, Canada. His publications include an edited collection, *Ovid and the Renaissance Body* (2001), a critical edition of *Emanuel Ford's 'Ornatus and Artesia'* (2003), and essays on early modern queerness, drama and non-dramatic literature. His volume of essays, *Prose Fiction and Early Modern Sexualities, 1570–1640* (with Constance Relihan) is forthcoming. He is at work on a monograph on erotic ethnography, travel, and popular prose romances in early modern England, and on a volume of essays on the Mediterranean and early modern England.

Robert Deam Tobin is associate dean of faculty and professor of German at Whitman College in Walla Walla, Washington. He is the author of *Warm Brothers: Queer Theory and the Age of Goethe* and *Doctor's Orders: Goethe and Enlightenment Thought*, as well as numerous articles in English and German on topics in gay and lesbian studies and German culture. He is currently working most intensively on the history of homosexuality in the late nineteenth and early twentieth centuries in Germany.

Theo van der Meer is an independent scholar and author of several books and numerous articles on the early modern history and modern of homosexuality in The Netherlands.

Wilhelm von Rosen obtained his PhD from the University of Copenhagen in 1994 for his thesis on Danish gay history from 1628 to 1912, *Månens kulør. Studier i dansk Bøssehistorie*. He has written articles in Danish and English on Hans Christian Andersen, the politics of gay liberation, and Denmark's gay history. Since 1970 he has been archivist, now senior researcher, at the Danish National Archives.

Preface

George Rousseau

We forget how swiftly our fields of inquiry alter unless we take the long view. When, little more than a decade ago, Kent Gerard and Gert Hekma edited and published their then seemingly mammoth 553-page anthology of essays entitled *The Pursuit of Sodomy: Male Homosexuality in Renaissance and Enlightenment Europe* (a double issue in 1988 of the *Journal of Homosexuality*; 1989 as a Harrington Park Press volume), the countries represented were confined to Western Europe. Even so, the book's span then appeared to be an embarrassment of riches. Britain and the Netherlands were well documented, largely because the available contributors happened to be working on those countries, but there was also discussion of Iberia, Italy, France, Germany and Scandinavia, and two general chapters were called 'overviews.' The Americas were omitted, as were Africa, Asia and the Middle East. Some scholars, even in those dark ages of 1988–89, were wondering about these distant hinterlands in the early modern world but no one then seemed serious about burning bridges to publish research about them. At least no one came forward and no one was included.

All this has now changed. The current volume covers practically the whole terraqueous globe from China to Peru. No country, no geographical region, it seems, any longer escapes the gaze of gay masculinity except the dark heart of the African Congo. Western Europe continues to be represented in fine detail, Switzerland and Denmark included, but it is the chapters on Russia, Japan, Southeast Asia and the precolonial Americas which are new and destined to have the greatest impact by dint of a genuine comparative basis for the further analysis of homosexuality in early modern history. Other books since 1988–89 have discussed Asia and the Americas: one can compile lists of their titles and contents. But it is these ever-larger geographies reaching east of the Baltic and Black Seas and west of the Atlantic Ocean that now permit new dominant strains crying out for comparison. Whatever the basic content is of 'gay masculinity' (and that content is surely pluralist and multi-layered) in the new global village of the twenty-first century, it is surely comparative: a polyphony of attitudes and discourses, codes and practices. For this reason, among others, the great broadening of geographical spread found here must be saluted. Once this book has been read, its contents digested, it will become clear why a Western,

Eurocentric view of gay masculinity – and *non*-gay as well – is now outdated and no longer adequate for the serious retrieval of this field. It would amount to tunnel vision.

What is it that these scholars primarily retrieve? The essays, several written by the same authors who contributed to the 1988–89 venture mentioned above, all imply victims and scapegoats: the *oppressed* and persecuted, omnipresent in these national reappraisals, even if they themselves often cannot now speak, write or be heard. Likewise, for the retrieval of the liberated and emancipated, whether they were first *oppressed* and then allowed to be free, or whether – in much lesser degree – they were permitted to celebrate their diverse sexualities openly without censure. The attentive reader of these essays attuned to the polyphonous texture of historical discourse – especially the voices of the various participants including those who compile the discourse – also hears the din of the imagined, but often silent, voices of the persecuted. They cry out of their forgotten tombstones in the gaps of these pages. They are omnipresent even if unseen and insubstantial. For whatever else these essays amount to in the aggregate, they constitute a history of persecution – and prosecution – far more than a record of liberation. Epochs of extraordinary freedom and licence do emerge in historical moments here and there: late Muscovy in Russia, precolonial Southeast Asian societies, early Hindu cultures. Nevertheless, construed as a block of history 1550–1800 this is primarily a story about the *oppressed*: growing only slightly less so at the end of the period, circa 1800, than they were at its start in the sixteenth century when the arts of alchemy, astrology, black magic, hermeticism, sodomy, and witchcraft were far more commingled than they became in the more secular, if also sunnier, milieu of the Enlightenment. Yet the sad fact, as many of these essays confirm, is that as time marched forward from the Renaissance to the present the sexually persecuted continued to be so in most places: north and south, urban and rural, rich and poor. What differed were the forms and varieties of sexual oppression, and it may be that the new comparative study of gay masculinity, which a book like this enhances so much, is a call to integrate this material into the rest of the historical picture. Stated otherwise, decipher these essays for their rhetorics and vocabularies, for the wide variety of tropes of the *oppressed* – the victims and scourges – and you see that familiar patterns continue to reappear.

The degree to which all these geographical regions permitted gay genocide in the early modern period is noteworthy: Swiss, Dutch, Middle European, Asian, American. All these geographies purged their homosexuals as if the event were *de rigeur* a *rite de passage* without which the particular society could move forward or progress. Until the 1970s, however, it was almost impossible to discuss genocide neutrally and calmly: the subject was too explosive and politically charged, tantamount in some ways to the incredible abuse and exploitation of children today; the last taboo, it seems, in our brave new world in 2005.

Since the 1970s, however, much has been written about genocide and its horrors. But we still cover our tracks when treading delicately over the ground of sexual genocide, especially of the types found in this book. The mass murder of men who have loved other men seems shocking to us, whether in sixteenth-century Switzerland or Nazi Germany, yet continues – even now – to be a politically explosive subject in many quarters. It is asking the wrong question to inquire what it is about countries and their rulers that compels them to murder their homosexuals *en masse*. These new comparative essays demonstrate how much genocide was carried out in the name of religion and purification. Over and over again in these case studies of historical retrieval the subject is murder in the name of purging to cleanse, obliterating to purify. It is as if the anthropologist, among the scholars, is best poised of all to explain why such genocide was then permitted. Surely, the clues to same-sex genocide lie far from the spheres of national character and national stereotype: one doesn't want to be essentialistic on the matter but there must be something almost universal in the human psyche that solidifies itself, from time to time and almost hysterically, behind the empowered prosecutors and murderers. Genocide came early in Switzerland, later – in the 1730s – in the Netherlands, later yet in Germany. Yet in all these places the historical record reeks with the rhetoric of crimes purged, pollutions cleansed, decadence eradicated. It goes too far based on the available evidence to purport that all these devastations of a minority – men who loved other men or abused them – were merely the dark work of Christianity; if not the dirty work of church fathers themselves, then the hangings of those persecutors justifying oppression in the name of the church. The countries without purges and genocides are safer havens than the rest. But even the Netherlands – historically among the most tolerant of places on earth for sodomites and homosexuals – only became 'enlightened' about same-sex masculinity and love about a hundred years ago as the Dutch historians and sociologists have shown.

These illuminating essays also amount to mini-histories of violence: if not of groups pitted against other seemingly identical groups across national boundaries, then of individuals plotting against others. The essays push previous borders further by suggesting to what degree the history of homosexuality has entailed waves of violence: waves large and small, public and private, mostly perpetrating unspeakable acts in the name of traditional Christian doctrines and (in our lingo) developing family values. Yet it is hard to know how to understand the basis for the alleged treachery of homosexuals against church and state – doctrine and tradition – given that so few of them in history ever perpetrated anything palpably damaging; least of all threatening to these civic and religious institutions. If these essays do anything to sharpen our sense of same-sex masculinities in the early modern world, they teach us how much of that record entails an account of violence and perceived vice. The early modern homosexual, even the child sodomite, was not merely an inherent outlaw but a nocturnal bird of prey who had to learn to manoeuvre amidst violence of diverse types as his ordinary *modus vivendi* in a fundamentally hostile environment.

This should not imply that there were no openly gay sub-cultures. There were, as several of these essays demonstrate. Flourishing societies, social clubs, random meetings, informal networks, ritual practices: all existed in varying degrees, in the old world as well as new. It is not the variety and quantity of these networks in themselves that grabs the attention but the complex nature of the desire they embodied that gives pause. The further questions these new essays give rise to pertain to the emotions – the affect – as much as any sodomitical acts themselves. Which passions, for example, were implicated in this wide array of disparate acts occurring in diverse situations? What were the emotional consequences for the individuals involved of indulging or – alternatively – repressing these desires and passions? In what ways were the openly sodomitical subcultures in that early modern world reflective of an unattainable condition of human existence? A great deal has been made by anthropologists of the religious and totemic shame implicated in the act of anal penetration. What, however, are the emotional resonances of this shame and how have they infiltrated the intimate relations of same-sex male relations? How too do men who have *both* been fucked, and not necessarily fucked by each other, relate to one another, in 1600 as well as 1800?

Affect, whether as late Renaissance passion or late Enlightenment emotion, continues to loom everywhere in these essays, even if mutely so. The record of same-sex relations after 1800, or 1850, generally follows the patterns of heterosexual, or at least heteronormative, family arrangements. Before then, in the world of the Renaissance and Enlightenment, affect's role was less clear. These fascinating essays suggest – perhaps in order to accommodate the whole affective domain – that our category *homosocial* continues to be useful for early modern same-sex relations even if it is ambiguous and sometimes palpably confused. It is a category whose time has arrived. Even more so than homoerotic it spans the wide girth of male–male attachments on which any solid history of heterosexuality would need to be constructed. The chapters dealing with Russia, Japan, and Southeast Asia make the point plainly, whether on the wide-open Russian steppes of the Muscovite era or in the suffocating brothels of the Togugawa period. These essays, again and again, entice us to wonder: when did histories of homosexuality become histories of affect? Even if there is a discrepancy between the categories available to us for historical explanation and the common-sense belief many of us harbor that men emotionally involved with one another will be men in love – still, we wonder what roles affect has played in male-male relations. The Russian *probatimstvo*, or ritual brotherhood, is a telling example. It opens up new windows not merely on early modern friendships so crucial to the whole fabric of social life before 1800, but also on the sites where these rituals were played out: in schools, monasteries, churches, clubs, fraternities, and – of course – on land and at sea in the military.

All these authors comment on the nature of their experiences of retrieval: if not explicitly then by implication. And the consensus seems to be that the experience was illuminating for progressing their research and personally exhilarating for revealing something that had not been known before. It is hard not to sense their own degree of freedom in recovering and decoding their particular terrains, not least for the greater 'truths' they have uncovered about the past. Indeed, it would be fascinating to have first-person accounts of what this journey was like for each of the authors. Inevitably models of the West and East, of sexual decadence and sexual purity as well as sexual neutrality, have infiltrated their thinking. Yet the more urgent sense, by far, is the group's collective will to expand their field: same-sex masculinity in the early modern world. It is not merely their idea that histories of sexuality and gay studies have taken off which impresses. These authors also now recognize, each in his own way, that the retrieval of same-sex masculinity entails, as well, the recovery of a history of heterosexuality.

Finally, a coda about the use of the word *queer*. Queer was virtually non-existent in the 1988–89 collection yet appears with considerable frequency here: if not universally than at least in sufficient abundance to cause the reader to take notice and wonder what the new word signifies. The word appears in this book's title. Yet what is *queer*? How should it be defined? What has been its lexical trajectory? How loaded a term is it? Does it get lost in translation? The authors who use it here all differentiate it, in some essential way or other, from its sodomitical and homosexual lexical neighbors. *Queer* is certainly not an equivalent for liminal, ideological, culturelly relative, homoerotic, same-sex homosexual, all the words in this sentence used as adjectives rather than nouns. Nor is queer tantamount to the broad realms of the homosocial or homoerotic: queer appears to denote something wider and more fundamental. Its gesture is to open up rather than close down. Queer wants to be heuristic in ways that its ancestors homoerotic and homosocial once were but no longer are. Nor is queer gay: those who confuse them are bound to give offence. The word queer – based on the letter Q and its riddled place in the history of the alphabet – has profound political edge today even if no one is certain precisely where its nervous energy lies. These essays reflect these diversities and signs, and are stronger for so doing.

Finally, the afterlife of this book. Even the casual browser gathers that the essays are solid. I predict they will be read for a long time. However, it may be less clear what the underpinnings amount to: not merely methodologically but also ideologically. An in-depth comparative study of same-sex queer masculinities before 1800 is destined to open the Pandora's box of sexuality. Life without sex is much less enjoyable than with it; without reproduction life is impossible. Yet virtually every major social-Darwinian commentator since the late nineteenth century has remarked on the advantages to population and other culturally evolving institutions enabled by persons who love those of their own sex. Yet the below essays are not primarily a record of joy but, almost tragically, a catalogue of suffering, silencing, suppressing, murdering. Of histories of homosexuality – and we (the collective authors) hope, heterosexuality – there will be no end. This one will, in turn, be followed by others. The great virtue of this collection is that its geographical sprawl – from the Atlantic to the Pacific, Santiago de la Cruz to Siberia – ensures us (and with only a few exceptions) how monolithically oppressed same-sex groups in history have been. That this should be so must give us pause about the nature of the human condition itself. For what is human nature if it must have been so egregiously intolerant of queer masculinity for the largest part of its recorded history? No adequate answers exist. But one almost hears, in the distance, an aggrieved Terence, the great Roman playwright. He continued to believe that his own humanity was based on one simple fact: that nothing human could be alien to him because he himself was human. Same-sex love was always human. How then did it become so repulsive in human history?

Acknowledgements

The editors would like to acknowledge *The William And Mary Quarterly* for permission to include material from Richard Godbeer's article ' "The Cry of Sodom": Discourse, Intercourse, and Desire in Colonial New England', *WMQ* 52 (1995): 259–86.

The editors would like to thank all at the Women's Education, Research and Resource Centre at University College Dublin for their ongoing support and interest in this project with particular thanks owing to Ursula Barry, the Director, Ailbhe Smyth, Administrator, Jennifer Morawiecki and Dean Mary Lambkin formerly of the Faculty of Interdisciplinary Studies.

David Robinson and Randolph Trumbach were exceedingly generous both in sharing their knowledge of the field and in putting us in touch with other scholars and potential and actual contributors to this volume. We would also like to thank Ian Moulton for sharing his work with us.

Thanks too are due to the staff at Palgrave Macmillan, particularly Daniel Bunyard, Deborah Bennett and Luciana O'Flaherty.

Michael O'Rourke would like to acknowledge the support of a Government of Ireland Scholarship in the Humanities and Social Sciences, which he held between 1999 and 2002, and which greatly helped with his research for this book. He would also like to acknowledge the continuous support of his family for his work, especially the support of his father, who died as this book was being prepared.

Introduction: Siting Queer Masculinities[1]

Michael O'Rourke

Back to the future of the queer past

In many ways this book is a companion volume to a book we co-edited in 2003, *Love, Sex, Intimacy and Friendship Between Men, 1550*–1800,[2] which took queer masculinities and male–male emotional relations as its focus. However it shares, we think, a number of concerns with a recent edited collection published by the University of Wisconsin press, *Queer Frontiers: Millennial Geographies, Genders and Generations*,[3] a book which explicitly situated itself at the cutting edge of the second wave of queer studies. Like the editors of that volume we are interested in queer spaces, queer places, queer histories, and working toward a historical geography of sexuality. In his afterword to that collection, 'Back to the Future', Richard Meyer has much to say which resonates with the rationale for the present volume, and with our collective authors' attempts to write affective histories, to touch their male subjects. Meyer talks about a 'kind of dialogue of desires, an exchange between the present and the past' (348) where the queer present and the queer past touch. He goes on:

> Among other things that dialogue tells us that queerness is not an invention of the 1990s. Attempts to complicate (and multiply) the possibilities of gender and sexuality, to highlight the performative aspects of identity, and to oppose the tyranny of the norm are woven into the historical fabric of gay and lesbian life (349).

This book enacts just such a haptic conversation between past and present and attempts to complicate any simple understanding of early modern masculinity and the early modern sex/gender system during a period which was immensely important because it was a time of transition in both the practice and representation of same–sex relations. We also mobilize the word queer in the book's title in order to signal a radical critique of heteronormativity in the service of producing a more well-rounded history and geography of dissident sexualities and identities in the early modern world. In its summoning of queer sites across the 'terraqueous globe', as George Rousseau puts it in his preface, this book also hopes to suggest 'space[s] of future exploration' (349). We share Meyer's vision of queer history when he states:

> And yet, as the expanding field of gay and lesbian history attests, the queer frontier exists not only in the future but also in the past. At their best, contemporary constructions of queerness enable us to see the past differently, to recover otherwise lost representations, and to renew the collective and creative force of alternative sexualities (349).

The queer history the authors of the following essays retrieve is what Jonathan Goldberg calls 'the history that will be'.[4] Eve Kosofsky Sedgwick has famously argued that 'many of the major nodes of thought and knowledge in twentieth century Western culture as a whole are structured-indeed, fractured-by a chronic, now endemic crisis of homo/heterosexual definition'[5] but the block of time which falls under our view is a culture in which a homo/hetero divide simply was not operant, as Goldberg and others have shown.[6] This is not of course to say that men did not desire other men in the early modern world, nor is it to dismiss the possibility of male–male eroticism prior to the invention of homosexuality, *pace* Foucault's epigoni. It is rather to be more attentive to 'certain social and epistemological changes' in the seventeenth and eighteenth centuries, which paved the way for 'modern erotic identities'.[7] Like Valerie Traub's recent history of women's erotic desires and practices, this book is 'offered in the name of history as well as in the name of a different futurity' (35). Writing a 'history that will be' is also to turn a homo-affirmative lens on the past which also reinvents that past. Judith Butler makes similar claims for the word queer, when she asserts in *Bodies That Matter* that:

> If the term queer is to be a site of collective contestation, the point of departure for a set of historical reflections and futural imaginings, it will have to remain that which is, in the present never fully owned, but always and only redeployed, twisted, queered from its prior usage.[8]

The queer masculinities recovered in this book are just such si(gh)tings of collective historical and political contestation, a simultaneous looking back and glancing toward the future, the future of the queer past. We hope that the readers of this book will share Meyer's opinion when he concludes his own look back at *Queer Frontiers* by saying that, 'the future of queer cultural production and political activism will both draw on, and radically reinvent, the gay and lesbian past. In this sense, what lies on the queer frontier "is our history and the history we are just beginning to become"' (349).

Sitings

The essays that comprise this long overdue collection of comparative studies of same-sex masculinities all work at the intersections of space and (sexual) identity in the interests of mapping male sexuality in the early modern period.[9] It is not just about queer history then but also about queer geography, or more specifically, historical geography. By siting the localized and particularized histories of these queer men, we are also contributing to the project of queering the geographies of identities,[10] and indeed challenging the discipline of geography's heteronormative representation of the world (both the Anglo/Western and non-Anglo/Western worlds). In recent years there has been a rapid growth in human, social, and cultural geography in the analysis of nonheterosexual geographies[11] and the ways in which sex is spaced and space is sexed.[12] Not surprisingly, queer theorists influenced by Foucault[13] have emphasized the interlinking between spaciality, sociality, sexuality and historicity. Drawing on theorists of space such as Edward Soja, Henry Lefebvre, David Harvey, Georg Simmel, Manuel Castells as well as Foucault, analysts of nonheterosexual or nonheteromasculine geographies have alerted us to the socially constructed, oppressive, and sometimes violent ways in which heterosexual practices operate while offering alternative shapes for the way we imagine, practise and theorize the sex-space couplet. Yet these accounts are very often not concerned with periods before modernity. This book, alongside David Higgs edited collection *Queer Sites* and Rudi Bley's comprehensive overview of 'geographies of perversion',[14] seeks to relate the experiences of queer men to the regulative production of space as heterosexist space.[15] As George Rousseau points out in his preface the regulatory production of heterosexist space can be violent, even genocidal, but queers have also contested those spaces and carved out a niche for themselves in urban, metropolitan worlds from Moscow to Lisbon, Paris to Philadelphia. As the chapters in this book show space is constitutive of (and indeed constituted by) sexual practices and sexual categories. Higgs's volume (which has contributions from many of our authors) maps the contours of male sexualities in four European capitals: London, Lisbon, Moscow, Paris as well as Amsterdam and San Francisco. The essays in our volume similarly chart the terrain of male sexual experiences and identities in various urban locations, Western and non-Western, European and non-European. The way queer sexual subcultures emerge throughout these essays is always tied to the particular conjunction between space and sexual subjectivity. Jon Binnie has talked about consumption and the production of queer space in contemporary London and Amsterdam[16] and these chapters also consider how men in various countries used public and private spaces in urban (and sometimes rural, or even at sea) locations to satisfy their sexual needs: toilets, parks, fields, churches, schools, pubs, coffee houses, (molly) houses. In these homosocial spaces men met other men, engaged in sexual practices and formed friendship networks. Some may not have identified as homosexual; an important part of writing historical geography is to document the under-explored sexual interactions between what Randolph Trumbach, in his mapping of sexual London, calls the 'homosexual minority' and the 'heterosexual majority'.[17] Frank Mort and Lynda Nead's special issue of *New Formations* on 'Sexual Geographies'[18] sets out to 'explore the relationship between sexual identities and regimes and the spatial mapping of London at a number of key moments since the 18th century' (5). The historical-geographical approach of our authors draws on a similar impulse to consider the intricate relationships between sexual subcultures, all-male enclaves, urbanization and modernization[19] since 1550. The different place-specific practices of the men in the various countries we cover here is an invitation to further comparative analyzes of same-sex masculinities: in Africa, China, the Balkans, Italy, Spain and elsewhere. We believe that a historical–geographical approach to studying the history of sexuality offers an invaluable entry point for those attempting to 'account for intrasocietal differences and for the lived experiences of those following the most common script for same-sex sexuality in a particular time and place'.[20] As well as being important for comparative studies of same-sex desires and practices and queer history the following essays will also be indispensable to those working in the emergent field of queer diaspora studies,[21] which attends to 'the transnational and multicultural network of connections of queer cultures and communities'. While queer disapora studies is most often concerned with postmodern discourses we feel that the essays here encourage a comparative historical and literary[22] study of early modern sex and gender regimes which would help to move us away from nation-specific studies to consider the exciting prospect of transnational traffic among and between nations. These reborderizations are facilitated further by the overviews of current research not written (or available) in English which our authors provide and which help to shift the study of queer masculinities away from its Euro-centric focus. The multidimensional approach of our authors means that they offer us snapshots of the existing scholarship while also suggesting avenues for future research and ways in which we might interrogate our current methodologies for researching queer histories, thereby redrawing the map and offering new blueprints for doing queer history.

Masculinities

While the field of geography has overcome its reticence and squeamishness about sexuality in the last ten years the emergence of a surfeit of articles and books, much of it coming out of sociology,[23] in the same period on the subject of masculinity has engendered a substantial body of work analyzing what masculinity is and does. Michael Roper wrote in a review in *History Workshop Journal* in 1990 that despite the abundant interest in masculinity we 'still know precious little about its history'.[24] Fifteen years later we know a great deal more about the social construction and complex history of masculinity/ies. It continues to be a hot cultural issue and the last decade has witnessed the rise of masculinity studies as well as an anti-feminist backlash, debates about men in feminism and a so-called crisis in masculinity. Scholars have also looked at the gendered production of space and scrutinized men's social interactions, masculinized spaces and masculine gender performances in the early modern world.[25] It has now become a critical commonplace that we can no longer talk of masculinity in the singular any more than we can talk of homosexuality or heterosexuality rather than homosexualities or heterosexualities. This book draws on the insights of a number of scholars who have mapped male sexuality, most notably Alan Bray[26] and Randolph Trumbach, and our contributors have attempted to site the variegated facets of masculinity, including many forms of sexuality, sociality and eroticism, across the wide range of male–male relations. They also analyze the many institutional and political structures which helped to give shape to the construction and development of male sexual identities and practices in the early modern world including class, nationalism, capitalism and imperialism. The masculinity turn in sociology and other disciplines (social history is most relevant to the current volume) has begun from the Foucauldian premise that sex and gender are socially constructed and caught up in a nexus of power/knowledge. As a result of feminism and gay and lesbian studies and their politicization of masculinity and their more nuanced debates on gender relations and heterosexuality, recent years have seen the emergence of considerations of multiple masculinities (indeed the array of masculinities is broadened in this volume to consider female masculinities,[27] the ways in which women produce and perform masculinity) in both Western and non-Western sex–gender systems. The historicization of western masculinities owes much to Randolph Trumbach's research which problematizes the neat linkage of two biological sexes, two genders, and two sexual orientations on which the modern sex–gender system is buttressed. He and others have argued that prior to the eighteenth century all persons were thought capable of desiring men and women and engaging in sexual acts as long as the heteropatriarchal privilege of penetrating women or youths was not disturbed. In or around the turn of the eighteenth century this sex–gender system underwent a massive transformation resulting in the modern Western binarized, dyadic sexual system. This instantiation of both compulsory heterosexuality and hegemonic masculinity can be attributed to several factors: among them the Protestant reformation, European imperialism and colonialism, incipient capitalism, secularization and urbanization. As Alan Bray has shown, the topography of the household was also instrumental in this change. Sharing a bed with another man, once a sign of intense male friendship and intimacy, could now be (mis)read as evidence of a sodomitical identity.[28] This social construction of masculinity has been built on a scaffolding of masculine privilege and the subordination of women and the nonheterosexual. The achievement of heterosexuality is predicated on a rejection of femininity and same-sex desires and modern masculinity shores itself up by 'killing the queer',[29] as we see time and again in these pages. Yet as Judith Butler shows in *Gender Trouble*[30] the 'heterosexual matrix', a gendered order 'oppositionally and hierarchically defined through the compulsory practice of heterosexuality' (151) is always haunted by its abjected other. Several of the essays here support the idea that in the final decades of the seventeenth century something changed: 'the sodomite had been a temporary aberration, the homosexual was now a species'.[31] The history of same-sex masculinities produced here then, is as much about writing the history of its twin, heterosexuality, and the integration of these histories should be a governing conceptual frame for all future premodern historiography. Equally important is historicizing how the (hetero)norm came to be the norm, especially since failures of the norm to reproduce itself already forms the ground of our queer analyses.

In conclusion we would note that the present volume is in no way meant to be comprehensive, nor indeed do all the contributors reach the same conclusions about early modern masculinities and dissident sexualities; 1550–1800 is by no means a unified queer period. Some readers will be disappointed that we have little to say about siting queer women although we do think that the discussion of the congruence between the oppression of women under heteropatriarchy and male same-sex desires in the production of hegemonic masculinity and the extension of the category of masculinity to include female masculinity in Judith Halberstam's terms are a start. Undoubtedly a book which would systematically analyze queer femininities during these timelines would yield an altogether different trajectory to the one outlined here for the men. Due to pressures of space we have not been able to include essays on Spain,[32] Italy,[33] Africa, China,[34] the Balkans. We would hope, however, that this volume will encourage other scholars to produce cartographies of queer desires for those regions and that they would also look at Hindu, Islamic, and Buddhist cultures.

Queer

A final note on the use of queer. We are not being modish or theoretically fashionable by using this word in our title. Not all of our contributors embrace the term. Some prefer not to use it. Others use it in radically different ways: some as a substitute for lesbian/gay/bisexual; some as a more open category for erotic desires, acts and affectivities which fall outside the domain of what Foucault calls alliance; and some as a term signifying a deconstructive reading practice.[35] That the word queer is collapsible onto gay male in this volume is, in many ways, unavoidable. This is, after all, a book about queer masculinities. However, we think that such a book should not simply be about men whom we would now recognize as homosexual, and we opt, as some of our authors do, for a more capacious usage of the word queer. For us, queer designates a range of acts, identities, propensities, affectivities and sentiments[36] which fissure heteronormativity. Only the word queer can adequately capture the fluidity, and amazing plasticity of the labile categories of gendered identifications and sexual identities available in this deeply resonant period.

Notes

1 Michael O'Rourke would like to acknowledge the support of a Government of Ireland Scholarship in the Humanities and Social Sciences, which he held between 1999–2002, and which greatly helped with the research for this chapter.

2 (Basingstoke: Palgrave, 2003).

3 (Madison: University of Wisconsin Press, 2000), ed. Joseph A. Boone, Martin Dupuis, Martin Meeker, Karin Quimby, Cindy Sarver, Debra Silverman, and Rosemary Weatherstone.

4 Jonathan Goldberg, 'The History that Will Be', in *Premodern Sexualities*, ed. Louise Fradenburg and Carla Freccero (New York: Routledge, 1996), 3–21.

5 Eve Kosofsky Sedgwick, *The Epistemology of the Closet* (Berkeley: The University of California Press, 1990), 1.

6 Jonathan Goldberg, *Sodometries: Renaissance Texts, Modern Sexualities* (Stanford: Stanford University Press, 1992).

7 Valerie Traub, *The Renaissance of Lesbianism in Early Modern England* (Cambridge: Cambridge University Press, 2002), 14.

8 Judith Butler, 'Critically Queer', in *Bodies That Matter: On the Discursive Limits of Sex* (New York: Routledge, 1993), 228.

9 Queer Theory draws heavily on spatial metaphors. On mapping see *Mapping Male Sexuality: Nineteenth Century England*, ed. Jay Losey and William D. Brewer (Madison: Fairleigh Dickinson University Press, 2000); Chris Perriam, 'Mapping Spanish "Queer" Cultural Identities', *Journal of Romance Studies*, 2, no. 1 (Spring 2002): 103–10; Clare A. Lyons, 'Mapping an Atlantic Sexual Culture: Homoeroticism in Eighteenth-Century Philadelphia', *William and Mary Quarterly* 60, no. 1 (January 2003): 119–54; Frank Mort, 'Mapping Sexual London: The Wolfenden Committee on Homosexual Offences and Prostitution, 1954–57', *New Formations* 37 (Spring 1999): 92–113; Robyn Wiegman, 'Introduction: Mapping the Lesbian Postmodern' in *The Lesbian Postmodern*, ed. Laura Doan (New York: Routledge, 1994), 1–20.

10 Francisco Valdes, 'Mapping the Patterns of Particularities: Queering the Geographies of Identities', *Antipode* 34, no.5 (2002): 974–87.

11 For an overview see Jon Binnie and Gill Valentine, 'Geographies of Sexuality – a Review of Progress', *Progress in Human Geography* 23, no. 2 (1999): 175–87

12 See Gill Valentine, 'Queer Bodies and the Production of Space' in *The Lesbian and Gay Studies Handbook*, ed. Steven Seidman and Diane Richardson (London: Sage, 2002), 145–60 and Alison Blunt and Jane Wills, *Dissident Geographies: An Introduction to Radical Ideas and Practices* (Essex: Prentice Hall, 2000) esp. 128–66.

13 On Foucault-space see Sally R. Munt, 'Framing Intelligibility, Identity, and Selfhood: A Reconsideration of Spatio-Temporal Models', *Reconstruction* 2, no. 3 (Summer 2002) <http://www.reconstruction.ws/023/munt.htm>.

14 David Higgs, ed. *Queer Sites: Gay Urban Histories Since 1600* (London: Routledge, 1999); Rudi Bleys, *The Geography of Perversion: Male-to-Male Sexual Behavior Outside the West and the Ethnographic Imagination, 1750–1918* (London: Cassell, 1996).

15 See David Bell and Gill Valentine, 'Introduction: Orientations' in *Mapping Desire: Geographies of Sexuality* (London: Routledge, 1995), 1–27 and *Queers in Space: Communities, Public Places, Sites of Resistance*, ed. Gordon Brent Ingram *et al.* (Seattle: Bay Press, 1997).
16 Jon Binnie, 'Trading Places: Consumption, Sexuality and the Production of Queer Space' in *Mapping Desire*, ed. Bell and Valentine 182–99.
17 Randolph Trumbach, 'The Heterosexual Male in Eighteenth-Century London and his Queer Interactions' in *Love, Sex, Intimacy and Friendship between Men, 1550–1800*, ed. Katherine O'Donnell and Michael O'Rourke (Basingstoke: Palgrave, 2003), 99–127 and *Sex and the Gender Revolution: Volume One: Heterosexuality and the Third Gender in Enlightenment London* (Chicago: University of Chicago Press, 1998).
18 Frank Mort and Lynda Nead, ed. 'Special Issue: Sexual Geographies', *New Formations* 37 (1999).
19 See also Jan Löfström, 'The Birth of the Queen/the Modern Homosexual: Historical Explanations Revisited', *Sociological Review* 45, no. 1 (1997): 24–41 and Henning Bech, *When Men Meet: Homosexuality and Modernity* (Cambridge: Polity, 1997).
20 Stephen O. Murray, 'The Comparative Sociology of Homosexualities', in *The Lesbian and Gay Studies Handbook*, ed. Seidman and Richardson (London: Sage, 2002), 83–96.
21 See Anne-Marie Fortier, 'Queer Diaspora', in *The Lesbian and Gay Studies Handbook*, ed. Seidman and Richardson (London: Sage, 2002), 183–97.
22 For a similar collection see Tom Betteridge ed. *Sodomy in Early Modern Europe* (Manchester: Manchester University Press, 2002).
23 The *locus classicus* is Bob Connell's *Masculinities* (Sydney: Allen & Unwin, 1995). The corpus of work on masculinities is too vast to put bibliographic shape on. Especially helpful to us were, Richard Collier, *Masculinities, Crime and Criminology: Men, Heterosexuality and the Criminal(ised) Other* (London: Sage, 1998); *Engendering Men: The Question of Male Feminist Criticism*, ed. Joseph Boone and Michael Cadden (New York: Routledge, 1990) and *Masculinity Studies and Feminist Theory: New Directions*, ed. Judith Kegan Gardiner (New York: Columbia University Press, 2002).
24 Michael Roper, 'Recent Books on masculinity: Introduction', *History Workshop Journal* 29 (Spring 1990): 184–6. For a more recent overview see Helen Berry, 'Scrutinizing Men: Current Trends in the History of British Masculinity, 1600–1800', *History Workshop Journal* 52 (Autumn 2001): 283–7.
25 See Brian Cowan, 'What was Masculine about the Public Sphere? Gender and the Coffeehouse Milieu in Post-Restoration England', *History Workshop Journal* 51 (Spring 2001): 127–59 and Karen Harvey, 'Gender, Space and Modernity in Eighteenth-Century England: A Place Called Sex', *History Workshop Journal* 51 (Spring 2001): 159–80.
26 Alan Bray, *Homosexuality in Renaissance England* (London: Gay Men's Press, 1982).
27 Judith Halberstam, *Female Masculinity* (Durham: Duke University Press, 1998).

28 Alan Bray, 'Homosexuality and the Signs of Male Friendship in Elizabethan England' in *Queering the Renaissance*, ed. Jonathan Goldberg (Durham: Duke University Press, 1994), 40–62.
29 See David Coad's *Gender Trouble Down Under: Australian Masculinities* (Valenciennes: Presses Universitaires de Valenciennes, 2002), 40–5.
30 Judith Butler, *Gender Trouble: Feminism and the Subversion of Identity* (New York: Routledge, 1990).
31 Michel Foucault, *The History of Sexuality*, Vol. 1, *An Introduction*, trans. Robert Hurley (New York: Vintage Books, 1980), 43.
32 See *Queer Iberia: Sexualities, Cultures and Crossings from the Middle Ages to the Renaissance*, ed. Josiah Blackmore and Gregory S. Hutcheson (Durham: Duke University Press, 1999) and 'Forum: Return to Queer Iberia', ed. Sidney Donnell and Gregory S. Hutcheson, *La Corónica* 30, no. 1 (Fall 2001) esp. 260–5.
33 For Venice see Guido Ruggiero, *The Boundaries of Eros: Sex Crime and Sexuality in Renaissance Venice* (Oxford: Oxford University Press, 1985); For Florence see Michael Rocke, *Forbidden Friendships: Homosexuality and Male Culture In Renaissance Florence* (New York: Oxford University Press, 1996); and for Siena see Ian Moulton's introduction to his new edition of Antonio Vignali's *La Cazzaria* (New York: Routledge, 2003).
34 On Africa see Stephen O. Murray and Will Roscoe, *Boy Wives and Female Husbands: Studies of African Homosexualities* (New York: St. Martin's Press, 1998). On China see Matthew H. Sommer, *Sex, Law and Society in Late Imperial China* (Stanford: Stanford University Press, 2000).
35 We would like to thank Tom King for pointing this out to us.
36 By focusing on male affect and love we are following recent trends in the field. See especially George E. Haggerty, *Men in Love: Masculinity and Sexuality in the Eighteenth Century* (New York: Columbia University Press, 1999) and Caleb Crain *American Sympathy: Men, Friendship, and Literature in the New Nation* (New Haven: Yale University Press, 2001). An especially important article is Anne G. Myles's 'Queering the Study of Early American Sexuality', *William and Mary Quarterly* 60.1 (January 2003): 199–202.

1

Searching in the Dark: Towards a Historiography of Queer Early Modern and Enlightenment (Anglo) Ireland

Chris Mounsey

Searching for what?

I believe and hope that I was asked to write this essay reviewing the study of male–male relationships in the Early Modern and Enlightenment (Anglo) Ireland because of my delight in finding rapprochements and syntheses between apparently opposing views. The syntheses of which I speak, that have in the past been between philosophy and literature, between literary theory and textual scholarship, do not follow any predetermined (say, Marxian) pattern. They are sometimes rather ragged and ungainly, but always, I hope, challenging and stimulating. Such syntheses are best characterized by William Blake's ideas from *Milton* and *Jerusalem*: that it is self-defeating to try to progress by excluding or negating past beliefs. Blake argues that should you move forward by stating 'that old idea was wrong' but 'this new idea is right', you miss out on the dynamic forces that fire progress. Moving forward by negation, Blake argues, is the progress of normatizing discourse.[1] To the present case, it is anathema to queer discourse, which seeks to accommodate all variant forms, modes, approaches and techniques.

Herein lies, of course, a foundational opposition, a point at which my argument may be deconstructed before it begins. Queer does not want normatizing discourse. Queer rejects normatizing discourses. Queer progresses by opposing normatizing discourse. But I draw your attention to the paradox (rather than try to pretend it does not exist) since it is queer *par excellence* to found queerness on a paradox rather than upon a solidly logical structure. For within the paradox lies the kernel of truth (or its foundational myth, or whatever you want to call it). Queer rejects normatizing discourse, while at the same time calls for all people to be queer. Queer 'normatizes' in its demand for queerness, which is anti-normal. And herein lies a queer methodology, which is exemplified in the diverse essays in this book, as well as in much of the work that has gone on and is going on under the banner of Queer Historiography.

Following the method of Jonathan Goldberg's *Sodometries*,[2] I shall begin with a modern metaphor before moving to (Anglo) Irish Early Modern and Enlightenment history and the debates it raises. Queer theory in terms of historical research, I would suggest, is like the AIDS quilts that have recently adorned our cities. Each piece of the quilt is made up of memories, the recovered, represented memories of a life now gone. In turn, each memory is made up of the memorialized and the memorializer, in a dynamic equilibrium, the one owing its existence in the quilt to the other. Sometimes the memorialized will be clearly visible in the design, sometimes more shadowy as the memorializer is brought to the fore. As pieces of a quilt, none are constructed with the design of the others in mind. All are separate. But all are part of the quilt, and the whole is greater than the sum of its parts. Although the pieces are stitched together only at the last minute, and may make uncomfortable bedfellows (the individual designs jarring with each other) each is as valuable as each other in demonstrating diversity that is the *raison d'être* of a quilt.

In the same way each method that makes up the methodology that is queer history is a separate piece of a whole that is greater than the sum of its parts. In terms of research into the history of male–male relationships, each method recovers the past, now more clearly, now with more emphasis on the method of recovery. The success of a method (which must lie in the clarity of the ideas expressed to the mind of the reader) is, of course, to be desired. But it is not the goal of the methodology as a whole, which is to celebrate diversity and dissonance. The queer rather than the normative.

I offer the idea of the AIDS quilt as something of a caveat since a number of recent historical studies of male–male relationships have begun with just this sort of review of queer work to date, but with the intention of offering the new method as the best way, while negating the others. So Cameron McFarlane's excellent *The Sodomite in Fiction and Satire*, ends his review with a comment that introduces and recommends his own approach at the expense of other approaches: 'Because each of these historians is, in his own way attempting to document the cultural *visibility* of homosexuality in this period, they each necessarily operate with a fixed and abstract notion of what "homosexuality" is: that is, they know what they are looking for'.[3]

Rather than cultural visibility, McFarlane chooses to centre his study on 'sodomitical practices', defined as:

> ... the nexus of ideas, relations, behaviors, discursive practices and meanings that could be set in motion under these signs. ... sodomy was not a self-evident category, but ... was discursively constituted and reconstituted and that these discursive formations enabled specific, often violent, political structures.[4]

And an interesting, persuasive study it makes. But there seems to be no need to criticize others in order to show value in one's own work. Perhaps the historians McFarlane criticizes do 'know what they are looking for' – because they are looking at history in a different way, such that for them, the objects they were searching for may have existed. One might not agree with the method, or the conclusions, but the experience of others may lead to heuristic conclusions. Like the brief sexual encounters between gay men searching each other out in the dark, there could just be a momentary frisson of pleasure at their meeting, however incompatible, if they met in the light.

We might extend this metaphor into a paradigm of the process of queer historiography. I suggested, in a discussion with Michael O'Rourke at Newman House, that a short ramble in Iveagh Park demonstrated to me why Gerard Manley Hopkins had not enjoyed teaching at University College, Dublin.[5] The park, I told him, offered too many 'dappled places', too much temptation for a priest in revolt against the expectations made of his sexuality. Michael looked at me blankly until I explained that it seemed to me that the tree-lined alleys in the park were ideal for cruising.[6] In turn he explained that since he was straight, he had never engaged in this type of activity, so he had never looked at the Iveagh Gardens in that light.

Of course it cannot be certain that Hopkins' dislike of University College, Dublin was based on his fear of giving way to sexual desire. It was possible, since cruising is not a modern phenomenon, but has been documented from as early as the entrapment of William Brown on Moorfields in 1726.[7] My suggestion had been based not upon what I could see in the park, but the way in which I looked at it. Michael's inability to see the park in the same way was not blindness, but lack of a particular expectation. What was important about the two views of Iveagh Gardens was that it gave an opportunity for dialog. Together we could go on to discuss the viability of my reading of the park from our differing perspectives.

It is this respect for difference that is not only a founding principle of Queer Theory, but also the method of its progression. It does not function by the meeting of opposites and the discarding of one in favor of the other. Nor by the synthesizing of new positions between two diametrically opposed viewpoints. It functions by the casual meeting of strangers who, as Nietzsche admonishes, must remain 'best enemies' if they are to find something like the truth.[8]

When confronting the task of writing on the history of Early Modern and Enlightenment male–male relationships in (Anglo) Ireland, one finds very little work done on it. Apart from the new and exemplary laws in Ireland on homosexual rights, almost nothing has been published about homosexuality in Ireland. This being so, one might be surprised to find there is a current methodological argument about how to study Irish homosexuality. What I shall do is explore two cases, one early modern: the Castlehaven Case, and one from the middle of the eighteenth century: the case of George Stone and George Sackville. The first is the site of much scholarly debate. The other is, to the best of my knowledge, a newly discovered case. I hope to use the problems that have arisen in the study of the first to throw some light on how one might discover a queer method of approach to the second.

Searching in Early Modern (Anglo) Ireland

The Castlehaven case, the sodomy trial of Mervin Touchet, Baron Audley and Earl of Castlehaven[9] has never been out of print. Lurid accounts of the case and attempts by the Earl's family to re-establish their dignity appeared from the day of his execution in 1631. I shall restrict myself to the debate about how to understand the case with reference to two recent scholarly versions of the story, one by Rictor Norton in *Mother Clap's Molly House*,[10] the other by Cynthia Herrup in *A House in Gross Disorder*.[11] What distinguishes these accounts of the case is that Norton's methodology is based in his unswerving essentialism, while Herrup concentrates her version on the overlapping discourses of government and the law, typical of the social constructionist.

Briefly the facts of the case are these: Mervin Touchet was brought to trial, on the insistence of his son, for the crimes of committing sodomy with four of his servants and assisting in the rape of his wife, and his son's wife. Touchet was tried and found guilty by a court of peers sitting at Westminster and beheaded.

Norton's six-page description of the events that led up to the execution are all he needs to capture the experience of his subject's oppression as an Early Modern homosexual. Norton, being a modern homosexual knows what was going on between master and servants as he has shared the experience. Homosexuality, for the essentialist, is a transhistorical category, and thus he can confidently declare: 'Meanwhile, Florentius (sometimes Lawrence) Fitz-Patrick and Castlehaven were buggering each other in the mansion at Fontain (later Fonthill) Gifford in the County of Wilts.'[12]

Furthermore, as a modern homosexual looking back at the treatment of his historical forefather, he may rise to outrage that:

> The outcome [of the trial] was a foregone conclusion because of Castlehaven's suspected Roman Catholic allegiance; in the words of the Attorney General: 'when once a Man indulges his Lust, and Prevaricates with his Religion, as my Lord Audley has done, by being a Protestant in the Morning, and a Papist in the Afternoon, no wonder if he commits the most abominable Impieties.' He was the ideal victim to be prosecuted for what many regarded as the 'Jesuit perversion.'[13]

He may then further demonstrate the transhistorical nature of the experience of the homosexual since, as he argues that:

> The legal precedent therefore clearly established the principle that homosexuals can be convicted and executed for acts which take place between consenting adults in private, even if penetration cannot definitely be proven, and even if the only accusation comes from the confession of one of the men involved.[14]

However, the facts of the case go some way to detract from this type of reading. As Norton himself points out, Touchet was not solely tried for sodomy, but also for the rape of his wife. In support of his position, Norton argues: 'Undoubtedly Castlehaven deserved punishment for having assisted in the rape of his wife, but he would never have been prosecuted for that had he not been a homosexual and a suspected Papist.'[15]

Norton might have added to this list of 'defects' that Touchet was Irish, particularly since Touchet's dalliance with the papacy was brief, and that Touchet's son, who brought the case against his father, was an out and out Catholic. Why should a court find against a man who was a Catholic only for a brief spell, when the case against him was brought by another Catholic?

While Norton's approach must be praised for its readability and passion, his departure from the facts of the case, and his inattention to the context of the trial, call for another type of approach to answer the questions left by his conclusions. Not even the jury could agree with Norton that Touchet was a sodomite, only 15 found him guilty of sodomy while all 26 found him guilty of rape.

Such an approach comes from the much more detailed account of the Castlehaven case by Cynthia Herrup. Where Norton searches for the transhistorical homosexual, Herrup searches for the perceptions of race and class. The strength of Herrup's argument derives from the fact that she does not divorce the Touchet case from its contemporary history. The most important issue at the time, she argues, was the effects of the Protestant Plantations, which have reverberated about the island of Ireland ever since, and define the tension inherent in the term (Anglo) Ireland used in the title of this essay. Herrup's case begins from the premise that in the Touchet case: 'The accusations ... swiftly became a test of the custodial obligations of the King as well as a constitutional struggle over the meaning of good paternal governance and good legal practice.'[16]

And in evidence for her position, she states that: '[The prosecution] saw in Castlehaven's behavior confirmation for anxieties about the degrading results of Catholic and Irish seductiveness. ... in 1630, Castlehaven had been punished for being more tolerant of Irish tenants than the Articles of Plantation allowed.'[17]

For this reason, Norton's avoidance of the influence of Touchet's Irish title could be argued to miss much of the point of the double accusation of rape and sodomy. Touchet was a bad manager of his entire estate. The situation outside his house (that he had neglected to turn Catholics off his lands), was reflected inside his house in his relations with his servants (sodomy and the giving of excessive gifts) and wife (rape). He paid with his life because it was a difficult time in Anglo Irish relations. Touchet was guilty since:

> An intricate hierarchy of gender, age, and status designed to inculcate obedience and self-discipline structured life within most genteel households in early modern England. ... Heads of household were expected to instruct their inferiors as well as to protect them. Superiors were to guide and to discipline their charges, but most important, to teach by example.[18]

In Norton's favor, as Herrup points out: 'Castlehaven was no more an Irishman than he was a Wiltshireman, ...' Although, as she goes on: ' ... but once again, what he was mattered less than what he could be made to seem. His family's embrace of Ireland was a means through which the King's attorneys might encourage people to question the Earl's loyalties.'[19]

Therefore, Herrup may draw her conclusions from the contemporary perceptions of the Irish by the English: 'For many Englishmen and women, the Irish embodied anarchic, traitorous, and infectious possibilites of the old faith. ... The English dismissed the Irish as barbaric and immoral at the same time that they portrayed them as boundlessly seductive.'[20]

Returning to facts, however, Herrup becomes victim to the problem that besets the social constructionist researcher into homosexuality in history. She has only the trial records on which to base her opinions. There are no incontrovertible facts to the case, and historians must rely on intuition (as does Norton) or fall foul of the problem of a 'crime' which few can comprehend, let alone put into clear speech when asked to testify to it under oath. Herrup attempts to make a virtue of this:

> We like to think of trials as structured quests for facts. But adversarial law is as much about style as about fact, about obfuscating as much as clarifying, about self-interest as much as objectivity. ... Regardless of fact and even law, the best performance is the most convincing one. And the most convincing performance is usually the one most strategically attuned to the fears and ideals of the judge and jury.[21]

Herrup's reliance solely on the evidence of a law case is true to social constructionist method, but we lose sight of Castlehaven as a person and as a homosexual. Like Virginia Woolf on the train to Richmond, this reader craves for the person that gave rise to the description.[22] Once again, Herrup attempts to make a virtue of the problem, and to go no further in her attempt to reclaim the person from the historical facts:

> Rape and Sodomy are not, of course, merely symbols of disorder – they are acts with real consequences for real people. If such crimes figuratively threatened the family and the state, they also actually harmed unwilling participants. But what makes acts into crimes is not intrinsic qualities, but the circumstances of their occurrences. So intimately do the circumstances attend the result, that in a sense, they themselves become the crime.[23]

Thus her book argues that the case against Castlehaven was so insecure in matters of law and evidence, that it must have been something else (English perceptions of Castlehaven's Irishness) that gave rise to the guilty verdict. Herrup draws on circumstances and reads these English perceptions in terms of the discourses of legal practice, national law, religious law, requirements of manhood (the code of patriarchy), requirements of the peerage (the code of honor). Castlehaven himself remains a mere shadow.

This is all well and good, but even Herrup cannot live in the sort of world in which discourse rules and the person is a mere chimera. In her introduction she thanks her partner, with whom she shares her house, thankful that it is in no way disordered. The comment is touching, but at the same time one is left wondering what Castlehaven's house might have been like. Can historical method discover nothing? Norton believed he had discovered a homosexual with whom he shares some common characteristics. But to do this he had to disregard some of the context and some of the facts. To overcome these problems and to bring in all the context, Herrup loses the person that was Mervin Touchet.[24]

In the similar and contemporary case of Francis Bacon, Lisa Jardine and Alan Stewart go as far as to reject out of hand the charge of homosexuality that has dogged Bacon's biography. In their 637-page biography of Bacon, the charge is explored for only a page and a half. They conclude, in despite of contemporary rumours and family papers that strongly suggest Bacon's behavior to his servants was similar to Castlehaven's, that Bacon was merely the victim of scandal mongers:

> What is intriguing about these attacks [on Bacon] is the easy way in which they conflate the questions of 'bribery' and 'sodomy'. Both D'Ewes and Aubrey [in his *Brief Lives*] are in fact talking of the relationship between Bacon and his servants, a relationship which they see as unhealthy. ... The nature of the intimate relationships between high-ranking men in the patronage and friendships that sustained Jacobean England meant that sodomy was a charge that spread out in all directions – from patron to client, from master to servant. It may be that association with Buckingham left men open to this sort of accusation. ... Whatever the case, it was a charge that stuck to Francis Bacon to this day.[25]

The reasoning displayed here picks up a few threads of the much lengthier debate in Alan Stewart's earlier work on homosexuality.[26] In one sense Jardine and Stewart's argument about Bacon's sexuality is watertight. There is no physical evidence and no documentary evidence of these relationships being more than accusations made against people who were physically closetted together because of their work. In another sense, it lacks openness to the possibility of homosexuality, or that homosexuality might have been less rare than has previously been thought. By failing to follow up on the possibility that Bacon was a homosexual Jardine and Stewart might be accused of telling a partial story. But the decision about how much of what type of evidence is necessary for a certain ascription of homosexuality is a difficult one to make. To return to the Touchet case, I will therefore offer a methodology for reading 'possibilities' from context plus whatever shreds of evidence present themselves, while remaining open about the fact that the readings are no more than possibilities. In this sense, I hope that the reading is both indebted to Norton's essentialism and to Herrup's social constructionism.

From the evidence presented at the trial, we have witness statements that he had sexual relations with his male servants, and that he assisted in the rape of his wife. The problem with evidence from witnesses is that it comes from their perspective, and it is framed by lawyers who are keen to make a plausible case. If we take the Countess of Castlehaven's evidence at face value, we reach a similar conclusion to the court. Touchet made his servants show her their private parts on their wedding might, and later held her arms while one of the servants raped her. Taken on its own, we might read this as evidence that Touchet was a bisexual voyeur who had used his rights as the patriarch of the household to violate his wife. However, the question remains why the Countess waited six months before bringing the charge against her husband, and after she had had a child by Skipwith, the Earl's servant.

Read alongside other evidence from the trial, we might reach a different conclusion. First we must remember that it was not the Countess who brought the case against Touchet, but the son of his first marriage. He was keen on protecting his entailed inheritance from being given away to favorites or to the Countess's bastard child. Next, Giles Broadway, another servant, testified that the Earl had lain with him in sexual dalliance but had not penetrated him, emitting rather, between his thighs (Norton, 1992: 9). This might be taken as evidence that the Earl was incapable of holding a firm enough erection for penetration.[27] Similarly we might accept Skipwith's evidence that the Countess enjoyed sex. By adding these to the Countess's evidence, we might reconstruct the sexual life of Fonthill Gifford in another and queerer way. On the wedding night of the Earl and his second wife, we might suggest, he attempted to have sex with her and failed to penetrate. He was either incapable because he was not inclined to have sex with women since he was essentially homosexual and preferred men, or simply because he was getting old. The Countess, in this story, might have been disappointed and declared that she liked sex and could not do without it. Rather than being enraged, it is possible that the Earl and she came to the agreement that they might both benefit from continuing his practice of sleeping with his servants. Witness statements at the trial concur that there were regularly three or four in the Earl's bed. If there was such an agreement, the Earl's holding the Countess's arms behind her while Skipwith penetrated her sounds less like rape and more like consensual, if queer sex. But it would not look good if the fact of the Countess's consent came up in court. Nor was it likely to be believed, in the ideological climate of the Early Modern period, which required the passivity of women in sexual, as well as other matters. Thus it is possible that she lied about being raped, though was truthful in the description of being held by the Earl while Skipwith penetrated her.

Likewise, it would be unlikely to be believed that Touchet was a sodomite – as the jury's majority verdict demonstrates. People, and juries are people, only believe what they can think possible. The lack of a case against Francis Bacon even at the nadir of his power, only ten years earlier, showed that such things were difficult to believe of the aristocracy. Thus we find a reason why of the Countess's case of rape might have been added to the charge of sodomy in an adversarial court. However, to charge the two together might make Touchet look so thoroughly debauched that the prosecution was running the risk of having the whole case disbelieved. Thus we have a reason why Touchet's Irish connections were so important. He may have been a peer, but he was an Irish peer, the ideology of which could be highlighted to the prejudices of the English jury to explain his queer sexuality. Touchet's bed was in as much disorder as his Irish estates – full of seductive Irish Catholics and devoid of dour Scottish Protestants. It is therefore perhaps no surprise that after his execution the Touchet family lost their English Baronies and lands while retaining the Irish earldom and lands.

By employing in this way a combination of personal and political (essentialist and constructionist) strategies to the reading we can begin to tie in some of the threads that will not fit in when only one method of reading is employed. The reading remains provisional, but it attempts to be true both to the life and expectations of Mervin Touchet and his Countess, as well as the lives and expectations of the English jury that convicted him. It is also bound to the contexts both of contemporary history and of the time of writing this essay. For when before would it have been possible to argue seriously that the Countess might have enjoyed sex, and not necessarily with her husband?

Searching in Enlightenment (Anglo) Ireland

Figure 1. Frontispiece to *The Female Parliament*. ([London], 1754). Courtesy of the British Library.

The case of George Stone and George Sackville in 1754 reverses the facts of the Castlehaven case in terms of the rule of (Anglo) Ireland. In this case it was the English Primate of all Ireland and the son of (and chief Secretary to) Lionel Sackville the Viceroy of Ireland who were accused of homosexuality. The accusation might or might not be a metaphor for the misrule of Ireland by the English, or might bear some truth as to the sexuality of the two men. Although there was no law case, accusations of homosexuality were levelled at Stone and Sackville in broadsides, in pamphlets and in two plays.

I have written elsewhere[28] at greater length about the history of this period in Irish history, and in particular about the propaganda war in which Stone and Sackville were vilified. Briefly, the Irish Patriots, led by Henry Boyle, made accusations against two of the most powerful Englishmen in Ireland. Together Stone and Sackville controlled the Irish Judiciary, the Irish Viceregal Court and the Irish Parliament. What led to the accusations was the Patriots upholding the power of the Irish Parliament to make its own decisions, and in particular over its right to decide how an Irish parliamentary budget surplus was spent without reference to the English Parliament and King. In the event the English party were defeated in the Irish parliament (by a mere five votes), and some historians have argued this was the first time that the Dublin middle classes began to see themselves as Irish.[29] In this sense, the accusations of homosexuality are, like the Castlehaven case, intermingled with notions of self-determination in the heterogeneous society that was (Anglo) Ireland.

Since the accusations were made in a propaganda war, they might easily be understood to be metaphorical. The Irish Patriot Henry Boyle, named 'Roger' in the pamphlets, is seen as a good farmer, while Stone and Sackville are depicted (literally in the frontispiece of a play *The Female Parliament*)[30] as homosexuals fighting over a good-looking young man.[31] In another play, *The Harlequins*,[32] they lead the dancing together. Read in a social constructionist way, all three depictions would be read as non-descriptive, and as functions of the discourse of political banter. Homosexuality would be understood as a metaphor for misrule.

Nevertheless, there is grist to the essentialist mill also. Henry Boyle was well-known to have built up the ruined and mortgaged estates of his father (who was called Roger) into profitable concerns. Of George Stone it was claimed in *The Female Parliament*, that he 'roll'd through the Street with a Ganymede in his Pontiff Chariot.' Read in a literal way, such evidence would suggest the essentialist reading would be more heuristic and that there was as much truth in the accusation against Stone as the description of Boyle.

Of course, much had changed in the history of homosexuality between the Castlehaven and Stone and Sackville accusations. The Molly House trials of 1726 had established homosexuality as a subculture. It might therefore be argued that Stone and Sackville had set up a similar institution in Dublin. However, no other evidence of it has yet been forthcoming. Nevertheless, the fact that Stone remained unmarried, while Sackville was married (conveniently?) in September 1754 could be used as evidence about their sexuality. Or it might be evidence of nothing at all.

What is important, however, is that we should not make the move of G.F. Russell Barker in the *Dictionary of National Biography* entry for George Stone, which reads:

> The appellation of 'the beauty of holiness,' which was given to Stone, ... on account of his good looks, was not confirmed by any singular excellence in his moral character. But though he did not conform to the decencies of his profession, he was probably innocent of the grosser charges which were brought against him by his numerous enemies. ...

In the face of the kernels of truth behind the metaphors, even the evidence of rumor should be taken seriously in the case of historical accusations of homosexuality. Since this sexuality was so forbidden as to be a capital offence, such that it cannot even be mentioned by name in the DNB article written a hundred and fifty years after the fact, it is not likely to be easily gleaned from contemporary historical documents. Homosexuality is a form of invective that is still used against enemies,[33] but this does not mean that accusations of it must always be discounted as baseless. In the case of Stone and Sackville, it might never be known for certain whether they were homosexuals. However, following the essentialist method we can conclude that they did have a sexuality, homo or hetero or bi. Following the social constructionist method we can be certain that sexuality was a typical device to be used as a charge against them in a propaganda war. With more space and more detailed examination of the facts from both perspectives, we might be able tease out a series of possible stories that fit all the facts and comes as close as possible to saturating the context. The degree to which we believe these men were homosexuals will also depend upon our own historiographical position. We too are complicit in the judgement made upon the past. All these things considered, we may progress without negation. We can discuss the validity of 'each others' arguments, and if we find the slightest agreements between the different approaches, we shall have become 'best enemies', and may have reached a kernel of truth.

It would seem to me to be foolish to cease to explore male friendships for erotic elements simply because there might be another explanation, and because the researcher might simply be looking at himself in the research material. But if each piece of research is carried out with careful consideration for the political significance of the closeness of the individuals, as well as with an awareness of the potential for sexual charge between the participants, then a more complete picture might emerge. If the political can explain away the sexual, then all well and good. If not, then the sexual ought to stand. For however much constructionists might want the sexual to be reduced to the textual, the essentialist argument remains suggesting that the sexual will exist willy-nilly.

It is two methods together acting simultaneously but pulling in opposite directions that makes the methodology queer. It is the constant refining process of apparently opposed work that makes the methodology queer. It is the meeting in the dark that makes the methodology queer.

Notes

1 Chris Mounsey, 'Christopher Smart and William Blake: A Distinctive Mode', Tom Woodman ed. *Early Romantics: Perspectives in British Poetry from Pope to Wordsworth* (Basingstoke: Macmillan, 1998).
2 Jonathan Goldberg, *Sodometries: Renaissance Texts: Modern Sexualities* (Stanford: Stanford University Press, 1992).
3 Cameron McFarlane, *The Sodomite in Fiction and Satire: 1660–1750* (New York: Columbia University Press, 1997) 14.
4 *Ibid.*, 20.
5 Katherine O'Donnell made this point about Hopkins in her introductory remarks at the 'Queer Men: Historicizing Queer Masculinities, 1550–1800' conference held at Newman House, St. Stephen's Green, Dublin in July 2001.
6 See OED 'cruising' *spec.* b.
7 Alan Bray, *Homosexuality in Renaissance England* (New York: Columbia, 1982).
8 See Friedrich Nietzsche, *Thus Spake Zarathustra*, tr. Thomas Common, [www.concordance.com/cgi-bin/1wrdr.pl] '10. War and Warriors'.
9 The Barony of Audley was an English title, and Castlehaven an Irish.
10 Rictor Norton, *Mother Clap's Molly House, The Gay Subculture in England 1700– 1830*, (London: GMP, 1992) [Cited as Norton].

11 Cynthia B. Herrup, *A House in Gross Disorder: Sex, Law and the 2nd Earl of Castlehaven* (Oxford: OUP,1999) [Cited as Herrup].
12 Norton, 28.
13 Norton, 29.
14 Norton, 30.
15 Norton, 30.
16 Herrup, xiii.
17 Herrup, 81.
18 Herrup, 13.
19 Herrup, 16.
20 Herrup, 19.
21 Herrup, 55.
22 See Virginia Woolf, 'Mr. Bennet and Mrs. Brown', (L.& V. Woolf: London, 1924).
23 Herrup, 61.
24 In the sister volume to this collection, *Love, Sex, Intimacy and Friendship between Men, 1550–1800*, eds Katherine O'Donnell and Michael O'Rourke (Basingstoke: Palgrave Macmillan: 2003), Nicholas F. Radel, argues in 'Can the Sodomite Speak: Sodomy, Satire, Desire and the Castlehaven Case' a view that comes tantalizingly close to the mixed methodology which I suggest here. He writes that

> If sodomy were only a symbolic crime, then what did the law's concern with bodies mean? And if sodomy appears only or primarily in the midst of other social or political disruptions, what did it mean that the judges appealed to individual agency to press the case against Fitzpatrick. (161)

Nevertheless, by following Cynthia Herrup's methodology, he cannot maintain the agency of sodomy, and in the end, his approach reduces the acts between upper class men and their servants to power relations. While he succeeds admirably in getting around the silence which surrounds homoerotic sex in the Early Modern period, he has to conclude, in the voice of the servant, 'If I can't [sic] speak what is being done to me or even what I am doing willingly, then, in some sense, I seem to be doing nothing at all or something else altogether.' (163)

25 Lisa Jardine and Alan Stewart, *Hostage to Fortune: The Troubled Life of Francis Bacon* (London: Victor Gollancz, 1998) 568.
26 Alan Stewart, *Close Readers: Humanism and Sodomy in Early Modern England* (Princeton: Princeton University Press, 1997).
27 It need not be, since Broadway might have been trying to protect himself and his provider from the death penalty.
28 See Chris Mounsey, 'Running with the Hare and the Hounds' in *New Hibernia Review Iris eirennach nua*, Vol. 4, No, 3 Autumn 2000, pp. 65–77.
29 Declan O'Donovan, 'The Money Bill Dispute', *Penal Era and Golden Age* (Belfast: Ulster Historical Foundation, 1979) 87.
30 *The Female Parliament. A seri-comi-farcical entertainment, never acted in Eutopia before ... With several pieces of chocolate-scandal, tea-calumny, and midnight slander, entirely new* (Printed next Door to the Saddle on the Right Horse: [London or Dublin], 1754).

31 See Figure 4.
32 *The Harlequins. A comedy*. (George Lion: London [in fact Dublin], 1753).
33 A picture in *The Times* newspaper soon after the bombing of the World Trade Center in New York, showed an American bomb about to be dropped upon Afghanistan inscribed with the words 'Hijack this Fags'.

2

Faust's Transgressions: Male–Male Desire in Early Modern Germany

Robert D. Tobin

Faust, the scholar who made a deal with the devil in order to experience life as fully as possible, has come to be seen as the quintessential German, one who particularly exposes the dilemmas and traumas of modernity. But there is another persistant aspect of the Faust legend that has been neglected in the scholarly literature. Specifically, male–male desire and references to sodomy have steadily accompanied accounts of the Faust story, from Klinger and Goethe to Thomas Mann and his son Klaus. In Friedrich Maximilian Klinger's novel of 1791, *Fausts Leben, Taten und Höllenfahrt* [Faust's Life, Deeds, and Journey to Hell], Faust's dealings with the devil bring him in contact with sodomitical popes. In Johann Wolfgang von Goethe's *Faust*, the relationship between the protagonist and Mephistopheles is close enough that many interpreters have found a homoerotic tinge to it; in any case, Mephistopheles ends up smitten with the boyish angels in the final scenes, as Margarethe and the Eternal Feminine rescue Faust from the jaws of Hell. Klaus Mann's *Mephisto* (1936) is based upon the story of the homosexual actor, Gustav Gründgens, although the novel transforms this homosexuality into interracial sadomasochism. Thomas Mann also alludes to homosexuality in his masterpiece, *Doktor Faustus* (1941), in which the protagonist, the composer Adrian Leverkühn, has an erotic friendship with the gallant violinist, Rudi Schwerdtfeger. The constancy of this homosexual component to Faust's story suggests the relevance of issues of sexuality for the development of modernity in Germany. Specifically, the emergence of same-sex desire as a structure of identity accompanies the modernization of Germany.

The rhetoric of individual cases

Intriguingly, two accusations of sodomy are among the only traces documenting the life of the historical Faust, who lived in what is now Germany probably between 1480 and 1540. In a letter written on August 20, 1507, Johannes Tritheim, the Abbot of Sponheim, wrote to Johannes Virdung, court astrologer at Heidelberg, that Faust had been expelled from the town of Kreuznach because he had misused his position as schoolmaster to take advantage of the schoolboys 'in the most lewd way.' In addition, the records of the city of Nuremberg show that on May 10, 1532, residency was denied to 'Doctor Faustus, the great sodomite and necromancer.'[1] Besides Faust, there are in this period many other individual cases of men who were accused of sodomy or rumored to prefer men sexually. While their actual sexual behavior is not knowable, the accusations and rumors themselves suggest that sexual desire was coming to be seen as a significant factor in a person's identity.

Probably more ink has been spilt on the subject of the sexuality of Johann Joachim Winckelmann (1717–68) than on any other German figure from the eighteenth century. Among the details that are certain is that Winckelmann moved from Germany to Rome, where he made a name for himself as a great art critic. Thirteen years after his arrival in Rome, on the way back to Germany for a brief visit, he was killed in Trieste by an unemployed cook improbably named Arcangeli. The murder could have resulted from a robbery gone wrong; on the other hand, it could have been part of a sexual situation.

Even in Winckelmann's own day there were rumors that he was sexually attracted to men. Casanova claimed to have discovered Winckelmann in a state of undress with another man, although the art historian explained to the famous lover that appearances were deceiving, that he was not in fact sexually interested in the young man, but that he was merely investigating how the Greeks had lived in order to understand their art better.[2] The aesthetician Friedrich Wilhelm Basileus Ramdohr, who wrote extensively on same-sex desire in his book *Venus Urania* (1798), cited Winckelmann as a prime example of a man whose erotic attractions lay with other men: 'It has often been said that the immortal Winckelmann felt the influence of an obscure physical sexual sympathy in his enthusiastic dependence on delicate male beauty.'[3] Clearly indicating where his own sympathies lay, Ramdohr exclaimed, 'Shame on him who suspects shame here! It was natural, it was open, which proves the involuntary and, as far as the enthusiast is concerned, very probably completely unconscious impulse of sexual sympathy.'[4] There is ample evidence, therefore, that Winckelmann's contemporaries regarded him as being sexually attracted to men in a way that set him apart from others.

The historian Johannes Müller (1752–1810) is now also known, if at all, for his predilection for handsome men. In their day, his histories of Switzerland were tremendous successes, although they are now hard to locate. Even in the early nineteenth century, Karl Friedrich Graf Reinhard remarked to Goethe that the 'red thread' that united the historian's work was the love of men for each other.[5] Müller's travails became public as a result of the so-called Batthiany affair, which transpired in Vienna in 1802 and 1803. A pupil, Fritz von Hardenberg, bilked the scholar out of a small fortune by inventing an admirer, 'the Count von Batthiany'. Hardenberg brought letters from the fictitious lover, letters that among other things encouraged Müller to lend money to his bright young pupil. Upon the discovery of the fraud, Müller had to leave Vienna embarrassed and broke. Goethe, who wrote in support of Winckelmann, also tried to help Müller by offering him a position in Weimar. Now, although his scholarly work is no longer so well known, Müller's sexuality still exerts a certain fascination. Astonishingly enough, he shows up in such popular gay anthologies as Martin Greif's *Gay Book of Days*.[6] In the academic arena, current interest has also focused on his sexual orientation and his era's responses to that orientation.[7]

There were also rumors about the sexuality of Friedrich II (Frederick the Great), King of Prussia. Friedrich's own father cast aspersions on his son's manliness when he declared him to be an effeminate fellow. Some of Friedrich's own publications led credence to the notion that he was interested in male–male desire. He penned anti-clerical poetry, such as the following poem, 'Le Palladion,' that had Catholic priests advocating sodomy:

> Wise Socrates demanded it
> From Alcibiades, who was certainly
> A good Greek; so behaved
> Euryalus and Nissus with each other.
> Am I supposed to cite more examples for you?
> There is the great Caesar, who the world
> Called the bridegroom of all Roman women,
> And who was at the same time the wench of Roman men.[8]

Although this passage relies primarily on the classical Greco-Roman tradition in justifying same-sex desire, Friedrich concludes his argument scandalously by comparing Jesus' relationship with the disciple John to that between Zeus and Ganymede.

Voltaire had perhaps begun the rumors about the enlightened monarch's sexual persuasions, accusing Friedrich of favoring good-looking soldiers with private audiences. But the rumors about the King persisted, as can be seen in one of the first biographies of Friedrich, by Anton Friedrich Büsching, which provided the following information about the royal tastes:

> For reasons of which I cannot be certain, he had begun early to develop a distaste for women and to avoid their company ... Because of this, he lost much sensual pleasure, but regained it through the company of men, and had retained from the history of philosophy that it was said about Socrates the he had loved the company of Alcibiades.[9]

The implications of Büshing's remarks were clear to Friedrich's famous physician, Johann Georg Zimmermann, who found it necessary to repeat and refute precisely this passage in a chapter of his *Fragmente über Friedrich den Große:* [Fragments on Frederick the Great, 1790], entitled 'On Frederick's Allegedly Greek Taste in Love.' Managing simultaneously to defend Socrates's honor and to take a swipe at the Jesuits, Zimmermann rephrases the concern as follows:

> It was rumored: 'He loved many of his pages, many an Antinous, many a beautiful youth, not actually as Socrates had loved the handsome Alcibiades, but as the Jesuits, according to the King's own story, so often loved their beautiful pupils.'[10]

All of this Zimmermann refutes with an obscurely complicated story about a medical condition that affected the King's genitals and that eventually required 'a cruel cut!'[11] This apparent disfigurement of the genitalia allegedly left the King so embarrassed that he avoided all amorous dalliances with women. Whether or not this story is true, it indicates that people in the era openly discussed their sovereign's sexual peccadilloes.

There are bound to be disputes about the accuracy of such accounts of personal behavior. Moreover, definitional questions emerge: even if these men were sexually attracted to other men, who is to say whether they belonged to a category that would today qualify as being 'gay' or 'queer'? Nonetheless, it is certain in the most prominent of their cases – Winckelmann, Müller, and Friedrich II – that their behavior was noted in its own time as remarkable and worthy of comment. This suggests that sexuality was coming to be seen as a quality of identity by the end of the early modern period.

Institutions

At least since Foucault, historians of sexuality have been more interested in the role of institutions in creating sexualities than in the arguable case histories of prominent individuals. Medicine, the nation-state, and its laws are some of the most obviously significant institutions that helped constitute sexuality in early modern Germany.

Not coincidentally, it was a doctor, Zimmermann, who felt obligated and entitled to explain Friedrich's sexuality to the world. In the early modern period, medicine gradually assumed the prominence in matters of sexuality that it was to exhibit so supremely in the nineteenth century. Already in 1688, Paulus Zacchia wrote on pederasty from the perspective of forensic medicine. He was convinced that pederasty commited on a male was 'certainly the most serious' crime.[12] A century later, medical attention was repeatedly directed to the subject of male–male desire. Heinrich Detering has uncovered an anonymous 1789 account, 'Nachricht von einer seltsamen Irrung eines menschlichen Triebes' [Report on a Strange Deviation of the Human Drive], which describes the existence of men whose desire is directed toward other men. The author cries out, 'Would that psychologists, physicians, and students of nature considered it worth the trouble not to overlook completely a subject on which the lifelong happiness of a person depends and which, were it to spread more widely, would necessarily interest the state!'[13] In an era in which the pursuit of happiness would be considered an unalienable right, any factor that would affect the lifelong happiness of an individual would become an aspect of identity.

By the end of the early modern period, therefore, there were clear calls for medical experts to devote their attention to same-sex attraction. In 1791, Karl Phillip Moritz's journal *Das Magazin zur Erfahrungsseelenkunde* [The Magazine of Experimental Psychology] published two accounts on the mental and spiritual health of men who had mysteriously deep feelings for other men. The first called upon medical science to look into the matter more closely, and the second responded by offering possible cures.[14] In a survey conducted between 1791 and 1794, H.B. Wagnitz reported that sodomites were among the inmates of Germany's insane asylums. His numbers are small (0.5 percent of inmates), but they indicate the beginning of institutional medicine's interest in the category of sexual deviance.[15] In 1796, Johann Valentin Müller published his *Entwurf der gerichtlichen Arnzeywissenschaft* [Proposal for a Forensic Medicine], which devoted an entire chapter to the subject of sodomy, understood to include onanism and tribadism, as well as sexual acts between men.[16]

Many of these medical writers mention the state's interest in studying sexual behavior. Detering's anonymous 'Nachricht' is certain that the state will need to focus on the phenomenon of male–male love because it could contribute to depopulation.[17] Johann Valentin Müller voices the same concern.[18] Ramdohr also refers to 'the disadvantageous effects on the population of the state' in his discussion of Greek love.[19] Thus, as the modern nation-state emerges in Germany (primarily through Prussia) toward the end of the early modern period, there is increasing institutional interest in the surveillance and governance of sexuality as an instrument of population control.

The most obvious manifestation of this state interest in sexuality was located in the law, which on this subject remained remarkably stable throughout the early modern period in Germany. One official document regarding same-sex desire was pertinent in the German-speaking world from the early sixteenth century to the beginning of the nineteenth century. In 1532, the penal code of Emperor Charles V, the *Peinliche Gerichtsordnung*, set the tone for the treatment of sexual perversion in the courts of the Holy Roman Empire: death by fire for immoral behavior between people and animals, men and men, and women and women.[20] The *Peinliche Gerichtsordnung* applied throughout the Empire until Napoleon dissolved it in 1806; shortly thereafter, some German principalities began adopting modernized legal codes from the French that decriminalized non-commercial consensual sexual activities between adults, resulting in a brief period in the early nineteenth century when same-sex activity was not a crime, at least in parts of Germany, for instance Bavaria.[21] Even Prussia, which remained the most conservative on this front, decreased the penalties for sodomy so that it was no longer a capital crime.[22] More research needs to be done on the extent to which sodomy was actually prosecuted in the early modern period in Germany, and whether the extreme penalties actually diminished the likelihood of frequent prosecution.[23] But the precipitous legal shift from capital crime to legal activity in some

German principalities suggests a changing status for sexual activity in the constitution of the individual.

Significantly, female–female sexual acts were penalized just as severely as male–male ones. Thus, there was not the judicial blindness toward same-sex activity among women that was to characterize German and English law in the late nineteenth century and that has given rise to the notion of 'lesbian impunity.' Similarly, the medical authorities writing on sodomy usually included sexual acts between women and whatever they felt to be non-normative sexual acts between men and women in the larger category of sodomy.[24] Although this article concentrates on male–male sexual acts, there were clearly precedents at the time for regarding sexual acts between members of the same sex as belonging to the same category of transgression.

Demographic and historical trends

Accompanying the development of institutions like medicine, law and the nation-state, a number of demographic and historical trends helped construct sexuality in the early modern period. Population growth and urbanization, particularly in Berlin, set the stage for the appearance of subcultures centering on male–male desire. Tourism and colonialism left particular inflections upon identities that were emerging in these subcultures. And a radical shift in the conceptualization of gender – from a 'one-sex system' to a 'two-sex system' – affected the self-understanding of men who desired other men and ushered in the notion of the 'third sex.'

The state interest in population control corresponded to an actual increase in population throughout the early modern period in Europe. The populations of Paris, Amsterdam, and London grew to over half a million each, allowing for subcultures to develop that focused on male–male desire. Germany, which suffered from the ravages of the Thirty Years' War in the seventeenth century, rebounded especially dramatically in the eighteenth century. Berlin began to emerge as a city that could compare with the large cities in Western Europe. Detering's anonymous 'Nachricht' declared that the city in which its author lived had a number of pederasts, but that there were far more such men in another, unspecified larger city: 'In a large city, which I don't want to mention by name, there is supposed to be an entire community of such misattuned lovers, who bring ever more men into their fraternity in order to find more nourishment for their lusts.'[25] Conceivably this city with its predatory vampiric boy-lovers might be outside Germany; reports of the scandalous behavior of sodomites in

London were mentioned in the Berlin press in January of 1793 and republished in Leipzig in 1796 under the title 'Außerordentliches Beispiel der großen Verdorbenheit der Sitten in England' [Extraordinary Example of the Great Decay of Morals in England].[26] Whether the city was in Germany or in another country, it is clear that people of the era were aware that increased urbanization allowed for the emergence of subcultures built around male–male desire.

If the city mentioned in the 'Nachricht' was in Germany, it was probably Berlin. The most significant evidence regarding a sodomitical subculture is the volume entitled *Briefe über die Galanterien von Berlin* [Letters on the Gallantries of Berlin, 1782], attributed to Johannes Friedel (1755–89). Friedel claims to have found communities of so-called 'warm brothers,' who at first seem to him to be merely exceptionally close friends but then turn out to be involved with each other romantically. He also stumbles across organized male prostitution:

> You'll find here houses which exist under the honorable name of boy tobacco shops [*Knabentabagie*] in which young men of fourteen, fifteen and more years of age come to pass the time ... You'll find procurers and procuresses who wander about on the streets and look for children, as well as grown-up youths, attract them to such houses and make their profit thereby.[27]

Johann Valentin Müller credits Friedel, citing the *Briefe* to argue that sodomy 'is brazenly practiced in large cities and in certain public houses handsome youth suffer the same lot as beautiful girls.'[28] Johann Valentin Müller's citation of Friedel suggests that those who lived in the late eighteenth century did not find it impossible that Berlin was in fact home to a subculture of men who desired other men. More recently, James Steakley has, upon analyzing Friedel's *Briefe*, concluded that 'a fairly continuous homosexual subculture is in place by the late eighteenth century' in Berlin.[29]

With the growth of cities came the accumulation of wealth. In the eighteenth century, a new group of affluent men were able to discover male–male love while travelling, particularly in Italy. Johann Georg Krünitz included an entry on pederasty in his encyclopedia of 1784, in which he informed readers that such practices were particularly common in Italy:

> Pederasty is more common in Naples than in any other city in Italy. Climate and leisure encourage this unfortunate practice ... Lord

> Tilney, who died in 1784 was a great pederast and for that reason made Naples his home for 25 years. To avoid a criminal trial that threatened him in England because of his favorite passion, which no race hates more than the English, he left his homeland forever and lived from his 18,000 pounds Sterling with the splendor of a great lord. He was usually in Florence in the summer and in Naples in the winter, where he threw splendid parties and satisfied his passions until his death.[30]

Winckelmann, of course, also fits into the Northern European tradition of looking for male–male love in Italy, a pattern that Robert Aldrich has studied more thoroughly in his work, *The Seduction of the Mediterranean*.[31]

Goethe, too, observed Italian sensuality first hand. In a letter of 29 December 1787, Goethe wrote to his friend and employer, Karl August, Duke of Sachsen-Weimar, that he had discovered 'a remarkable phenomenon that I have seen nowhere as strong as here, it is the love of men amongst themselves.'[32] Goethe had a number of other connections to draw between male–male desire and Italy: he had translated Cellini's autobiography, which specifically discusses accusations against the artist of sodomy. He also translated one of Richard Payne Knight's travel journals to Sicily for inclusion in his study of Phillip Hackett, the Prussian artist who spent much time in Italy. While this journal does not mention sexuality in any particular way, Knight, who was infamous in the eighteenth century because of his *Discourse on the Worship of Priapus* (1786–87), was part of a male-centric and phallus-obsessed world of northern European connoisseurs that vibrated with homosocial and homosexual tensions.[33] Given the associations in Goethe's writings between male–male desire and Italy, it is not surprising that he includes the following couplet specifically among his Venetian Epigrams:

> Boys I have also loved
> But I prefer girls;
> If I'm tired of her as a girl,
> She can serve me as a boy as well![34]

Whether one believes Goethe's claim that he has loved boys or not, it is typical for an eighteenth-century German that he would position this love in Italy.

From the touristic fantasy it is only a small step to the colonialist imagination. Research has shown that the colonial effort also played a role in the reconstitution of sexuality in the early modern period.[35] In the German-language realm, a document that Friedrich II commissioned Cornelius de Pauw to write about the New World is informative. Friedrich's request that de Pauw write the document itself shows that the Germans were interested in the exploratory activity characterizing this era, although they lacked a consistent colonial effort. The fact that de Pauw emphasized the high incidence of homosexuality and effeminacy among Native American men shows that for the Germans colonialism affected ways of thinking about and representing sexuality.[36]

The German observation of the colonial endeavor gave early modern writers and thinkers the opportunity to use motifs from the colonized world as they tried to describe male–male sexuality. In his novel, *Siebenkäs* (1796), John Paul (1763–1825) locates male–male desire outside of Europe. The narrator of the novel hopes to see his characters 'imitating the Tahitians, who exchange names as well as hearts with their beloveds,' even when these beloveds are of the same sex.[37] Here Jean Paul is alluding to a long tradition of finding (homo-)sexual liberation in the South Pacific, a tradition that took hold especially firmly in the eighteenth century.[38] Closer to home, Jean Paul cites in his novel Alberto Fortis's 1778 account of life in the Balkans, where, according to Fortis, something like same-sex marriages took place:

> They have even made it [friendship] a kind of religious point, and tie the sacred bond at the foot of the altar. The Sclavonian ritual contains a particular benediction for the solemn union of two male or two female friends in the presence of the congregation.[39]

Early modern Germany found in the newly discovered world and the exotic parts of the old world a space in which to conceptualize male–male desire.

As colonialism and industrialization advanced in Germany and Western Europe, gender structures also changed. Thomas Laqueur has argued forcefuly that in the eighteenth century a major shift took place in the conceptualization of gender in northwestern Europe, from what he calls the 'one-sex system' to the 'two-sex system.'[40] This gender shift had a strong effect on sexuality, as Randolph Trumbach argues. In the one-sex system, the boy, an underdeveloped man, was virtually exchangeable with the woman, meaning that many if not most men might occasionally have sex with a younger man instead of a woman. In the two-sex system, no such equation applied. Instead, men who desired men began to think of themselves as female souls residing in male bodies. They inverted their gender, claiming the position of a woman in a heterosexual relationship. All desire in this way of thinking remained heterosexual, passing from the masculine to the feminine and vice versa. This view, then, produced in the early modern period what Trumbach calls the 'birth of the queen' in an essay by that name: the emergence of a class of men who understand their desires for other men in terms of gender inversion.

In the German-speaking realm, gender inversion as an explanation for same-sex attraction comes out most clearly in the writings of Ramdohr. In his three-volume book *Venus Urania* of 1798, he argues that love – as opposed to friendship – is characterized by a union of the masculine and the feminine. Provocatively, however, he insists that these two categories do not overlap entirely with the categories of man and woman. Articulating the ways in which the masculine and the feminine can create a household, he claims rather astonishingly for this time and place that 'men can live with men in domestic harmony, or women with women, or finally men with women; in every case of this sort one is the leader, ruler, actor, while the other is the submissive, responsive part.'[41] Ramdohr's explanation of same-sex desire as a product of gender inversion coincides nicely with Trumbach's theories on the emergence of the third sex at the end of the early modern period in western Europe.

Intellectual and cultural trends

Intellectually, the early modern period is characterized by a rediscovery of the classical tradition, a tradition that provided a sturdy vocabulary of concepts like 'Greek friendship' for discussing same-sex desire. This emphasis on the classical tradition for the justification and explanation of same-sex desire results in the emergence and popularization of a classical canon of same-sex desire that would survive through the present day. Friedrich II's 'Palladion,' with its references to Socrates, Alcibiades, Nissus, Euryalus, and Caesar, is just one example of this standard classical canon of male–male desire. Friedel's *Briefe* of 1782 are redolent in classical language, referring to 'Socratic lovers' following the pattern of Zeus and Ganymede.[42] The anonymous 'Nachricht' of 1789 provides a similar analysis.[43] Such explanations of male–male desire would become a mainstay in the Western tradition in the following centuries, in part because outside of the classical, philological tradition there was very little discursive space for a discussion of same-sex desire in artistic, scholarly, and popular publications.

At the beginning of the early modern period in Germany, allusions to same-sex desire in classical texts reprinted in the early modern era tended to be ignored or even translated out of existence. Sven Limbeck has demonstrated how pederastic references in Plautus comedies were completely removed from sixteenth- and seventeenth-century translations and performances.[44] Until the eighteenth century, scholars like Johann Matthias Gesner and Moses Mendelssohn defended Socrates from the accusation of pederasty; the physician Zimmermann took this line in his defense of Friedrich II. In the second half of the eighteenth century, however, following the example set by Voltaire, thinkers like Johann Georg Hamann and Herder began to acknowledge that homoerotic desire played a large role in classical writings.[45]

The earliest German-language essay devoted entirely to the subject of same-sex desire is Christoph Meiners's 'Betrachtungen über die Männerliebe der Griechen' [Observations on the Male Love of the Greeks], a thirty-page text that was included in the Göttingen philologist's collected essays, *Vermischte philosophische Schriften* [Various Philosophical Writings] of 1775. In this essay, the prestige of classical antiquity provides cover for a discussion of male–male love. Meiners finds the 'enthusiastic love of the beauty of the male sex' to be one of the 'characteristic customs or passions' of the Greeks.[46] Following the French *philosophes*, he attributes the development of this peculiar passion to the poor treatment of women in a society where only men were educated and enjoyed freedom of movement. He is also suspicious of the gymnasia, 'in which the most beautiful youth revealed to the lustful eye all the charms of their unclothed bodies.'[47] Meiners adds that the magnificent art of the Greeks contributed to making them all connoisseurs of the male body.[48] Ultimately, according to Meiners, the custom goes back to the heroic friendships common in the days of Chiron and Achilles, Achilles and Patroclus, and Orestes and Pylades.[49] Such friendships are in no way feminine, but rather characteristic of 'raw, warlike peoples,' including the indigenous peoples of the Americas, according to Meiners.[50] With the increasing refinements of Greek society, these friendships took a new turn and 'began very early to decay among the Greeks into unnatural lust.'[51]

Winckelmann famously based his principles of artistic taste on Greek painting and sculpture. He infuses his analysis of classical art with a great appreciation of the sensuality of Greek culture and its appreciation of the body. Whereas critics of Greek love tended to condemn the practice of exercising naked, Winckelmann has nothing but praise for the gymnasia:

> Their exercises gave the bodies of the Greeks the strong and manly countours which the masters then imparted to their statues without any exaggeration or excess. The young Spartans had to appear naked every ten days before the Ephors, who would impose a stricter diet upon those showing signs of fat.[52]

Following Winckelmann, Ramdohr's analysis of same-sex love in *Venus Urania* is framed entirely as a question of Greek aesthetics.

Literary figures also made extensive use of the classical tradition for discussions of same-sex desire. The novelist Wilhelm Heinse made one of the earliest defenses in the German tradition of male–male love when he noted in his foreword to his translation of Petronius' *Satyricon*: 'Who would prove to the Greeks that the pleasures that they took with beautiful Ganymedes should not have delighted them more than the pleasures with their women.'[53] This passage is reminiscent of Christoph Martin Wieland's casual aside in his most famous novel, *Agathon*, regarding the Greek custom of kissing boys instead of girls: '"O unhappy one!", he [Socrates] said to the young Xenophon, who could not understand that it was a dangerous thing to kiss a beautiful boy, or – to speak in accordance with our customs – a beautiful girl.'[54] In 1774, the poet Johann Wilhelm Ludwig Gleim defended Heinse against Wieland's accusations of immorality by pointing out that Wieland's own early poetry had introduced German youth to the idea of Greek love and encouraged them to acquire Ganymedes of their own.[55] Wieland's poem, 'Juno und Ganymed' [Juno and Ganymede], published anonymously in 1765 as part of *Comische Erzählungen* [Comical Stories], was filled with rococo bantering about the relative merits of male and female lovers.

The most extraordinary example of sexualized heroic, 'Greek' friendship found in the German literary tradition of the eighteenth century is Schiller's fragmentary play, *Die Malteser* [The Maltese], which he began in 1795. Set among the Knights of Malta, 'the plot is simple and heroic, as are the characters, who are at the same time exclusively masculine,' Schiller wrote to his friend Wilhelm von Humboldt.[56] Two of the main characters of the play, Crequi and St. Priest, were to be lover and beloved, following what Schiller refers to in his notes as the 'love of the Greek youths for each other.'[57] Schiller explicitly indicates that this love is sexual: 'Their love is of the purest beauty, but it is however necessary not to remove from it the sensual character with which it is attached to nature. It may and must be felt that it is a transfer, a surrogate, of sexual love, and an effect of a natural drive.'[58] Schiller makes clear that the two knights fall into two separate categories, the lover and the beloved: 'But only one is the lover, the active one; the younger and beloved behaves passively.'[59] Clearly, Schiller is not making any effort to hide the sexuality of male–male relationships in the Greek tradition.

Many of the discussions of Greek love center on the notion of friendship, which was itself enjoying a vogue at the end of the early modern period. The cult of friendship was particularly strong in England and Germany, while Voltaire remarked that he did not find it especially well developed in France.[60] By the mid-eighteenth century, German gentlemen were expressing tender feelings for each other in words that were virtually indistinguishible from the vocabulary of lovers. This cult of friendship produced effusive declarations of love, sometimes going so far as mimicking marriage proposals. The poet Gleim sent the following ditty to Friedrich Jacobi:

> I want to be a girl:
> Then he would marry me;
> He wouldn't lack for friends
> Nor for love, nor for wine:
> I want to be his girl![61]

Jacobi himself was to write to the novelist Jean Paul, 'I feel just like you that the friend should love his friend like the wife loves her husband, the [female] lover her [male] beloved.'[62] By the end of the early modern period, the cult of friendship was allowing for radical reconceptualizations of relationships between members of the same-sex.

Sedgwick wryly observes that scholars have for years tried to ignore the language of friendship with the following 'rule': 'Passionate language of same-sex attraction was extremely common during whatever period is under discussion – and thus must have been completely meaningless.'[63] But in fact eighteenth-century readers objected to the tone of the more demonstrative male–male letters, suggesting that they were not completely innocent in their own era. Anna Louise Karsch's critique of the effusive *Briefe von den Herren Gleim und Jacobi* [Letters of the Messieurs Gleim and Jacobi] shows that the language of friendship was provocative in its own day: 'There are too many kisses in this work to avoid slander, suspicion and mockery.'[64] Similar concerns greeted Müller's letters to Karl Victor von Bonstetten, which are monuments to the cult of friendship. They were so tender and intimate that their editor had to reassure readers that this friendship was 'of the strictest, purest virtue' and was 'in every other respect identical to that friendship that produced the best and greatest things in antiquity.'[65] The phrase, 'in every other respect,' implies that the Greek friendships were not necessarily 'of the strictest, purest virtue' and admits that one could and did imagine that Müller's letters were signifiers of sexual desire. Given these contemporary misgivings about friendship, it seems highly likely that same-sex desire played a role in the cult of friendship.

The novelist Jean Paul is said to have coined the term 'Freundesliebe' [love of friends].[66] His fantasies of male–male love take place in the masculine context of sailors and warriors dying in each other's arms. In his novel *Siebenkäs*, the character Siebenkäs has an intense relationship with his double, whose name is Leibgeber. This relationship culminates when the two of them 'lay clasping each other on the high tide of life, like two shipwrecked brothers, who swim in the cold waves, embracing and embraced, and who hold nothing more than the heart, of which they are dying.'[67] A subsequent so-called 'dream within a dream' ends with the image of bloody warriors bonding sensually together:

> Finally the smoke parted in billows above two bloody people who lay in each other's wounded arms. It was two sublime friends who had sacrificed everything for each other, themselves first of all, but not their fatherland. 'Lay your wound on mine, beloved!'[68]

Added to this kind of appeal are a number of lachrymose scenes in which the narrator addresses dead friends of his, and cites specifically the British tradition of friendship, exemplified in the letters of Swift, Arbuthnot and Pope, as models.[69] This tradition of friendship builds on the eighteenth-century interpretations of Greek love to provide a fertile field for homoerotic fantasy.

An additional cultural development that accompanied the rediscovery of the classics was an increasing aestheticism. This too became associated with male–male desire, particularly in a Greek context. Winckelmann argues that an appreciation for beauty requires an openness to masculine beauty as well:

> I have observed that those who are only aware of beauty in the female sex and are hardly or not at all affected by beauty in *our* sex, have little innate feeling for beauty in art in a general and vital sense. The same people have an inadequate response to the art of the Greeks, since their greatest beauties are more of our sex than the other.[70]

As part of his defense of Winckelmann, Ramdohr finds that art connoisseurship is frequently associated with male–male desire:

> This appearance of physical sexual sympathy with the enthusiasm for youthful male beauty should not be used as a reproach to art lovers, among whom it is found most frequently. It is in no way shameful, for they are often not aware of its effect on them.[71] This linkage of the Greeks, friendship, a sense for aesthetics, and an appreciation of masculine beauty is a foundation for much modern gay self-construction.

Conclusion

The early modern period in Germany more or less encompasses the span of time between the life of the historical Faust (1480–1540) and Goethe's writing of his version of *Faust* (roughly from 1770 to 1830). During this time there is an increase in public discussion about a number of men, such as Winckelmann, Müller, and Friedrich II, who were said to desire other men sexually. At the same time, institutional structures gradually make way for the emergence of an identity based on sexuality. Medicine becomes increasingly interested in the phenomenon of same-sex desire, while the law eventually removes the death penalty from sexual acts between members of the same-sex, and even briefly decriminalizes them entirely. More generally, urbanization, tourism, colonialism, and the rise of the two-sex system inflect the emergent sexual identity in ways that will make it specifically modern. Finally, this developing sexual identity is related in many complex ways to the rediscovery of the classics, the cult of friendship, and the birth of aesthetics.

These structures are the foundation upon which the sexual identity of people who were attracted to members of their own sex in the nineteenth century would be built in Germany. This is important, because much of the research in medicine, law, and homosexual activism that concerned homosexuality took place in the German-speaking realm.

Karl Heinrich Ulrichs campaigned ceaselessly for the rights of the 'third sex' that he called 'urnings' in the 1860s and '70s. Karl Maria Kertbeny coined the term 'homosexual' in an open letter to the Prussian Minister of Justice urging the decriminalization of sodomy in 1869, the same year in which Carl Westphal devoted an article to the subject of gender inversion that Foucault has argued signals the 'birth of the homosexual.'[72] If the homosexual was indeed born in the nineteenth century and in a German medical journal, then the many factors outlined in this article suggest that its conception took place in the early modern period and at least in part in Germany. Perhaps the modern construction of homosexuality is one more product of the transgressions of that early modern German, Faust.

Notes

1 Both cases are cited in Theodore Ziolkowski, *The Sin of Knowledge* (Princeton: Princeton University Press, 2000), 47.
2 Jacques Casanova, *Histoire de ma vie*, 8 vols (Wiesbaden: Brockhaus, 1961), 7: 197.
3 Friedrich Wilhelm Basileus Ramdohr, *Venus Urania*, 3 vols (Leipzig: Goschen, 1798), 2: 134.
4 Ramdohr, 2: 134.
5 Cited in Paul Derks, *Die Schande der heiligen Päderastie* (Berlin: Verlag rosa Winkel, 1990), 343.
6 Martin Grief, *Gay Book of Days* (Secaucus, NJ: Mainstreet Press, 1982), 17–18.
7 See, for instance, Simon Richter, 'Winckelmann's Progeny,' in Alice A. Kuzniar (ed.), *Outing Goethe and His Age* (Stanford: Stanford University Press, 1996), 33–46.
8 Reprinted in Joachim Campe (ed.), *Andere Lieben* (Frankfurt: Suhrkamp, 1988), 112.
9 Anton Friedrich Büsching, *Character Friedrichs des Zweytens*, 2nd edn (Halle: Witwe, 1788), 22.
10 Johann Georg Zimmermann, *Fragmente über Friedrich den Großen* (Leipzig: Weidmann, 1790), 85–6.
11 Zimmermann, 70.
12 Paulus Zacchia, 'Zu Fragen der gerichtlichen Medizin. Über die Knabenschändung,' in Joachim S. Hohmann (ed.), *Der unterdruckte Sexus* (Lollar: Aschenbach, 1977), 205.
13 Heinrich Detering, '"Zur Sprache kommen": Eine homoerotische (Auto-) Biographie 1789,' in Gerhard Härle (ed.), *Grenzüberschreitungen: Friedenspädagogik, Geschlechter-Diskurs, Literatur-Sprache-Didaktik* (Essen: Blaue Eule, 1995), 271.
14 *Das Magazin zur Erfahrungsseelenkunde*, ed. Karl Phillip Moritz, 1783–92. Facsimile Edition, ed. by Anke Bennholdt-Thomsen and Alfredo Guzzoni (Lindau: Antiqua, 1979). The particular articles include 'Aus einem Brief,'

Magazin 8.1. (1791), and under the rubric 'Seelenheilenkunde' in *Magazin* 8.2 (1791). For a less sensitive reference to 'the disgusting suspician of pederasty,' see 'Auszug aus dem Leben H. Cardus,' *Magazin* 6.1. (1788): 79.

15 Heinrich B. Wagnitz, *Historische Nachrichten und Bemerkung über die merkwürdigsten Zuchthäuser in Deutschland*, 2 vols (Halle: Gebauer, 1791–94), 2.2: 14.

16 Johann Valentin Müller, 'Entwurf der gerichtlichen Arzneywissenschaft, 1796,' in Joachim S. Hohmann (ed.), *Der unterdruckte Sexus* (Lollar: Aschenbach, 1977), 211–24.

17 Detering, 'Zur Sprache kommen,' 276, see also 271.

18 Johann Valentin Müller, 134.

19 Ramdohr, 2: 138.

20 Cited in Derks, 140.

21 See Derks, 163, for a province-by-province explanation of the changing legal status of sodomy in Germany. For a discussion of the situation particularly in Bavaria, see Isabel V. Hull, *Sexuality, State, and Civil Society in Germany, 1700–1815* (Ithaca: Cornell University Press, 1996), 349–50.

22 James Steakley, 'Sodomy in Enlightenment Prussia,' in Kent Gerard and Gert Hekma (eds), *The Pursuit of Sodomy* (New York: Harrington Park Press, 1989), 163–75.

23 Brigitte Ericksson refers to late nineteenth-century research claiming that there were over one hundred sodomy trials. Brigitte Ericksson, 'A Lesbian Execution in Germany, 1721: The Trial Records,' in Salvatore J. Licata and Robert P. Petersen (eds), *The Gay Past: A Collection of Historical Essays* (New York: Harrington Park Press, 1985), 41–56. Steakley cites a study of 43 males and one female charged with sodomy between 1700 and 1730, of whom nine individuals were executed for bestiality and three for same-sex activities. Hull provides documentation on the prosecution of sexual crimes overall, but usually without bringing out sodomy charges specifically.

24 For more information on female–female sexuality in Germany, see Ericksson.

25 Detering, 'Zur Sprache kommen,' 276.

26 Reprinted in *Capri: Zeitschrift für schwule Geschichte* 22 (August 1996), 31–3.

27 Johann Friedel, *Briefe über die Galanterien von Berlin, auf einer Reise gesammelt von einem österreichischen Offizier 1782*, ed. by Sonja Schnitzler (Berlin: Eulenspiegel, 1987), 142–3.

28 Johann Valentin Müller, 134.

29 Steakley, 170.

30 Reprinted in *Andere Liebe*, 19.

31 Robert Aldrich, *The Seduction of the Mediterranean* (London: Routledge, 1993).

32 Johann Wolfgang von Goethe, *Goethes Werke: Herausgegeben im Auftrage der Großherzogin Sophie von Sachsen*, 142 vols (Weimar: Böhlau, 1888; reprint, Tokyo: Sansyusya, 1975), 4.8: 314–15.

33 George Sebastian Rousseau, *Perilous Enlightenment: Pre- and Post-Modern Discourses: Sexual, Historical* (Manchester: Manchester University Press, 1991), 68–137.

34 Goethe, 1.5.2: 381.

35 Jonathan Goldberg, *Sodometries* (Stanford: Stanford University Press, 1992), 177–222.
36 Susanne Zantop, 'Dialectics and Colonialism,' in W. Daniel Wilson and Robert C. Holub (eds), *Impure Reason* (Detroit: Wayne State University Press, 1993), 305 and 307.
37 Jean Paul (= Johann Paul Friedrich Richter), *Werke in drei Bänden*, ed. by Norbert Miller (Munich: Hanser, 1969), 1: 474.
38 Robert Aldrich, 'Weiße und farbige Männer,' *Forum: Homosexualität und Literatur* 7 (1989) 5–24.
39 Alberto Fortis, *Travels into Dalmatia* (New York: Arno Press, 1971), 56–7.
40 Thomas Laqueur, *Making Sex: Body and Gender from the Greeks to Freud* (Cambridge, MA: Harvard University Press, 1990). See also Linda Schiebinger, *The Mind Has No Sex? Women in the Origins of Modern Science* (Cambridge, MA: Harvard University Press, 1989).
41 Ramdohr, 1: 174.
42 See, for instance, Friedel, 141.
43 Detering, 'Zur Sprache kommen,' 277.
44 Sven Limbeck, 'Plautus in der Knabenschule: Zur Eliminierung homosexueller Inhalte in deutschen Plautusübersetzungen der frühen Neuzeit,' in Dirck Linck, Wolfgang Popp, and Annette Runte (eds), *Erinnern und Wiederentdecken* (Berlin: Verlag rosa Winkel, 1999), 15–67.
45 Derks, 59–60.
46 Meiners, 1: 64.
47 Meiners, 1: 82.
48 Meiners, 1: 86.
49 Meiners, 1: 83.
50 Meiners, 1: 83.
51 Meiners, 1: 88.
52 Johann Joachim Winckelmann, *Reflections on the Imitation of Greek Works in Painting and Sculpture*, trans. by Elfriede Heyer and Roger C. Norton (La Salle, IL: Open Court, 1987), 7–9.
53 Karl Heinrich Urichs, *Forschungen über das Räthsel der mannmännlichen Liebe*, ed. by Hubert Kennedy, 12 vols in four (Berlin: Verlag rosa Winkel, 1994), 2 (Inclusa): 53.
54 Christoph Martin Wieland, *Werke*, ed. by Fritz Martini and R. Döhl, 5 vols (Munich: Hanser, 1964), 1: 665.
55 Derks, 234.
56 Siegfried Seidel (ed.), *Briefwechsel zwischen Friedrich Schiller und Wilhelm von Humboldt* (Berlin: Aufbau, 1962), 1: 174.
57 Friedrich Schiller, *Sämtliche Werke*, ed. by Gerhard Fricke and Herbert G. Göpfert, 5 vols (Munich: Hanser, 1965), 3: 173.
58 Schiller, 3: 172.
59 Schiller, 3: 173.
60 Marie François Arrouet Voltaire, *A Philosophical Dictionary*, ten volumes in two (New York: Conventry House, 1932), 1:514.
61 Cited in Hans Dietrich, *Die Freundesliebe in der deutschen Literatur* (Leipzig, 1931; reprint, Berlin: Verlag rosa Winkel, 1996), 30.
62 Cited by Dietrich, 33.

63 Eve Kosofsky Sedgwick, *Epistemology of the Closet* (Berkley: University of California Press, 1990), 52.
64 Cited by Richter, 36.
65 Johannes von Müller, *Sämtliche Werke*, ed. by Johann Müller (Tübingen: Cotta, 1811–15), 4: ix.
66 Dietrich, 34.
67 Jean Paul, 1: 713.
68 Jean Paul, 1: 648.
69 Jean Paul, 1: 495.
70 Johann Hoachim Winckelmann, *Writings on Art*, ed. by David Irwin (London: Phaidon, 1972), 92.
71 Ramdohr, 2: 133.
72 Michel Foucault, *The History of Sexuality. Volume 1*, trans. by Robert Hurley (New York: Vintage, 1980), 43.

3
The Historiography of Male–Male Love in Portugal, 1550–1800

David Higgs

In its broadest sense the historiography of male homosexuality in Portugal from mid-sixteenth century to the start of the nineteenth is nourished by evidence on the topic from any perspective. In fact the richest documentation prior to the abolition of the Portuguese Inquisition (Holy Office) in 1821 derives from sodomy trials before it.[1] The interpretation and ambiguities of those trial records are a challenge to historians. The records of the Portuguese Inquisition are housed in the National Archives in Lisbon.

Further information can be gleaned from legal and police records and literary sources. More details may be culled from ecclesiastical archives. Mott also located one example of the most rare type of documents for same-sex relationships before 1800: namely personal letters, diaries and memoirs. A 1664 one-sided correspondence exists from a self-identified man making an offer of gay sex to another individual who preserved and then used the letters to attempt to maul him by invoking the Inquisition. The letters written by a sacristan in the Algarve go from amorous declaration to bitter recrimination that someone to whom the writer was generous was now mocking him *to women*.[2]

Very little material from the Portuguese records for the 'abominable sin' (*pecado nefando*) has been printed. Even less has been translated into English. The trials provide insights into how the inquisitors understood the temptations of sin. Here I shall deal with Inquisition documentation, which at first spoke of sodomy as a sin but in the last set of the Byelaws, that of 1774, called it a crime. Information is thus overwhelmingly found in the documentation amassed by those bent on the repression of sodomy, but even more so of scandalously public homosexual behaviors.

One can distinguish between two major categories. The first comprises the cases dealing with age-unequal encounters where a younger partner usually under 20 years of age is sodomized by an older male. A central motif for Lisbon and to a lesser extent Oporto is that dependent or vulnerable male adolescents were sexual objects: page boys, lackeys, messenger boys, street porters, and runaways. Indeed it may be that seventeenth-century 'street kids' were disproportionately queer. In 2001 it has been claimed as many as 25 to 50 per cent of 'street kids' are queer in a large Canadian city, many of them runaways from family disapproval of their orientations.[3] As in Florence of the fifteenth century a boy who had been receptive in sodomy might later marry and have children.[4]

The second category comprises assumptions revolving around the effeminate *fanchono* ('fairy') identity, often with campy speech and sisterly sociability, of men who sought to be bottoms to virile men and retained that desire as they aged. The first was a power relationship while the second was one driven by desire. The *fanchonos*, that is penetrable youths and men, were certainly a category to be denied full recognition with 'worthy men' – *homens bons* – both in the informal world of male sociability in the world on the move as well as in that of the records of the Inquisition. In a phallocratic world where many males lacked regular access to sex with women, using a *fanchono* to come to orgasm was not considered destructive to a clearly male gender. The *fanchonos* may have associated with female prostitutes and shared the same cruising grounds which, in Lisbon, were especially the market area by the side of the Tagus. There is scant evidence of anything like co-resident and egalitarian sexual intimacy between two men. A 25-year-old servant admitted in a trial of 1630 'putting his own tongue in the rear orifice' of the 33-year-old governor of Cape Verde from between 30 to 40 times.[5] That was certainly a sexual relationship between two adults but one that was unlikely to be egalitarian. In 1622 a witness noted of a monk who was a cook in his convent who was known to entice his partners with offers of food and drink, and 'that people said that a friar of Saint Anthony's convent was a sodomite *or* [my emphasis] a *fanchono*'[6] Foreigners perhaps felt more liberated than Portuguese. One of only three individuals sentenced to death prior to 1668 by Évora was a Moorish slave in 1575:

> And they both dined and went to bed, and the said António Luís began to embrace and to kiss him calling him brother and saying other sweet words and putting his hand on his shameful parts. And

> then António Luís put himself on top of he the confessant and slept with him carnally like a man with a woman, putting his nature in the back passage.[7]

The documentation is informative on desire and has at least something about queer domesticity, dinner and endearments. Attitudes in Portugal towards homosexuality current over time among the educated as much as those of the unlettered changed dramatically in the centuries between the reign of John III (1521–57) when the Portuguese Inquisition began its activities, and the passage of the partnership ('Unions in fact') legislation by the majority of the deputies in the National Assembly in Lisbon in February, 2001.

Clerical discourse

The clerical discourse on male homosexuality was found both in pastoral injunctions, sermons, and manuals for confessors of the period 1550–1800 as well as in the pre-sentencing discussions among inquisitors. In a profoundly Catholic culture change was measured, in the first instance, by what the clergy of that time taught on the topics of sin and sexuality. We can also assume that in future the intersection of studies of what Mark D. Jordan calls 'liturgy queens' and male–male sexual behaviors may offer rewarding subjects of investigation about priestly queer conduct.[8]

The Inquisition was established in Portugal in 1536 and was operational by 1540. Various men and youths and some women were denounced for sodomy, and one female and fewer men than those accused were arrested and tried for the sin of sodomy from the 1560s on during the life of the tribunals down to their final abolition in 1821. From 1580 to 1640 Portugal was part of a dual monarchy in which the Spanish king was also king of Portugal. In practice the seventeenth century was the era in which there were the most arrests. The Philipine period saw orders for increasing severity against sodomy in the Portuguese world. Philip II ordered in January 1596 a trial for sodomy with three partners and similar acts with four others to proceed to sentence against a *fidalgo* in India without further consultation: the execution of nobles or sentence to appear in a public auto da fé had to be referred to the crown.[9] In July 1611 and January 1614 the crown reiterated that sentences to 'natural death' could be rendered against sodomites by civil judges simply on the strength of the inquisitorial decision and without seeing the trial documentation.[10] There were signs of a 'homosexual panic' in Inquisitorial practice: in October 1620 the Inquisitor General wrote to the king that sins of sodomy and witchcraft were spreading in the kingdom and it was necessary to respond with rigorous punishment to avoid great ills.[11] In August 1624 and again in 1628 there were calls for punishments to appease an angry divinity and to satisfy public opinion.[12] In 1631 it was said that divine anger has been revealed by 'things which have taken place against this monarchy' and that the remedy is punishment of 'evil sins of a scandalous and bad quality.'[13] The height of the campaign against sodomy took place after the restoration in 1640 of a Portuguese dynasty, the Braganza family.

The study of evolving clerical commentary on matters of sexuality is informative.[14] Rodrigo do Porto published various manuals of confessors and penitents in the sixteenth century (1549, 1552, 1579). He had much to say on 'pollution', particularly if ejaculation resulted from fantasizing about someone or the wish to 'carry out this vile delectation', although he excused involuntary nocturnal emission or 'flux' of semen. He addressed these thoughts particularly for the adolescent male: 'Whence they say that the chaste youth is a martyr without shedding blood, because of the continence of a man youth, which according to the scriptures is only given by God to man.'[15]

The publications of one late Inquisitor General and Confessor of Queen Maria I, Inácio de São Caetano (1719–88) addressed with some precision issues of sexual behaviors and included among them same-sex practices. This penitential literature with the approval of the state offered the paradigm of repentance and chastity as the desirable lifetime option for males who felt attracted to sexual relations with their own sex. Six volumes (in Portuguese) of the *Idea Of A Perfect Priest Instructed In His Obligations And Instructing His Flock In Solid Piety* (1772–85) could be complemented with his *Compendium Of Evangelical Moral Theology To Train Worthy Ministers Of The Sacrament Of Penance And Spiritual Directors, Much Extended In This Second Printing* (1784) 6 vols. He stressed that spiritual directors should be aware of the uses, customs and royal laws in force in the kingdom and that they should explain truth in Portuguese and not in Latin.

As a youth São Caetano had been a military cadet and had probably heard and seen more than spiritual exercises. There was a long discussion of impurity and he warned his clerical readers against it not only for temporal goods and bodily health but because of the damage this vice caused to the soul of whoever gave himself up to it. In volume three of the *Compendium* he dealt with sexuality, and there he discussed masturbation. Among other points he wrote that done with small boys incapable of deception it is, in practice, inseparable from the desire for sodomy.

Modern sexology holds that the most common form of human sexual activity over a lifetime is masturbation to orgasm, either in solitary, mutual or collective circumstances. It can be a component of foreplay, or as a complement to other techniques of coming to climax, at least among those capable of having an orgasm. Although prior to the Second World War and particularly in the nineteenth century there were commentators like Richard von Krafft-Ebing who associated masturbation with the cause of homosexual behavior, in the twentieth century it was more common to view masturbation as equally prevalent among heterosexuals and homosexuals. I am unaware of any claim prior to 1700 that masturbation engendered *fanchonos*. Arlindo Monteiro noted in 1922 that sodomy was, in fact, the least common homoerotic sexual practice, exceeded by both fellatio and masturbation.[16]

Laws against masturbators figured in the *Ordenanças Filipinas* Book Five, title 13, section 3 as 'Those who commit the crime of softness with themselves or with another of the same or of a different sex', and was also punished by the 12 October 1606 law which laid out the punishment as prison, flogging and sentence to the galleys for up to seven years for commoners. If they were nobles it was exile to Angola for seven years, which would avoid scandal. For those with a position in the royal household they were to be erased from the book of those with such positions and would lose their nobility. If they should revert to masturbation they could see their punishment increase into the death sentence, although in that case it should not be carried out without an authorization from the prince (section 13 of the *Ordenanças,* supra and the same 1606 law).[17] We can notice that these drastic measures speak of the crime rather than the sin and do not stress the fact of seminal discharge.

Such excessive measures against the most common sexual practice of humanity instantly make us ask whether they were ever applied. There is certainly no case known to me in the Portuguese historical literature. On the contrary, what is very common in sodomy trials before the Inquisition is the frank admission of repeated masturbatory acts between partners as individuals deny dispensing intra-anal semen. When priests were accused of abusing their sacerdotal authority in order to masturbate another person, or to be masturbated by that individual, the activity was then usually called in the documentation '*molicies*' (a word deriving from the Latin Mollitia meaning softness) or, rather more appropriately, indecent touchings (*'tocamentos torpes'*). This leads one to think that the laws were a kind of judicial Gongorism, grotesque in its exaggeration of the gap from judicial prohibitions and social reality.

Just as the church considered masturbation as a sin so the law was to consider it a crime although in practice confessors and judges took this lightly. This reaches back to the deeply-rooted campaigns against masturbation in the confessional manuals of Catholic Europe.

By the last third of the eighteenth century things were quite different. After 1760 the pursuit of lay sodomites was rare indeed. Priests who made sexual advances to penitents or to servants were reported and investigated, and so too was a child rapist.

During the eighteenth and nineteenth centuries a medicalized discourse emerged, dating from Tissot and others, which taught that 'wasteage' of seed was bad for health. Melo Franco argued in that way in 1794 in a book published in Lisbon.[18] It has been argued that this is a Protestant-based posture where semen, like capital, should be accumulated. However it figured in much Catholic penitential writing. The age cohort of prepubescent boys had its own internal lines of interdiction: 'good' boys knew it was not pious to masturbate, and non-playing boys were uninterested in doing so with partners. Others saw masturbatory activities as age complicit: it was outside of the grown-up world, and above all was self consciously a preliminary to more adult activities with the opposite sex. In demonstrating that masturbation is a mortal sin Caetano included among other causes the sight of bodies of the same sex. He also warned against touching the body, excepting boys who do so unintentionally when swimming, but if they do so deliberately it is sinful.

Medical discourse

Towards the end of the nineteenth century the kind of medicalized investigations, which were the Portuguese contribution to an international movement, included some historical references to time before 1800. Adelino Silva's 1896 book on sexual inversion was the first work on homosexuality to be published in Portugal. Subsequently Francisco Ferraz de Macedo, Arlindo Camillo Monteiro, Asdrubal António d'Aguiar and others would publish texts dealing with male homosexuality.[19] That of Monteiro in 1922 was significantly published in a limited edition of five hundred copies all of which were signed by the author. A note printed on the front page says it was for the use of the lettered and libraries. It was not reprinted and is quite rare. Monteiro used Medieval chronicles, Inquisition records and police statistics for sources on lesbians and homosexual males. He referred to some earlier studies of particular sodomy cases before the Inquisition like that of the conde de Vila Franca in the mid-seventeenth century. He also considered the sociology of those denounced in inquisitorial documentation and compared that with modern police reports. Monteiro used many judgemental adjectives and did not address changing attitudes over time. The second part of his book also contained a lengthy medicalized discussion of homosexuality and numerous quotations from foreign authors.

In the last third of the twentieth century after the fall of the authoritarian government in 1974 there was a marked liberalization of topics for historical investigation, and that included work published on the history of Portuguese male homosexuality. The same period saw the emergence of a vocal LGBTQ intelligentsia who looked to the past to understand the developing genderizing of Portuguese attitudes towards sexual identities, age relations in queer sexual systems, and the antecedents of egalitarian and committed couples of the same sex. This was in the context of a political movement trying to achieve legislation to recognize on-going co-resident relationships. In tandem with those investigations went explorations of transgressiveness, queer images and behaviors and the limits on the social space for sexual dissidences. Much remains to be explored in the twenty-first century on these and other topics.[20]

The best post-1974 studies of male–male sexuality based on Portuguese Inquisition records are those by the Brazilian anthropologist Luiz Mott.[21] Other scholars who have published valuable studies of individual cases are João Alves Dias and Alberto Vieira.[22] They revealed the need for a more systematic guide to the diverse documentation about the 'abominable sin' in Inquisition trials, preliminary enquiries, denunciations and other references.

There are few signs that Queer Theory affected the writing of the history of homosexual males by Mott, Dias or Vieira. There is also the model of literary studies like that in *Queer Iberia* where homosexuality is discerned in poetry and chronicles produced in the time span prior to 1550.[23]

In general the topic is dominated by the traditional paradigms of Iberian and Mediterranean masculinities: that is the role-playing around sexual practices between adolescents or effeminate receptive men and virile insertive adults. The sexual dynamics are genderized into highly stressed top/bottom roles. In the Inquisition documentation the stress falls on the accusations and confessions of anal penetration. The prisoner denies this or advances alternative, less reprehensible, behaviors. The purpose of the trial is to bring the sodomite to confess his active or passive (*paciente*) activities. The Inquisition is the Mother of Lies in the sense that denials, protestations of repentance, and accusations of others, and substitution of a lesser sexual practice to a major one are all commonplace. However, whether those confessions are *true* in a literal sense is much less important than that the confessants thought their depositions were plausible representations, since the inquisitors always discuss whether they seemed to merit credit.

Within the parameters of plausibility then they point to a seventeenth-century Portuguese male–male sexology. I use the clumsy albeit shorter form than homosexual because the latter carries the baggage of urnings, medicalization and civil rights that has accumulated since 1867.

In 1644 at the height of the anti-sodomy drive in Lisbon various accounts surfaced of a nobleman then aged 30 and married who lived in the district of São Roque near Rato who was a large and light-complexioned man, Francisco Correa de Lacerda. He recalled a page of the count of Paneguião with whom he was active, penetrating him and having an orgasm in his anus, and later the pageboy, by then aged 21, confessed that and other incidents both of sodomy and of a lot of masturbation. The page João Botelho had started to work at age 11 for a priest who also was involved with him sexually and who had offered him to the '*fidalgo mancebo*' (young nobleman) Francisco Correa de Lacerda. This Lacerda confessed he had sodomized another boy aged about 15 making plain in his account the vulnerability of the youth, a runaway pageboy.

He said further that

> three or four months ago in this city on the steep street that goes from the Hermitage of Our Lady of Purity to the houses on Rato place he was with a lad whom he had heard it said was called Bayros and does not know his name nor where he was from and being both of them alone at night he the confessant put his virile member in the rear vase of the said lad Bayros who was standing up facing the rampart, and inside the said rear vase he spilled his seed, and with this lad nothing else happened: he was fifteen years old with a long face with some freckles, and blonde curly hair and dressed in a woollen cloth and with a cape that is also old, and the reason he knew him was because the boy had worked for some days for the countess of Palma and ran away and when a lackey of the countess met him in the street and ran after him the lad hid himself in the

> house of he the confessant, and there he talked to him and on the same night they went to the said site to commit the said sin as has been said, and does not know where the said lad now resides in this city but heard it said that he was going around as a porter, treated badly, in the Loreto district.[24]

What these and other accounts make plain is that vulnerable male adolescents were sexual objects for more powerful men just as were women. Bayros was a ragamuffin who could be sodomized. In the conditions of the Portuguese world with its frequent absence of white women, its stress on premarital chastity for girls, and the numbers of pages, apprentices, and young boys on ships and other largely male work situations there was a widespread 'faute de mieux' attitude to same-sex practices to orgasm. The runaway page 'paid' for his refuge by being receptive in anal sex after a conversation in which this was agreed.

In a larger sense the sexual classifications went from the basis of male–female to those of class and race and place in the social hierarchy. The social 'qualities' of persons were recalled by the terminology of new and old Christians or that of white or black – 'all white men free of the infected nation' – meaning without Jewish ancestors, and enumerations of those who were vile or of 'lesser condition' who could not carry a sword: 'I order that apprentices of mechanical skills, lackeys, outriders, sailors, boatmen, and bargemen, negroes, and other persons of equal or inferior condition cannot wear a sword ...' (Alvará of 24 May 1749).[25]

Lowly individuals were more often encountered in the sodomy records than those higher in the social scale.

The confession of sodomites was the closest thing we can get to a self-revelatory gay *autobiography* in the seventeenth century. Of course there were older poetic and literary renditions of individuals engaging in homoerotic activities, especially being sodomized (the *fodinculos*) but not composed in the first person.[26] However it is important that we understand the limits of a confession to the Inquisition: this was not the self-indulgent recall of past exploits by a raconteur. Instead a prisoner stood before a crucifix and priestly interrogators in the knowledge that what he was saying may bring him continuing imprisonment, confiscation of property, torture with the *strappado*, punishment by flogging or to serve as a galley slave, and even lead to his death, burning of his corpse and the scattering of his ashes to ensure that he could not be part of the Resurrection.

Machos are polyvalent in the traditional system, both married men (*casados*) and bachelors (*solteiros*): that is, they penetrate. Like female or male rape this is aggressive. During a visitation to the city of Lagos on 2 June 1620, a 14-year-old, António, came forward who lived in Aljezur. He said that in September of the previous year going out to watch over some cows belonging to his cousin he was joined by Bartolomeu Lourenço, 20 years old, 'who lunged at him and embraced him and threw him on the ground saying that he wanted to sleep with him from behind.' He resisted. Bartolomeu threw him down and being unable to pull down his britches he cut them with a knife. He put António on all fours and took him from behind. He made him spread his legs and kissed the nape of his neck saying as he did so 'Ah, My soul!' 'And immediately he put his nature into his behind and knew him carnally spilling seed inside the behind of he the confessant.' As the historian Borges Coelho wrote, a poor illiterate boy probably would not confess in these terms but the notary made a narrative of what he was told about the rape: we notice the classic paradigm of the prepubescent vulnerable boy being a sexual object for a vigorous youth in all likelihood not yet married, the element of violence and threat with a knife, and the endearment as he sodomized the boy in a country setting where he could not escape. The visitation enabled António to complain about his violation eight months earlier: we cannot know if he was acquainted with his rapist or whether there were any prior sexual practices short of forcible sodomy between them.[27]

Did egalitarian male–male love imagery exist in Portugal between the sixteenth to the eighteenth centuries? There is the whole vexed question of 'passionate friendship', which may have included some physical intimacy but equally could have had none at all. Moreover polite conventions excluded any reference to such genital activities.

'Good' Christian machos were represented by the Virgin Warrior Ideal in Portuguese culture by the imagery of the Infante Dom Henrique.[28] They were exalted by good celibate priests. The married macho should keep to Pauline prescriptions.

Old men were assumed to desire celibacy: see the citation even among pagans of the elderly Sophocles in Plato's *Republic*, glad at his freedom from sexual desire.[29] Christians were offered the example of the Saints. In the name of aesthetics and propriety the old were thought beyond/above sex. There is also the shameless (because wishing to be receptive) old bottom, hoping to be penetrated anally, or to suck off the prime macho. In the traditional system there are virtually no examples of old–old male couples.

Seventeenth-century male–male genital practices were just that, and seen as a product of the temptation of the demon.

The question the twenty-first century asks of the sixteenth, seventeenth and eighteenth is whether there was an ethnogenesis, a sense of community, or complicity? Mott (1989) argued that there was. In Portugal or at least Lisbon there was clearly the *fanchono* identity at least a century before that of the English mollies.

The modern lesbian and gay identity which rejects functional bisexuality in favor of being exclusively gay or lesbian was unknown in Early Modern Portugal, save in the form of the *fanchono*, the fairy, who is throughout the sexual curriculum receptive, as in the words of Rafael from Madeira in 1570: 'The *fanchonos* are receptive in anal sex [*pacientes*], and never does a *fanchono* commit this sin with another *fanchono*.'[30] A witness from Rafael's trial said he was: 'well built. He seemed to be a woman in his talk: it was effeminate and *fanchono*. Whatever man saw him lost his head for him ... he was very good in bed.'[31]

A *fanchono* can also be a man and a father but remains the effeminate bottom, seeking throughout his life to be fucked. A *fanchono* may be a never married man. The clean-shaven swishy (young) priest is at least a potential but non-playing *fanchono*, may be a de facto one, or of course may be a stern moralist. Catholic values that govern behaviors were least effective in the big cities of Lisbon and of Oporto. Variables governing conduct were family control and the presence of predatory males. Friendship in such a setting could be support, and might also be sexual.

The Inquisition Byelaws of 1640 included Chapter 25 on those who commit the abominable crime of sodomy. After considering those who confessed freely or furtively the sixth article referred to those who were openly queer in their behavior:

> 6. And being someone so debauched publicly, and scandalous or inculpated with such circumstances that they greatly aggravate his faults, as would be to provide a lodging for committing this offence, or to be a third party in abetting it, or if the person perseveres in it for many years, committing it anywhere that the person finds oneself, shall be punished with a public arbitrary punishment despite having come forward oneself because in these terms the accused does not receive a greater punishment in the infamy of having a public punishment than from that which derives from the scandal which he had given with the debauchery of his faults.

Here the backdrop of a putative 'out and proud' identity in its seventeenth-century formulation is made the target of infamous public punishment.

A substantial inquiry which did not, however, lead on to a full trial, was the case of a butcher from the village of Malpica, near Castelo Branco. In the initial denunciation forwarded in 1796 the octogenarian commissioner recalled an earlier scandal in 1781 when the same butcher, Lopes, nicknamed the cudgel (*cacheira*) was denounced for his enticements of the two sons of a man now dead. It was assumed that he must have some physical disorder in his genitalia, and particularly to have female organs, to wish sexual commerce with males: 'as it was presumed that he was a hermaphrodite the judge ordered him to be examined, but it was found that he only had the masculine sex'.

Now a tailor came forward to denounce him again for his passion for young men. The priest reported that Lopes had done this:

> ... with João Tiago with the one as incubus and the other as sucubus, and that for the same sin he invited, and had invited the majority of the youth of this place of whom many are married and that he had not made this revelation despite having heard the Edict of the Holy Office because he did not know what was the 'abominable crime' and sodomy. This is the case which has spread and is spreading in this place of Malpica ...[32]

Clearly the priest was making a lame excuse for not having earlier denounced the butcher so keenly interested in Malpica's youths. The commissioner pleaded various ailments to be excused from carrying out more investigations into the more than 15 years of sexual enticements by the butcher to local bachelors. Lisbon sent out a questionnaire for the investigating commissioner to use, of which question three asked:

> If it was known, or had heard say, that somebody committed the abominable crime of sodomy in such a depraved manner and so publicly that by this horrible crime had caused public scandal in the place where the individual lived and among the persons that know the individual, enticing for this aim some persons and whether of both sexes.

This produced informative replies that show how in a semi-rural setting Lopes conducted himself. A 40-year-old married peasant (*lavrador*) born and brought up in the same village with Lopes described him as:

> a meat cutter in the slaughterhouse, accustomed to invite to his house bachelor men, and youths, and it was said that they there committed the abominable crime of sodomy, with him being passive. Some fathers reprimanded their own sons and forbade them to go to the house of the above mentioned.

The tailor who had lived for most of his life in Malpica repeated what he denounced in the butcher adding that he had actually seen one occasion when a muleteer called João Tiago was still a bachelor. Another married man from the village said that the butcher invited the young bachelors to his house so that they would sodomize him. The fourth witness, another peasant, married and native of Malpica, said that these sessions were a public scandal in the village. A fifth man, aged 20 and a mason, said that Lopes offered the youths food and drink as a preliminary to the 'abominable crime'. This was hearsay but it caused a scandal in the village. A shoemaker in his sixties born in the same village said that Manuel Lopes the Cudgel caused scandal by his pursuit of the young bachelors, and that his nick-name was She-Wolf (*a Loba*). The investigating commissioner repeated that Lopes was passive with the unmarried youths (*moços*) when he was a widower:

> he is poor and despised, and lives from being a butcher, and that for the last year or more nothing has been heard of this allegation (*que cessou aquela fama*) ...

This was written in Monsanto on April 1 1799. A number of other residents then testified about the opinion held of him: they all emphasized that he was despised for his libertinism and bad behavior. The commissioner added that his occupation of butcher (*carniceiro*) is 'of the most vile in these our lands'.

The priests who helped in the investigation agreed that there was no doubt of the facts, and that this was 'murmured' by everybody. Thus the widower butcher known as She-wolf was a disgrace: almost 20 years earlier he had been examined to see if he had normal genitalia. Clearly he was reproved and scandalous. Equally evident was that some unmarried youths of the village were accomplices in parties with food and drink, which led to their sodomizing the host. There was here clearly a situation on the very edge of that tolerated by village standards, but one that took place in his own house. At the price of scandal and public contempt the widower kept his dirty but necessary job and was able to pursue his sexual prey. Investigations abruptly concluded in 1799, probably because the Inquisitors noted what the reader two hundred years later sees. There was no clear evidence or witness from any participant in the sodomy, save the tailor who claimed to have seen the muleteer João Tiago *in flagrante*. When questioned, the then married João Tiago said nothing about it. The investigators thought he was not telling the truth. No other witnesses could or would name the '*moços solteiros*' and none of the latter actually volunteered or testified to committing an offence, which would cause them to be liable to punishment. Probably there was here a kind of village solidarity against an external intrusion of moral retribution. Collective community disapproval over the butcher's appetite for the unmarried young men in the village was one thing, but it was quite another to denounce and ruin a man born and raised in their community and whom many had known all their lives.[33]

Another enquiry from the 1790s, this time of a Portuguese immigrant in his fifties in Minas Gerais, Brazil, also had references to attempts to verify if his genitals were those of a man or a hermaphrodite. In 1796 a secular priest normally resident in São José in Minas, but who made his denunciation at the Carmelite monastery in Rio de Janeiro, identified a habitual and recidivist receptive sodomite, Manuel José Correia. The priest claimed the individual, also from São José and at present in the city of Rio, was notorious for 'illicit dealings with men in the abominable sin of sodomy, being the patient.' He enumerated nine partners: two free and two slave mulattoes, and five white men. Because of the notoriety of these 'insults' he was ordered into the presence of the local judge ordinary and two doctors who examined his body in São José. They attested he was anatomically male 'a complete man' – and not a woman. The priest said he was denouncing Correia in Rio because he knew of this sin which could bring about the excommunication of the accused, and that he was troubled by the 'most grave scandal' aroused by the appetites of the denounced.

The accused man was a militia captain who had already fled to the coastal city having sold almost all his property. The priest who made the denunciation before the Carmelite Nascentes in Rio in November 1796 had been anxious for the arrest of the sodomite the year before, in Minas, as laid out in a letter to the commissioner sent from São José do Rio das Mortes. Further enquiries were ordered from Lisbon. These revealed that the denouncer priest, Doutor Manuel Rodrigues Pacheco, had avoided the follow-up investigation. It also transpired that a brother of Pacheco and the accused had a lawsuit for damages, which added to more than nine thousand cruzados. That dispute produced the accusation that Correia was a hermaphrodite [*Emafrodita*] and that led to the medical examination of his genitalia. In the document the word for man – homem – is decorated with glitter marks around the h, and the final letter is raised with a cross stroke and glitter marks. This commissioner, José de Soira de Azevedo Ferreira e Araújo, entered into the kind of detail often missing on the raw denunciation. The accused man was known to have many enemies because he was extremely effeminate.[34] To the priest it seemed sufficient to note that a flamboyantly womanish man would have many enemies because of being what he was. Furthermore he was a pious Catholic who paid for Church festivals in the mother church [Matriz] of São José. He had in his house a shrine, which was the best in the whole district. The accused was born in Coimbra, Portugal and had come to the region when very young. He had never been known to show any sexual interest in women. He was said to be impotent and that was adduced as a reason why he invited men to his house so that, in the action of 'becoming het up' ['*na ação de se esquentarem*'] the accused might have an orgasm, ['*ter poluição*']. The accused was now over 50 years of age, and sickly. Lisbon issued no further instructions to the Brazilian commissioner. The documents do not say but seem from their dates and locations to show that the accused man had gone to Rio from São José having sold up property, and then returned to São José, during the years 1795 to 1801. It was the financial dispute more than his undoubted homosexual appetites that got him into trouble with the civil justice. Moreover his flamboyant effeminacy became a weapon for his enemies against him.[35]

In the same way the judicial examinations by doctors of the genitalia of the widower butcher from Malpica or the 50-year-old from Coimbra who had never had anything to do with women and who was very effeminate point to the same physiological considerations. The Enlightenment sought to look at the male body for signs of the feminization, which 'explained' why a man might wish to be sodomized. There were no calls for a 'medical examination' in the seventeenth-century trials when the sentences spoke of temptations by the Demon.

Thirty sodomites were executed, and the number of other full trials leading to lesser punishments like whippings, confiscations of property, exile from the kingdom for periods of time or life was approximately 400 over the entire life of the Lisbon tribunal, which was responsible for central Portugal and for Brazil.

The grand total number of names listed in the Cadernos do Nefando and the denunciations, sometimes together with additional accusations like blasphemy, was over 6,000. The Inquisition was initially established in 1536 and finally abolished in 1821 so there is not much point mounting an elaborate quantitative machinery to deal with this evidence over hundreds of years. The predominance of urban over rural cases in the documentation may simply mean there was less such behavior in the country, or perhaps such behavior was less likely to be denounced. *Excel* would not be much use. What is of interest is the degree of detail in the records on a subject, which is usually concealed by fear or disgust.

The percentage of the adult population which is primarily homosexual in orientation is hard to establish in any society at any time in the past: a 1994 US study advanced 2.8 per cent of adult males in the population and 1.4 per cent of women, with more having reported at least some homosexual experience over the age of 18. Assuming similar levels in Portugal before 1800 in a society that was primarily rural with one major city there were perhaps 50,000 male homosexuals *avant la lettre* and 25,000 lesbians around 1789. Given the problems caused by same-sex activities most of these individuals would refuse or hide those desires, or would perhaps be extremely vigilant over revealing their orientation to others. Despite the artificiality of the calculation it does show that the 6,000 denunciations, the 400 trials and enquiries and the 30 executions for the nefarious sin during the life of the Portuguese Inquisition record only a tiny part of the homosexual men in Portugal in the period considered, 1550 to 1800.

A text in the registers of the General Intendency of Police in Lisbon dated 23 September 1794 provides a brief vignette of a loving relationship between two young men, one of whom was a messenger boy named José da Silva who had been dismissed from the service of the Marquis of Nizza. He was taken into the household of a high court judge Manuel de Matos and a son of that official who was a cadet in the Mecklemberg cavalry regiment installed Silva in his own bed, living scandalously, and practicing the most lubricious actions, which, the official writing the text noted, for modesty's sake he omitted. As a result Silva was put into the workhouse in the Saint George Castle in Lisbon, whereupon the cadet having won over the corporal of the guard which patrolled the workhouse was able to achieve Silva's escape one night, and the messenger boy returned to the house of the said cadet and continued in the same impropriety which had caused him to be imprisoned in the first place. He was arrested a second time and again put in the workhouse to learn one of the trades taught there. The police official noted that the cadet had displayed all the excesses of those that men seek when they are possessed by a dominant passion in favor of any woman who has captivated them.[36] One may underline that the text does not use the word sodomy although that word is written in pencil in the margin of the register, doubtless by a subsequent cataloger. It spoke of depravity (*'relaxção'*) as analogous to 'a dominant passion in favour of *any* [my emphasis] woman.'

Perhaps elite cadets could for a time behave in a city setting in a way which would be unthinkable in the countryside. Perhaps the cadet Matos considered himself to be in love with Silva, perhaps the messenger boy reciprocated. It took constraint to prevent them sleeping together in sexual intimacy. The police report does not give us any information on the subsequent lives of those two young men.

It has been advanced that during the century of light there was an increase in sexual repression in Western Europe related to the growth in the capitalist bourgeoisie.[37] However Portugal had scarcely no repression compared to Britain where in the same time span some sodomites were hanged. It appears that individuals who avoided outright scandal might escape serious penalties. Like the Judge who presumed hermaphrodism in the widower butcher nicknamed She-wolf from the village near Castelo Branco who chased after unmarried youths, the referent to homosexual affection involved a feminine component. Presumably this police investigation was not carried on by the Inquisition because the accusation was not of a specific form of sexual activity, that of anal intercourse, and neither the messenger boy nor the young officer were telling what happened in bed. The police were not concerned with the physical forms of affection exchanged by the two youths ('for modesty's sake, &c') but rather in the outrage to public decency in the openness of a same-sex love.

Late eighteenth-century Lisbon saw numerous cross-dressing actors taking the part of women on stage in the theaters because Queen Maria I did not think it decent for females to do so. This gave opportunities for effeminate cross dressers to perform. The professional opportunities then permitted these transvestites to appear without beards, imitating the gracefulness of women, and some of them growing luxuriant heads of hair and declaiming their lines in a falsetto and playing the love scenes in a way that lent itself to double-entendres. In 1789 a play at the Salitre theatre *Nas Viajantes Ditosas* provided opportunities for some well-known female impersonators. Monteiro in 1922 constantly harped on difference between effeminates and virile homosexuals.[38]

My reading of the Inquisition documents convinces me that the notion of a type of man whose preferred sexual activity was with other males was indeed current from 1550 to 1800. The most common word for this in Portuguese was *fanchono,* but at least for a time in seventeenth-century Lisbon *bobija* was current much like bugger in English and used as a noun or a verb, (*bobijar*).[39] Social pressures and perhaps self-image might make *fanchonos* marry women but in those instances we would not hear of those relations which were non-physical or which were very occasional and strained to produce the children so necessary for economic security in early modern Europe. Once children had been produced the husband could refuse 'venery' which was not for reproductive aims.

Conclusion

Attitudes expressed in Portuguese public discourses towards sexual activities between males during the period 1550 to 1800 in Portugal were affected by the Counter Reformation, the Scientific Revolution and the Enlightenment, but the informal and ubiquitous oral lore of masculinities was unchanging.

Young boys had a curiosity about the sexual maturation of their own and other male bodies and this might lead to what one country rapist from Guarda diocesis called in 1795 the 'boys' game.' He claimed to have participated in sodomy when he was eight years old and to have become accustomed to it. He admitted to having violated nine young boys who only came forward years later once he had injured a child so badly that his conduct became a scandal. He was married at that time.[40] An adolescent without strongly masculine secondary characteristics, especially a beard, was considered a potential sexual object by some sexual predators. Unprotected adolescents, especially lower-class orphans or servants, might find themselves forced to be receptive in sodomy. Elite boys were spared a functional feminization, which would disgrace their lineage and precipitate a reaction from kin.

On the other hand there were groups of adult men who even in their self-definition projected themselves as effeminates who wanted to be sodomized by 'real' men. They might well be friendly to each other, their 'sisters' or 'girlfriends,' but they would not be sexual partners of other *fanchonos*. This was thus an identity but also a prohibition. From the subsisting documentation there seem to be virtually no examples of egalitarian sexual commerce between mature males in the documentation.

That makes all the more intriguing the incident explored by Boswell both in the journal of Montaigne from his travels in Italy in 1580–81, and a report of the Venetian Ambassador from Rome. Montaigne wrote that two Portuguese in the church of Saint John of the Latin Gate married at Mass, took Communion together, after which they were sleeping and eating together. The Ambassador said the men married each other thus defiling the holy name of matrimony, and adding they lived together 'like husband and wife.' He also noted that they had gone to the flames, as they deserved: a reference to the punishment of burning at the stake, which had the biblical authority of the fate of the cities of the plain.[41]

The praxis of the Inquisition evolved in the sense that by the second half of the eighteenth century only individuals involved in behaviour that remains criminal at the start of the twenty-first – homosexual rape – were pursued and punished. Despite clerical homophobic discourse the reality was that a relatively benign repression of Portuguese homosexuals existed in the Early Modern Period.

Notes

Abbreviations:

ANTT National Archives of Portugal, Lisbon.
IL Inquisition of Lisbon Document.

All translations from the Portuguese are by David Higgs unless otherwise noted.

1 See the important article by Luiz Mott, 'Inquisição e Homossexualidade,' in Maria Helena Carvalho dos Santos (ed.) *Inquisição* (Lisbon: 1989) vol. II, 475–508 with numerous references to the call numbers of Inquisition trials and other documentation.

2 See Luiz Mott, 'Meu menino lindo: cartas de amor de um frade sodomita, Lisboa (1690)' in *Luso-Brazilian Review*, vol. 38, no. 2, (Winter 2001) 97–115. These love letters, which are not translated from Portuguese, reveal an extensive vocabulary of same-sex affectionate terminology.

3 John Sinopoli, 'Sex trade bill forgets queers: youth and prostitution' in *Xtra!* 15 November 2001, 11.

4 Michael Rocke, *Forbidden Friendships: Homosexuality and Male Culture in Renaissance Florence* (New York: Oxford, 1996).

5 Luiz Mott, 'Crypto-sodomites in colonial Brazil' translated by Salima Popat' quoting IL 12,248 in Pete Sigal (ed.) *Infamous Desire: Male Homosexuality in Colonial Latin America* (Chicago: University of Chicago Press, 2003) 189.

6 A. Borges de Coelho, *Inquisição De Evora Dos Primórdios A 1668* (Lisbon: Caminho, 1987) vol. 1, 268.

7 Coelho, I, 268.

8 Mark D. Johnson, *The Silence of Sodom: Homosexuality and Modern Catholicism* (Chicago: University of Chicago Press, 2000).

9 Isaías Rosa Pereira, *A Inquisiçao em Portugal. Séculos XVI–XVIII – Período Filipino*, [Lisbon] Vega [1993] 180–1.

10 Rosa Pereira, 170–1.

11 Rosa Pereira, 111.
12 Rosa Pereira, 161.
13 Rosa Pereira, 168–9.
14 Angela Mendes de Almeida, *O Gosto Do Pecado: Casamento E Sexualidade Nos Manuais De Confessores Dos Séculos XVI e XVII* (Rio de Janeiro: Rocco, 1922).
15 Almeida, 1992: 106.
16 Arlindo Camilo Monteiro, *Amor Sáfico E Socrático Para Uso De Letrados E Bibliotecas*, Lisbon, Instituto de Medicina Legal de Lisboa, 1922, 250, citing Magnus Hirschfeld, Albert Moll and others.
17 *Ordenações Filipinas, Livros IV e V*, reprint of the Rio de Janeiro edition (1870) by Candido Mendes de Almeida (Lisbon: Fundação Calouste Gulbenkian, 1985) 1163.
18 Francisco de Melo Franco, *Medicina Theologica* 1794, republished São Paulo, 1994, 72.
19 See the articles on Aguiar and Macedo by Robert Howes in R. Aldrich and G. Wotherspoon, *Who's Who in Lesbian and Gay History from Antiquity to World War II* (London and New York: Routledge, 2001).
20 António Fernando Cascais (ed.) *Indisciplinar a Teoria. Estudos Gays, Lésbicas e Queer*. (Lisbon, Fenda, 2004).
21 See the article on Luiz Mott by Robert Howes in R. Aldrich and G. Wotherspoon, *Who's Who in Contemporary Gay and Lesbian History from World War II to the Present Day* (London and New York, Routledge, 2001) 294–6.
22 Alberto Vieira, 'O Estudo do Quotidiano e Sexualidade na Ilha de São Miguel no Século XVII. O Processo do Conde de Vila Franca' in M. Helena Carvalho dos Santos (ed.), *Inquisição* (Lisbon: Universitária Editora, 1989) vol. II, 1989, 817–40.
23 Josiah Blackmore, 'The poets of Sodom' in J. Blackmore & G.S. Hutcheson (eds) *Queer Iberia: Sexualities, Cultures and Crossings from the Middle Ages to the Renaissance* (Durham: Duke University Press, 1999) 195–221.
24 ANTT IL Livro 134, fol. 372r.
25 A. J. Russell-Wood, *Fidalgos and Philanthropists*, (London Macmillan, 1968) 246, note 1.
26 Blackmore & Hutcheson, op. cit, pp. 195–221.
27 Coelho, I, p. 268.
28 Peter Russell, *Prince Henry 'the Navigator' A Life* (New Haven: Yale University Press, 2000); H. B. Johnson, *Dois Estudos Polémicos*. (Tuscon, Fenestra, 2004).
29 Plato, *The Republic* translated with notes and an interpretive essay by A. Bloom (New York: Basic, 1968, 5).
30 Dias, op. cit. 157.
31 Mott 'Inquisição e homossexualidade' op. cit. 489.
32 ANTT IL Livro 321, unpaginated investigation.
33 A modern ethnographer reporting on community attitudes in Alentejo in the 1960s wrote that 'Homosexuals are biologically, so to say, outside the male sex and their fate is considered below that of a criminal.' José Cutileiro, *A Portuguese Rural Society* (Oxford: Clarendon Press, 1971) 102.
34 por ter genio de mulher e muito extravagante ...
35 IL Liv. 321, unpaginated: March 1795, 20 November 1796, 24 November 1797, July 1801.

36 ANTT. Intendência Geral de Policia. Liv. 4, fol. 184v–185r.
37 Jacques Solé, *L'amour En Occident À L'époque Moderne* [Brussels] Complexe, [1984] based mainly on British, French and Italian examples with no mention of the Portuguese world.
38 Monteiro, *Amor*, p. 242.
39 Mott's reading was *botija* which means jar. IL 6554.
40 ANTT IL 9737.
41 John Boswell, *Same-Sex Unions In Premodern Europe* (New York: Villard, 1994) 264–5 and notes for texts in original French and Italian.

4

'Are Those People Like Us' – Early Modern Homosexuality in Holland

Theo van der Meer

Introduction

In 1730 the discovery of a network of men who engaged in homosexual behavior set off an unprecedented series of sodomy trials in the Dutch Republic. Between 1730 and 1732, some 350 men were prosecuted. About 100 of these suffered the death penalty.[1]

Despite the fact that men had suffered arrests and severe penalties for sodomy in the Low Countries ever since the late Middle Ages, in 1730, many believed that sodomy, the *crimen nefandum*, the unmentionable vice, was hardly known, much less 'perpetrated', in this country. Since the Reformation the Reformed Church in The Netherlands had kept silent on this subject at least as far as its own flock was concerned.[2] In contrast to France and England sodomy was hardly mentioned in literature, not even in libertine novels.[3] If talked about at all, sodomy was thought to be a Catholic, or, more particularly, an Italian vice.

The idea that people in this country barely engaged in sodomy had been reinforced since the early seventeenth century by legal authorities. Until then occasional death sentences – burning at the stake or decapitation – had occurred in public. Yet, from the early 1600s in accordance with the notion of a *crimen nefandum* most men convicted on such charges had been executed in secret (by strangling at a stake) 'so that it would remain covered that these atrocities were committed in this country.'[4] Corpses of such culprits had been thrown into the sea or buried under the gallows, 'to put away from us all memory of this evil.'[5] In case of death penalties often only summary verdicts were left and actual trial records were destroyed. It was only jurists who sometimes published for a limited, professional audience about sodomy in legal commentaries.

The events of 1730 did not just mean that the Republic entered an era of persecution of homosexual behavior – waves of arrests like the one in that year repeated themselves several times during the eighteenth and early nineteenth centuries – but also changed the meaning of the *crimen nefandum*. The discovery of networks of sodomites in which men of all social strata participated, as well as of public and private meeting sites, the realization that many participants had developed an effete body language and a sodomite-lingo – in short subcultural phenomena – caused homosexual behaviour to become part of public discourse.

Following the discoveries the administrative council in the province of Holland issued an edict instructing local courts to execute convicted sodomites publicly.[6] The prosecutions were accompanied by scholarly and popular publications. Ministers of the reformed church began to publish books, because, as one of them wrote, there was a time to be silent and a time to speak out and, with the discovery of the sodomite networks, the latter had now begun.[7] They especially addressed the issue as to why sodomy had 'suddenly' become so widespread. Literary and other journals followed suit, sentences were published and even advertised abroad. Street-singers produced ditties, sung at the occasions of the public executions. Poems honoring the pursuit of the courts and some prints picturing the recent discoveries and executions were sold.[8] Extensive trial records from that date onwards were kept, not least of all to show posterity that everything had been done 'to wipe this vice' from the face of the earth.[9] Whereas knowledge about homosexual behavior previously had been considered dangerous since it might provoke unnatural desires, from 1730 onwards, knowledge was thought to deter people from engaging in such behavior. Yet, rather than putting an end to the violation of certain bodily boundaries, new ones emerged, which would eventually separate men from women and the majority from a minority. The prosecutions, the social organization of homosexual behavior and the sodomites' reaction to persecution, as well as the public's response to all of these, gave a shape to the subjective experience of homosexual behavior.

Despite the claim, made in 1730, that sodomy had hardly been known by previous generations, from the final quarter of the seventeenth century onwards, a steady increase in the number of sodomy trials occurred as well as trials related to blackmail. A couple of times they included between four and ten men. The year 1730 marked a turning point as far as the number of people prosecuted on sodomy charges were concerned. Series of arrests repeated themselves: in 1764,

1776 and between 1795 and 1798 in various cities and provinces. Aside from such series, there were incidental trials as well. Altogether, in the eighteenth century some 800 sodomy trials were held in The Netherlands. In only about 1 per cent of these cases were women prosecuted because of lesbian activities.[10] About 200 men suffered the death penalty because of sodomy and about as many again were sentenced to solitary confinement.[11] In 1811 the enforcement of the French penal code in the Netherlands formally decriminalised homosexual behavior. Yet, based on a public indecency statute in that law, in the first decades after 1811 on average about as many sodomites were prosecuted as in the decades since 1730.[12]

Despite the fact that persecution of homosexual behavior in The Netherlands was much more severe than in England or France, and despite the avowed determination in 1730 to wipe out this vice once and for all, for a variety of reasons authorities in The Netherlands never wanted to unleash relentless witch hunts of sodomites. As a result, persecution came about as purges, whose meanings in the end were highly symbolical, yet crucial for the way in which the discourses on homosexual behavior eventually would evolve. They drew a line between permissible and impermissible behaviour that would force people on both sides of the line to define or redefine themselves in terms of their desires, sex and gender.

Social organization of same-sex behavior

Though sodomy trials had not been as uncommon as many wanted to believe in 1730, some profound changes had taken place in the previous decades that can explain the shock and amazement that met the discoveries in that year. Until the beginning of the early modern period, in parts of Europe and also in the Low Countries, same-sex contacts usually were characterized by hierarchical differences, most commonly expressed in disparate ages, although it seems unlikely that such behaviour was as widespread in the Dutch republic as it was for instance in Florence in Italy, where intergenerational sexual activities were part of male sociability and socialization.[13] Moreover, intergenerational differences between same-sex partners seem to have been just one of the ways in which hierarchical differences between such partners manifested themselves in The Netherlands. While some verdicts from the fifteenth to the late seventeenth century explicitly mention that the culprits had sought sex with youths or at least minors, others mention that the men convicted had been after other men, without specifying an age.[14] In some cases, like in that of the polish officer Sigismundis Pape in 1684, it all remains rather ambiguous: he stood accused of having been sexually involved with both a 10- or 11-year-old boy and a 21-year-old private.[15]

In The Netherlands prior to the late seventeenth century, such same-sex contacts usually had come about within individual circumstances, as between a master and an apprentice in a workshop, or indeed between an officer and a private, or as a result of initiatives taken by someone in a superior position. In the 1670s a former mayor of Utrecht for several years had sexual contacts with two young boys whom he had met on separate occasions when they were still in their early teens. The sexual contacts evolved from fondling, to masturbation, actual sodomy and even flogging.[16] Not surprisingly, in cases of actual sodomy, the person in the superior position penetrated the one who because of his station in life or because of his age was inferior. In trial records of those days there was no mention at all of specific meeting sites, codes that showed up in the later sodomy trials.

Such features of same-sex contacts rapidly changed in the final quarter of the seventeenth century, not just in the Republic but, as studies by Randolph Trumbach, Alan Bray and Michel Rey have shown, also in urban areas in England and northern France.[17] Perhaps, research would show, such changes occurred in the old cities of western parts of Germany as well.

From the final quarter of the seventeenth century onwards references are to be found of cruising sites in cities in the Republic. Public conveniences were mentioned, as well as public buildings like the city hall in Amsterdam, or places such as commodity exchanges in that city and in Rotterdam, parks, squares and city ramparts. From the early eighteenth century onwards in the major cities there were also pubs, brothels and private parlours for men who desired their own sex.[18] Some in The Hague offered *rendez-vous* to customers who brought their own 'trade' (to use a somewhat anachronistic term) or had sent for one. One man who offered such occasion also acted as a go between for gentlemen who required sexually available servants, not just in The Hague but in nearby cities such as Delft and Leiden as well.[19]

References were made to gestures men would use at these cruising sites to get in touch with other men. In a cruising park in The Hague men were rumoured to use handkerchiefs, in front of the city hall at Dam Square (since 1806 the Royal Palace) in Amsterdam, men would walk around with their arms akimbo, and hit another who did the same with an elbow, if the other was to his liking. Inside the city hall they would step on somebody's foot. Since sodomites shared many of their meeting sites like Dam square with female prostitutes, it is not difficult to see where some of these gestures may have come from. It could of course also create misunderstandings: as early as 1702 a man in a park in The Hague interpreted such a gesture made to him by another man as an invitation to go with him to the whores.[20] Though courts would appreciate these gestures as secret codes, much like those of freemasons, they rather reflected a body language. Many of these gestures were also described in *artes amandi* and they related to courtship and gender in a way that was deeply rooted in culture, and as such barely used consciously. Being asked about signs, some suspects said that they were not aware that these existed.[21]

There are many references to effeminate behavior, speech, gestures, and dress in the trial records after 1675. Some men were said to speak in a 'girlish' way. All through the eighteenth century sodomites prinked themselves up and some were said to dress in an effeminate manner. Even if eighteenth-century dress did not look very masculine from a twentieth-century perspective, for a man selling rags at fairs in the 1790s, to be dressed in 'a light frock with brown stripes, a white vest with red little dots, dark trousers, white stockings and shoes with ribbons [and] a triangular black shining hat with a black little rose, a black lus with a yellow button attached to it,' seems a bit over the top.[22] Occasionally some men would stroll around in female attire, like a prominent official of a church in Utrecht (convicted in 1730) who in the 1720s had been thrown out of his rooms by his landlord after he had found him dressed as a shepherdess.[23] Although most major cities hosted pubs where sodomites used to meet, there are no indications that they were in any way similar to the London molly houses, or that visitors to these pubs enacted there the same charades as their London counterparts. Yet, some must have been aware of the habits in London. One man arrested in The Hague in 1730, although Dutch, had been a regular in Mother Clap's molly house, but had left England after the raid on that house in 1726.[24] He had told others in Holland about his experiences in London. In the 1720s a group of sodomites used to meet in a park in Haarlem under a large oak tree and held elections to choose a ringleader who had first choice of partners.[25] Though minors did not disappear altogether from the scene (many had their first sexual encounters while still being adolescents), their place was mostly taken by young adults who, next to serving upper-class men, often also engaged in homosexual activities with one another. Whereas in the first case they would still by and large keep to a division of active and passive roles, in the second they would exchange them. Other adults would do the same with their social equals.

At the core of these networks, participants would maintain strong personal and often also economic ties – and there were jealously guarded love affairs. Two men put on trial in 1730 in Amsterdam and The Hague respectively, were said to have a contract, which they called a marriage contract, in which they promised only to have sex with others with each other's consent.[26] In the 1790s two young men from The Hague, offered sexual services to very high-ranking officials, yet also had set up a household for themselves and, when they split up, one of them wrote heart-wrenching letters to the other, full of jealous comments as well as desperate pleas to come back.[27] By 1826 in love letters found on a man arrested for public indecencies, the modern Dutch colloquial for boyfriend is used. Both the author of the letter and the addressee already had boyfriends, but neither was happy with his. The writer of the letter wrote about the jealousy and suspicions of his lover, and related an incident that had nearly turned violent. His meeting with his new friend seems to have been a passionate one: 'the last kiss you gave me ... still scorches my soul.'[28]

The emergence of subcultures at the end of the seventeenth century not only reflects a change in actual same-sex behaviour but also a profound change in desires. When homosexual contacts moved from hierarchical relationships and a strict division of active and passive roles into more egalitarian relationships, in which active and passive roles could be exchanged, it mirrored the transformation from a culture which in every respect (class, age, sex) had been based on hierarchical differences into a more egalitarian one, at least one in which egalitarian ideologies began to play a role. It was part of a rising modernity in which, among other things, an affective individualism and the 'modern' individual, a new interiority, or subjectivity itself, began to emerge. Whereas at first hierarchy itself had been eroticised, the new egalitarian culture also brought along a new economy of desires, in which gender became the central focus of subject and object choice. Sodomites may or may not have been effete – quite a few were, as can be gleaned from the records – but often they clearly desired masculine men, that is those who did not wear wigs, had an upright posture and were pockmarked. This new economy of desires may not have replaced the older system completely, but at least settled itself next to it, and to some extent may have competed with it. It was the persecutions of 1730 that forced this emerging individual to define himself in terms of his sex, gender and desires.

Discourses

One of the issues addressed in the books that were published in 1730 was the apparent sudden emergence of homosexual behavior in the Republic. The idea rested upon what were thought to be the causes of this behavior as well as the particular position the Republic was supposed to hold in God's schemes. As the Bible told, the fall of Sodom and Gomorrah was the inhabitants' punishment for what was known as their excess of diet: indulgence in wealth, food and dressing. It had been gluttony that had caused homosexual behaviour to emerge in Sodom. Gluttony had led the inhabitants of Sodom into all kinds of debauchery and had finally resulted in homosexual practices. The fact that the Republic in the seventeenth century had become a prosperous and powerful nation was a reward for its inhabitants' sobriety and restraint. It was considered to be proof of the fact that The Netherlands, as a Protestant nation, had become a new Israel and the Dutch had become God's new chosen people. The sobriety shown by the Dutch was also proof that homosexual behavior – unlike in Catholic countries with their excessive lifestyles – simply could not exist in the Republic. However, prosperity was also a mixed blessing. Life itself was God's continuous test of man to resist temptations and gluttony.

In the first quarter of the eighteenth century, the Republic was perceived by its inhabitants as a nation in political and economical decline after its Golden Age. Though historiography has made clear that in many respects this was not true, there were tremendous problems that were inherent to the Republic's basically still medieval political and economical structures. Yet, especially in the discourses that emerged around the prosecutions, the perceived decline was attributed to man's personal doings. With their free will, the Dutch had given in to gluttony and for this they were punished. When it was discovered in 1730 that sodomy was widespread in the country, it was considered to be the result of indulgence in lesser sins, like card playing, gambling, indulgence in food, drink, and debauchery.[29]

Modern concepts have divided mankind into fixed categories of sexual human beings; eighteenth century concepts implied that every human being – given the right or wrong circumstances – could indulge in homosexual behavior. As late as 1777 an anonymous author wrote that the seed of sodomy hid in each and everybody.[30] That idea originated in the then reigning sexual ontology, an apparently seamless unity of notions concerning sex and sexual differences, nature, masculinity and femininity, psyche and the body, as well as polity.[31]

Calvinism from its very rise was much less hostile towards lust, as Catholicism had been, at least up until the time of the Counter Reformation. Calvinism rejected celibacy as unnatural and it did not consider procreation as the sole or primary purpose of sex between spouses. Indeed, procreation was divinely commanded but sex as a means to create companionship between married partners, contributed to the creation of the environment in which best to raise the offspring.[32] Carnal desires and pleasures were both a prerequisite for procreation and a reward for spouses whose marriage was according to a celestial plan. If such desires were a necessity for the survival of mankind, hunger and thirst, cold and warmth, fatigue created necessary desires for food, refreshment, dress and leisure. Yet, there was a dangerous side to all of this. Fulfilment of such needs could easily result in excess and hedonism. Indulgence in physical needs could turn into debauchery and finally into unnatural behaviour. Sexuality did not represent a unity within itself, but was part of a dichotomy according to which corporeal needs could either be fulfilled with restraint or result in gluttony. With the discovery of the sodomite networks in 1730 it was made clear that sodomy itself was the ultimate form of hedonism. It resulted from 'lesser sins' that over a number of years, despite the warnings of its teachers, had affected the country.[33]

Whether sex served procreation or companionship between spouses, it could only mean that the purpose of physical differences was to unite male and female. After all 'she' was flesh of 'his' flesh, bone of 'his' bone and as such they were one 'flesh', whereas males were each other's alien. Therefore, between males there could be no love but just 'filthy greed'. In marriage man and wife owned one another's bodies; indulging in sodomy meant that man stole his body from his wife. Besides, as St. Paul had taught the Corinthians (6:13), the body was not for fornication but for God and it was the temple of the Holy Spirit. Hedonism, debauchery and ultimately sodomy, polluted this temple. The sodomite committed a terrible theft by taking away his body, which was not rightfully his, from God, thus betraying the stewardship over his body.[34]

In this discourse, nature and consequently sex and sexual differences represented a moral order as much as a physical one. Nature was the place in which God had revealed Himself and His purpose, which, as one judge in a sodomy trial in 1797 put it, for all living beings meant to continue the existence of their species. Where animals could only obey their natural instincts, human beings also possessed reason and free will. Through reason and the study of nature man could behold the divine plan and through his free will he could either live in accordance with this plan or place himself outside its boundaries.[35]

Nonetheless, if the body was a temple to be kept clean from hedonism, man was by nature better equipped to restraint than woman. After all, as medical teaching of the time made clear, women either had an incomplete male body or, at the very least, a body that would cause her insatiable lust, unless she submitted herself to hierarchy between the sexes within the confines of marriage.[36] Femininity, and consequently female honor, was constituted by chastity; masculinity or male honour by sobriety and restraint.

In this discourse desires were understood to be only corporeal. Once somebody got caught in a downwards spiral of gluttony, the mind lost control over the body. As one pamphleteer wrote in 1730, a vice once tasted, singed the senses and made a man crave for its repetition, for more and for worse.[37] Once a man had perpetrated sodomy, he would hold on to it. All through the eighteenth-century sodomy trials, suspects were asked under what circumstances they had begun with their behaviour and more importantly, for how long they had 'held on' to it. Such an understanding of desires may be appreciated as a psychology that is a psychology of excess based on a separation of mind and body. This psychology also meant that nature, as a moral order was highly versatile. Despite his male body, a man could give in to gluttony. Like a woman he could become insatiable and he could become unmanly.

Perhaps most striking about all of this is the fact that there was very little that was new about it. Until 1730, without so much as actually mentioning sodomy, the biblical text of the fall of Sodom and Gomorrah had served to preach restraint and sobriety and to warn against gluttony. All the aforementioned elements about sexual differences and gender had already been present in medieval moral teaching about sexual and other behavior, about desire, restraint, chastity, and about marriage.[38] Moreover, the discourse also fitted a thousand-year-old political and social one, which equated civil virtue and incorruptible statesmanship with masculine self-control, and also embraced concepts of sex and gender. By the end of the sixteenth century this discourse had been given new impetus with the emergence of neo-Stoicism in Europe.[39]

The explicitness about these subjects in 1730 and the fact that they were all put together could perhaps best be appreciated as a *grande finale*. The discourse rather applied to a former era in which desires were related to hierarchy than to desires related to egalitarianism and gender. Therefore such explanations could not and would not last. From 1730 onwards the sodomy trials and all that was related to them, also meant that a process of transformation began.

The interrogations of suspects and the trial procedures paralleled the Catholic confession since the Counter Reformation, in which, according to Michel Foucault, the desire for knowledge first emerged.[40] Prosecutors in many ways resembled confessors, in this case preparing culprits for eternity. The evidence they acquired often went far beyond what was needed to convict a suspect or to track down others. Though trial procedures by their very nature focussed on actual criminal – in this case sexual – acts and unlike the Catholic confession hardly on feelings, thoughts, dreams or impulses, in the course of the eighteenth century, prosecutors began to reach beyond the acts and to look for personal motives and the life stories behind them. The latter was epitomized in the words of a prosecutor who in 1797 ordered a delinquent, after he had confessed his transgressions, to tell about his life 'from his childhood to the present.'[41] By exploring individual motives the ontology and understanding of homosexual behavior therein was also gradually transformed. At the same time the ritual of public executions played a decisive role in this process of transformation.

Public executions were theatrical dramas in which everybody – authorities, the culprit and the public – played its own role, and in a language composed of signs and symbols,[42] they generated meanings around homosexual behavior. In the Republic, in the early modern period people could be executed by hanging, decapitation, garrotting, and breaking on a wheel. Each form related to the social position of the person to be executed, to his or her sex, to the crime he or she had committed, and to the level he or she was to be robbed of his or her honor. Decapitation was the least infamous of all capital punishments, mostly reserved for capital offenders from the upper classes, and in 1730 explicitly rejected as a way to execute sodomites. Garrotting was the usual punishment for women who had perpetrated a capital crime, as well as for men who were guilty of particularly cowardly crimes, or who were sentenced for high treason. Whereas sodomites were also usually garrotted, their punishment related to the way in which their crimes were perceived: they had become like women, they were cowards and they had betrayed the Republic.[43]

Public executions were highly stylized events that lasted for several days. Paraphernalia like 'blood robes' and the 'verge of justice' worn by the dignitaries on the day of the executions, as well as the homage paid to them by guards of honor, underlined their majesty. Justice was most triumphant when the delinquent behaved like a remorseful sinner and those who died with tranquillity were the darlings of both their judges and the public. It also made the public accept the fact that justice was done, which in turn legitimized the power of the authorities.

As noted before, prosecutions in The Netherlands in the eighteenth century came about as purges whose meanings were highly symbolic. Sure enough, executions were meant to punish the delinquents and to deter others. Yet, since only a small number of all of those who engaged in homosexual behavior were executed, and given the kind of ceremonies that surrounded the executions, they can also be considered as cleansing rituals that had to reconcile a polluted universe with mankind. As the anthropologist Mary Douglas has said, cleansing rituals are a form of mutual exorcism.[44] At the scaffold, the sodomite became an expiatory sacrifice who had to suffer for all similar acts. Since the seed of sodomy hid in each and everybody, the executions also had to exorcise such desires. Moreover, if a sodomite was somebody who had given in to the utmost gluttonous desires, it could only have happened because the whole country had indulged to some extent in gluttonous practices. Therefore, the executions also became a ritual of common penance for the polity.[45]

Even if many attended the executions for mere sensation, the poems that were published in 1730, on the occasion of the executions, reflected upon everything that was required. They stressed the fact that all had given in to a certain degree of gluttony, and therefore, that all were more or less guilty of the emergence of same-sex desires. The discourses in 1730 constructed sexual orthodoxy by attributing characteristics of unnatural desires to sodomites. Despite the fact that all were more or less guilty, the poems expressed wonder at why the delinquents had fallen prey to their desires. Rudely, they raised the question why sodomites favored 'a sewer' over 'a clean woman's lap'. Why had sodomites betrayed the beauty of women? Why had they betrayed the desirability of women and in fact become women haters? At the same time the poems sang the praise of the 'fair sex', and how sodomites had grieved that sex by giving up on it. Such statements implied, of course, that the sexually orthodox knew how to appreciate the desirability and beauty of women, that they abhorred the 'sewer', and consequently could not desire males. Thus, through the persecutions not only sodomites were defined, but also the male populace at large had to define itself in terms of its gender and desires. After all, such barriers between that populace and sodomites were still rather flimsy yet in the course of the eighteenth century more recognizable features were given to sodomites.[46]

Remarkably absent from most of these publications in 1730, were references to the effeminate appearance of sodomites, despite the fact that trial records from that year show that effeminacy was wide spread among sodomites. Perhaps the absence of such references was due to the fact that traditionally, and, despite everything that happened, also in the literature of a major part of the eighteenth century, effeminacy was a hallmark of a womanizer, the fop and also of an upper-class libertine, not of a sodomite.[47]

Nonetheless, the discourses that had begun in 1730 soon made the effeminacy of sodomites its central focus and in the 1750s effeminacy became the hallmark of the sodomite. 'One could recognize those folks,' a young man who had prostituted himself said in 1752, 'because there does not grow a beard on their cheeks, that their eyes are whorish, their speech is drawling and their movement wriggling.'[48] A decade later, a jurist wrote in a similar fashion that sodomy resulted in 'that effeminate posture, that drawsy eye, those whorish cheeks which one clearly observes in all those inhuman humans and which in some even affects their speech.'[49] Besides, when at first desires were understood to be mostly corporeal in a psychology that separated the mind from the body, in the new discourse mind and body became united. Homosexual behavior became as much attributed to inner proclivities as to corporeal desires. If anything, it turned sodomites into a recognizable species, as the same jurist made clear: 'if the eye is the mirror of the soul and inner emotions intimate outwardly inner proclivities in the face, so are those who without prejudice pay attention to physiognomy not to be blamed.'[50] While penal reformers in the Republic followed Beccaria in his objections to the death penalty, in the case of sodomy they required severe punishments that would stress the gender deviance of the culprits. Most of these reformers came up with suggestions such as next to having them incarcerated in women's prisons, flogging sodomites while they were dressed as women, and having them occasionally shown to the public in that attire.[51]

Thus, the discourse also created a new psychology that fitted the emerging 'modern' individual. Both inwardly and outwardly, sodomites were thought to be like women, yet not like any woman. After all, there was still the effeminate womanizer, who needed to be distinguished from the sodomite. Sodomites, were like whores, like lewd women, that despicable species, who had given up their chastity.

The sodomite was a 'he whore' as an English author by the mid-eighteenth century wrote.[52] By the end of the eighteenth century, a predominantly political discourse that embraced concepts of sex and gender had changed into a sexual discourse with political dimensions that understood human beings as sexually desiring subjects. In the eye of the beholder, sodomites – both inwardly and outwardly – increasingly came to represent a separate genus. Unlike nineteenth-century discourses, which emphasized the congenital (medical) origins of homosexuality, this eighteenth-century discourse still considered such a condition as a moral one that individuals acquired by their own doings. However, unlike in 1730 when 'the rise' of sodomy was attributed to the nation as a whole, in such new approaches, homosexual behavior and desires became more and more individualized. Men who gave in to such desires were themselves held responsible for both their desires and their doings, and at the scaffold they no longer had to carry the burden of all the nation, but only to suffer for their own sins.

Emerging category

It was such cultural meanings that sodomites appropriated while, at the same time, through discursive resistance, they gradually bended them to their own benefit. From that, new meanings arose, that became the very basis of a subjectivity that allowed men who desired their own sex, at least among one another to speak with their own moral voice.

Once arrested, people who had engaged in homosexual behaviour had few excuses for what they had done. Many said they had been seduced, mostly in their early pubescence, and typically they would agree with their prosecutors that ever since they had held on to it. In the 1770s the Court of Holland was told about a man who had related to his wife that he had been seduced at the age of 14, that he damned the day it had happened, but that afterwards he could not stop these activities.[53]

Yet, within their own circles these men would develop legitimacy for their behaviour that twisted existing cultural meanings into more positive ones. It was especially devout men who did so. By the mid-eighteenth century, men appeared in court who among one another had called on the biblical elegy of David for Jonathan, in which he sang that his love of Jonathan was more wonderful to him than the love of women.[54] The very same men also found excuses, at least for themselves, by claiming that they had been born with their desires. No less than a church minister, who stood on trial in 1757, had according to witnesses said that he had inherited his desires from his mother, because when she was pregnant with him she had lusted strongly for her absent husband. She had passed on her desires to her yet unborn child.[55] By framing his thoughts within existing pre-scientific knowledge – according to which a foetus could be physically influenced by the strong emotions and sexual appetites of the mother – he provided himself and others with the strongest possible argument. It also outraged his prosecutors because, sharing this pre-scientific knowledge, they had no means to challenge the argument. In the following decades, others claimed congenital origins for their desires as well, putting more and more emphasis on an innate gender deviancy. By the end of the eighteenth and in the early nineteenth centuries men began to refer to their 'inborn weakness', which obviously still bore reminiscences to earlier discourses on lack of restraint. The difference was that since these men thought themselves to have been born with this weakness, they could not help their condition. 'It is a weakness that is innate to us,' in 1826 the man who also used a still current colloquialism for boyfriend, wrote to his male lover. Speaking out on behalf of people like himself, he raised a moral voice by adding that God had created no human being for its damnation.[56]

With such excuses sodomites showed a growing self-awareness in the sense that they thought to form a separate category. In the early eighteenth century, most men who were arrested still referred to other men they only knew in terms of their behavior. They would say that so and so also existed in 'a filthy manner' or talked about a (high placed) gentleman 'whose cart does not go straight either.'[57] By the end of that century, sodomites talked about men who were 'members of the family',[58] asked one another 'are those people like us?',[59] indeed about 'you and me' and 'thousands like us.'[60] In 1826, the man whose love letter I quoted above rang a notorious modern bell. He also wrote to his lover: 'you cannot trust any human being in this world, but those who are members of the family are the greatest bitches of all.'[61] With their sense of belonging to a separate category and their ideas about innate effeminate characteristics and desires, these men had turned themselves into a separate genus. Implicitly, such feelings and notions anticipated the scientific discourses of the second half of the nineteenth century, which claimed the existence of a third sex.

Conclusion

Especially since Michel Foucault published the first volume of his history of sexuality in 1976, historians have placed most emphasis on medical discourses that began in the second half of the nineteenth century. It was these discourses that, according to these historians, generated an entirely new concept of the existence of a third or intermediate sex: men with an innate female soul or inverted sex drives, or at least with a congenital moral pathology. In turn these discourses are supposed to have inspired the emergence of new subjectivities, meaning more or less exclusive same-sex desires and identities.

Research shows rather that, in north-western Europe, in terms of desires, subjectivity and of physical and social realities, modern homosexuality began to emerge in the late seventeenth century. It also shows that notions about the existence of a third sex, both among men with same-sex desires and among their adversaries, had already become part of popular lore by the early nineteenth century. In other words, half a century later the medical profession did not just invent a new category, but gave 'scientific' articulation to pre-existent folk knowledge.

Our understanding of the world today and the order we perceive in it is by and large based on sexual differences and sexual identities, which also create at least the illusion of human equality. Far into the early modern period, the world was understood by its hierarchical features. Sexual and gender differences were subservient positions in general hierarchical distinctions. Hierarchy was supported by the pursuit of honor. Honor, by definition, was first and foremost a public virtue. It related to 'the good feelings others have about us', as one jurist put it in the seventeenth century.[62] Honor depended not only on people's behaviour, but also on intricate sets of interdependencies: class, gender, family, employer, profession and neighborhood dictated how honorable persons were and how they would perceive themselves and others. Such a society was by virtue a society in which inequality reigned, since honor was not equally distributed. A person, a class, a family, a sex, a profession, a generation could claim to be more honorable than others or indeed deny them honor.[63]

From the end of the seventeenth century onwards personal conscience was becoming a disciplinary force as well. This affected people's social behavior, yet its emergence as an inner force also reflected profound ontological and psychological changes, indeed changes in psychological habitus, creating interiority and subjectivity.[64] The emergence of personal conscience gave rise to what Lawrence Stone would call affective individualism.[65] In other words, at the end of the seventeenth century the modern individual *as* an individual began to emerge: the individual who began to know him- or herself and others by its sex and gender, by its desires, and who could speak with its own moral voice, claiming its own moral authority over itself, as opposed to the state or church. Beginning in the late seventeenth century it was such ontological and psychological changes that set the conditions for the – in itself undisputed – success of the medicalization of (homo)sexuality in the second half of the nineteenth century.

Homosexual desires emerged at the end of the seventeenth century, not in medical or even explicitly sexual discourses, but in discourses that were related to inherent tensions in any hierarchical society. Inequality was met, or to a certain extent balanced, by social resentment and discourses that dealt with some ways to overcome inequality. By the end of the seventeenth century, this began to result in new forms of cultural relationships, foremost between and within the sexes. This 'gender revolution', as Randolph Trumbach would have it, resulted in more egalitarian relationships between men and women and also gave rise to homosexual desires.

Notes

Abbreviations

HG = Hooggerechtshof (High Court)
HvH = Hof van Holland (Court of Holland)
MA = Municipal Archive
NA = National Archive
ORA = Oud Rechterlijk Archief (Old Court Archive)
RA = Rechterlijk Archief (Court Archive)

1 See the contributions by Leo Boon, Dirk Jaap Noordam, Arend Huussen, and myself in Kent Gerard, Gert Hekma (eds), *The Pursuit of Sodomy in Renaissance and Enlightenment Europe*, (New York, London: The Haworth Press, 1989). Also Theo van der Meer, 'Sodomy and the Pursuit of a Third Sex in the Early Modern Period', in Gilbert Herdt (ed.), *Third Sex/Third Gender. Beyond Sexual Dimorphism in Culture and History* (New York: Zone Books, 1994) 137–212 and 528–41.
2 Van der Meer, 'Sodomy', 178–9.
3 Donald Haks,'Libertinisme en Nederlands Verhalend Proza, 1650–1700, in Gert Hekma, Herman Roodenburg (eds), *Soete Minne en Helsche Boosheit. Seksuele Voorstellingen in Nederland 1300–1850* (Nijmegen: SUN, 1988), 85–108.
4 *Resolutien Staten van Holland en Westvriesland* (1730) 430.
5 MA Rotterdam, Schepenarchief 250, 200^{r-v}.
6 *Groot Placaet-boek. Inhoudende de Placaten en Ordonnantien van de ... Staten Generaal der Verenigde Nederlanden, ende van de ... Staten van Hollandt ende Westvrieslandt, Sesde Deel* ('sGravenhage, Isaac & Jacobus Scheltus, 's Lands Drukkers, 1746).

7 Henricus Carolus van Byler, *Helsche Boosheit of Grouwelyke Zonde van Sodomie*, (Groningen, 1731), Voorberigt 29–30.
8 Van der Meer, 'Sodomy' 181.
9 *Resolutien Staten van Holland en Westvriesland* (1730) 430–1.
10 Theo van der Meer, 'Tribades on Trial. Female Same-sex Offenders in Late Eighteenth Century Amsterdam,' in John Fout (ed.), *Forbidden History. The State, Society and the Regulation of Sexuality in Modern Europe* (Chicago and London: The University of Chicago Press, 1992) 189–210.
11 See note 1.
12 Theo van der Meer, 'Private Acts, Public Space. Defining Boundaries in Nineteenth Century Holland', in William Leap (ed.) *Public Sex/Gay Space* (New York: Columbia University Press, 1998) 223–45.
13 Michael Rocke, *Forbidden Friendships. Homosexuality and Male Culture in Renaissance Florence* (New York and Oxford, Oxford University Press, 1996).
14 Van der Meer, 'Sodomy', 148–51.
15 NA HvH 5337.1.
16 MA Utrecht, Secretariaatsarchief II–2236.
17 Alan Bray, *Homosexuality in Renaissance England* (London: Gay Men's Press, 1982); Michel Rey, 'Police et Sodomie à Paris au xviiie Siècle: du Péché au Désordre', in *Revue d'Histoire Moderne et Contemporaine*, 29 (1982), 113–24. 'Parisian Homosexuals Create a Lifestyle, 1700–1750: the Police Archives', in Robert P. Maccubbin (ed.), *'Tis Nature's Fault: Unauthorized Sexuality During the Enlightenment* (Cambridge: Cambridge University Press, 1987). Randolph Trumbach, 'London's Sodomites: Homosexual Behavior in the Eighteenth Century', in *Journal of Social History*, 11 (1977), 1–33; 'The Birth of the Queen: Sodomy and the Emergence of Gender Equality in Modern Culture', in Duberman, Vicinus and Chauncey jr., *Hidden from History*: Reclaiming the Gay and Lesbian Past New York: 129–40; *Sex and the Gender Revolution: Heterosexuality and the Third Gender in Enlightenment London* (Chicago, London, University of Chicago Press, 1998).
18 Van der Meer, 151–3.
19 NA, HvH 5420.3.
20 NA, HvH 5374.1.
21 Van der Meer *Sodoms Zaad*, (Ansterdam: SUN, 1995) 153–4.
22 MA Utrecht, Secretariaatsarchief II–469[27].
23 MA Utrecht, Secretariaatsarchief I 2244–1730[1].
24 See note 19.
25 Leo Boon, 'De Grote Sodomietenvervolging in het Gewest Holland, 1730–1731', in *Holland. Regionaal Historisch Tijdschrift*, 8 (1976) 140–52.
26 MA Amsterdam, 5061 – 536, 25[v].
27 MA Dordrecht, ORA 312.
28 NA, HG – 395, 1258.
29 For a survey on contemporary publications on sodomy see Lucien von Römer, 'Der Uranismus in den Niederlanden bis zum 19. Jahrhundert, mit besondere Berücksichtigung der grossen Uraniervervolgung im Jahre 1730,' in *Jahrbuch für Sexuellen Zwischenstufen*, 8 (1906) 365–512.
30 *Nadere Bedenkingen over het Straffen van Zekere Schandelyke Misdaad*, (Amsterdam, 1777).

31 Gilbert Herdt, 'Representations of Homosexuality: an Essay on Cultural Ontology and Historical Comparison,' in *Journal of the History of Sexuality*, 1 (1991) 481–504, 603–32.
32 Donald Haks, *Huwelijk en Gezin in Holland in de 17e en 18e Eeuw. Processtukken en Moralisten over Aspecten van het Laat 17de en 18de-eeuwse Gezinsleven* (Utrecht: Hes Uitgevers, 1985) 9–11.
33 Van der Meer, 'Sodomy', 181–9.
34 Van Byler, *Helsche Boosheit*, 1731, p. 129. Van Byler was not the only one who wrote in this way about sodomy, but his was the most scholarly of the books that came out in 1730–31.
35 MA The Hague, RA – 11.
36 Thomas Laqueur, *Making Sex. Body and Gender From the Greeks to Freud* (Cambridge Massachussetts and London: Harvard University press, 1990); Herman Roodenburg, '"Venus Minsieke Gasthuis", Over Seksuele Attitudes in de Achttiende-eeuwse Republiek', in *Documentatieblad* 18 (1985) 119–41.
37 Jacob Campo Weyerman, *Godgeleerde, Zeedekundige en Historische Bedenkingen over den Text des Apostels Pauli (Rom. 1–27)*, (Amsterdam, 1730) 2–8.
38 Van der Meer, *Sodoms Zaad*, 380. Cf. 'Petty Bange, Voorstellingen over Seksualiteit in de Late Middeleeuwen', in Hekma & Roodenburg (eds), *Soete Minne* (Nijmegen: SUN, 1988) 42–60.
39 Dorinda Outram, *The Body and the French Revolution. Sex, Class and Political culture* (New Haven and London: Yale University Press, 1989) 69–71.
40 Michel Foucault, *The History of Sexuality, Volume I: an Introduction* (New York: Random House, 1978).
41 See note 27.
42 Anton Blok, 'Theatrische Strafvoltrekking onder het Ancien Regime', in *Symposion, Tijdschrift voor Maatschappijwetenschap*, 1 (1979) 94–114.
43 Van der Meer, 'Sodomy', 189–92.
44 Mary Douglas, *Purity and Danger. An Analysis of the Concepts of Pollution and Taboo*, (London, New York: Ark Paperbacks, 1989).
45 Van der Meer, 'Sodomy', 189–92.
46 Van der Meer, *Sodoms Zaad*, 385–96.
47 Randolph Trumbach, 'Sodomy Transformed: Aristocratic Libertinage, Public Reputation and the Gender Revolution of the Eighteenth century', in *Journal of Homosexuality*, 19 (1990) 105–24. Also, Dorothee Sturkenboom, *Spectators van Hartstocht: Sekse en Emotionele Cultuur in de Achttiende Eeuw*, (Hilversum: Verloren, 1998).
48 MA Utrecht, Secretariaatsarchief I 2244–1751[1].
49 Franciscus Lievens Kersteman, *Hollandsch Rechtsgeleerd Woordenboek* (Amsterdam, 1768) 528.
50 *ibid.*
51 Van der Meer, 'Sodomy', 193–4.
52 Randolph Trumbach, 'Gender and the Homosexual Role in Modern Western-culture: the 18th and 19th Centuries Compared', in Anja van Kooten Niekerk and Theo van der Meer (eds), *Homosexuality, Which Homosexuality*, (Amsterdam and London: An Dekker and Schorer, Gay Men's Press, 1989) 149–70.
53 NA, HvH 5506.4.

54 For instance Christiaan Schaaf, who stood trial in 1749 but was acquitted: NA, HvH 5458.9.
55 NA, HvH 5472.
56 See note 28.
57 See note 19.
58 NA, HvH 5515.1.
59 MA Amsterdam, 5061 – 539, pp. 328–66.
60 See note 27.
61 See note 28.
62 Simon van Leeuwen, *Het Rooms-Hollands-regt*, (Amsterdam, 1676) 469–76.
63 Cf. Lotte van de Pol, 'Prostitutie en de Amsterdamse Burgerij: Eerbegrippen in een Vroegmoderne Stedelijke Samenleving', in Peter te Boekhorst, Peter Burke, Willem Frijhoff (eds), *Cultuur en Maatschappij in Nederland 1500–1850. Een Historisch-antropologisch Perspectief* (Meppel, Heerlen: Boom, 1992) 179–218.
64 In *Sodoms Zaad* (1995) I deal extensively with issues like honor, shame, public reputation, etc. Cf. Norbert Elias, *The Civilizing Process* (Oxford: Blackwell, 1994).
65 Lawrence Stone, *The Family, Sex and Marriage in England 1500–1800*, (New York: Harper Colophon Books, 1977).

5

Almost Nothing: Male–Male Sex in Denmark, 1550–1800

Wilhelm von Rosen

Erotic and sexual love between men was a comparatively late phenomenon in Denmark's social life. Not until well into the nineteenth century did negotiated sexual acts involving consenting adults, as opposed to violence, rape, and abuse of social or physical superiority, become a part of the social fabric. And even recorded instances of sexual coercion were fairly rare.

The law

The legal situation was not complicated.[1] Until the Reformation in 1526 sodomy, like other crimes against religion, was solely a matter of canon law dealt with by the ecclesiastical courts as a reserved sin. Contrary, however, to other formerly canonical offences relating to marriage, religion, and the use of the reproductive organs, the prohibition on sodomy did not become national law until the promulgation in 1683 of *Danske Lov* (the Danish Code). That the prohibition on sodomy did not become national law properly speaking until this comparatively late date must be due to the ease with which the judiciary was able to handle the comparatively few cases that occurred, on the legal basis of the Bible ('God's Law') and foreign law (Carolina).

From a judicial point of view there was not much difference between sodomy with a man (or a boy) and sodomy with an animal. All of the known cases of sodomy from the seventeenth century concerned bestiality with the exception of four cases. One or possibly two of these, in 1613 and 1628 respectively, led to execution.[2] In the other two instances of sodomy with men/boys from the second half of the seventeenth century (1663, 1673–74) sentence could not be passed. The small number of cases, as well as the unproblematic lack of a 'proper' legal precept, must mean that sodomy was not a crime of importance to the authorities. Which does not mean that it was not a serious crime.

The Danish Code of 1683 was a work of compilation. The Sixth Book contained the penal law. One of the very few articles not found in earlier legislation was the article dealing with sodomy (art. 6-13-15): 'Conduct which is against nature is punished with burning at the stake.' Adoption of this article cannot be explained by sodomy being of particular concern to the government, but was rather the result of a professional desire to achieve completeness. The Danish Code was prepared by a number of Royal Commissions with law professors in a prominent position. The article on sodomy was included in Chapter 13, 'On Laxity,' which also dealt with rape, incest, fornication, etc., but not with other formerly canonical offences such as usury, perjury and sorcery. The Danish Code thus indicates a development from the religious concept of carnal offences as sins, a spiritual danger excluding the individual from God and the state of Grace, towards a more secular understanding of crimes of the flesh as acts detrimental to society – besides, still, offences against God and Nature. Sexual conduct was now a matter regulated by the state and the government in a way which it had not been before the Reformation. To a large extent the actual governmental control was entrusted to the clergy, which after the introduction in 1660 of absolute monarchy became a corps of civil servants appointed by the king and the central government.[3]

The Danish Code was also the King's Code. This meant that interpretation of law was a royal prerogative reserved for the courts of law and the government. Commentaries by jurists on the Sixth Book were not published until the 1760s. Thus it was not until the publication in 1791 of Professor Christian Brorson's *Essay on the Interpretation of the Sixth Book* that the crime described as 'conduct which is against nature,' was discussed in print by a jurist.[4] Brorson explained that a sentence to death at the stake could only be passed, 'without exception,' when the crime had been consummated which presupposed, 'the thing inside the thing and the effusion of semen' (res in re et effusio seminis). Less punishable crimes of this sort were to be punished arbitrarily.[5] The comments by Brorson and other commentators had practical relevance only in cases of bestiality; there seems not to have been any formal prosecution for sodomy with a man or a boy between 1663 and 1820 – except for two cases in the 1740s. From the 1750s the death penalty for sodomy (i.e. bestiality) was commuted by Royal Pardon to life imprisonment.

The Sixth Book of the Danish Code remained in force until 1866. Royal pardon as an administrative routine, and arbitrary punishment[6] for sexual acts between men, did not become relevant until after 1820, especially when from the 1830s such acts were dealt with, in a routine fashion, by the courts of law.

The cases of 1613 and 1628

The earliest known case of sodomy with a man is the execution of the priest, Peter Johannes of Brandstad in Scania, in 1613.[7] The bishop, a few years later, in a record of memorable events in the diocese, described the priest: 'Everybody talked about his immorality which was so reckless that he abandoned the natural conduct with women and defiled himself with sodomitical intercourse with males (paiderastia).' Rumors led to the priest being interrogated by the local authorities. The result was communicated to the king (Christian IV) who ordered the bishop to have him defrocked, imprisoned and charged. Six months later Peter Johannes was sentenced to death and the king decided that for this 'unheard of act' he should burn at the stake, 'as a serious warning to others.'[8]

In October–November 1628, within an interval of one month, two Scotsmen – a lieutenant-colonel and a private – were burned at the stake in Copenhagen. The only source of this event is the executioner's two bills. They list the expenses but do not state the crime, nor the names of the condemned. Had the crime been bestiality, the burned animal(s) would have been mentioned in the bills. In theory the two Scotsmen may have been executed for sorcery or incest. However, the circumstances (two men, the nature of the punishment) point to sodomy with a man.

Whatever the crime, 1628 was an ominous year, the lowest point in King Christian IV's participation in the Thirty Years War. More than half of his kingdom, the peninsula of Jutland, was occupied by general Wallenstein's imperial troops. Famine, disorder, and moral dissolution accompanied military disaster and defeat. Christian IV, as well as Wallenstein, employed Scottish mercenaries. Since no lieutenant colonel is 'missing' from the payroll of the Scottish regiments in the king's service, it seems probable that the two executed Scotsmen were prisoners of war.

A few weeks after the execution of the two Scotsmen, but without any direct connection to it, the king appointed a commission of bishops and professors of divinity to prepare a statute on the religious discipline of the population: *Statute on the Authority of the Church over the Unrepentant* (1629). It was necessary, the royal order explained, to consider, especially now, how God's wrath and surely imminent revenge and punishment might be averted. Orthodox Lutheranism explained military defeat and famine as God's punishment for the ungodly conduct of the population. The statute appointed the clergy as 'servants' in matters of morals, namely as supervisors who warned, admonished, and often initiated prosecution. In the 1740s, after severe criticism from the courts the priestly supervision of morals was reduced.[9]

The exemplary punishment and the spectacular 'publicity' surrounding the executions in 1613 and 1628 are, as we shall see, in obvious contrast to the administratively ordered discretion and 'silence' of the eighteenth century.

The cases of 1663 and 1673–74

Both of the instances of sodomy that we know of from the second half of the seventeenth century took place in a military setting. That the sodomitical conduct became known to the authorities was undoubtedly because it involved victims who considered themselves raped and abused.

Soldiers employed at the extensive works of fortification around Nyborg Castle were housed in the town of Nyborg. In August 1663 Sergeant Claudi Amberg shared a bed with a 13-year-old boy, Hans Claussen, who later in a military court explained that Amberg had committed an immoral act with him while he was asleep. When he woke up the sergeant had threatened him, promised gifts and money, and put his male member in his behind. The boy became ill, but recovered after a week. Sergeant Amberg did not confess. Consequently the court sentenced him to undergo torture, 'so that the truth may be brought into the light of the day.'

It is not known how the matter with Sergeant Amberg ended. The commanding general in Nyborg reported the case to the Commander-in-Chief of the Danish army and asked what should be done. Neither he nor the War Office answered. Six weeks later the general in Nyborg wrote to the king and complained that he had not received an answer to his inquiry. The War Office then ordered him to resume proceedings in the military court. Renewed interrogation did not lead anywhere and again the commanding general wrote to his superiors in

Copenhagen and asked what he should do with the 'boy-molester' (Knabenschänder) – 'was he to be chased away or to be punished in some other way?' The War Office probably did not answer. The sentence to undergo torture seems not to have been carried out. Being chased away was not a serious punishment. It was, however, an easy way out.

The exploits of Captain Frederik von Basse in the early 1670s were less disputed. In December 1673 Basse left his company in Norway[10] and fled to 'another kingdom.' His wife, who was related to one of the most powerful noble families in Denmark–Norway, complained to the viceroy that 'untrue' accusations made by soldiers from her husband's company was the reason for his flight. She asked the viceroy to appoint a commission of inquiry and, if the allegations turned out to be true, to grant her a divorce from Basse. The viceroy knew all about it; a few weeks previously he had reported to Copenhagen, to the Commander-in-Chief of the army, that Basse had left, 'because he did things I cannot mention.'

The desired commission was appointed. Its main purpose was probably to establish the grounds for an immediate divorce. Interrogation of nine soldiers from Basse's company revealed that for two years he had regularly abused his authority as an officer to force and threaten the soldiers into 'bodily intercourse in a sodomitical manner.' To one of the soldiers it had happened ten times. It is not possible to determine the degree of coercion or consent, since it was in the interest of the soldiers to emphasize that they had been coerced. In principle they risked being prosecuted for sodomy. But this seems not to have happened. Except for the divorce, the matter concluded with Basse's departure to another kingdom. In this case as well as in the case of the sergeant who did not confess, the authorities were probably relieved that there was or could be found an easy way out.

Nowhere in the documents of these two cases from the second half of the seventeenth century is there a mention of God or a reference to the committed acts as crimes against religion. To the military authorities the problem was probably a matter of disorder, the offence a rare type of violence, as well as distasteful and best forgotten. The circumstances surrounding these instances of sodomy were otherwise very ordinary. They took place within, and were facilitated by the power structure of the army, which, like the hierarchy within households, did not allow for a subordinate to say no. Basse had five children and when he fled his wife was pregnant.

The cases of 1742 and 1744

The only two known instances of sex between men in the eighteenth century are very dissimilar, especially in that the first concerned consensual sex between adults, the other what would now be termed paedophilia. Little is know about the first, much more about the second case, which deserves a more detailed account because it very clearly illustrates the attitudes of officialdom to sex between men.

A soldier named Jacob, married for 20 years, committed acts of gross filthiness with Peter Jessen, an apprentice. There were witnesses and they both confessed to having done something shameful with the mouth, as well as masturbated. But they denied having committed the Levitical sin (anal intercourse) and consequently could not be sentenced according to article 6-13-15 of the Danish Code. Jacob was sentenced in 1742 according to martial law to run the gauntlet 16 times (300 men) and to life imprisonment, reduced by royal pardon to two years. What happened to Peter is not known.[11]

These events took place in Åbenrå, a town in the Duchy of Slesvig (Southern Jutland). From another, later case it is known that in 1821 there was in Slesvig a vulgar word for men who were rumored or known to have indecent relations with other men, 'Schwanzerspiller', Low German for 'cock-player' – or queer.[12] One might, on this flimsy evidence, hypothesize that in the culturally and economically more developed Duchies of Slesvig and Holstein, close to (and part of) Germany, there developed earlier than in the Kingdom of Denmark a social role connoting an individual and a personality with a particularly bad taste that went further than being a mere legal subject.

1744: Boring Village

In 1744 two men from the village of Boring in Jutland, 72-year-old Rasmus Væver and 18-year-old Laurids Frandsen, were discovered in a field in compromising circumstances by Laurids Frandsen's father.[13] Because of the 'particular love' of Rasmus for Laurids, demonstrated over the years by numerous gifts and the promise of an inheritance, Laurids' father had come to suspect that Rasmus Væver was a hermaphrodite, and that he had seduced his son. After the discovery in the field Rasmus Væver was subjected to an examination of his genitals. It turned out that he was indeed a man. The local vicar took down a statement to the effect that for the past 10 years Væver had regularly had interfemoral sex with Laurids. Although Rasmus Væver undoubtedly had feelings for Laurids, these are best characterized as the feelings of a rapist for his victim. Their sexual relationship began when Laurids was raped as an 8-year-old boy; the gifts were payment for Laurids' silence and for continued sexual abuse, and they were supplemented by threats. Rasmus Væver and Laurids Frandsen were taken into custody and tried for 'sins against nature.'

The counsel for the prosecution argued that their crime constituted sodomy, and that they should be sentenced to the stake according to article 6-13-15 of the Danish Code, while the counsels for the defence argued that sodomy presupposed 'res in re' (i.e. anal penetration). The judge took the very unusual precaution of asking the central judicial authority in Denmark, the *Danske Kancelli* (the Danish Chancellery) in Copenhagen, for advice. The Chancellery instructed the judge and formulated the sentence to be passed. This was a breach of the informal division of power between the courts of law and the executive branch of government, and definitely outside the limits of competence of the Danish Chancellery. Besides this case it is known to have happened only in a very few and inconsequential instances.

Rasmus Væver was sentenced arbitrarily to two years of hard labor followed by banishment from the Province of Jutland. Laurids Frandsen was discharged. It was accepted that because of his youth and lack of knowledge, he could not have realized that he had committed a sin.

The sentence was based on an opinion drawn up by the Procurator General (legal advisor to the Danish Chancellery), J. S. Wartberg. Wartberg made a distinction between sodomy as referred to by the *arsenokoitai* in 1 Cor. 6,9, cf. Levit. 20,13, and *peccatum onaniticum*, the sin of weakness, committed by the *molles* (1 Cor. 6,9). This last was again divided into three categories, of which the last fitted perfectly the case under consideration: a) masturbation with oneself or with another man, b) *peccatum onaniticum* perpetrated by married couples, and c) 'when the member is inserted between the thighs and semen is expelled.' If everyone who committed these sins, were to be put to the stake, Wartberg wrote, the extinction of a large part of the human race would be the consequence. He added, not quite correctly, that no theologian or jurist had ever been of that ungodly opinion.[14]

Wartberg severely castigated the vicar for his 'blind zeal.' He was the one who on his own initiative had reacted to the rumors in his parish by investigating the incident in Boring, and then instigated formal prosecution:

> On the contrary, all rational and enlightened theologians agree that Christianity and *prudentia politica* (political wisdom) demand that a priest, in case of such rumours, should never investigate the matter in public, much less pass the matter on to the courts for investigation or prosecution. The priest should, as far as possible in secret, investigate the origin of the rumour, reproach the sinner for his abomination, castigate, teach, and exhort him to convert and to abandon his sin, and try to repress the rumour.

In order to prevent rumors from spreading further by the hearing of an appeal before the Provincial Court, the Prosecutor General arranged that the sentence was immediately confirmed by Royal Order-in-Council. The scandal and the inspirational effect of any rumor was what worried the government.

Wartberg's attitude as expressed in his legal opinion and the irregular course of the case in 1744 go a long way to explain why instances of sex between men (sodomy or not) brought to court must have been very few, and why so few cases have been found in the archives. Wartberg's outline of what 'Christianity and political wisdom' required in such cases, probably referred to the Statute of 1629 on the Authority of the Church over the Unrepentant which in 1683 had become part of the Second Book of the Danish Code. According to article 2-9-8, sins and vices that were difficult to suppress and to prove in a court of law, such as drinking, gambling, swearing, 'abuse of intercourse', etc. were to be handled by the clergy in the way outlined by Wartberg. The priest and his helpers were to keep such matters secret and were forbidden to keep records (2-6-26). This extremely discreet administration of possible instances of rumored or discovered sex between men contrasts starkly to the harsh measures taken in the complex of sodomy trials in the rural Osterdeel Langewoldt jurisdiction of the Netherlands in the 1730s, and with other sodomy trials in rural Netherlands in the following period.[15]

For all practical purposes, that is, for judicial and administrative purposes, sodomy and other genital sexual acts between men did not occur in Denmark in the eighteenth century.

Queers out of the question

> *Even so, if it was out of the question, then it was out of the question, and no more matter, then one simply must not speak or think, even to oneself, about it. It would have to be a forbidden subject to*

> *be said or thought on the matter. And if there was no more to be said or thought on the matter.*[16]
>
> Charlotte Bingham

One would expect that the number of sodomy cases would be small, in absolute terms, in a comparatively small population (in 1769: 0.79 million),[17] but two in one century may seem to be fewer than reality. It is possible that one or two more cases may be dug out from the records, and it is probable that queer sexual conduct was more widespread than indicated by (only) two known court cases. However, the hypothesis begs the question of 'reality'.

The case of 1744 illustrates that Christianity and the precepts of the Bible was a real and a serious consideration, but also that silence rather than deterrence was, explicitly, the policy adopted by the eighteenth-century Danish government. The two cases referred to above came to court only, because witnesses and a zealous vicar impeded governmental control of events. The government was convinced that the politically wise method to prevent sodomy and the 'Onanitic sin' was to prevent scandalous discourse. Therefore Laurids Væver was given a mild sentence, deprived of his right to an appeal, and, by being sentenced to exile, removed forever from the province. This method of prevention was not applied to other comparable crimes, such as bestiality and fornication.[18] In practical terms the policy of silence was carried out, especially in Copenhagen and the provincial towns, not by the clergy but by the police. As can be seen from a few but rather uncontrollable and spectacular cases during the first two decades of the nineteenth century, suspected sodomites were informally warned and advised to leave the town, a so-called *consilium abeundi*. This was an expedient without legal foundation (except in absolutist rule) and its use can only have been exceptional. By the mid-1830s the authorities gave up and a series of regular court cases began.

To impose silence and to avoid discourse in order to prevent certain acts from being committed – to not make them known to those who do not know but might be tempted out of curiosity[19] – reflects a very old mentality connected with sodomy as the crime not to be mentioned among Christians. But the policy was also, and possibly more relevant here, in harmony with the basic tenets and the mentality of the Enlightenment and the Age of Reason. The dispersing of knowledge and education based on reasoning (and on revealed Reason) were the tools of societal management and the agents for change. Presumably this reasoning could also work through prevention of knowledge and, incidentally, it corresponds antithetically to the Foucauldian concept of discourse = power. In the eighteenth century the basic tool of education for the young of the general population was the sermon on Sundays and Martin Luther's Catechism according to which it was a sin to even think of transgressions of the Sixth Commandment, much less to enumerate or warn against the various ways in which it could be done.

It is obvious that records of criminal court cases are insufficient and dangerous sources when we ask for a description and an estimate of the actual sexual conduct of the (male) population. This is especially so when, to cover two hundred years, we have only six documented instances of men having had sex with each other.[20] But certainly, there were men who had sex with other men and with boys. In all probability they were few and it did not happen often, if we compare with the later age of modern and urban homosexuality. In principle of course, interpretation and generalization depends on which ontology of homosexuality one employs.

In his history of the phallus as a symbol of the (male) 'homosexual radical,' the psychoanalytically oriented psychiatrist Thorkil Vanggaard[21] referred to the above-mentioned case of 1744 and added that in an age where men slept together with other men and with boys, nobody would pay attention to what happened in these many shared beds, especially when zealousness might lead to criminal prosecution and have extremely serious consequences. Vanggaard was not aware that the short abstract of the case that he had found, reflected an exceptional occurrence, but presumed that Rasmus Væver's and Laurids Frandsen's conduct was, more or less, widespread. It is not important that Væver and Laurids did not live in the same household and did not have sex in a bed but in the fields and during daytime and early evenings. Nor is it conclusive that in contemporary sources not even the faintest allusion to such activities between males sharing the same bed has been found. (Wartberg's estimate referred to above, points to 'a large part of the human race,' but also includes solitary masturbation and married couples; Wartberg's taxonomy did not include the concept of a man having sex with a man.) On sober consideration, however, it seems likely that, besides economy (beds were an expensive commodity), common sleeping arrangements, rather than being an opportunity for sex, served to control the whereabouts and the activities of the young, the unmarried, and the hierarchically lower-placed members of the household. In an orderly household it was probably the master and the matron who decided who slept with whom in which bed. Not to mention that sounds would be heard in the small houses of the age and that soiled sheets could not go unnoticed. Two men in one bed was not a script for sexual intercourse.

To conclude: until the early nineteenth century the policy of silence was successful. Sex between men had no relevance and no place in Danish social life. It occurred (extremely?) seldom and, when it did, it was probably characterized by abuse rather than by negotiation and consent.

Queer literary efforts

> *Denmark is a very small and a very petty country. Everybody knows everybody. The highest god is the fear of men, and the greatest fear is to become ridiculous. These dimensions are the undoing of the country: Denmark disappears into Copenhagen; Copenhagen becomes a provincial town.*[22]
>
> Søren Kierkegaard

Need one say that Denmark was not Italy, and Copenhagen not Paris? Voltaire, a contemporary who had sharp eyes, observed in 1764:

> On sait assez que cette méprise de la nature est beaucoup plus commune dans les climats doux que dans les glaces du septentrion, parce que le sang y est plus allumé, et l'occasion plus fréquente: aussi, ce qui ne parait qu'une faiblesse dans le jeune Alcibiade est une abomination dégoutante dans une matelot hollandais et dans un viviandier moscovite.[23]

Denmark belongs to the 'Icy North.' From a European perspective it was provincial and rustic. The vast majority of the population lived in the countryside. The capital, Copenhagen, in 1769 had 80,000 inhabitants,[24] too few to sustain a sodomitical subculture[25] but sufficient for discursive sodomy and pederasty to emerge as a tale of Ancient Greece and as calumny disguised as Italian vice.

Far away from the peasants of the village of Boring in Jutland, educated citizens in Copenhagen read the essays of the playwright Ludvig Holberg (1684–1754), the intellectual and literary giant of the age – and, by the way, a friend of Procurator General Wartberg. It is probably not relevant that Holberg was unmarried, nor that Wartberg, also unmarried, when he died, left the largest wardrobe Copenhagen had ever seen. In one of his essays, *Epistle No. LIV*, Holberg in 1748 introduced a new age, and males as sexual objects, by asking and answering the question: Had Socrates been devoted to pederasty?[26]

It was certainly a foregone conclusion that Socrates had not been devoted to pederasty which Holberg – ever an educationalist – explained as 'a shameful and unnatural love for young men, a vice with which a number of Greeks of that time were infested.' The problem as presented by Holberg concerned the relationship between 'unnatural vices' and friendship, a man's 'special love' for another man. The one should not be mistaken for the other, as Voltaire also later argued in his essay on 'The So-called Socratic Love.'[27] Moreover, it was Plato who, according to Holberg, had been devoted to pederasty and had sought to exonerate himself by slandering Socrates. For how could, Holberg asked, a 'delicate gentleman' like Alcibiades allow himself to be debauched by such an ugly person as Socrates?

Holberg's lengthy arguments in defence of Socrates must, at least to some of his readers, have seemed a bit silly. He breached rules of formal logic in the same way that a character in one of his celebrated comedies had done in order to prove to his poor mother that she was in reality a stone. Also, his reference to Plato's *Faidon* as a source may have been wilful misdirection, since he clearly took his examples from Plato's *Symposium*. But then he may have written his essay without consulting anything and mixed up *Faidon* (on the death of Socrates) and *Faidros* (on Love).

In his introduction of pederasty into Danish literature, Holberg did not question the precepts of contemporary morality and law, nor did he discuss whether pederasty was beneficial or harmful to society and the individual, a question that at the time began to be argued outside of Denmark, notably by Montesquieu. But he did, implicitly, perceive morality as historically variable by removing pederasty from religious concepts and from the Christianity of daily life in Denmark, and locating it, safely, in Antiquity and among the heathens, that is, in the centre of the humanist mentality of the educated elite. To publish an essay on this subject was naughty and in line with international tendencies, but tempered by an undoubtedly necessary derogatory choice of words.[28]

A queer murderer

In a 'Moral Tale,' a short story published in 1781, Dorothea Biehl, Denmark's earliest advocate for women's emancipation, went further than mere derogatory vocabulary. Her 'weapons' were calumny, slur, and insult. Dorothea Biehl (1731–88) was a successful author of plays and comedies in the vein of Holberg in which she argued for the acceptance of women as beings capable of thinking, reading and writing. With age she also became somewhat bigoted.

In her autobiography (published in 1909) Dorothea Biehl freely admitted that the 'Moral Tale' with the title, 'The False Friend,' was an act of revenge. A few years previously the managing director of the Royal Theatre, Hans Wilhelm von Warnstedt, whom she, not without hesitation because of a face that 'indicated a black and deceitful soul,' had accepted as her true friend, had returned one of her plays with 'an extremely offensive letter.' Warnstedt had excluded her from the Royal Theatre through 'sly schemes and crafty intrigues.' She had been deprived of every hope of future income. However, 'The False Friend' was a *succès fou*. Volume II of Moral Tales sold 200 copies. Everybody in Copenhagen knew that Don Varini, a papal courtier and the villain of the tale, was Warnstedt.

And Don Varini was thoroughly villainous. Hiding 'a conceited, false, ambitious, ungrateful and hating heart' behind a mask of modesty and loathing of vice, he cultivated the naive and romantic scholar, Don Carlos, whose friendship and feelings he pretended to reciprocate. In reality he slandered and undermined Don Carlos and prevented him from obtaining a deserved position that could alleviate his poverty. Because Don Carlos was a morally superior being, Don Varini came to hate him so much that he paid a pair of scoundrels to murder him. But justice was fulfilled: by mistake they killed Don Varini. His fate was an example, which demonstrated to 'malicious hearts' that their wickedness was in vain.

Don Varini's real motive for ingratiating himself with Don Carlos was that he wanted him to become a tutor to the young Sebastiano and thereby further his prospects. The real Sebastiano had to be the ballet dancer, later actor, Frederik Schwarz. In 1767 or shortly afterwards, when Schwarz was 14–15 years old, Warnstedt had become his patron, instructor and friend. In Miss Biehl's Moral Tale Don Varini had taken notice of Sebastiano, 'a young boy' of 14 or 15 years who performed in the houses of the rich and the powerful by playing the zither. Don Varini took so much pleasure in him that he did not rest until he had established a closer relationship: 'This pleasure turned into a violent passion of the mind and led to that shameful confidence for which fire fell from the Heavens and destroyed Sodom and Gomorra.'[29]

Thus, to his biographers in the nineteenth and twentieth centuries, Warnstedt became an early example of the artistic degenerate and homosexual in the history of the Danish theatre.[30] Contemporaries seem not to have assigned any credibility to the moral tale. Warnstedt and Schwarz both continued in their careers. Warnstedt remained as managing director of the Royal Theatre for ten more years, then became Danish minister to the court in Lisbon and was later Master of Ceremonies at the royal court in Copenhagen. He did cause a scandal, however, when on the way to Portugal he married a rich widow. And it was hardly a secret that the well-known actor, J. P. Frydendahl (born 1766), was his illegitimate son. Schwarz too continued in his profession and became one of the most prominent actors and directors of his age. Did Warnstedt, within a few years after siring an illegitimate son, commit sodomy with Frederik Schwarz? There is no reason to accept that Miss Biehl would know anything about that.

Dorothea Biehl in her treatment of sodomy, which she only mentioned in a delicate but unequivocal biblical paraphrase, picked up the theme from Holberg. Sodomy was a vice that in principle had no connection to friendship but became mixed up with it anyway. In her tale sodomy and Don Varini's 'violent passion' for Sebastiano was the spectacular antithesis to Don Carlos' true feelings of friendship for Don Varini, the very reason why he was cheated by a false friend (and nearly murdered by him) as she herself, a woman, had been by Warnstedt. It was not Dorothea Biehl's intention to expound on the relationship between morality and sodomy, for sodomy was indisputably immoral and unacceptable. Her intent was to get revenge and to contribute to Copenhagen's *cronique scandaleuse*. In this she succeeded, probably because it made sense to her readers that there might be something 'sodomitical' to a friendship between two males, especially, perlaps, when they were of different ages and the environment was the theatre.

It seems to have been agreed upon in the eighteenth century that sodomy was an Italian phenomenon. In accordance with this observation Dorothea Biehl placed her tale in Rome. 'This vice is considered less terrible by Italians than by any other people.' But although all righteous persons loathed those who surrendered to this awful vice, they were, wrote the advocate of women's emancipation, particularly despicable in the eyes of women.

Many years later Warnstedt alluded to all this when he wrote to his nephew and warned him against allowing his daughters to learn to write: 'Incredible evil springs from the writings of women. She has neither good nor evil intent; she writes and lets her imagination carry her away for a quarter of an hour, sends it away, and remains completely unworried about the consequences.'[31]

The end of the beginning

Whatever Holberg himself may have had in mind, and because of Dorothea Biehl's furious frustration in friendship, their tales linked together in one discourse the unacceptable and criminal act of pederasty and the acceptable emotionality of a special friendship. In spite of the normative difference they were brought together. This can be seen as the first appearance in Denmark of the important nexus within the later concept of congenital homosexuality between the feelings and the acts. In the words of the German physician Casper in 1852: 'the strange *psychological* aspect of this disgusting aberration. [....] The sexual inclination of a man for a man is in many cases [....] congenital.'[32] The romantic friendship of the eighteenth and early nineteenth century was not homosexuality in disguise but rather a conception of the male Self which contributed to changing, later in the nineteenth century, the often violent and hierarchically determined act of sodomy into the comparatively more democratic homosexuality.

Real queerdom did not emerge in Denmark until the nineteenth century. French and German immigrants together with local actors and ballet dancers formed a small circle of pederasts, which was effectively, and very secretly, dissolved by the authorities in 1814. In the 1830s hunger and deprivation led to boy prostitution within the large central prison in Copenhagen. And in the 1850s Copenhagen became large enough to sustain a small pederastic subculture, which had its nightly meeting ground in precisely the same spot that is today visited by adventurous queers. It came gradually and began fairly quietly.

Notes

1 On the legal theory and practice of sodomy in Denmark, see Wilhelm von Rosen, 'Sodomy in Early Modern Denmark: A Crime Without Victims', *The Pursuit of Sodomy: Male Homosexuality in Renaissance and Enlightenment Europe,* ed. Gert Hekma, and Ken Gerard, (New York: Haworth, 1989) (= *Journal of Homosexuality 16,* No. 1/2). For an overview in English of Denmark's gay history, see von Rosen, 'A Short History of Gay Denmark 1613–1989: The Rise and the Possibly Happy End of the Danish Homosexual', *Nordisk Sexologi 12* (Copenhagen: Dansk Psykologisk Forlag, 1994) 125–36. von Rosen, 'Denmark', *Gay Histories and Cultures: An Encyclopedia, 2nd* edn, ed. G. E. Haggerty, (New York, 2000), 251–4. The standard work on Denmark's gay history is von Rosen, *Månens Kulør. Studier i*

Dansk Bøssehistorie 1628–1912 I–II (Copenhagen: Rhodos, 1993); summary in English, 793–818. The following is to a large extent based on *Månens Kulør* where detailed references to sources and secondary literature can be found.

2 There are no known cases of sodomy from the sixteenth century.

3 See von Rosen, *Månens Kulør*, 73–5.

4 The commentary by C. D. Hedegaard (1760) was almost entirely an uncritical and largely irrelevant recapitulation of commentaries on German law by Damhouder (1601) and Carpzow (1636).

5 Christian Brorson, *Forsøg til den Siette Bogs Fortolkning i Christian den Femtes Danske og Norske Lov, samt Straffene efter de ældre Love* (Copenhagen, 1791), 379.

6 Arbitrary punishment refers to sentences that differed from the punishment prescribed by the casuistic formulas of the Danish Code.

7 Scania (Skåne) is now the southernmost province of Sweden.

8 Laurids Laursen, (ed.), *Kancelliets Brevbøger 1609–15*, (Copenhagen: Rigsarkivet, 1916), 622–3, 653. G. Carlqvist, *Lunds stifts hedaminne 1. ser. I* (Lund, 1943), 60. Kornerup, Bjørn, 'Til Lunde Stifts Kirkehistorie i det 17. Aarh.', *Vetenskapssocieteten i Lund Årsbok* (Lund, 1943), 22. Alex Wittendorff, (review of Wilhelm von Rosen, *Månens Kulør*, 1993), *Historisk Tidsskrift 94* (Copenhagen, 1994), 152–4.

9 Tyge Krogh, *Oplysningstiden og det magiske. Henrettelser og korporlige straffe i 1700-tallets første halvdel* (Copenhagen: Samleren, 2000), 179, 181.

10 Until 1814 Norway was part of the Danish–Norwegian Dual Monarchy.

11 Krogh, 159, 482.

12 *Månens Kulør*, 308.

13 *Månens Kulør*, 79–120.

14 Cf. commentaries on German penal law by Damhouder (1562), Carpzow (1636) and Böhmer (1732). Especially the last was probably known to Danish jurists at the time.

15 E.g. L. S. A. M von Römer, 'Der Uranismus in den Niederlanden bis zum 19. Jahrhundert, mit besonderer Berücksichtigung der grossen Uranier-vervolgung im Jahre 1730', *Jahrbuch für sexuelle Zwischenstufen VIII* (Leipzig: Spohr, 1906), 366–511. A.H. Huussen, Jr., 'Sodomy in the Dutch Republic during the Eighteenth Century', Robert P. MacCubbin, (ed.), *Tis Nature's Fault. Unauthorized Sexuality during the Enlightenment* (Cambridge University Press, 1987), 168–78.

16 Charlotte Bingham, *The Season* (London: Mass Market Paperback, 2001), 237.

17 The number refers to the Kingdom of Denmark, i.e. without counting the population of Norway and the Duchies of Slesvig and Holstein, *Statistisk årbog 1965* (Copenhagen, 1965), Table 4.

18 Silence as a principle of prevention was, however, informally prescribed for self-mutilation and forgery of banknotes.

19 The inspirational effect of discourse was, according to C. D. Hedegaard, *Forsøg til en Tractat angaaende Den Danske Criminal-Ret, 2nd edn*, (Copenhagen, 1760), 661–2, the reason why the Danish Code did not specify the different ways in which sodomy could be committed.

20 Or 16, if we count Captain Basse's exploitation of his men.

21 Thorkil Vanggaard, *Phallós. A Symbol and its History in the Male World* (London: Cape, 1972). Cf. von Rosen, 'Vanggaard, Thorkil,' Aldrich, Robert, and Wotherspoon, Garry (eds), *Who's Who in Contemporary Gay and Lesbian History* (London and New York: Routledge, 2001), 417.
22 N. Thulstrup, (ed.), *Søren Kierkegaards Papirer VIII, 1,* (Copenhagen, 1917), A 630 [1848].
23 Voltaire, *Dictionnaire philosophique I* (1764), ed. Julien Benda et Raymond Naves, (Paris, 1937), 26.
24 *Statistisk Årbog 1965* (Copenhagen, 1965), Table 4.
25 See E. W. Monter, 'Sodomy and Heresy in Early Modern Switzerland', *Journal of Homosexuality 6* (New York: Haworth, 1981–82): 42, 51.
26 Ludvig Holberg, *Epistler I*, ed. F. J. Billeskov Jansen, (Copenhagen, 1944), 234–6.
27 Voltaire, *Dictionnaire Philosophique I*, 22.
28 *Månens Kulør*, 127–32.
29 Charlotte Dorothea Biehl, 'Den falske Ven eller hertil og ikke længere', *Moralske Fortællinger II*, Copenhagen, 1781), 88.
30 e.g. Wladimir Ørbæk, *Hans Wilh. Warnstedt* (Copenhagen, 1936), 10–11.
31 Ørbæk, 60–1 and *Månens Kulør*, 170–9.
32 Johan Ludwig Casper, 'Ueber Notzucht und Päderastie', *Vierteljahrsschrift für gerichtliche und öffentliche Medicin 1* (Berlin, 1852) 62; reprint in J. S. Hohmann, *Der Unterdrückte Sexus* (Lollar, 1977); emphasis by Casper.

6
A State of Sin: Switzerland and the Early Modern Imaginary

Helmut Puff

In late medieval and early modern Europe, the Swiss were frequently caricatured along sexual lines. The injurious term 'cow-Swiss' carried with it the allegation of bestiality.[1] In *De Nobilitate et Rusticitate* ('Of Nobility and Peasantry'), written in 1451, Felix Hemmerli presented sexual intercourse between Swiss men and their cattle as a virtually ubiquitous phenomenon. According to this canonist, Swiss men avoided 'the company of their wives.' Instead, they populated barely habitable mountain areas, sharing their lives with cows. Shockingly, according to Hemmerli, the Swiss had resigned 'themselves to these dogged rumors. They [did] not suffer anymore from the accusations and even [did] not feel obliged to apologize or bring charges against their defamers.' Hemmerli's overt specification of bestiality amongst the Swiss peasantry deployed a rhetoric congruous with descriptions of same-sex relations common in the same period. His description of sexual acts 'against nature' centered around the explicit mention of that which, according to the same author, should be left unspoken: 'It would be better if we fell silent, put the finger on our mouth, and rejected these aspersions entirely. Then, this well-known talk would really be silenced.'[2]

Bestiality's relationship to language was as problematic as sodomy's.[3] Enunciations thereof were suspended between verbal proliferation and censure. Slurs often served as a prime means to voice what theologians had declared unspeakable (though, at the same time, they greatly contributed to a growing discourse on these sins). Bestiality, like sodomy, was anything but a peccadillo. According to Thomas Aquinas, cross-species intercourse was the worst among all sexual sins, worse even than same-sex sexual acts.[4] The many men who were executed for sexual intercourse with animals, and also for sex with other men, testify to the severe retribution brought upon both types of offenders.[5] The crime's severity is further evidenced by the fact that some men turned themselves over to the authorities in order to be punished, sometimes years if not decades after they had committed the act. One can only conjecture that these self-declared criminals expected to be cleansed of a sin that burdened their existence. According to several competing and overlapping value systems, sex with animals thus emerges as an extremely severe offense. In light of bestiality's sinfulness, it worked extremely well as a vehicle for defamation of the Swiss – well fit to ridicule a people perceived as rural. For outsiders, bestiality slurs were therefore convenient in daily interactions. But the Swiss themselves also embraced stock images of the sexualized 'foreign'.

Swiss men frequently voiced suspicions of people from regions where Romance languages were spoken. French and Italian men were labeled 'buttfuckers' (*arsbruter*), for example, or similarly obscene slurs alluding to sexual relations between men.[6] Men whom urban courts tried for sodomy claimed to have 'learnt' homoeroticism from *welsche*, a derogatory term reserved primarily for speakers of Italian but also for other Latin peoples. In a period of increasing cross-cultural contacts, intensifying mercantile exchange, and growing mobility across the Alps (above all that of Swiss mercenaries), defendants regularly explained their sexual behavior via genealogies of seduction that led to regions south or west of the Alps. Though confessions of this kind did not protect the accused from a death sentence, these explanations must have struck a chord in a culture and society like Switzerland which rallied around notions of a moral as well as sexual probity often labeled 'German.'[7]

After having been seized by the authorities in Zurich for theft, Jacob vom Schloss was found to have had a string of lucrative erotic liaisons with men his superior in age and social status. In the dock, he attributed his ruin to the *welsch*. Having confessed that the first man to have seduced him in Geneva was a notary at the court of Savoy, Jacob proceeded to warn 'every honest man ... that he does not send his children to the *welsch*, neither the French, the Savoyards nor others, since they try hard to cheat us Germans of our children [literally: shit on our children] and introduce such viciousness to us.'[8] Jephat Scheurmann confessed in 1609 to having been 'seduced' as a young man while 'in foreign countries.' He mentioned an apprentice from Fribourg as his preceptor. The precise wording is of interest here. Scheurmann stated that 'he was brought into this vice,' as if an alien force had intruded on his core self. He attributed his failure to protect his innocence of sodomy to youthful ignorance: 'he did not know that it was a sin.'[9] Once seduced, Scheurmann was seduced again in his hometown, Zofingen, and proceeded to seduce others. Still others had acquired what they described as a habit away from home while traveling in Italy (Rome and Milan are mentioned specifically).[10] Whereas foreigners often viewed bestiality as a typically Swiss sin, the Swiss themselves constructed the *Romania* as a haven for sodomites. Their descriptions are replete with anxieties about foreign intrusions while also pointing toward inexpressible desires.[11] Like bestiality, sodomy characterizes a people out of sync with God's order. Like the practice of bestiality, sodomy threatened to wreak havoc on a polity. If the sins associated with the Old Testament city of Sodom could not be uprooted, this region might suffer a similar fate for having aroused God's wrath.

From the vantage point of a history of insults and perceptions of the 'other,' a specifically Swiss 'sexual culture' can indeed be said to have existed during the early modern period. In this configuration, the sexual and the political were intimately intertwined. The supposed dissemination of bestiality among Swiss men and the supposed equanimity with which charges of bestiality were met, according to Hemmerli's and others' partisan diagnosis, were in fact part and parcel of a whole cluster of negative labels attached to this people in late medieval and early modern Europe. The Swiss attracted a great deal of injurious attention. Popular songs as well as humanist treatises labelled the Swiss as proud, arrogant, avaricious, and, more than anything, rebellious. To be sure, their polity was a constitutional oddity. Neither a monarchy nor an aristocracy, the Swiss Confederacy came to be seen as a peasants' state; that is, a political entity lacking a divinely ordained government and therefore unruly, barbarous, uncivilized, and violent. Their lowly origins notwithstanding, however, the Confederates proved victorious over their mightiest enemies in the military conflicts of the war-prone era before and after 1500, at least until they suffered defeat in the battle of Marignano (1515). The highly publicized wars in Northern Italy propelled images of fearsome Swiss warriors to distant places all across Europe. Their reputation as great soldiers made Swiss mercenaries an early modern *cause célèbre*, admired and feared at the same time.[12]

In anti-Swiss polemic, the Confederacy's constitutional peculiarity surfaced in frequent comparisons that likened the Swiss to the Hussites or Turks, bellicose foes of Christianity, advancing the cause of the Antichrist. When Emperor Maximilian I published a 'Manifesto against the Confederates' in April of 1499, the term 'unnatural,' meant to describe Switzerland's misconstrued political order, also carried religious and sexual connotations, characterizing the Swiss as 'heretics' and villains *in sexualibus* (though the document mentions neither bestiality nor sodomy explicitly).[13] As Tom Brady points out, those who rebeled against their rulers thought of themselves as 'turning Swiss.'[14] Claudius Sieber-Lehmann speaks of a downright 'war of insults' when neighboring territories shifted allegiance or, like Basel, became a member of the Confederacy in the early sixteenth century.[15] These exchanges may in fact have helped to forge a sense of commonality among the widely divergent regions of Switzerland.[16]

An upstart in the European theater of states, the Confederacy was also reputed to be an El Dorado for criminals of all persuasions. Apparently, it did attract shady figures like the nobleman Richard Puller von Hohenburg. Having lost all his Alsatian possessions due to various criminal charges (including sodomy), Puller von Hohenburg became a citizen of Zurich. There, he and his servant Anton Mätzler were discovered to have engaged in same-sex eroticism and were burnt at the stake as sodomites in 1482. Hereby the city council, urged by Zurich's Swiss compatriots, was able to avoid a feud over Hohenburg's possessions with a close ally of the Confederacy, the city of Strasbourg.[17] During the fifteenth and sixteenth centuries, city officials, literati, and humanists therefore increasingly sought to counter these negative perceptions. By a variety of measures, they dressed up the Confederacy's image, among other reasons to bring legitimacy to this state. Various historiographical projects, for instance, provided the Swiss with an elaborate foundational myth.[18]

During the Reformation, confessional allegiance opened another combat zone, this time within Switzerland. Divided between Catholic and Reformed cantons, the Swiss polity became the forum for an exchange of sexual slurs on a grand scale. Catholics accused Huldrych Zwingli, Zurich's Reform theologian, of being a thief and a sodomite, a 'villain of the penis' (*zärsbösewicht*) who had 'fucked' a mule (or a cow, or a mare) in Paris. The charge of bestiality against Zwingli was a sexual slur befitting his country of origin (as opposed to the 'Italian' sin of sodomy). At the same time, the defamer, Hans Seiler of Solothurn, reified the foreign connection of 'sins against nature' by artfully setting the scene in Paris. According to Pia Holenstein and Norbert Schindler, this accusation was so successful that within a short period of time, the 'cow-fuckers' became a widely used slur for adherents of the Reform.[19]

At the same time, Protestant pamphlets disseminated images of an 'Italian' Catholic Church infested with a great number of sins, sodomy prominent among them. One of the most successful and widespread Protestant slurs against a Catholic clergyman, the bishop Giovanni della Casa, originated probably in Zurich in the middle of the sixteenth century. Pier Paolo Vergerio, an Italian and recent convert to the cause of Protestantism, exposed the 'fact' that Della Casa had published a poetic 'praise of sodomy' before becoming a censor and inquisitor for the cause of Catholic Reform. Protestant authors reiterated this disparaging anecdote endlessly in a variety of Latin and German publications until the end of the *ancien régime*.[20] The ultimate sin of sodomy was made to symbolize the ultimate depravity of Roman Catholics in general and Roman Catholic prelates especially.

Sexual slander functioned as one of the most versatile vehicles for enunciating the so-called ineffable. Historians would be well-advised to study this startlingly creative discourse. Read against the grain, defamation unveils powerful images in which notions of male–male sexuality pervaded a great variety of discourses.

Above all, polemical discourse was meant to mobilize potential constituencies. In Reformation Basel, the council issued decrees requesting that the French religious refugees who resided in the city encourage their servants to comport themselves as 'good Protestant people' and not like 'sodomites.' A certain but imprecisely defined habitus and style of clothing was considered rife with vaguely defined sexual connotations and indecent in the highest measure.[21] A deeply rooted cultural reflex against everything Latin or *welsch*, as the derogatory expression goes, is discernible in encounters with France and, above all, with Italy, the true homeland of sodomy. Ironically, these were countries whose social and sartorial codes also provided much-admired models north of the Alps.[22]

What emerges from the above considerations is the conceptual similarity of two sexual sins. Sodomy and bestiality were twin concepts that had a name in common. The vernacular term for both acts was 'heresy' (*ketzerie*) – a term referencing religious as well as sexual unorthodoxy. The sodomite was not like the 'heretic' merely by way of comparison. In Swiss German, the 'heretic' *was* a man who had sex with an animal or with a person of his own sex (like the English 'bugger', a term which originally denoted a religiously unorthodox group).

The research on queer masculinities in Switzerland has been attentive to this conceptual double entendre. In a pioneering article, originally published in French in 1974, E. William Monter investigated court proceedings in a comparative framework; that is, he explored both sodomy and bestiality trials. Moreover, he did so in two locations, Geneva, a city with few rural holdings where bestiality was practically unknown, and the rural canton of Fribourg where charges of bestiality were prevalent. The author demonstrates how persecutions for sexual 'heresy' and for witchcraft were in fact linked – a link he attributed to 'the unusually high degree of religious motivation behind these two governments during the sixteenth and seventeenth centuries' before a more secularized state did away with these trials altogether. Problematically, religion – typically associated with the premodern – functions as a blanket explanation in this argument, with little consideration given to the ways in which rulers and subjects inhabited the religious. In fact, governmental political authority greatly increased with the various Reforms, inducing city councils, for instance, to control public enunciations of what passed as illegitimate sexuality.[23] Stephanie Krings studied 29 cases of sodomy and bestiality proceedings in St. Gallen between 1463 and 1742, three of which centered on charges of same-sex sexual acts. Interestingly, male–male sexuality was considered a more severe offense than bestiality.[24] William G. Naphy's work on the Republic of Geneva sheds light on Geneva's ruling elite and their approach to a variety of sexual delicts.[25]

So far, the occasional studies on homoeroticism have largely been inspired by the two paradigms of social and legal histories. Much remains to be done. Swiss cities were a center of humanism in the north and the forms of male sociability in this context warrant an in-depth analysis.[26] My study, *Sodomy in Reformation Switzerland and Germany, 1400–1600*, tries to broaden this horizon by working toward a cultural history of sodomy in a German-speaking context. Ultimately, I intend to contextualize notions of queer sexuality in the age of Reforms and its concomitant religious, political, and ideological shifts. This means looking at the resonances between sodomy trials and religious pamphlets, artistic discourse and defamation on the streets. Significantly, such a study requires reading the Protestant politics of matrimony into the politics surrounding sodomy.

The configuration of highly public images this article took as a starting point suggests that a case might indeed be made for a specifically Swiss history of male–male sexuality. To date, there is little in terms of an existing historiography on queer masculinities for early modern Switzerland.[27] Yet the question of whether the history of queer sexuality truly follows borders – borders that were relatively unstable during the early modern period – must be asked. Don't we need to query the very notion of broadly conceived national, cultural, or geographical commonalities and their relevance to a phenomenology of erotically charged interactions between men? The answer to this question depends on how we frame what we desire to know. If an investigation of queer masculinities foregrounds the analysis of patterns of friendships, sexual alliances, and self-descriptions, one should expect to find only small, though potentially intriguing, deviations from sensibilities, sociabilities, and sexualities documented for other areas of Europe.[28]

As one can surmise from the research published thus far, the patterns of erotic attachments between men were, like in other areas of Europe, often intergenerational. At the same time, trial documents reveal that, unlike in the South (in cities like Florence or Venice), little significance was attached to the question of who penetrated whom (if anal intercourse was at issue).[29] What mattered most to the judges was the age of the participants. If one partner was considered a child or an adolescent, he often escaped death or other forms of punishment. As in other parts of Europe, persecution primarily targeted the poor and foreigners; few members of the elite were ever brought to court.[30] Yet the overall number of men persecuted for same-sex sexual acts remained low, much lower than in fifteenth-century Italian cities. This held true even after the *Constitutio Criminalis Carolina* of 1532 had been promulgated, when criminal persecution of sodomy for the first time gained an unmistakably clear legal basis in the German empire and in many areas of Switzerland, though this law code's subsidiary status caused application to vary from canton to canton. Unlike in the aforementioned Italian cities, however, the death penalty was meted out regularly. The threat of executions with their potentially disruptive effects on communities (if members of a particular community were executed) placed severe limits on indictments for same-sex relations. Episodic persecutions of homoeroticism thus remained the rule throughout the early modern period in Switzerland.[31]

Nonetheless, the early modern state apparatus could weigh on its subjects with destructive force. This can be illustrated by the exceptional case of Kyburg, a region in the hinterland of Zurich. Between 1694 and 1698, 22 of 24 male defendants were executed for sodomy. These trials revealed that large numbers of men shared sexual pleasures as adolescents – a wave of persecution which ended only when the *Landvogt* Johann Conrad Heidegger had been replaced.[32] Such an upsurge in executions for sodomy testifies to the ability of early modern institutions to exert power brutally whenever there was a will to 'discover' and punish networks of men perceived as sodomites. This exceptional event also testifies to a shift in the discourse on sodomy.

The relevant documents distinguish *sodomia* for male homoeroticism from *bestialitas* for bestiality – wordings indicating a shift toward professionalization in law enforcement and, concurrently, differentiation of offenses.

As queer studies have so aptly demonstrated, researchers benefit from embedding research on social acts and sexual pleasures among men in linguistic, cultural, and political particulars. Future studies on Switzerland might help to dethrone hegemonic models of queer masculinities derived from research on English and Italian contexts. The promise of darting a glance at queer masculinities in this part of Europe lies in investigating a region which, at least during the early modern period, constituted a somewhat unique polity. As we have seen, the Confederacy was the recipient of highly sexualized disparagements from its neighbors. Yet between 1550 and 1800, the imagery conjured up by Switzerland underwent a profound transformation. What had been viewed as Europe's 'wild west' in the fifteenth and sixteenth centuries emerged as one of Europe's favorite travel destinations in the eighteenth.[33] The image of the noble peasant replaced that of the unruly mercenary. Enlightenment thinkers elevated the inhabitants of the Alps, formerly decried for their supposedly outrageous sexuality, to models for all of humanity, supposedly close to the prescribed natural ways of living, hailing them as harbingers of democracy: in short, a people whose lifestyle had kept them from the (sexual) depravities of modern civilization. The new projection was a desexualizing one and, by contrast to earlier images of the Swiss, a very queer metamorphosis indeed.

Those who took the seductive identification of Switzerland with nature's beauties all too literally, or rather physically, were considered troublemakers, however, and treated as such. When Johann Wolfgang von Goethe (1749–1832) swam naked in a lake with two friends, the brothers Christian and Friedrich Leopold Counts of Stolberg, during their first trip to Switzerland in 1775, these nature- and poetry-loving young spirits 'scandalized the civilization-loving Swiss with their natural exercises' (*Naturübungen*) (though, according to Goethe's autobiographical *Dichtung und Wahrheit*, they had taken precautions to hide their youthful, 'shining' bodies from the gaze of others).[34] As a result, the Counts broke off their trip and left Zurich. Kurt Eissler speaks repeatedly of 'the homosexual meaning Switzerland had for' Goethe in his psychoanalytic study of the poet.[35] As Paul Derks has shown, such a reading gives an all too unsubtle and ahistorical spin to a flurry of evocative experiences and literary passages that celebrate the beauty of the male body framed by what remade Switzerland's image in eighteenth-century Europe, the country's sublime landscape.[36]

Notes

My thanks go to Matt Johnson and Steve Gutterman for feedback on this article.

1 Thomas A. Brady, *Turning Swiss: Cities and Empire, 1450–1550* (Cambridge: Cambridge University Press, 1985) 58; Susanna Burghartz, *Leib, Ehre und Gut: Delinquenz in Zürich Ende des 14. Jahrhunderts* (Zurich: Chronos, 1990) 131; Matthias Weishaupt, '"Kuhghyer": Eine historisch–anthropologische Untersuchung zur sexuellen Schmähpraxis und Schandsymbolik in der spätmittelalterlichen Eidgenossenschaft (1350–1520),' in *Zürcher Mediävistik: Bulletin* (WS 1999/2000) 68.

2 Felix Hemmerli, *De nobilitate*. Translated after Claudius Sieber-Lehmann and Thomas Wilhelmi (eds.), *In Helvetios-Wider die Kuhschweizer: Fremd- und Feindbilder von den Schweizern* (Bern: Paul Haupt, 1998) 53-4.

3 I am using sodomy to denote male–male sexual acts in this context. In Latin texts of the period under consideration, the term *sodomia* or *vicium sodomiticum* can cover a much wider terrain of non-procreative sexual acts (including cross-species sexuality). At the same time, in a number of contexts, the same term refers to male–male eroticism primarily. See Mark D. Jordan, *The Invention of Sodomy in Christian Theology* (Chicago: University of Chicago Press, 1997).

4 Thomas Aquinas, *Summa Theologiae: Pars Secunda Secundae* (Torin: Marietti, 1952) 676 (quaestio 154, articulus 12).

5 For Zurich and Lucerne comparative figures are available that roughly compare to my own calculations, see Gerold Meyer von Knonau, *Der Canton Zürich, historisch–geographisch-statistisch* (St. Gallen: Huber, 1844-1846) 155; Kasimir Pfyffer, *Der Kanton Luzern, historisch–geographisch–politisch geschildert* (St. Gallen: Huber, 1858) 19, 379. See also Pierre Olivier Lechot, 'Puncto Criminis Sodomiae: Un procès pour bestialité dans l'ancien Evêché de Bâle au XVIIIe siècle', in *Schweizerische Zeitschrift für Geschichte* 50 (2000): 123–40.

6 Staatsarchiv Zürich (StAZ), A 27.3 (*Kundschaften und Nachgänge* 1500–1520), July 1518; StAZ, A 27.35 (*Kundschaften und Nachgänge* 1579), Wilhelm von Mühlhausen 1579; Staatsarchiv Luzern (StALU), COD 4435 (Turmbücher), 197r (1561).

7 See Hans Conrad Peyer, *Verfassungsgeschichte der alten Schweiz* (Zurich: Schulthess Polygraphischer Verlag, 1978) 19. In the early modern period very few areas of the Swiss Confederacy were non-German speaking.

8 StAZ, B VI 245 (*Rats- und Richtbuch* 1513–1519), 79r/v. See also, Staatsarchiv Solothurn (StASO), DS (*Denkwürdige Sachen*) 33, 35r.

9 StALU, COD 4500 (*Turmbücher*), 152r (1609).

10 StASO, Vergichtbuch (*Ratsmanual rot* 19) 1478–1552 (Hans Pröpstli 1525), 170–1.

11 Cf. Dominic Sieber, 'Calvinistische Passionen, konfessionalisierte Körper: Zur Autobiographie des Zinngießers Augustin Güntzer (1596–1657?)', in *sowi* 24 (1995): 5–11.

12 See, for example, Thomas Platter's autobiographical text in which he relates his life as a wandering student. He was frequently welcomed and given food or housing when people in various regions of Germany learnt he was Swiss. Thomas Platter, *Hirtenknabe, Handwerker und Humanist: Die Selbstbiographie 1499 bis 1582* (Nördlingen: Greno, 1989) 23, 26, 29, 33. Responses to the Confederacy were in part conditioned by social and educational status. Humanists and members of the elite were more likely to engage in anti-Swiss polemic.

13 Maximilian I, 'Manifest gegen die Eidgenossen (22. April 1499)', in *In Helvetios*, 88–91, here 90. See the frequent references to Turks and Muslims in this context.

14 Brady, *Turning Swiss*.

15 Claudius Sieber-Lehmann, 'Schimpfen und Schirmen: Mülhausen, Basel und die Eidgenossen', in *Eidgenössische 'Grenzfälle': Mülhausen und Genf*, ed. Wolfgang Kaiser, Claudius Sieber-Lehmann, Christian Windler (Basel: Schwabe, 2001) 115–55, here 120–1. With regard to bestiality, 122–35.

16 Claudius Sieber-Lehmann, *Das eidgenössische Basel: Eine Fallstudie zur Konstruktion herrschaftlich-politischer Grenzen in der Vormoderne* (Basel: Habilitationsschrift, 2002).

17 Heinrich Witte, *Der letzte Puller von Hohenburg: Ein Beitrag zur politischen und Sittengeschichte des Elsasses und der Schweiz im 15. Jahrhundert sowie zur Genealogie des Geschlechts der Püller*. Beiträge zur Landes- und Volkskunde von Elsass-Lothringen. Vierter Band (Heft 16–20) (Strassburg, 1895); Christine Reinle, 'Konflikte und Konfliktstrategien eines elsässischen Adligen: Der Fall des Richard Puller von Hohenburg († 1482)', in *'Raubritter' oder 'Rechtschaffene vom Adel'? Aspekte von Politik, Friede und Recht im späten Mittelalter*, ed. Kurt Andermann (Sigmaringen: Thorbecke, 1997) 89–113.

18 Edgar Bonjour and Richard Feller, *Geschichtsschreibung der Schweiz vom Spätmittelalter zur Neuzeit* (Basel: Schwabe, 1962).

19 Pia Holenstein, Norbert Schindler, 'Geschwätzgeschichte(n): Ein kulturhistorisches Plädoyer für die Rehabilitierung der unkontrollierten Rede', in *Dynamik der Tradition*, ed. Richard van Dülmen (Frankfurt am Main: Fischer, 1992) 63–4.

20 Winfried Schleiner, 'Burton's Use of *praeteritio* in Discussing Same-Sex Relationships', in *Renaissance Discourses of Desire*, ed. Claude J. Summers and Ted-Larry Pebworth (Columbia: University of Missouri Press, 1993) 159–78.

21 Wolfgang Kaiser, 'Les "étranges fantaisies" des Welch: Les débuts difficiles de la communauté réformée de langue française à Bâle (XVIe–XVIIe siècles)', in: *Religion et identité*, ed. Gabriel Audisio (Aix: Publications de l'Université de Provence, 1998) 82.

22 For France, see Rebecca E. Zorach, 'The Matter of Italy: Sodomy and the Scandal of Style in Sixteenth-Century France', in *Journal of Medieval and Early Modern Studies* 26 (1996): 581–609. For context, see Lionello Sozzi, 'La polémique anti-italienne en France au XVIe siècle', in *Atti della Accademia della Scienze di Torino: Classe di Scienze Morali, Storiche e Filologiche* 206 (1972): 99–190.

23 E. William Monter, 'Sodomy and Heresy in Early Modern Switzerland', in *The Gay Past: A Collection of Historical Essays*, ed. Salvatore J. Licata and

Robert P. Petersen (New York: Harrington Park Press, 1985) 41–55, here 49; first published as: 'La Sodomie à l'époque moderne en Suisse romande,' in *Annales esc.* 29 (1974): 1023–33.

24 Stefanie Krings, 'Sodomie am Bodensee: Vom gesellschaftlichen Umgang mit sexueller Abartigkeit in spätem Mittelalter und früher Neuzeit auf St. Galler Quellengrundlage', in *Schriften des Vereins für Geschichte des Bodensees und seiner Umgebung* 113 (1995): 1–45.

25 William G. Naphy, 'Sodomy in Early Modern Geneva: Various Definitions, Diverse Verdicts', in *Sodomy in Early Modern Europe,* ed. Tom Betteridge (Manchester: Manchester University Press, 2002) 94–111; id., *Plagues, Poisons, and Potions: Plague Spreading Conspiracies in the Western Alps, c. 1530–1640* (forthcoming).

26 See, however, Helmut Puff 'Männergeschichten / Frauengeschichten: Über den Nutzen einer Geschichte der Homosexualitäten', in *Geschlechtergeschichte und Allgemeine Geschichte,* ed. Hans Medick, Anne-Charlotte Trepp (Göttingen: Wallstein, 1998) 165–9. On Theodor de Bèze, see Winfried Schleiner, '"That Matter Which Ought Not To Be Heard Of": Homophobic Slurs in Renaissance Cultural Politics,' in *Journal of Homosexuality* 26 (1994): 41–75.

27 Most of the existing literature is focused on the late medieval period when urban courts started to prosecute same-sex sexual relations. Hans-Rudolf Hagemann, *Basler Rechtsleben im Mittelalter,* 2 vols. (Basel: Helbing & Lichtenhahn, 1981/1987); Helmut Puff and Wolfram Schneider-Lastin, 'Quellen zur Homosexualität im Mittelalter: Ein Basler Projekt', in *Forum Homosexualität und Literatur* 13 (1991): 119–24; Wolfram Schneider-Lastin and Helmut Puff, '"Vnd solt man alle die so das tuend verbrennen, es bliben nit funffzig mannen jn Basel": Homosexualität in der deutschen Schweiz im Spätmittelalter', in *Lust, Angst und Provokation: Homosexualität in der Gesellschaft,* ed. H. Puff (Göttingen: Vandenhoeck & Ruprecht, 1993) 79–103; Andreas Niederhäuser, *Homosexuelle Lebenswelten im Spätmittelalter* (Zurich: Beiträge der Koordinationsstelle Homosexualität und Wissenschaft, 1994); Helmut Puff, 'Localizing Sodomy: The "Priest and Sodomite" in Pre-Reformation Germany and Switzerland', in *Journal of the History of Sexuality* 8 (1997): 165–95; id., 'Überlegungen zu einer Rhetorik der "unsprechlichen Sünde": Ein Basler Verhörprotokoll aus dem Jahr 1416', in *Österreichische Zeitschrift für Geschichtswissenschaften* 9 (1998): 342–57.

28 Only in 1648 did Switzerland achieve recognition of its political independence from the Holy Roman Empire, though de facto the Confederacy had acted independently since the fifteenth century.

29 Cf. Michael Rocke, *Forbidden Friendships: Homosexuality and Male Culture in Renaissance Florence* (Oxford: Oxford University Press, 1996).

30 In 1626, Hans Walther von Castanea, son of a wealthy merchant, was urged by his kin to flee the city in order to avoid being prosecuted for sodomy and other charges. Urban authorities took Castanea's escape for a confession of guilt and sentenced him to death in absentia. Yet the charges were so vague that they seem to have been fabricated. The whole scandal was related to conflicts over the inheritance of Hans Georg von Castanea and his business. See Staatsarchiv Luzern (STALU), Archiv 1, Personalien, AKT 113/302; Kurt Messmer, Peter Hoppe, *Luzerner Patriziat: Sozial- und*

wirtschaftsgeschichtliche Studien zur Entstehung und Entwicklung im 16. und 17. Jahrhundert (Lucerne: Rex-Verlag, 1976) 344–6, 348.

31 See my *Sodomy in Reformation Germany and Switzerland, 1400–1600* (Chicago: University of Chicago Press, 2003), chapters one, two, and four.

32 Staatsarchiv Zürich, B VII 21.2. Cf. Erich Wettstein, *Die Geschichte der Todesstrafe im Kanton Zürich*, Ph.D. (Winterthur: H. Schellenberg, 1958) 80–3.

33 Cf. Petra Raymond, *Von der Landschaft im Kopf zur Landschaft aus Sprache: Die Romantisierung der Alpen in den Reiseschilderungen und die Literarisierung des Gebirges in der Erzählprosa der Goethezeit* (Tübingen: Niemeyer, 1993).

34 Johann Wolfgang von Goethe, Dichtung und Wahrheit, in: *Werke: Hamburger Ausgabe*, vol. 10 (Munich: Beck, 1988) 152–4. I have used the following English translation: *The Autobiography of Goethe: Truth and Poetry: From My Life*, ed. Parke Godwin (New York: John Wiley, 1849), vol. 2, part 4, 81–3, here 81. The poetry in question that incited the three men to such exuberant behavior is Gessner's.

35 Kurt R. Eissler, *Goethe: A Psychoanalytic Study 1775–1786* (Detroit: Wayne State University Press, 1963), 373. See also 370 and 374 as well as further references to homosexuality in other chapters.

36 Paul Derks, *Die Schande der heiligen Päderastie: Homosexualität und Öffentlichkeit in der deutschen Literatur 1750–1850* (Berlin: Verlag rosa Winkel, 1990) 259–62.

7
Can We 'Queer' Early Modern Russia?

Dan Healey

Can we 'queer' early modern Russia?[1] To historians of Russia, the question is a jarring one. It contains two problematic notions for Russianists. To begin with the more familiar one, we must consider what sort of 'early modern' Russia existed, and whether its characteristics can easily be equated with those of Western Europe. This discussion would compare and contrast European historical conditions with the political, social, economic and cultural development of Muscovy (the principality centered on Moscow which came to dominate the eastern Slavs in the fourteenth century). Under many rubrics this discussion would suggest that Russia's situation was different. Muscovy was a sprawling territory on the border zone between the European and the Asian worlds, and in the thirteenth and fourteenth centuries it was subject to Mongol domination. The Muscovite prince (tsar of Russia from the accession of Ivan IV, The Terrible, in 1533) claimed to be an autocrat, and his noble servitors spoke of themselves as 'slaves.' The peasants were subject to a serfdom that increased, not lessened, its grip during the sixteenth and seventeenth centuries and was not abolished until 1861. Orthodoxy made Russia different, too. Using vernacular and looking to Byzantium for inspiration, Russian Orthodoxy denied Roman claims to lead Christianity. Until the seventeenth century Russia skirted the intellectual ferment of the Western Renaissance. Russia's 'early modernity' looked very different from that of European societies on the Atlantic coastline. These are issues that have received much airing in English-language historiography about Russia.[2] Classical historiography in Russian does not employ the label 'early modern' at all.[3] For the purposes of this essay, the temporal limits of early modern Russia are taken to be from about the mid-fifteenth to the early eighteenth centuries, or from the reign of Ivan III that marked the consolidation of Moscow's hegemony over neighbouring principalities, to the rule of Peter I, The Great, whose reforms transformed Muscovy into the European great power of Imperial Russia.

The second troubling notion in our question – that we could use the word 'queer' to describe anything Russian before the very recent past – has been the subject of far less commentary. Discussions have focused on the modern era. A debate is taking shape among scholars of literature and history about the applicability to Russian experience of concepts derived from Western European and US sex/gender systems. The unproblematic importation of 'queer' appears to some as a new form of cultural imperialism. To cite one example, the use of queer as a conceptual framework for thinking about Russians has been citicized for telling us more about an American sociologist writing in the 1990s about her search for the 'queer in Russia,' than about Russian sexualities as such. The apparent absence of a well-defined, Western-style gay identity in contemporary Russia is allegedly romanticized as a feature of our (Western) past and future. Thanks to an historical detour, Russian same-sex oriented people (in this romantic view) enjoy a prelapsarian queerness that avoids the limitations of the modern homosexual identity.[4]

Yet even Brian Baer, the literary scholar who raised this criticism, finds a sensitive and nuanced queer reading of Russia indispensable.[5] As an historian working with the documented past, I have defended the utility of queer theory as a lens enabling a nuanced and culturally sensitive view of dissenting genders and sexualities as they emerged on Russia's turbulent path to modernity. Earlier accounts of Russia's history of same-sex relations referred to 'homosexuality' in an unsophisticated and unproblematic fashion. By avoiding conceptual reductionism, and attuning our ears to the fluidity and variety of gender and sexual dissent apparent in the sources, historians can offer new insights into Russia's gender cultures that unsettle monolithic narratives of heterosexuality.[6] They can also enrich historians' concepts of dissent, social disobedience and resistance in Stalin's Russia – concepts that have remained underdeveloped until recently because of conservative political science models of dissent widely held among Russianists.[7] Exploring Russia is also potentially a means to challenging some of the Anglo-American presumptions behind queer as a conceptual tool.[8]

Many literary scholars of Russia are less interested in tracing the varieties of sexual and gender identity, and are more concerned about a narrowly modern concept of homosexuality and its place in Russia's 'high culture'. They implicitly argue for a Russian sexual 'Sonderweg', a special path in the modernization of same-sex love that emphasizes the Russian educated elite's aesthetic, metaphysical and philosophical bracketing of this theme.[9] The sexual sonderweg is undoubtedly an important way to understand the cultural reception of sexological categories in early twentieth-century Russia, and does resonate in contemporary mentalities for some members of Russia's so-called 'sexual minority'. Yet the political implications of the sonderweg thesis are troubling. Elsewhere I have asked whether a politics focused on the elevation of same-sex love to a 'high culture' plane is the most effective guarantee of the right to sexual expression in contemporary Russia.[10] Discussion about the queering of Russia is only beginning, and the terms of the discussion are still nascent. No satisfactory translation exists in Russian for the English 'queer' and this fact has led authors who are interested in thinking about 'strange' or 'transgressive' love in Russian culture to cast about for alternative labels.[11]

For the sake of this essay, let us hypothesise that 'queer' or something resembling it is a useful category of historical analysis, one that can be applied to Russia of the 'early modern' era. Let us imagine that a young Ph.D. candidate is waiting in the wings with a dynamite topic, ready to begin the queering of early modern Russia. What are the institutional, intellectual and methodological barriers standing in her way?

Perhaps the simplest description of the problem confronting our imaginary graduate student would be to say that, until very recently, there was a chasm between Russian and queer studies. The linguistic, palaeographic and source-criticism skills our budding student needs to approach the queering of early modern Russia would have to be passed on to her by a generation that has had little or no contact with gay, lesbian, or queer theoretical perspectives. The reasons for the virtual absence of these approaches in Russian studies are complex. It is not the case that the scholarly community working on Russian is overtly homophobic but, rather, that institutional frameworks have until recently suppressed serious interest in sexualities. The intellectual conditions in which scholars of Russia worked until the collapse of communism in 1991 included a sex-phobia that was replicated on both sides of the iron curtain. Inside the USSR, authoritarian information controls denied researchers access to relevant materials for biographical and historical studies of sexualities, in accordance with a dogmatic Stalinist prudery. Russian scholars did not dare address the topic, and foreign researchers, hoping to retain access to a Soviet visa, and finding little in card catalogs to encourage such an interest, did not ask the relevant questions. In the Anglo-American world, Cold War considerations encouraged Russianists in political science, sociology and history to focus on conventional politics, and even those working on the distant past needed to stress the relevance of their interest to the imperative of 'knowing the enemy.' In the post-Cold War era the decline of academic study of Russia's distant past has been precipitous. Of the 70 Russian history positions posted in the United States from 1991 to 2002, only four went to scholars working on Russia before 1850. During the same years, when US universities conducted searches for European early modernists not one early modern Russianist was hired.[12]

Such an environment has hardly been encouraging for the development of studies of early modern Russian gender and sexualities. To take one relevant sub-field of social history, historians of Russia were slow to delve into women's history, while their colleagues in French, German, British and American history forged ahead in the 1970s. Much ground was recovered, it must be said, in the 1980s and the field of Russian and post-Soviet women's studies has expanded rapidly. Our Ph.D. candidate would be well advised to seek a sympathetic supervisor, perhaps from among the cohort of historians of Russian women who have emerged as the Cold War has waned.

The young scholar intent on studying queer early modern Russia would encounter an interesting array of problems once she arrived in Moscow or St. Petersburg to conduct her research. There is still a strong legacy of Stalinist homophobia in Russia's historical profession. The Ph.D. candidate might find, to take one practical example, that her Russian academic sponsors (who guarantee visa and archival arrangements on payment of fees) are unenthusiastic about taking her on with an explicitly 'queer' project title. Similarly when she arrives to work in archives that are critical to her topic, openness could be a tactical error, particularly with regard to Soviet-trained directors who grant specialized access and some older staff who run reading rooms. Just as foreign researchers used to do in the 'bad old days', our young candidate might choose to develop an anodyne general title for her project that ensures access without drawing unsympathetic attention to her interests.

All is not completely bleak in this regard, however. Very recently, a small number of academics inside Russia, some of them working in collaboration with Western scholars of gender and sexuality, have begun to publish essays and document collections in Russian on themes in the history of heterosexuality. Russian readers, once shocked to see any mention of sex in print, have during the 1990s become jaded by exploitative journalism on the subject. Perhaps as a result of this weariness with commercial writing about sex, there is a rising demand for more intelligent discussion of Russia's sexual heritage. Our Ph.D. candidate will find a new cohort of scholars, by and large not yet in positions of power in Russia's academy, but who will be eager to hear about her interests and assist her with her research.[13] Another positive feature of the post-Communist research environment is the new accessibility of provincial archives. Enterprising scholars are benefiting from the warm welcome and the enlightened and generous attitudes often extended to foreigners by archivists outside Moscow and St. Petersburg.

What topics could a researcher intending to apply queer perspectives to Russia's early modern past consider working on? What sorts of sources are available for this kind of work? As a Russianist surveying the field with a queer eye, I offer some suggestions about what we currently know and what topics might be worthy of further exploration. My comments are based on themes in popular culture, on space and the regulation of sexuality, and lastly on ritual and emotion as potentially productive areas of research.

Popular culture

In his pioneering articles on Russia's gay history and culture, Simon Karlinsky describes a heritage of exuberant and uninhibited homosexual relations between men, which he finds in sources on medieval Kievan Rus' (tenth to thirteenth centuries) and later Muscovy.[14] Karlinsky goes so far as to characterize the Muscovite period as possibly 'the era of the greatest visibility and tolerance for male homosexuality that the world had seen since the days of ancient Greece and Rome.'[15] The 'open homosexuality of the Russian peasants' was supposedly mirrored at court, where a succession of rulers reportedly indulged in homosexual relations that supplemented or eclipsed their conjugal duties with their wives. No indigenous legislation apparently prohibited the sin of Sodom during the Kievan and Muscovite eras, while churchmen's admonitions expressed outrage but did not seem to reflect popular sentiment. Muscovy, in Karlinsky's enthusiastic reading, was a historical 'gay' paradise, one he associates with the durable gay-friendly reputations (constructed by homosexual emancipationists in the nineteenth century and much recycled since then) of ancient Greece and Rome.

Karlinsky's brief discussions of Muscovite homosexuality must be acknowledged as path-breaking and subversive when contrasted with the traditionally de-homosexualized accounts of the age produced during the Stalin and post-Stalin eras.[16] His accounts, however, are founded on a problematic source base and deserve to be tested against other kinds of evidence. Karlinsky's claims for the prevalence of homosexuality among Russians rely primarily on foreigners' reports of what they saw as visitors to Muscovy. Unlike comparable European societies of this era, Muscovy left a relative paucity of indigenously produced secular sources, and Russianists have traditionally relied on foreigners' accounts to generate a picture of social life.[17] What these foreigners said about widespread mutual male sexuality in Muscovy may well be accurate, but their statements need to be contextualized. Karlinsky himself acknowledges that European visitors came from societies that punished sodomy harshly.[18] Yet the impact of early modern European views of sodomy (which were far from monolithic)[19] on these foreigners' impressions of Muscovy remains unexplored. Also relevant to any development of our thinking about these foreigners' accounts is the wider cultural matrix they fit within. Outsiders' assessments of Moscow were part of a complex and evolving tradition by which an 'Eastern' Europe was constructed as only just within the Christian orbit, yet at the same time as Other to a 'civilized' West.[20] There is scope for the further exploration of the place of sodomy in this symbolic distancing of West and East.[21]

Claims that sodomy was widely practised by rulers and elites in Muscovy depend on sources that tell us more about the symbolic status of male–male sexuality than about actual same-sex love in this society. Karlinsky's thesis of toleration for sodomy in early modern Russia fails to acknowledge that many of the statements concerning homosexual relations between tsars and subjects come from propagandistic texts. These documents were often created by Muscovites involved in clan-based struggles for power during the chaos created by Ivan the Terrible, or later during the dynastic breakdown of the late sixteenth and early seventeenth centuries. For example, the sources on Ivan the Terrible's rumored sodomitical relations with Fedor Basmanov are tracts written by Muscovites and foreigners castigating the tsar's bloodthirsty regime.[22] Charges such as these often mix same-sex relations with other forms of deviance including the practice of witchcraft, associations with minstrels (condemned by Orthodoxy) or desecration of Orthodox religious symbols and holy places by invaders. When Tsar Dmitrii (ruled 1605–06) was deposed by the Shuiskii clan the corpse of this Western-looking tsar was dragged through Moscow's streets by the genitals and heaped on a table with that of a supposed sexual partner,

Petr Basmanov.[23] In Muscovite political symbolism same-sex love between men could be an emphatically negative charge.

The actual value attached to everyday sexual intimacies between men may not, however, have been as negative, as a recently discovered petition of 1616, held in Swedish state archives, suggests. In this document an unnamed petitioner complains (to someone in authority who is also unnamed) that a man called Fedor exploited his youth and 'stupidity' to have sex with him over four years. Fedor then extorted hefty sums of money from him by threatening to tell his father about their relations. The author does not complain about the nature of the sexual relationship but rather about the extortion he has suffered.[24] Whether as symbol of political disgrace, or as a facet of everyday intimacy, sodomy in early modern Russia had complex meanings that cannot be lightly equated to an imagined gay golden age of classical antiquity.

Karlinsky's interpretation also suffers by downplaying the significance of Russian Orthodoxy. The numerous religious texts available for the period deserve more careful attention from historians of sexual diversity. These texts are significant because Muscovites created them themselves, and thus they can tell us something about how early modern Russians thought about sexually transgressive behaviour. Eve Levin's study of early Orthodox ecclesiastical material – penitential manuals and especially guides to clerics for questioning the faithful during confession – situates 'homosexuality' among the sexual practices regarded by clerics as 'unnatural', along with sodomy (anal intercourse regardless of the gender of partners), bestiality and masturbation.[25] Levin notes some of the characteristics of 'male homosexuality' in the Orthodox world that these manuals reveal. Priests asked questions that betray a hierarchy of sexual practices, from masturbation to anal penetration, which valued the preservation of masculine gender roles. The Church regarded acts that did not imitate male–female copulation as relatively harmless. Younger men were treated more leniently when 'sin' between men was under consideration.[26] The penitential guides, if examined systematically by scholars familiar with the social and cultural history of same-sex relations in other jurisdictions, would probably yield further insights about popular eroticism between Muscovite men. A recent Russian-language publication of these guides suggests two themes that could be pursued. Muscovite priests of the fifteenth century thought that men saw in the male youth (*otrok*) a fair substitute for 'women and girls' with whom they might have sex.[27] An examination of age thresholds in male–male erotic bonds could at least be posited from these penitential guidelines, and the results compared with what we know about Renaissance England and Italy. Another intriguing set of prohibitions surrounds cross-dressing and effeminization, and these deserve greater attention from historians of clothing and manners in comparative perspective.

The best-known historian of women for Russian-language readers, Natalia Pushkareva, has written about sources for the early history of Russian heterosexuality, which could perhaps also be productive for the study of transgressive sexual behaviors. She has proposed that literary depictions of sexual relations (dating from the late Muscovite era) and collections of popular sayings and folklore (gathered in the early nineteenth century but reflecting pre-1700 attitudes) are useful sources on the sexual culture of Muscovy.[28] The frequency with which anal imagery occurs in these sources deserves careful scrutiny. Among the other sources Pushkareva has examined – probably less likely to turn up anything for queer researchers – are medical writings (for cures for sexually transmitted diseases) and extremely rare personal letters or notes from this period. (About 750 birch-bark documents survive from early Rus': court rulings and official lists, supplemented by a handful of letters; but Pushkareva notes that only two of these letters deal with intimate relations between spouses.)[29] Another source, again tending to emphasize heterosexuality, consists of advice manuals, the most famous for our period being the *Domostroi*.[30] Yet even those documents which do not directly relate to same-sex relations provide context for the determined researcher. If such materials could be read in conjunction with the other kinds of sources discussed here, the queering of early Russian popular culture could begin.

Space and its regulation

The vast and relatively undifferentiated natural environment of the northeastern European plain encouraged Russians to think creatively and perhaps unusually about space.[31] Many historians who have thought about same-sex relations in Russia have noted the importance in Russia of homosocial institutions and the space they produced and maintained for the creation of 'queer sites.'[32] More investigation of the Muscovite antecedents of modern Russia's homosocial institutions, and inquiry into their spatial character, would undoubtedly yield new insights about Russian constructions of masculinities and about mutual male sexuality.

The regulation of homosociability offers an initial way to approach same-sex relations in these spaces. In Muscovy, two key homosocial institutions were men's monasteries and the military. From the Kievan era, monastic regulation demonstrated an awareness of the possibility of sex between men or between men and boys, as Levin's work in this area attests.[33] Levin argues that it was not the object-choice in sexual encounters between monks that worried monastic leaders, but the fact of sexual contact in an environment so constructed to exclude women and therefore supposedly the temptation to lustful sin. (Paradoxically, the dietary advantages of life in religious communities may have stimulated and not suppressed libidinous appetites.) Penitential manuals for monastic confessors present a menu of acts deemed to endanger the souls of men together: touching one's own genitals, showing them to another man, sleeping in the same bed with a fellow monastic. In the late tsarist decades a regime of mutual scrutiny operated in Orthodox monasteries and seminaries to deter male–male intimacies.[34] It would be profitable to compare what may be gleaned from earlier monastic regulation with what could be discovered about the planning, construction and operation of monasteries and other religious communities, to develop an understanding of the homosocial world of these spaces, and the same-sex relations they harbored.

The masculine world of war was another homosocial arena in Muscovite society. It was not until Peter the Great's Military Articles of 1716 that sodomy was formally prohibited between soldiers in Russia. Peter's re-casting of Muscovy's comparatively irregular and ill-equipped standing armies consolidated Russia's acceptance of the lessons of the European military revolution.[35] Military life before Peter, despite the adoption of standing armies in the mid-seventeenth century, was generally marked by patron–client hierarchies, and supported by the soldier's own economic resources or activities in agriculture and commerce.[36] A potentially productive line of research for historians of gender and sexuality might inquire into the structuring of Muscovite military formations, their recruitment, training, and periods when men were quartered in barracks and billeted among the population at large.[37] Looking just beyond our period, further investigation into the reconstruction of masculinity brought by Peter the Great's transformations of military organization is certainly possible given the array of sources surviving from his activist reign.[38]

Military and political leadership was closely interconnected in Muscovy, and the tsar's court was another social environment with a pronounced homosocial character. Among the many ranks and titles in this environment, both tsar and tsaritsa had 'companions of the bedchamber', individuals of the same sex who slept in the same chamber (and even the same bed) with their sovereign. 'Spalniki' of the seventeenth century 'slept in the tsar's chamber with him every night in turn in groups of four.' The same source primly notes that 'many of them are married people'; it also says that children of the nobility and gentry might be selected for this rank. The tsar relied on these companions to convey messages and carry out secret commissions; they accompanied him on excursions to monasteries and summer residences. 'Postelnitsy' (companions of the bed) and 'masteritsy' (craftswomen, i.e. sewing companions of the tsaritsa) similarly kept the bed of the sovereign's wife warm, and were selected from the upper gentry and nobility. A queer reading of these roles would undoubtedly point to the determination expressed in the sources to ward off any hint of sexual misconduct in the description of such same-sex intimacies – a determination perhaps indicative of the expectation that readers would imagine them.[39]

Another related form of courtly masculine homosociability surrounded the traditions of hunting and falconry. Under Alexis I (reigned 1645–76) the summer palace complex at Kolomenskoe outside Moscow became the headquarters of the tsar's falconers. In 1650 Alexis found it necessary to issue instructions enjoining these men to maintain 'accord and friendship' amongst themselves, 'that there should be no discord of any kind between them', and that junior falconers should be kept under the surveillance of older hunters.[40] What disturbances lay behind these instructions is unclear. More work could be done to examine the court for its same-sex formations and their implications for intimacy and sexuality.

Religious, military and courtly homosociability do not exhaust the range of single-sex spaces in Muscovite life. The appearance of the commercial bathhouse in seventeenth-century Moscow left a trail of regulations about the segregation of the sexes, yet this quintessentially Russian institution has not received sustained professional historical attention.[41] Brothels apparently existed in towns well before their licensing in the nineteenth century, although little is known about them. Mechanisms for the regulation of public spaces in the era are poorly understood and more research on criminality, and on the work of secular and ecclesiastical courts would be welcome (Recent social histories of the seventeenth century have addressed legal issues such as property disputes, but notions of criminality and punishment are under-researched.)[42] Domestic space too had its homosocial elements:

the seclusion of elite women in Moscow's palaces appeared to set up a rigid gender divide in private life, yet the Domostroi frequently mentions moments when men and women were required to mix to ensure the proper functioning of the Muscovite household.[43] Specialists with a queer eye could no doubt expand what is currently known about same-sex relations in Muscovy by examining these themes in well-known sources for evidence of the formation and regulation of homosocial spaces.

Ritual and emotion

The themes dealt with so far have stressed the tracing of mutual male sexuality in history through representations of, and locations for, sexual acts. These approaches, while very helpful in uncovering previously ignored patterns of behavior, do not necessarily reveal much about the emotions that usually accompany sexual encounters. Historians of Muscovy are beginning to explore the range of emotion women and men felt for each other.[44] Mutual male (or mutual female) relations remain to be examined for the character of friendship, of loving affection and sustained devotion. For the historian, the most promising window on these emotions are the religious and popular institutions of ritual brotherhood and sisterhood (in Russian, *pobratimstvo* and *posestrimstvo*).

In the early twentieth century, homosexual intellectuals began to scrutinize brotherhood rituals in eastern and southeastern Europe with a view to recovering pre-modern patterns of homosexual affection.[45] John Boswell noted that during the homophobic wave of the mid-twentieth century, modern social science regarded ritual brotherhood with extreme discomfort, and distorted its discussions of the phenomena by refusing to acknowledge any homosexual content in these relationships. Boswell suggests that the intelligentsia of southeastern Europe adopted similar attitudes hoping, it appears, to be perceived as 'civilized' and modern.[46] It is hardly surprising that Russian scholarship about *pobratimstvo* was marked by similar attitudes, and that Stalinist homophobia intensified intellectuals' predisposition to see ritual brotherhood in Russian history through these filters. The myth that Russia was a sexually chaste nation interposed between a degenerate West and an East permeated by vice was a cultural trope that enabled tsarist and Soviet intellectuals to ignore or ascribe to foreign Others any manifestations of same-sex love they discussed.[47] Russian rituals of *pobratimstvo* and *posestrimstvo* are thus ripe for re-examination by scholars willing to eschew the homophobia that surrounds Western and Russian discourses on the topic.

One prominent Russian scholar of nineteenth-century peasant behaviour has discussed the origins and character of religious and popular *pobratimstvo*.[48] M. Gromyko is silent about the potential for same-sex love in ritual brotherhood, but her work presents readers with an array of early literary, religious and ethnographic sources for the study of this form of friendship. The *bylina*, or traditional heroic poem, celebrated the deeds of warriors who defended ancient Russia from its many enemies. Brotherhood appears in these poems as a frequent marker of mutual affection and care. Some poems refer to sworn brotherhood between experienced fighters and younger warriors, while others present such relations between men of equal standing and age who have supported each other through battles and ordeals. Of the social roots of this oral poetic tradition, Gromyko notes, 'Naturally among these armed bands the need to establish relations of supreme friendship [*sverkhdruzheskie otnosheniia*], strengthening and intensifying the concept of comradely mutual assistance and support, was especially pronounced. Torn from their communities and families, warriors sought ties that would take the place of family. The sworn brother was [as some poems explicitly said] 'more than one's own blood' [*pache rodnogo*].'[49]

Gromyko also discusses Russian Orthodox religious documents, some as early as the eleventh century, which mention *pobratimstvo*. Among these texts are a significant number of sixteenth- and seventeenth-century prayer books presenting various ritual forms for celebrating brotherhood. Some of these Muscovite books also discuss impediments to marriage between men and women whose families are already linked by ritual brotherhood.[50] As part of a reform to make Russian religious observance more closely conform to Byzantine Orthodox practice, Muscovite Patriarch Nikon excluded rituals of brotherhood from the list of recognized offices in 1658. (The influences under which Nikon removed these particular rites certainly deserve investigation.)[51] Despite Nikon's reforms, state decrees of 1667 still took *pobratimstvo* into account. Local practice of the ritual continued in popular usage but also in churches. Gromyko cites one example of a parish register recording acts of brotherhood as late as 1801 in southern Russia.[52] Ethnographers gathered considerable data on the persistence of brotherhood rituals among the peasantry and lower orders of townsmen as late as the 1880s. These observers emphasized the benefits of mutual assistance and emotional intimacy, especially between partners in the same occupation or among those who traveled far from home to seek a living.[53]

How might a queer-sensitive historian interpret *pobratimstvo*? The pan-European and vast temporal sweep of John Boswell's study of 'same-sex unions' obscures national and historical variety, and his argument that these relations masked or contained erotic content appears speculative. Indeed, I have argued for the Russian case that *pobratimstvo* needs to be considered separately from same-sex eros, and on its own terms (if such a thing is possible), without anachronistically reading into it modern models of companionate marriage.[54] Yet Boswell's approach did broadly contextualize ritual brotherhood, and it made reflexive homophobic denial of the rite impossible for scholars and churchmen. The problems in Boswell's final book should not blind us to its subject matter, nor lead us to abandon it as a hostage to US culture wars over gay marriage. For Russianists interested in approaching the topic of ritual brotherhood, the late Alan Bray's work on friendship in early-modern English culture (published posthumously by University of Chicago Press) offers a sophisticated and sensitive model. Bray in fact disagreed with my 1999 argument that historians must begin by separating the sworn brother from the sodomite: '[T]he two I think had always potentially been brothers.' He argued that traditional society faced the troubling question that male sociability might lead to 'the sinful but unavoidable lust of the sodomite' by responding 'with ritual and with humour and by both denial and displacement.' Bray posited that the decline of *pobratimstvo* (and its Western analogues) was linked to the transformation of ideals of friendship from a traditional notion of 'particular affection' to a modern, Kantian 'undifferentiated moral benevolence.'[55] Bray's hypothesis about traditional particular friendships finds some resonance in Russianists' thinking about affective ties. Eve Levin has proposed that friendship in Muscovy before 1700 was an important locus of emotional support in a culture that virtually treated marriage as 'a business transaction' rather than a bond of affection.[56] The courtly practice of adopting, sponsoring and sometimes dropping royal favourites could also be re-examined with the intersection between intimacy and sponsorship that characterized these special relationships.[57] Whether the history of Russian friendship followed Western trajectories remains to be explored. But for our imagined Ph.D. candidate hoping to queer the history of Muscovy the themes of ritual and emotion would furnish more than enough material upon which to base a ground-breaking scholarly study.

Some final thoughts

Naturally, this brief survey of a handful of themes does not exhaust the possibilities for re-writing the history of early modern Russia from queer perspectives. There are in all likelihood sources and themes that have been ignored or that remain unknown that would add to this sampling. For me, one of the greatest pleasures in working on modern Russian approaches to homosexuality was the discovery of previously unidentified materials. A scholar delving into Russian same-sex relations for an earlier era would almost certainly experience the same pleasures of discovery.

What would be the significance of 'queering' early modern Russia? An important effect, modifying Karlinsky's thesis, would be to show how same-sex relations were a complex and profound part of Muscovite culture. This would not of course be the same thing as a celebration of Muscovy as contender for 'gay paradise' status in a queer historical canon. Instead, the elaboration of the sites and rituals of homosociability and mutual male (and mutual female) love in Muscovy would challenge existing assumptions about Russia before Peter the Great. The charge made by many Russians since the early 1900s, that homosexuality is a foreign import, and that Russia was (and is) somehow innocent of such vices or immune to such diseases, would be further undermined.[58] Such new work could also add complexity to the 'sexual sonderweg' thesis, by expanding what is known about pre-modern forms of sexuality between men and how elites before the late nineteenth century regarded it.

Successful scholarship in this area could also stimulate historians of early modern Russia to think less about masculinity as a biological given, unworthy of exploration. The history of manhood is in its infancy in Russian studies.[59] Further investigation of this theme is crucial to the revision of casual assumptions about Russia's men as naturally predisposed either to war-making or conversely (and controversially) to a 'slave mentality.'[60] The construction of masculinities in Muscovy's political, economic and social life is sure to attract the attention of young scholars, and their work will suffer without more sophisticated understandings of mutual male sexuality than those presently available to them. Virtually uncharted territory, early modern Russia awaits its queer historians.

Notes

1 I acknowledge with pleasure the suggestions and advice given by Michael O'Rourke and Lindsey Hughes. Professor Hughes generously drew my attention to several features of Muscovite civilization and to recent scholarship relevant to same-sex sociability and intimacy; rather than acknowledge many instances individually I thank her here for her energetic assistance with this paper. Any mistakes are of course mine alone.

2 James H. Billington, *The Icon and the Axe: An Interpretive History of Russian Culture* (New York: Vintage, 1966); Daniel H. Kaiser and Gary Marker, eds, *Reinterpreting Russian History. Readings 860–1860*s (New York: Oxford University Press, 1994).

3 Russian historians traditionally refer to Kievan Rus' (ca. 800–1240), the 'Mongol Yoke' (1240–1480), Muscovy (1480 to ca. 1700) and Imperial Russia (to 1917).

4 Brian James Baer, 'Russian Gays/Western Gaze: Mapping (Homo)Sexual Desire in Post-Soviet Russia', *GLQ: A Journal of Lesbian and Gay Studies* 8.4 (2002): 499–520, commenting on Laurie Essig, *Queer in Russia: A Story of Sex, Self and the Other* (Durham & London: Duke University Press, 1999).

5 Brian James Baer, 'Vozvrashchenie dendi: gomoseksual'nost' i bor'by kul'tur v post-sovetskoi Rossii, [The Return of the Dandy: Homosexuality and Culture Wars in Post-Soviet Russia]' *O muzhe(n)stvennosti*, ed. Sergei Ushakin (Moscow: Novoe Literaturnoe Obozrenie, 2002) 556–81. See also his comments in 'Russian Gays/Western Gays' and idem, 'The Other Russia: Re-Presenting the Gay Experience', *Kritika: Explorations in Russian and Eurasian History* 1.1 (2000): 183–94.

6 Dan Healey, *Homosexual Desire in Revolutionary Russia: The Regulation of Sexual and Gender Dissent* (Chicago: University of Chicago Press, 2001).

7 Dan Healey, 'Sexual and Gender Dissent: Homosexuality as Resistance in Stalin's Russia', *Contending with Stalinism: Soviet Power and Popular Resistance in the 1930s*, ed. Lynne Viola (Ithaca: Cornell University Press, 2002).

8 For a discussion of the effects of globalization studies on queer studies, see Elizabeth A. Povinelli and George Chauncey, 'Thinking Sexuality Transnationally', *GLQ: A Journal of Lesbian and Gay Studies* 5.4 (1999): 439–50.

9 This current of thought is best captured in Evgenii Bershtein, '"Psychopathia sexualis" v Rossii nachala veka: politika i zhanr', *Eros i pornografiia v russkoi kul'ture/Eros and Pornography in Russian Culture*, eds M. Levitt and A. Toporkov (Moscow: Ladomir, 1999); but see also Ol'ga Kushlina, 'Zelenyi krai za parom golubym...,' *Novoe literaturnoe obozrenie* 35.1 (1999): 400–2, reviewing Konstantin K. Rotikov, *Drugoi Peterburg* (St Petersburg: Liga Plius, 1998).

10 Dan Healey, 'Olga Zhuk, *Russkie amazonki: Istoriia lesbiiskoi subkultury v Rossii XX vek.* [review]', *Kritika: Explorations in Russian and Eurasian History* 3.2 (2002): 362–8.

11 Diana Lewis Burgin, *Marina Tsvetaeva i transgressivnyi eros: Stat'i, issledovaniia* (St. Petersburg: Inapress, 2000); N. M. Solntseva, *Strannyi eros: Intimnye motivy poezii Nikolaia Kliueva* (Moscow: Ellis Lak, 2000). Another recent focus for the queering of Russian culture is in Dostoyevsky studies.

See e.g. Susanne Fusso, 'Dostoyevsky's Comely Boy: Homoerotic Desire and Aesthetic Strategies in *A Raw Youth*', *Russian Review* 59.4 (October 2000) 577–96.

12 'The *Kritika* Index: The Shrinking Past', *Kritika: Explorations in Russian and Eurasian History* 3.4 (Fall 2002): 575–6. Despite these constrictions there has been a wealth of imaginative research on Muscovy; see Robert O. Crummey, 'The Latest from Muscovy', *Russian Review* 60.4 (October 2001): 474–86.

13 These scholars include contributors to A. L. Toporkov, ed., *Seks i erotika v russkoi traditsionnoi kul'ture* (Moscow: Ladomir, 1996), and Levitt and Toporkov, eds, *Eros i pornografiia v russkoi kul'ture*.

14 Simon Karlinsky, 'Russia's Gay Literature and History (11th–20th Centuries)', *Gay Sunshine* 29/30 (1976): 1–7; idem, 'Introduction: Russia's Gay Literature and History', *Out of the Blue: Russia's Hidden Gay Literature*, ed. Kevin Moss (San Francisco: Gay Sunshine Press, 1996).

15 Karlinsky, 'Introduction: Russia's Gay Literature and History', 16.

16 His work was rapidly put before Russian readers as Soviet strictures crumbled: S. Karlinsky, 'Gomoseksualizm v russkoi kul'ture i literature', *Tema* 2.1 (1991): 4–5; idem, '"Vvezen iz-za granitsy…"? Gomoseksualizm v russkoi kul'ture i literature,' *Erotika v russkoi literature. Ot Barkova do nashikh dnei. Literaturnoe obozrenie. Spetsial'nyi vypusk*, eds I. D Prokhorova, S. Iu. Mazur, and G. V. Zykova (Moscow: Literaturnoe obozrenie, 1992).

17 Arthur Voyce, *Moscow and the Roots of Russian Culture* (Norman, Oklahoma: University of Oklahoma Press, 1964); note also N. L. Pushkareva, ed., *'A se grekhi zlye, smertnye…': Liubov', erotika i seksual'naia etika v doindustrial'noi Rossii (X-pervaia polovina XIX v.)* (Moscow: Ladomir, 1999), 138–46.

18 Karlinsky, 'Introduction: Russia's Gay Literature and History', 16.

19 Alan Bray, *Homosexuality in Renaissance England* (London: Gay Men's Press, 1982); Michael Rocke, *Forbidden Friendships: Homosexuality and Male Culture in Renaissance Florence* (New York & Oxford: Oxford University Press, 1996).

20 Larry Wolff, *Inventing Eastern Europe: The Map of Civilization on the Mind of the Enlightenment* (Stanford, Ca.: Stanford University Press, 1994).

21 See e.g. Rudi C. Bleys, *The Geography of Perversion: Male-to-Male Behavior Outside the West and the Ethnographic Imagination, 1750–1918* (New York: NYU Press, 1995). For comments on Muscovy see Dan Healey, 'Moscow', *Queer Sites: Gay Urban Histories since 1600*, ed. David Higgs (London: Routledge, 1999) 38–60, especially 39–40.

22 J. L. I. Fennell, *The Correspondence between Prince A. M. Kurbsky and Tsar Ivan IV of Russia 1564–1579* (Cambridge: Cambridge University Press, 1963), 243 n. 1.

23 Chester Dunning, 'Who Was Tsar Dmitrii?', *Slavic Review* 60.4 (2001): 705–29; see 708, 724.

24 See A. A. Selin, '"Golubaia" chelobitnaia' [A 'gay' petition] <http://www.gay.ru/science/history/chelobit.htm>, accessed 20 May 2002.

25 Eve Levin, *Sex and Society in the World of the Orthodox Slavs, 900–1700* (Ithaca and London: Cornell University Press, 1989), 197–211.

26 *Ibid.*, 201–2.

27 Pushkareva, ed., *'A se grekhi zlye, smertnye…'*, 13–116.

28 Pushkareva, ed., *'A se grekhi zlye, smertnye...'*, 5–9. On seventeenth-century literary sources note also D. S. Likhachev, 'Individualism in Muscovite Literature', *Reinterpreting Russian History: Readings 860–1860s,* eds Daniel H. Kaiser and Gary Marker (New York: Oxford University Press, 1994) 197–205.

29 Simon Franklin, 'Literacy in Kievan Rus'', *Reinterpreting Russian History: Readings 860–1860s,* eds Daniel H. Kaiser and Gary Marker (New York: Oxford University Press, 1994) 73–9; Pushkareva, ed., *'A se grekhi zlye, smertnye...'*, 7.

30 Carolyn Johnston Pouncy, ed. and trans., *The Domostroi: Rules for Russian Households in the Time of Ivan the Terrible* (Ithaca and London: Cornell University Press, 1994); Nancy Shields Kollmann, '"What's Love Got to Do With It?": Changing Models of Masculinity in Muscovite and Petrine Russia', *Russian Masculinities in History and Culture,* eds Barbara Evans Clements, Rebecca Friedman, and Dan Healey (Basingstoke and New York: Palgrave, 2002) 15–32.

31 Jeremy Smith, ed., *Beyond the Limits: The Concept of Space in Russian History and Culture* (Helsinki: Suomen Historiallinen Seura, 1999).

32 Levin, *Sex and Society in the World of the Orthodox Slavs;* Rotikov, *Drugoi Peterburg*; Healey, 'Moscow.'

33 Levin, *Sex and Society in the World of the Orthodox Slavs*, 290–2.

34 Healey, *Homosexual Desire in Revolutionary Russia*, 25–6.

35 Healey, *Homosexual Desire in Revolutionary Russia*, 79–80.

36 Richard Hellie, *Enserfment and Military Change in Muscovy* (Chicago: University of Chicago Press, 1971); idem, 'The Petrine Army: Continuity, Change and Impact,' *Canadian-American Slavic Studies* 8.2 (1974): 237–53.

37 An anonymous letter sent to Tsar Alexis I in 1661 noted that demoralized deserting soldiers were creating chaos in Moscow, gambling, drinking and committing sodomy with small boys; see Philip Longworth, *Alexis, Tsar of All the Russias* (London: Secker and Warburg, 1984) 145. This letter is apparently indigenous and not a foreigner's comment on Moscow's 'barbarism'.

38 Lindsey Hughes, *Russia in the Age of Peter the Great, 1682–1725* (New Haven, Ct. & London: Yale University Press, 1998); Kollmann, '"What's Love Got to Do With It?"'.

39 Grigorii Kotoshikhin, *O Rossii v tsarstvovanie Alekseia Mikhailovicha* (St. Petersburg: Tipografiia Glavnogo upravleniia udelov, 1906) 24–5, 29, 33. This report on Muscovy, composed for Swedish paymasters in 1666–67 by a Moscow government official turned spy, appears to emphasize the sexual probity of the companions of the bedchamber. I am particularly grateful to Lindsey Hughes for drawing my attention to the spal'niki.

40 Longworth, *Alexis, Tsar of All the Russias*, 65.

41 On Russia's baths, see however Nancy Condee, 'The Second Fantasy Mother, or All Baths Are Women's Baths', *Russia – Women – Culture,* eds Helen Goscilo and Beth Holmgren (Bloomington & Indianapolis: Indiana University Press, 1996); and I. A. Bogdanov, *Tri veka peterburgskoi bani* (St Petersburg: Iskusstvo-SPb, 2000).

42 Nancy Shields Kollmann, 'Convergence, Expansion, and Experimentation: Current Trends in Muscovite History-Writing', *Kritika: Explorations in Russian and Eurasian History* 2.2 (2001): 233–40. For an excellent new discussion of Muscovite investigations in cases of rape, see Daniel H. Kaiser,

'"He Said, She Said": Rape and Gender Discourse in Early Modern Russia', *Kritika: Explorations in Russian and Eurasian History* 3.2 (2002): 197–216.

43 The seclusion of Muscovite women was perhaps exaggerated by foreign observers whose views betray an Orientalist and sexualizing imagination. See Isolde Thyret, *Between God and Tsar: Religious Symbolism and the Royal Women of Muscovite Russia* (Dekalb, Il.: Northern Illinois University Press, 2001).

44 Pushkareva, ed., *'A se grekhi zlye, smertnye...'*, 507–16; Kollmann, '"What's Love Got to Do With It?"'.

45 John Boswell, *Same-Sex Unions in Premodern Europ*e (New York: Villard Books, 1994), 269–70.

46 Boswell, *Same-Sex Unions*, 262–79.

47 Healey, *Homosexual Desire in Revolutionary Russia*, 251–7.

48 M. M. Gromyko, *Traditsionnye formy povedeniia i formy obshcheniia russkikh kres'ian XIX v.* (Moscow: Nauka, 1986), 70–92; see also this author's *Mir russkoi derevni* (Moscow: Molodaia gvardiia, 1991).

49 Gromyko, *Traditsionnye formy povedeniia*, 79.

50 Families embroiled in precedence disputes (*mestnichestvo*), offer a possible tangential source of information about *pobratimstvo*; on these sources see Nancy Shields Kollman, *Kinship and Politics: The Making of the Muscovite Political System, 1345–1547* (Stanford: Stanford University Press, 1987).

51 I am indebted to Stephen Morris for his advice to me on Nikon's reforms.

52 Gromyko, *Traditsionnye formy povedeniia*, 81.

53 Gromyko, *Traditsionnye formy povedeniia*, 82, 86–7.

54 Healey, 'Moscow,' 41–2.

55 These quotations are taken from a letter to me by Alan Bray, 24 July 1999. Further on Bray's conception of the relationship between sexuality, friendship, and ritual brotherhood: Alan Bray, 'Homosexuality and the Signs of Male Friendship in Elizabethan England,' *History Workshop* 29 (1990): 1–19; idem, 'A Traditional Rite for Blessing Friendship', *Love, Sex, Intimacy and Friendship Between Men, 1550–1800* Katherine O'Donnell and Michael O'Rourke, eds (Basingstoke: Palgrave, 2003) 87–98; idem, 'Epilogue', *Sodomy in Early Modern Europe,* ed. Tom Betteridge (Manchester: Manchester University Press, 2002) 164–8.

56 Levin, *Sex and Society in the World of the Orthodox Slavs*, 301.

57 *Pobratimstvo*-like relations (slightly later than the scope of this essay) may be discerned in the correspondence between Peter the Great and his favourite Aleksander Menshikov. On Muscovite favouritism, see Robert O. Crummey, *Aristocrats and Servitors: The Boyar Elite in Russia, 1613–1689* (Princeton: Princeton University Press, 1983), 135–63.

58 On the charges, see Karlinsky, '"Vvezen iz-za granitsy..."?'; Healey, *Homosexual Desire in Revolutionary Russia*, 48–9.

59 Eliot Borenstein, *Men without Women: Masculinity and Revolution in Russian Fiction, 1917–1929* (Durham and London: Duke University Press, 2000); I. A. Morozov and S. P. Bushkevich, eds, *Muzhskoi sbornik. Vyp. 1. Muzhchina v traditsionnoi kul'ture* (Moscow: Labirint, 2001); Barbara Evans Clements, Rebecca Friedman, and Dan Healey, eds, *Russian Masculinities in History and Culture* (Basingstoke & New York: Palgrave, 2002); Sergei Ushakin, ed., *O muzhe(n)stvennosti* (Moscow: Novoe literaturnoe obozrenie, 2002).

60 The contention that Russians are somehow given to a slave-like mentality has aroused fresh debate; see Daniel Rancour-Laferriere, *The Slave Soul of Russia: Moral Masochism and the Cult of Suffering* (New York & London: New York University Press, 1995); Marshall Poe, *'A People Born to Slavery': Russia in Early Modern European Ethnography, 1476–1748* (Ithaca: Cornell University Press, 2000).

8

Male Homosexuality in Early Modern Japan: The State of the Scholarship

Gary P. Leupp

Serious historical study of same-sex relationships came of age in the 1980s, heralded by Kenneth J. Dover's magisterial *Greek Homosexuality*, appearing in 1978.[1] Given its careful scholarship and warm critical reception, Dover's work emboldened historians to research homosexualities in classical antiquity, medieval and early modern Europe, and in the west in more recent times.[2] Such works as John Boswell's *Christianity, Social Tolerance and Homosexuality*, Michael Goodich's *The Unmentionable Vice*, and Alan Bray's *Homosexuality in Renaissance England* stimulated dozens of articles and monographs on sexual intimacy between males in the western world.[3] Work on non-western homosexuality lagged behind, although only by about a decade. In 1990 Bret Hinsch published his *Passions of the Cut Sleeve*, an examination of male–male relationships in premodern China. Since then a number of works have addressed the question of homosexuality in India, Islamic societies, Africa, and Japan.

Recent western work on the history of Japanese male–male sexuality Japanese sexuality has for well over a century attracted an unusual degree of western interest and so, not surprisingly, Japan's traditions of male–male sex received particular attention from western scholars even before the recent boom in studies of the history of homosexuality.[4] (The relative abundance of source materials has encouraged this interest; Hinsch notes the 'enormous literature on homosexuality' in Japan as compared with China.)[5] In 1986, a French scholar translated an unpublished work by the Japanese psychologist Watanabe Tsuneo (b. 1946), entitling it *La Voie des éphêbes: Histoires des homosexualités au Japon*.[6] Half of this slim volume consisted of material drawn from the pioneering work on male–male sex in Japan, *Honchô nanshoku kô* (Studies of *Nanshoku* in Our Country) written by the literary critic

Iwata Jun'ichi (d. 1940).[7] While covering the eighth through twentieth centuries, it focused on the late medieval period (fifteenth and sixteenth centuries) and on samurai sexual behavior. (As of about 1600 the samurai, or hereditary martial class, is thought to have constituted around seven per cent of the population. This remained the case up to the early 1870s.) An English translation of *La Voie* appeared in 1989 (entitled *The Love of the Samurai*), producing widespread interest.[8] But while Watanabe has published a number of works on issues of gender, sexual psychology, and men's studies (*danseigaku*), he has not published this work on pre-modern homosexuality in Japanese.[9]

In the same year that the English version of Watanabe's book appeared, Paul Schalow, an American scholar of Japanese literature, published a significant article on *Nanshoku ôkagami* (The Great Mirror of *Nanshoku*). This is a collection of homoerotic stories by the Osaka writer Ihara Saikaku, published in 1687. He followed up the next year with an annotated English translation of the work, based on his doctoral dissertation.[10] Schalow's translations of shorter works, with commentary, quickly established him as the leading western authority on 'male love' in Japan during the early modern period.[11]

Sociologist Stephen O. Murray, whose works on male–male sexuality span continents and millennia, contributed a chapter on 'Male Homosexuality in Japan Before the Meiji Restoration,' in a compilation on 'Oceanic Homosexualities' published in 1992.[12] Drawing heavily on my unfinished *Male Colors* manuscript, it provided an overview of the topic, emphasizing male prostitution as a corollary to the kabuki theater, samurai age-structured homosexuality, and the 'effeminization' of the youthful partner during the Tokugawa period.[13] (Murray associated the kabuki-centered homosexual tradition with the 'a rising, mercantile bourgeoisie).'[14] Eiko Ikegami's *The Taming of the Samurai* addressed the problem of violence rooted in homosexual love-triangles, unwanted approaches and rejections among samurai men and boys in seventeenth-century Japan.[15] Art historian Timon Screech discussed male prostitution in Tokugawa Japan in connection with his study of eighteenth-century erotica published in 1999.[16] The only other western scholar at the time significantly contributing to the study of the history of Japanese homosexuality, literature specialist Margaret Childs, confined her work to the fourteenth and fifteenth centuries.[17]

My own published contributions date from 1995.[18] In *Male Colors: The Construction of Homosexuality in Tokugawa Japan*, I attempted an overview of male–male intimate relationships during the Tokugawa shogunate (1603–1868), emphasizing the commodification of sexuality within the emerging capitalistic economy, and the development of a bourgeois homosexual tradition at variance with pre-existing monastic and samurai *nanshoku* traditions.[19] This was the first English-language work to broadly examine male homosexuality in the Tokugawa period, drawing on primary and secondary historical sources and attempting to position *nanshoku* within a comparative historical framework. In subsequent papers I amplified an argument I had made in *Male Colors*, namely that there was a conspicuous *decline* in the *nanshoku* tradition after around 1750; and also broached the topic of female–female sexuality in Tokugawa Japan.[20]

Gregory M. Pflugfelder, an historian at Columbia University, brought further sophistication to the field with his *Cartographies of Desire: Male–Male Sexuality in Japanese Discourse, 1600–1950*.[21] About half of this richly documented study deals with the Tokugawa period, wherein he too, finds a substantial 'commodification' of homosexual behavior. In addition, during the 1990s, western scholars interested in the topic of sexuality in Buddhist societies gave some attention to premodern Japanese homosexuality.[22] Thus at the opening of the new millennium, there was a critical mass of English-language scholarship on early modern Japanese male homosexuality, allowing those with a general interest in the history of sexuality to grasp the basic features of *nanshoku* and consider them in global historical perspective.

Meanwhile, Japanese scholars aside from Watanabe have begun to address the topic, inspired in part by the prolific western-language bibliography on the global history of homosexuality.[23] (Ujiie, for example, has been influenced by Alan Bray's *Homosexuality in Renaissance England*.)[24] The emergence of a gay rights movement in Japan also encouraged research on male–male relationships, although the relationship between the movement and academe is not nearly as close in Japan as it is in, for example, the US. A group to promote *Kuia Sutadiizu* (Queer Studies) was active in Tokyo by 1996.[25]

Recent Japanese work on the history of Japanese male–male sexuality

Ujiie Mikito, an archivist at the National Institute for Public Documents in Tokyo, has produced the most significant body of work on *nanshoku*. His *Bushidô to eros* (Bushidô and Eros) focuses upon male–male sexual relations within the samurai class in the castle-town of Edo (modern Tokyo) during the Tokugawa period, when the city (population over one million by 1700) served as the shogun's capital. *Edo no shônen* (Edo Youth) addresses in part the man–boy sexual relationships of the epoch.[26] In both, Ujiie highlights the problem of passion-driven violence.

Hanasaki Kazuo, a literary scholar and historian, author of numerous works including an *Illustrated Dictionary of the Great City of Edo*,[27] published an annotated collection of Tokugawa era works describing the *kagema chaya* (brothels featuring *kagema*, cross-dressing boys associated with the kabuki theater) in 1992.[28] Much of the content of the works Hanasaki makes available deals with the phenomenon of anal intercourse, and the numerous wood-block prints accompanying his texts generally show men and *kagema* involved in this activity. But Hanasaki provides no real analysis of the structure of homosexual relations, or the impact of kabuki-centered male prostitution in shaping bourgeois sexual behavior in the Tokugawa period.

Amateur historian Shibayama Hajime (b. 1926) published his three-volume work *Edo danshoku kô* in 1992–93.[29] This is a collection of essays about *nanshoku* in Edo during the Tokugawa period. It is addressed to a popular audience, with chapters treating samurai vendettas rooted in homosexual love-triangles, and the appeal of the kabuki *onnagata* (female role performer). Reminiscent of Iwata's *Honchô nanshoku kô*, it contains many passages from literature, speculations about past sexualities, and comparative observations pertaining to present-day behavior. Since the material in Iwata's book extends only into the Sengoku and Azuchi-Momoyama periods (1467–1598), this trilogy can be read as a continuation, of sorts, of Iwata's project.

Hiratsuka Yoshinobu's *Nihon in okeru nanshoku no kenkyû* (Studies of *Nanshoku* in Japan) appeared in 1987.[30] Lacking footnotes or a central thesis, it is another popular work explicating the content of Tokugawa-era homoerotic literary works, but also documenting the survival of *nanshoku* into the early twentieth century. Finally, Saeki Junko's Bishônen *kuzushi* (loosely, Thrown into Turmoil by Beautiful Youths) paraphrases passages from sixteenth and seventeenth-century literary works, such as *Denbu Monogatari* (ca. 1640), *Iro Monogatari* (ca. 1670), *Nanshoku ôkagami* (1687), *Hagakure* (1716), etc., pertaining to men's desire for boys.[31] The author herself states that hers is 'not an academic work.'[32] But *Bishônen kuzushi*, like the work of Shibayama and Hiratsuka, follows in the tradition of Iwata's *Honchô nanshoku kô* in popularizing awareness of the prevalence of *nanshoku* in premodern Japan, especially in on the early Tokugawa period.[33]

Throughout this literature produced by Japanese writers, the phenomenon of *nanshoku* is treated as *exotic* and remote from both the writer and reader's experience. Hanasaki, for example, feels obliged to conclude the introduction to his book as follows:

> I can't believe that anal coitus, which seems to be popular in Europe and America (having no personal experience, I only know this from films and publications), is the same as the homosexual behavior (*nanshoku fûzoku*) that came to flourish in Japan. But both males and females have backdoors, and if you consider the nature of copulation, wouldn't the experience have the same quality [for male–male partners as heterosexual couples]?[34]

Ujiie entitles his chapter on male–male sexual relationships in *Edo no shônen*, 'Another Country' (*Anazaa Kuntorii*), using the foreign expression to emphasize the distance between contemporary Japan and the world of *nanshoku.*[35] I have seen no serious academic work by self-identified gay or bisexual men linking historical scholarship on *nanshoku* to contemporary gay experience – no effort to root contemporary Japanese *dôseiai* ('same-sex love,' the usual rendering of the English 'homosexuality') in early modern practices.

Socio-cultural context of the historical study of same-sex relations

Conditions for the study of sexuality in Japan strike many westerners as favorable. The Japanese tend to have a matter-of-fact attitude towards sexuality in general, and serious scholars in Japan may devote their careers to (say) the study of prostitution in the Tokugawa era.[36] Censorship laws have been relaxed in the last decade or so, allowing for the publication of Tokugawa wood-block print erotica, among other things. Strong public interest in the history of sexuality insures book sales beyond the academy. But few university-trained historians have so far addressed the question of *nanshoku.*

This is not because Japan is a particularly homophobic country. Male homosexual situations occur in such genres of Japanese popular culture as television dramas and comic book series, sometimes in surprising contexts.[37] Comic books catering to adolescent girls, such as Takemiya Keiko's *Kaze to ki no uta* (Song of the Wind and Trees, in 17 volumes, published between 1977 and 1984), often center on intergenerational male–male sexual relationships, for reasons sociologists and psychologists endlessly debate.[38] Cross-dressing has been a cardinal feature of Japanese drama history, and cross-dressing entertainers appear routinely on Japanese prime time television with minimal attention given to their sexual identity. But university historians seem to find the topic of same-sex relationships of arcane or marginal interest, to be discussed in general volumes of *fûzokushi* (history of manners) or *sei seikatsushi* (history of sex life).

There is certainly some homophobia in academia; I once (in the mid-1980s) heard a distinguished Japanese historian remark that gay American men *deserved* to get AIDS. Another, when discussing the composition of a future seminar on gender and sexuality in history, responded to the suggestion that a certain western scholar doing work on homosexuality might be invited, simply mused, 'Hmm, foreigners seem very interested in that.' But it was clear that in her view, 'that' was not a very appropriate for Japanese scholars to address.[39]

Issues

Thus, the only recent truly academic work on the history of *nanshoku* in Japan has been done by Watanabe, a psychologist; Ikegami, an anthropologist (both publishing in western languages); and Ujiie, an archivist. Few of the other writers deal with major theoretical questions. But the journal reviews of my work, and publications by Schalow, Pflufelder and others, have raised a number of issues among western scholars interested in sexuality in early modern Japan.

Chronology and causality

Iwata found three distinctly articulated traditions of male–male sexuality in Japanese history: the first, associated with Buddhist monasteries, dating from the ninth century; the second, rooted in samurai society, from around the twelfth; and a third, emerging in urban commoner society, from the seventeenth century. Shibayama has a different periodization scheme: a 'Period of *Nanshoku* Based on Chigo Love,' from the ancient period to the Kamakura period (1185–1333), during which priests had relationships with *chigo* (preteen or teenage boys placed in temples as acolytes), and samurai with some of their attractive young retainers; a 'Period of *Nanshoku* Based on Love of Youths (*Shônen*),' in which theatrical troupes helped create a new ideal of beautiful youth as an object of admiration and sexual desire; and a 'Period of Heterosexual-Type (*joshikiteki*) *Nanshoku*,' beginning during the mid-eighteenth century, during which thoroughly feminine-acting boys, treated in many ways as courtesans, were the major objects of adult male homosexual desire; and finally, 'Modern *Nanshoku*,' from the last decades of the Tokugawa period into the present, in which the samurai *nanshoku* tradition has disappeared. By the late nineteenth century, Shibayama suggests, common urbanites' (*chônin*) influences and the widespread availability of commercial male–male sex (especially the services of the *kagema*) destroyed that tradition.[40]

Shibayama's periodization scheme plainly highlights shifts in the nature and appearance of the partner to be penetrated; it is, one might say, a 'top's' view of history.[41] But it gives little attention to class, and in particular to the spectacular increase in samurai numbers from 1200 to 1600, especially from the early sixteenth century when tens of thousands of men and boys were routinely encamped on battlefields, removed from lay society and its female component; and it does not adequately address the issue of power structures.

Pflugfelder has explicitly rejected a three-stage theory of Japanese homosexuality as a remnant of Tokugawa discursive constructions echoed by modern scholars, including Iwata, who 'have replicated these narrative tropes without recognizing them as historical artifacts that deserve critical scrutiny in their own right.'[42] He does not elaborate on this assessment, however, and such rejection probably reflects the postmodernists' disinclination to embrace 'metanarratives' in general. Yet there can be no denying the general sequence. The documentary record for male–male sexual behavior, which becomes quite rich from the tenth century, deals principally with priests and *chigo* and allows us to posit a 'first stage' of *nanshoku* from that century to ca. 1300. After that the record is augmented with many references to homosexual relationships among the samurai, particularly during the sixteenth and seventeenth centuries.

From the mid-seventeenth century, many sources depict urban commoner males involved in homosexual relationships with one another, with kabuki actors and prostitutes very often serving as the 'insertee' partners. The traditions overlap chronologically, but impact one another; for example, the *kyôdai musubi* or 'brotherhood bond,' committing a boy acolyte to an adult priest, becomes the model of the relationships between daimyo (barons) and their pageboy bed partners by the sixteenth century. Samurai sexual lives become transformed by obligatory urban residence and exposure to bourgeois culture from the early seventeenth century, and commercial sex gradually erodes the former conventions of long-term relationships, written 'brotherhood' contracts, and careful monitoring of the youthful partner. The sequence of articulated traditions suggests a causal linkage between conditions requiring the long-term separation of communities of men and boys from female company, and the occurrence – in the absence of powerful ideological constraints – of widespread sexual activity between males in those contexts.

Nature vs nurture

This thesis has proven to be controversial. Paul Schalow, in a review of *Male Colors*, alleged that, 'for Leupp, homosexual relations require explanation, for he assumes that they arise only from extraordinary circumstances, such as the absence of females.'[43] Margaret Childs accused me of holding the 'extreme social constructionist position that homosexual behavior is always the result of social conditions,' and the view that 'heterosexuality is essential and that homosexual behavior only emerges when that essential identity is somehow thwarted.'[44] Chris Berry also faulted me with the 'homophobic' assumption that one 'needs to account for an origin of homosexuality in Japan (but not of heterosexuality).'[45]

In fact, I explicitly indicate in *Male Colors* my belief that homosexual behavior and desire occur in all societies and eras, but that their incidence is not uniform among historical societies, and socio-economic and cultural factors may produce periods of flourishing, as well as periods of decline, of specifically constructed homosexual traditions.[46] Both Ujiie and Pflugfelder support this position when they describe the weakening of *shudô* or *nanshoku* after about 1750.[47] At a conference on 'Sexuality and Edo Culture, 1750–1850' held in August 1995 at Indiana University, Ujiie presented a paper in Japanese, later translated as 'From Young Lions to Rats in a Ditch: The Decline of Shudô in the Edo Period.'[48] This decline, Ujiie said, was indicated by a reduction in the numbers of pageboys retained for sexual purposes by the daimyo and the drop in male prostitutes' numbers, and was explained by late Tokugawa writers including Kyokutei Bakin (1767–1848) by such factors as the earlier marriages of samurai males, the waning of martial culture and the educational aspects of *shudô*, and the performance of the *genpuku* ceremony earlier in a boy's adolescence.[49]

At the same conference where Ujiie presented his paper, I suggested that the changing sex-ratios in Tokugawa cities contributed significantly to *nanshoku* decline.[50] Circa 1700 there were twice as many men in Edo (modern Tokyo) as women, although the ratio gradually equalized, and by 1868 fully half the commoner residents of Edo were female. This, I opined, probably influenced the construction of sexual desire and behavior. Pflugfelder later rejected 'the demographic determinism implicit in Leupp's analysis.'[51] In fact I had not attempted to provide any precise 'analysis' but merely raised for discussion the relationship between the dramatically changing sex-ratio and the diminishing volume of historical evidence for *nanshoku.* That this suggestion alone should have provoked some a heated response at the conference indicates the depth of emotion surrounding the nature/nurture question.

Reality vs. representation

Scholars treating this topic also differ on the relationship between *representations* of male–male sex and actual, historical sexual practice. In general, those in the field of literature and influenced by postmodernist deconstructionism tend to reject the attempt to reconstruct 'what really happened.' Rather, on the assumption that historical reality is ultimately unknowable, they limit themselves to textual analysis. Pflugfelder, for example, states that he is more concerned with *discourses* about behavior than 'the sorts of sexual acts that people engaged in.'[52]

In *Male Colors* I tentatively presented what became a controversial thesis, that male–male fellation rarely occurred in Tokugawa Japan; that it was regarded as somehow 'taboo;' that this taboo was rooted in neo-Confucian conceptions of deference based upon age and status; and that male–male sexual activity was almost always took the form of role-structured anal sex. I based this thesis on the lack of reference to male–male oral sex, not only in popular erotic fiction, but in medical texts and sex manuals, and in erotic art (which given its *raison d'être* – to titillate – probably depicts the full range of actions its consumers found familiar or appealing).[53] Some reviewers questioned how one could really *know* what went on behind closed doors, implying this practice must have occurred, but none produced substantial evidence for it in *nanshoku* relationships.[54] In this instance, the researcher on early modern Japanese sexuality can avoid addressing the issue of 'what happened between men' entirely (as something unknowable, or even irrelevant); assume that *nanshoku* necessarily entailed the range of physical activities associated with contemporary (western or Japanese) gay/queer lifestyles; or make judicious use of the sources representing *nanshoku* to sketch out tentatively the nature of male–male sexual relationships in an environment appreciably different from any known to the writer or his readers.

The historian, as opposed to the literary specialist, is perhaps more inclined to undertake the third option, but a strong trend has emerged within the field of history to confine inquiry to the 'history of representation.'[55] This is a cautious route, since the scholar can disavow any necessary connection between the representations he or she supplies and 'what really happened.' But even the presentation of texts is inevitably selective, and the reader, unless informed about the historical context of the text (which might mean grasping key facts about the archeological record, linguistics, class structure, demography, history of trade, etc.) will be unable to conceptualize the phenomenon under discussion. An understanding of *nanshoku* requires, in my view, an understanding of the Tokugawa four-class system; the neo-Confucian ideology widely promoted by the shoguns; the demographics of the cities; the organization of samurai households; the monk-acolyte relationships common in Buddhist monasteries; Shinto beliefs about pleasure, purity and impurity; the traditional practice of poor families selling children, etc. It was a very different 'male homosexuality' than we find anywhere today, including some features (sexual exploitation of preteen boys) that contemporary opinion would likely condemn, while excluding some behaviors (oral sex) regarded as 'normal' and pleasurable practices in much of the contemporary gay world.

Nanshoku and violence

Much of the work of Japanese writers has focused upon acts of violence associated with homosexual passion, especially from the seventeenth through mid-eighteen centuries. The first century of Tokugawa rule placed many in the samurai class under great stress, as they were obliged to shed their traditional position as warriors on call, and instead adapt to conditions of peace and reside in castle-towns. In many cases, samurai incomes were inadequate to support a comfortable urban lifestyle. Disillusioned by their loss of social position, and jealous of the wealth of the bourgeoisie, some formed criminal gangs.[56] For centuries the samurai had cultivated a sense of honor, and of class pride, and in the new circumstances of national peace, forced residence in castle-towns, and the emergence of a substantial middle class of merchants and artisans (who, while denigrated in the official neo-Confucian class system, were often far more comfortable than most samurai), many warriors vented their frustrations through violent acts justified as necessary for the defense of their honor. They became inclined to respond to any perceived slight or offense with brutal retaliation. Samurai could by law in any case cut down commoners with near impunity (for 'insolence'). In the context of a generalized culture of violence, wherein preservation of 'face' was of foremost concern, it is not surprising to find many accounts of triangular homosexual relationships producing fatal consequences, or of men's unwanted advances producing violently indignant responses, or of youths' refusals prompting bloodshed.[57]

The historian should not, of course, replicate the view expressed by some Confucian scholars of the Tokugawa era – that is, that male–male sexual passion constituted a threat to social order because of samurai males' penchant for expressing their sexual/romantic jealousies and injured feelings through their swordsmanship. But one cannot ignore the fact that in any early modern discussion of the characteristics of *nanshoku*, the latter was associated with well-known violent incidents.[58] Paul Schalow has suggested that in drawing attention to the popular (seventeenth-century) association between bloody incidents and 'homosexuality' in *Male Colors*, I 'methodologically' performed 'the equivalent of concluding from a survey of Grand Opera that heterosexuality per se is somehow intrinsically associated with murder and suicide ...'[59] In fact, having established the general atmosphere of tolerance for male–male sexuality in Tokugawa Japan, I merely posited the linkage to violence as one of several negative associations of *nanshoku* found in the literature. (Shibayama, Ujiie, and Ikegami have all emphasized this linkage more than I have.)

The wakashû's experience

One cannot attempt to understand the specific construction of male–male sexuality in Japan during the period we examine without considering the experience of the *wakashû*, the younger/receptive partner, which (as in the case of the Greek *eromenos*) is less well documented than the experience of the older, 'active' partner. There is, to be sure, ample evidence for cruel and exploitative relationships. Children of both sexes were often forced into prostitution, and literary sources attest to the suffering of the boy-prostitute.[60] (An early seventeenth-century manual of man–boy sex refers to two 'methods' of anal intercourse – 'dry insertion' and 'tearing the hole' – that cause 'severe pain' but are very pleasurable for the adult partner.)[61] But the atmosphere of 'political correctness' in the US may incline the scholar to depict the *wakashû* experience as *routinely* one of 'abuse' whether or not the sources demonstrate this.[62] Pflugfelder, for example, opines that men's interest in *wakashû* was 'unwanted' by the latter and regarded as an unpleasant fact of life.[63] But his own research, as well as my own and that of others, based on literary, biographical, legal, medical, and iconographic sources, plainly suggests that some youths *pined* for older lovers; provided sex without expectation of remuneration; and physically enjoyed anal penetration.[64]

The psycho-sociological dynamics of these relationships were certainly determined in part by neo-Confucian ideological constructs, feudal institutions, and notions of service that related to individual self-esteem in ways that may be unique to early modern Japan. A youth's submission to penetration (which in many other societies where homosexual cultures have flourished, including ancient Greece, invited ridicule or opprobrium) could be matter of *pride* in Japan (especially if the 'elder brother' was a man of status).[65]

Bisexuality

In *Male Colors* I suggested that the *nanshoku* tradition of Tokugawa Japan was essentially part of a *bisexual* eros; that men – at least the urban men upon whom my research focused – were generally attracted to women as well as boys; and that exclusive homosexuality, while known and discussed, was far less common than bisexual behavior.[66] The fictional Yonosuke, in Ihara Saikaku's novel *Kôshoku ichidai otoko* (Life of an Amorous Man, 1682), has sex with 3,742 women and 725 young males by the age of 54. He represents the consummate urban playboy – a type encountered throughout Tokugawa literature.[67] Nonliterary sources, such as English merchants' records in the early seventeenth century, make mention of Japanese men known to enjoy heterosexual activity as well as 'buggering boys.'[68]

Pflugfelder opposes use of the term 'bisexuality,' as a category 'which would not have been understood' in Tokugawa Japan 'in the same sense that [it is] currently understood,' arguing that premodern Japanese behavior 'often followed patterns quite different from those we associate with' contemporary bisexuality.[69] But it seems to me that 'we' even today *do not have* a clear conceptualization of bisexuality, or the 'patterns' it entails, and that, in the absence of a lucidly articulated contemporary bisexual identity and lifestyle, it is reasonable to allude to a figure like Yonosuke as bisexual *by definition*.[70] Murray also pronounces himself unconvinced that male bisexuality was 'generalized' in the cities, but complicates the issue by eliminating from consideration 'those renting bodies' – men, that is, who were not 'following [the ideal of] *wakashudô*' but merely satisfying lust in a brothel setting. He almost places the burden of proof upon the researcher to show that the majority of males involved significantly with other males in sexual intimacy were *not* exclusively gay.[71]

There were certainly men in early modern Japan who had exclusively homosexual lifestyles, including some of those referred to as *nanshoku-zuki* ('those who like *nanshoku*' – *nanshoku* aficionados, who were *particularly* fond of sex with boys), and all those referred to as *onna-girai* (women-haters). But these were in the minority, as they were in the Greco-Roman world. Comparative study of other historical societies to which scholars have imputed bisexual cultures may help to sharpen debate on the issue of bisexuality in Japan.[72]

Conclusion: the need for comparative studies

Sir George B. Sansom, one of the most important western scholars of Japanese history in the mid-twentieth century, observed in 1950 that western students 'cannot hope to approach the standard of scholarship of Japanese specialists in historical research,' but that they might make significant contributions in several areas, including translating Japanese works and popularizing Japanese studies in their own countries. Most importantly, western Japan scholars might 'make some useful contribution to the work of their Japanese colleagues' in 'comparative studies.'[73] Half a century later, we find foreign scholars pioneering in original research which does in fact meet the Japanese 'standard of scholarship;' there is no parallel in Japanese scholarship, for example, of Pflugfelder's analyses of medical and legal discourses on male–male sexuality between 1600 and 1950. This may be explained in part by an academic environment in the US more supportive of such work than one yet finds in Japan. Nevertheless, developments in the study of male intimacy in Japan in the west are bound to encourage more serious scholarship on the topic in the Japanese academy.[74]

A foreign historian's work on male–male relations in Japan is necessarily comparative. In eighteenth-century Japan, there were no molly houses, no venues for 'egalitarian' male–male sex; rather, there were tea houses (*nanshoku-jaya*) where men paid to bugger boys. In Japan, there were no laws or religious campaigns against specific sex acts; age-graded role-structured male sex was indeed associated with the samurai ruling class and the Buddhist clergy. But given some fundamental similarities between early modern Japan and early modern Europe, as well as conspicuous differences, studies of *nanshoku* provide a useful foil for the understanding of western (and other) homosexualities.[75] In both

Europe and Japan, between 1550 and 1800, sexual relationships in general came to reflect the values, and adapt to the requirements, of incipient capitalism, but in wholly different social, cultural, religious and political contexts.[76]

How, exactly, does the *nanshoku-jaya* of eighteenth-century Japan compare to the molly house in England? The *onna-girai* to the 'woman-hater' in England? The kabuki actor–prostitute to the boy-prostitutes who helped support English theater? Or Tokugawa shoguns' well-known homosexual relationships to those of some of the Stuart (or Bourbon) kings, and the public response to them? In investigating such questions, and many others involving comparisons with other societies, students of Japanese *nanshoku* can provide new insights into the *global* history of male–male intimacy before 1800.

Notes

1 Throughout this article, following Japanese practice, I place Japanese surnames before given names. I make exceptions for Japanese residing in the west who use the western order (such as Eiko Ikegami). Japanese historians typically periodize their history as follows: ancient period (to 1185); medieval (1185–1572); early modern (1572–1868); modern (1868–1945); contemporary (1945–present).

2 Kenneth J. Dover, *Greek Homosexuality* (Cambridge, Massachusetts: Harvard University Press, 1978).

3 Michael Goodich, *The Unmentionable Vice: Homosexuality in the Later Medieval Period* (Santa Barbara, Ca.: ABC-Clio, 1979); John Boswell, *Christianity, Social Tolerance, and Homosexuality: Gay People in Western Europe from the Beginning of the Christian Era to the Fourteenth Century* (Chicago and London: University of Chicago Press, 1980); Alan Bray, *Homosexuality in Renaissance England* (London: Gay Men's Press, 1982).

4 Interest in Japanese sexuality in general is reflected in the enormous popularity throughout Europe and North America of Pierre Loti's novel *Madame Chrysanthème* (1888), Clive Holland's novel *My Japanese Wife* (1895), the stage play 'Madame Butterfly' by John Luther Long and producer David Belasco (1900), Giacomo Puccini's *Madame Butterfly* (1904), etc. The first scholarly work on Japanese male homosexuality in a Western language was the short article by Jwaya [Iwaya] Suweyo, 'Nan sho k' (die Päderastie en Japon),' in the *Jahrbuch für sexuelle Zwischenstufen*, 4 (1902), 263–71. This essay dealt with what the author viewed as a rapidly disappearing phenomenon. Ferdinand Karsch-Haak (1906), Friedrich Krauss (1911), Edward Carpenter (1914), and other pioneer sexologists drew upon this work in describing the samurai tradition of male homosexuality. Later, stories by Ihara Saikaku pertaining to male–male relationships were translated into English by E. Powys Mathers; see *Comrade Loves of the Samurai* (London: John Rodker, 1928). Historian Donald Shively discussed the homoerotic atmosphere of the kabuki theater in 'Bakufu versus Kabuki,' in John W. Hall

and Marius B. Jansen (eds), *Studies in the Institutional History of Early Modern Japan* (Princeton: Princeton University Press, 1968), and in 'The Social Environment of Tokugawa Kabuki,' in James R. Reardon, William Malm, and Donald Shively (eds), *Studies in Kabuki* (Honolulu: University of Hawaii Press, 1978). Shively also discussed the bisexual fifth Tokugawa shogun; see Shively, 'Tokugawa Tsunayoshi, the Genroku Shogun,' in Albert Craig and Donald Shively (eds), *Personality in Japanese History* (Berkeley: University of California Press, 1970), 97–9.

5 Bret Hinsch, *Passions of the Cut Sleeve: The Male Homosexual Tradition in China* (Berkeley: University of California Press, 1990), 6.

6 Tsuneo Watanabe, and Jun'ichi Iwata. *La Voie des éphêbes: Histoires des homosexualités au Japon.* Trans. Michel Bon (Paris: Editions Trismegiste,1986).

7 Jun'ichi Iwata, *Honchô nanshoku no kô.* Ise: Kogawa shoten, 1974. *Nanshoku,* rendered by some as 'male love' or 'manly love,' refers to the age-graded, role-structured types of male homosexuality in early modern Japan. It is more or less synonymous with *wakashûdô* ('the way of youths'), often abbreviated to *shudô.*

Iwata (1900–45) and Minakata Kumagusu (1867–1941) were the pioneers of *nanshoku* study in the twentieth century; their correspondence from 1931 to 1941 is of much interest. See Kumagusu and Iwata, 'Morning Fog (Correspondence on Gay Lifestyles)', trans. William F. Sibley, in Miller, Stephen D. (ed.), *Partings at Dawn: An Anthology of Japanese Gay Literature* (San Francisco: Gay Sunshine Press, 1996), 135–71. Iwata's historical bibliography of materials pertaining to *nanshoku, Nanshoku bunken shoshi* (Kogawa shoten, 1973), remains an indispensable research tool.

8 Tsuneo Watanabe and Jun'ichi Iwata, *The Love of the Samurai: a Thousand Years of Japanese Homosexuality,* trans. by D.R. Roberts (London: Gay Men's Press, 1989).

9 Watanabe's *Toransu giendaa no bunka (Transgender Culture)* was published in 1989.

10 Paul Schalow, *'The Great Mirror of Male Love,' by Ihara Saikaku* (Harvard University Ph.D. dissertation, 1985), 2 vols; Schalow, 'Male Love in Early Modern Japan: a Literary Depiction of the Youth', in Martin Duberman, Martha Vicinus, and George Jr. Chauncy, (eds), *Hidden from History: Reclaiming the Gay & Lesbian Past* (New York: NAL, 1989); Schalow, 'Japan', in W. Dynes, (ed.), *Encyclopedia of Homosexuality* (New York: Garland, 1989); Schalow, trans., *The Great Mirror of Male Love,* by Ihara Saikaku (Stanford: Stanford University Press, 1990). See also Ihara Saikaku, *Tales of Samurai Honor* trans. Caryl Ann Callahan (Tokyo: *Monumenta Nipponica,* 1981).

11 Paul Schalow, 'Kûkai and the Tradition of Male Love in Japanese Buddhism', *Buddhism, Sexuality and Gender* ed. José Ignazio Cabezón (New York: State University of New York Press, 1992); 'The Invention of a Literary Tradition of Male Love: Kitamura Kigen's *Iwatsusuji*', *Monumenta Nipponica,* 48, 1 (Spring 1993); 'Spiritual Dimensions of Male Beauty in Japanese Buddhism', *Queer Dharma: Voices of Gay Buddhists* ed. Winston Weyland (San Francisco: Gay Sunshine Press, 1998).

12 Stephen O. Murray, *Oceanic Homosexualities* (New York: Garland Publishers, 1992), esp. 121–50.

13 Murray duly credited me (111, footnote 1), and indicated that he had made use of a draft of *Male Colors* I had provided him in 1989. But he apparently thought that my book would have the same title as the draft and be published in 1992, at the same time as *Oceanic Homosexualities.*

14 Murray, 146. Females were banned from the kabuki stage in 1642; thereafter, boy-actors and *onnagata* typically doubled as prostitutes. See *Male Colors*, 90–2.

15 Eiko Ikegami, *The Taming of the Samurai: Honorific Individualism and the Making of Modern Japan* (Cambridge, Massachusetts: Harvard University Press, 1995), 209–10, 290–1, 305–6, etc.

16 *Sex and the Floating World: Erotic Images in Japan, 1700–1820* (Honolulu: University of Hawai'i Press, 1999), 54–9; 84–6; 88–94, etc.

17 Margaret H. Childs, '*Chigo Monogatari*: Love Stories or Buddhist Sermons?' *Monumenta Nipponica*, 35, 2 (1980); *Rethinking Sorrow: Revelatory Tales of Late Medieval Japan*. Ann Arbor (Michigan: University of Michigan Press, 1991). Gregory Pflugfelder, in his 'Strange Fates: Sex, Gender, and Sexuality in *Torikaebaya Monogatari*,' *Monumenta Nipponica*, vol. 47.3 (1992) also discussed the sometimes homoerotic content of this twelfth-century novel.

18 I had, however, discussed master–servant homosexual relationships in *Servants, Shophands and Laborers in the Cities of Tokugawa Japan* (Princeton, New Jersey: Princeton University Press, 1992), 77, 98–9.

19 Gary P. Leupp, *Male Colors: The Construction of Homosexuality in Tokugawa Japan* (Berkeley: University of California Press, 1995).

20 'Male Homosexuality in Edo during the Late Tokugawa Period, 1750–1850: Decline of a Tradition?' in Sumie Jones, (ed.), *Imaging/Reading Eros: Proceedings for the Conference, Sexuality and Edo Culture, 1750–1850* (Bloomington, Indiana: Indiana University, 1996), 105–9; ' "The Floating World Is Wide": Some Suggested Approaches to Researching Female Homosexuality in Tokugawa Japan', in *Thamyris: Mythmaking from Past to Present* (Amsterdam), 5.1 (May 1998), 1–40.

21 *Cartographies of Desire: Male–Male Sexuality in Japanese Discourse, 1600–1950* (Berkeley: University of California Press, 1999).

22 John Stevens, *Lust for Enlightenment: Buddhism and Sex* (Boston and London: Shambala, 1990), 87, 97, 127, 139; Bernard Faure, *The Red Thread: Buddhist Approaches to Sexuality* (Princeton, New Jersey: Princeton University Press, 1998), 12–13; 208; 215–17; 227.

23 Tonô Haruyuki published an article on the relationships between the Heian courtier Fujiwara Yorinaga (1120–56) and young men. 'Nikki ni miru Fujiwara Yorinaga no nanshoku kankei', *Hisutoria*, 84 (September 1979); see also Tonô, 'Yorinaga to Takasue', *Izumi* (Osaka), 14 (July 1990).

24 Translated into Japanese as *Dôseiai no sekaishi: Igirisu Runesansu* by Taguchi Masao and Yamamoto Takao (Tokyo: Sairyûsha, 1993).

25 Kuia Sutadiizu Henshû Iinkai, eds, 'Kuia histutorii', *Kuia sutadiizu '96* (Tokyo: Nanatsu Mori Shoken, 1996).

26 Tokyo: Kodansha, 1995; Tokyo: Heibonsha, 1989.

27 Kazuo Hanasaki, *Ôedo monoshiri zukan* (Tokyo: Shufu to seikatsusha, 1994).

28 Kazuo Hanasaki, *Edo no kagema chaya* (Tokyo: Miki shobô, 1992).

29 The three volumes are: *Akujo hen* (Tokyo: Hihyôsha, 1992); *Wakashû hen* (1993); *Shikidô hen* (1993). *Danshoku* is an alternative reading of *nanshoku*.

30 Yoshinobu Hiratsuka, *Nihon in okeru nanshoku no kenkyû* (Tokyo: Ningen no kagakusha shuppan jigyôbu, 1987).
31 Tokyo: Heibonsha, 1992. Much of this material is available now in English. I translated the *Denbu Monogatari* as an appendix to *Male Colors* (205–17). William Scott Wilson translated sections of the samurai treatise *Hagakure*, as *Hagakure: The Book of the Samurai* (Tokyo: Kodansha, 1979).
32 Personal correspondence, August 28, 1995.
33 Some other non-academic contributions include Makoto Furukawa, 'Kindai Nihon ni okeru dôseiai no shakaishi', *Za Gei* (May 1992); 'Sekushuariti no henyô. Kindai Nihon ni okeru dôseiai no mittsu no ko', *Nichibei Josei Jânaru*, vol. 17 (1994); 'Dôseiai no hikaku shakaigaku: Rezubian, gei sutadiizu no tenkai to danshoku gainen', in Inoue, Toshi, Ueno, Chizuko *et al.* (eds), *Sekushuariti no shakaigaku* (Tokyo: Iwanami shoten, 1995).
34 Kazuo Hanasaki, *Edo no kagema chaya* (Tokyo: Miki shobô, 1992), 7.
35 Ujiie (1989), 121ff.
36 Anthropologist Ruth Benedict was reasonably accurate in reporting soon after the Second World War that 'We have many taboos on erotic pleasure which the Japanese do not have. [In Japan] [t]here is nothing evil about "human feelings" and therefore no need to be moralistic about sex pleasures.' See Benedict, *The Chrysanthemum and the Sword* (Boston: Houghton-Mifflin Co., 1946), 183–4. She adds that in Japan 'moralistic attitudes are inappropriate' towards relationships between 'adult men' and 'boy partners', 187–8.
37 Ôshima Nagisa's 1999 film *Gohatto* (Taboo), set in Kyoto in 1865, involving a samurai male–male sex plotline, and starring the popular actor 'Beat' Takashi, brought *nanshoku* into the cinematographic mainstream.
38 Win Lunsing, ' "Gay Boom" in Japan: Changing Views of Homosexuality?' *Thamyris: Mythmaking from Past to Present*, 4.2 (Autumn 1997), 272–5. On male homosexuality in women's comics see also Mark McLelland, 'The Love Between Beautiful Boys in Japanese Women's Comics', *Journal of Gender Studies*, 9.1 (2000).
39 Another older Japanese female scholar, a personal friend of mine, having heard of my intention to publish a book on *nanshoku*, called me to confirm rumor of a 'scandal.' She could not imagine why a *married* man would write such a book.
40 Hajime Shibayama, *Edo nanshoku kô. Shikidô hen* (Tokyo: Hihyôsha, 1993, 37).
41 Pflugfelder uses the term 'virile gaze' to refer to the way in which the 'elder brother' or male brothel customer apprehended the object of desire. See *Cartographies of Desire*, 35–6.
42 See his review in *Monumenta Nipponica*, 53, 2, 278.
43 Review in *Journal of Japanese Studies*, 23.1 (1997), 199–201
44 *Early Modern Japan: An Interdisciplinary Journal*, 6.1 (Summer 1997).
45 Chris Berry, Review of Gary P. Leupp, *Male Colors*: *Japanese Studies*, 18. 2 (September 1998), 208.
46 Leupp, *Male Colors*, 11, 198–201.
47 Pflugfelder, *Cartographies of Desire*, 92–6.
48 Mikito Ujiie. 'Shudô ni tsuite,' *Sexuality and Edo Culture, 1750–1850: Papers Presented*; Jones (ed.), 115–18.

49 Ujiie (1996), 116–18. From the *genpuku* ceremony, usually performed between ages 15 and 18, a teenage boy wore adult male clothing, and adopted the adult male haircut. From this point on, he was supposed to lose his homoerotic allure. *Male Colors*, 125–7.
50 Among the registered commoner population of Edo in 1733, there were 174 males for every 100 females. By 1832 the ratio was 120:100; in 1867, 101:100. See Leupp (1996), 105–9.
51 Pflugfelder, *Cartographies of Desire*, 137, n. 104.
52 Pflugfelder, *Cartographies of Desire*, 8.
53 Leupp, *Male Colors*, 191–4.
54 Ellis Tinios. Review of *Male Colors. Japan Forum*, 9, 1 (1997), 101–3; Margaret H. Childs, Review of *Male Colors. Early Modern Japan*, 6.1 (Summer 1997), 40–2; Paul Schalow, Review of *Male Colors. Monumenta Nipponica*, 23.1 (1997), 196–201. Pflugfelder's work subsequently provided several Tokugawa-era references to homosexual fellatio. *Cartographies of Desire*, 41, n. 50.
55 For a critique of postmodernists' rejection of history, see Ellen Meiksins Wood and John Bellamy Foster (eds), *In Defense of History: Marxism and the Postmodernist Agenda* (New York: Monthly Review Press, 1997).
56 Gary P. Leupp, 'The Five Men of Naniwa: Gang Violence and Popular Culture in Genroku Osaka', *Osaka: The Merchant's Capital in Tokugawa Japan*, James L. McClain and Wakita Osamu (eds) (New York: Cornell University Press, 1999), esp. 127–31.
57 Ikegami, 218–22.
58 *Male Colors*, 164–70.
59 Schalow (1997), 200.
60 See Robert Lyons Danly's translation of a chapter of Ihara Saikaku's 1682 work *Kôshoku ichidai otoko* (Life of a Sensuous Man), in which a male prostitute speaks candidly about the job, in Stephen D. Miller, (ed.), *Partings at Dawn: An Anthology of Japanese Gay Literature* (San Francisco: Gay Sunshine Press, 1996), 94–5; also Andrew Markus, 'Prostitutes and Prosperity in the Works of Terakado Seiken,' in Jones (ed.), 39–40.
61 Schalow (1992), 220.
62 Murray (1992), 144–5, n. 41.
63 Pflugfelder, *Cartographies of Desire*, 75.Similarly, the Japanese scholar Koike Togorô, in his *Kôshoku monogatari* (Tokyo: Kamakura insatsu, 1963), 266–7, assumes that Iemitsu, the third Tokugawa shogun (r. 1623–51) 'was forced to pear the pain of the passive partner' in his relationship with an older man during his boyhood.
64 See my review of Pflugfelder's *Cartographies* in *American Historical Review* (June 2001), 959–60, and Leupp, *Male Colors*, 178–82. Murray (1992, 125–7) also discusses at least some '*wakashû's* eager subordination' and 'eager[ness] to be loved' by men.
65 Jesuit missionaries who worked in Japan in the sixteenth century often noted that 'both the boys and the men who consort with them [sexually] brag and talk about it openly without trying to cover the matter up.' See Michael Cooper, comp. and ed., *They Came to Japan: an Anthology of European Reports on Japan, 1543–1640* (Berkeley: University of California Press, 1965), 46–7.

66 Leupp, *Male Colors*, 94f.

67 Ihara Saikaku, *Ihara Saikaku shû*, ed. Yasuoka Teruoka, and Asô Higashi (Tokyo: Shôgakukan, 1971), 103. For a very loose translation of *Kôshoku ichidai otoko*, see Kengi Hamada, trans., *The Life of an Amorous Man by Ihara Saikaku* (Tokyo and Rutland, Vt.: Tuttle, 1964). Hamada inexcusably omits one whole chapter of homoerotic content, but see 35–9.

68 See Derek Massarella, *A World Elsewhere: Europe's Encounter with Japan in the Sixteenth and Seventeenth Centuries* (New Haven, Connecticut.: Yale University Press, 1990), 239.

69 Pflugfelder, *Cartographies of Desire*, 5; also Pflugfelder, review of *Male Colors. Monumenta Nipponica*, 53.2 (Summer 1998), 276–80.

70 *Webster's New Universal Unabridged Dictionary* (New York: Simon and Schuster, 1983), defines a bisexual simply as 'A person who is sexually attracted by members of both sexes' (186).

71 Murray (1992), 137–43.

72 Eva Cantarella has discussed bisexuality in Greco-Roman society in *Bisexuality in the Ancient World* (New Haven: Yale University Press, 1992).

73 George B. Sansom, *Japan in World History* (Tokyo and Rutland, Vt.: Tuttle Books, 1951), 11–14.

74 Conferences on gender studies involving both Japanese and western scholars have become routine. The two-volume *Giendaa no Nihonshi* (History of Gender in Japan), published by University of Tokyo Press in 1994, grew out of a series of such meetings, at which westerners were more inclined to raise issues of same-sex attraction.

75 There are similarities in the Chinese and Japanese traditions of male–male sexuality, notably the validation of both 'passive' and 'active' partners in homosexual anal intercourse. But in Japan, one finds greater emphasis than in China on *age* as the determinant of sexual role. Leupp, *Male Colors*, 203.

76 See Leupp, 'Capitalism and Homosexuality in Tokugawa Japan', and Murray (1992), 146. On incipient capitalism in Tokugawa Japan, see Edwin O. Reischauer, and John K. Fairbank, *East Asia: The Great Tradition* (Boston: Houghton Mifflin Co., 1958), 641–2.

9

Colliding Cultures: Masculinity and Homoeroticism in Mughal and Early Colonial South Asia

Walter Penrose

The period between 1550 and 1800 witnessed the beginning of a collision of cultures in South Asia perhaps greater than the Himalayas themselves.[1] The process of Islamic conquest of Hindu lands had begun centuries before, and in the early sixteenth century the Portuguese established a 'maritime empire' in the Indian Ocean that ignited a long, confrontational process of European colonization.[2] In 1526, the Mongol dynast Babur defeated the Sultan of Delhi and established the Mughal Empire.[3] By the death of the Sultan Aurangzeb in 1707, Mughal rule reached its zenith after the conquest of southern India, but not without intense Hindu/Muslim struggle.[4] Early Mughal rulers, unlike Aurangzeb and later British colonials, largely tolerated the Hindu culture they encountered in South Asia, particularly with regard to gender variance and eroticism. Homoerotic poetry and artwork appear to have flourished in the Mughal period; even prescriptive Sanskrit sexual literature was translated into Persian for the subcontinent's new rulers' erudition and enjoyment. Mughal invaders have been called 'hedonistic' by James Saslow – their artwork, poetry, and even translated sex manuals celebrated human sexuality.[5]

Documenting precolonial ideas regarding gender and sexuality, however, does not necessarily lead to a utopia of same-sex desire and gender variance.[6] Misogyny, sex/gender segregation, caste/class/status issues, age, and varying religious prohibitions must be considered. Nevertheless, understanding the patterns of traditional life in South Asia which, at a minimum, tolerated organized forms of homoeroticism and gender variation can help us to see through the fallacious claims of Nationalist movements in South Asia that have appropriated the colonizer's sex/gender ideology, and called it native.[7] Age and/or status-differentiated male homoeroticism was celebrated in Mughal art and literature, male and female gender-variant individuals were incorporated into South Asian life, and gender roles appear to have been more fluid than today.

The introduction of Western ideology, a long process that peaked with direct British rule, changed traditional ways of life. The British officially annexed Bengal in 1765, and gradually spread their authority throughout the sub-continent in the late eighteenth and nineteenth centuries.[8] Analysis of sixteenth to nineteenth century Mughal literature and artwork, in conjunction with European travel accounts, reveals an expression of masculinity and sexuality in Mughal South Asia that is complex and distinct from postcolonial ideology. Behavior that compromised masculine status may be called 'queer,' but it was organized and regulated in a sanctioned fashion. An intensification of 'queerness' is evident with respect to gender variance and sexuality in colonial texts.

In order to demonstrate this intensification, I will divide this paper into four sections. First, I will discuss male–male eroticism and its relationship to masculinity in the Mughal Empire. Second, I will discuss Mughal-era gender variance and male homoeroticism that continued certain facets of Hindu social organization in a Muslim milieu, as well as British reactions to this social phenomenon. Third, I will discuss what both native and British authors perceived to be 'masculine' behavior in women of Mughal and successive court structures. In conclusion, I will analyze the complex and problematic relationship between South Asian queerness and colonialism.

Male homoeroticism and homosocial masculinity in the Mughal Empire

Despite Islamic celebration of homoerotic desire in poetry, Islam is not devoid of prohibitions against homoerotic sex.[9] The *Quran* proscribes homosexual behavior between men, but it provides a far lesser punishment than either Hebrew or Christian bible: 'If two men among you are guilty of lewdness, punish them both. If they repent and amend, leave them be. For Allah is Oft-Returning, Most Merciful' (4.16, trans. A. Yusuf Ali). Stories of Sodom and Gomorrah are interpreted as prohibiting sexual relations between men as well (*Quran* 7.80–4; 11.77–83; 15.51–74; 27.54–8). In the *Shariah*, Islamic law derived in part from *hadith* (sayings) of the Prophet Mohammed, homosexual behavior is condemned more harshly.[10] Homoerotic *desire*, nevertheless, was not considered sinful – in Islamic poetry, expressions of male–male desire are frequent, but references to homoerotic acts are rare.

An understanding of this complicated prohibition of the act of penetration coupled with the allowance of desire between males, and even tolerance that turned a blind eye to the doctrines of religion or tried to change them, is important to comprehend homoeroticism in Mughal India. Kidwai writes that guilt was difficult to establish, and one finds far less punishment of homoerotic acts in Islamic societies than in Europe at the same time (111). The *Shariah*, Islamic law, required 'incontrovertible evidence,' moreover, 'such as confession of four faithful eyewitnesses to the act of penetration' (111). In the seventeenth and eighteenth centuries, noted Orthodox theologians Shaikh Abdul Haq Muhaddis Dehlavi and Shah Waliullah advocated for the harshest of penalties. The emperor Akbar (d. 1605) is said to have forbidden homoerotic relationships, but his efforts were unsuccessful, and, though he issued a warning to one aristocrat, he later yielded (112–13). Other emperors had noted homoerotic attachments. The autobiography of Babur, the first Mughal ruler, indicates the rulers' infatuation with a 'boy' called Baburi.[11]

Although homoerotic acts are defined as a crime in the *hadith*, at the same time it is noted that 'the Prophet saw God as a beautiful youth with long hair and cap awry.'[12] Unlike the orthodox, who believed that... conformity with the *Shariah* (religious law) ensured salvation, Sufis believed that the personal experience of divine love was the true way (114). Kidwai writes that some Sufis were less inclined to follow the *Shariah* than others, and were called 'intoxicated Sufis' (114). Kidwai notes that in Sufi literature, homoerotic metaphors were employed to describe the relationship between Allah and man (115). 'By the twelfth century, the notion had gained ground that God's essence was unfathomable and his beauty could only be realized by contemplating his creations who were the witnesses (*shahid*) of his magnificence' (115). Admiring male beauty, in this strain of thought, could never be sinful. Sufism influenced male Persian poets, who extol the beauty of male youths.

Male homoeroticism was highly visible in the literature of Muslim South Asia. There is no evidence that I am aware of that such forms of desire were exulted in Hindu society. The homosocial conditions created by Islamic culture allowed for the expression of male–male desire in poetry.[13] Poetic traditions imported from Persia allowed for the celebration of age differentiated love between men and culminated during the Mughal era in a purely Indo-Islamic poetic form, the Urdu *ghazal*.[14] Urdu replaced Persian as the high literary language of the

Mughal Empire towards the end of the seventeenth century (118). *Ghazal* 'is written from the man's point of view who is always the lover, the wooer, or the pursuer and who proudly declares his chaste desire for the object of his love' only as long as 'he or she remains chaste.'[15] The object of the poetry was known as the *mushuq*, or the beloved, and was always referred to by masculine pronouns.

Ghazal sometimes addressed women with masculine pronouns, however, either to mask the identity of the beloved as a woman or simply out of convention. Due to this, heteronormative Urdu scholars in both the colonial and postcolonial periods argued that beloveds were all women referred to by masculine pronouns.[16] Naim persuasively argues that male–male eroticism cannot be denied in Mughal-era *ghazal*, however, citing, among others, the following reasons: 'Many verses contain a reference to an extremely masculine attribute, namely the down (*xat*) on the cheeks of pubescent boys' (122). Predominantly 'masculine' clothing items are mentioned in association with the couple, such as 'turbans, caps, swords, daggers, etc' (122). References are made to male homosocial milieus, such as the market. In some verses, the names of 'individual boys' are found, and other anonymous references to 'young boys,' are clear with respect to gender because of the terms used, such as *launda,* or 'boy' (122).

Rahman notes the stigmatization of passivity in Islamic cultures.[17] Nevertheless, he quotes a verse which he calls rare, 'ruthless honesty,' written by Abru (7): 'The boy who is chaste is persecuted and is made helpless by those who are strong. /He is the king in Delhi who lies beneath the lover.'

'Couplets about boy-love' describe a 'society which forbade women from meeting men openly and tacitly allowed men to make love to catamites or "boys of the bazaar" as Mir calls them in his autobiography' (7). The poet Nakish (d. 1838) referred to the 'mint' which his beloved, Meerzai, had in his trousers (7). The prohibitions against sexual reference adhered to by other Islamic poets were sometimes ignored in South Asian poetry.

Rahman stresses that the beloved in Urdu *ghazal* is a boy, an *amrad*, who, 'belongs, as it were, to the category of women: those who take the penis in the orifices of their body' (3). Rahman argues that the correct term for homoerotic relations in *ghazal* is *amrad parasti*, or 'boy-love,' *not* homosexuality (3). Kidwai, on the other hand, asserts that *amrad parasti* is the cause of much misconception: 'Orientalists as well as modern commentators have cited it to categorize all male–male relationships as age stratified.'[18] He argues that '[w]hat "boys" meant and whether all boys were adolescent is open to question' (121). 'The sexual roles assumed by the lover and the beloved are very rarely stated explicitly' (122). In later *ghazal*, Kugle argues, 'there is little evidence to fix the age of the masculine beloved,' in Urdu.[19] 'There are few linguistic or imagistic clues to determine whether "boy," "youth," or "young man" would be most accurate in translation' (35).

Kidwai questions Rahman's assertion that boys are considered like women because they take the penis into the orifices of their body. He notes that some beloveds were not 'so young as to be smooth faced' or beardless. In one poem, soldiers pursue an older narrator (121–2). Some of the relationships lauded in poetry appear to have lasted for a lifetime. Another beloved, Mukarram, for example, completed the days of ritual mourning for his lover which a Muslim wife must observe when her husband dies.[20] Regarding modern India, Cohen writes that:

> ... one is either *gandu* – one who is done to, up the ass – or *londebaaz* – one who delights (*baaz*) in doing young men (*londe*) ... Doing and being done to are usually distributed by relative age but renogiated as the play of a tryst shifts into the longer-range intoxication of ... deep love.[21]

This may have been the case with long-term male–male relationships in Mughal South Asia, but we can't be sure. Mukarram, as a beloved, grieves like a wife, not a husband.

The poet Abru (d. 1733) implies that a transition was made from beloved to lover in Mughal Delhi. Naim describes how Abru instructs a youth on how to 'dress and behave in order to entice lovers.'[22] Abru prescribed long hair, parted in the middle, avoidance of excessive sun, the application of pastes and oils to the skin at night, reddening of the lips with betel juice, the use of eye-liner, henna on the finger knuckles (but not palms), jewelry, perfume, flirtatiousness and planned neglectfulness, dignity not unlike that of a king treating his lovers like courtiers. When the right man comes along, Abru writes: 'Do everything that will give him pleasure.'[23] Abru advises the youth not to shave when 'down' begins to appear on his cheeks, as this is still 'spring' (167). When the hairs on his face became tough, he should then begin to shave until his lovers lose interest, due to the loss of his 'delicate bloom' (167). The youth was then to give up the 'desire to be adored,' and 'Mingle with lovers, make no special claims./Enjoy the company of the beauteous ones' (167–8). The latter are presumably youthful beloveds.

Abru taught the beloved how to perform his gender, as we see in Abru's poetry, and even how to transition to manhood.[24] The gender of the beloved youth in *ghazal* may be seen as existing somewhere *between* that of an adult male and a woman, as the clothing and adornment of the beloved illustrate. Richard Burton mentions that older men used henna to color their beards, while 'young men sometimes stain the hands and feet with it.'[25] Modern South Asian women wear henna on their hands. Manucci wrote that Mughal women used *mehndi* to color the hands and feet red.[26] Women are shown wearing henna in Mughal-era illustrations whereas adult men do not have reddened hands.[27] On the other hand, adult, mustached men wear skirted garments, pearls, turbans – items similar to those prescribed by Abru for the beloved.[28] Manucci indicates that the Sultan Aurangzeb's attendants carried perfumes as he rode in pomp to Kashmir, just as Abru prescribes that the beloved use perfume.[29] Beloveds wore clothing (i.e. turbans), pearls, and perfume like older men, but like women, henna on their hands. They were subordinated to men but also aspired to someday become them, most likely passive in sex, but expected to one day become active. Urban beloveds of *ghazal* were (if not slaves), youths in training to become men. 'Masculinities' are hierarchical, and the beloved did not exercise 'hegemonic masculinity.'[30] Yet, he might have aspired to someday exercise it. Beloveds had an identity based first of all on age.

Vanita argues for the existence of categories of sexual identity before the nineteenth century.[31] Even though 'the terms "homosexual" and "heterosexual" were not used, other terms were used to refer to those with a lifelong preference for erotic attachments to those of their own sex.'[32] Vanita writes that 'romantic attachments between men and between women' were often 'compatible with marriage and procreation,' and that a person's 'primary emotional attachment may be to a friend of his or her own gender' (xiii). Vanita discuss certain terms in South Asian languages which refer to same-sex love and predate 'any importation of nineteenth-century European psychologists' terminology' (xxi). In pre-colonial texts, for example, *chapti* 'was a word for sex between women as well as for the women who practiced it' (xxi). Mughal art does suggest that women carried on *both* egalitarian and gender-defined homoerotic relationships.[33]

The categories that one finds for Mughal-era men, however, are based first of all on some form of differentiation (age, status/class, and/or gender), and, secondly on sexual 'identities' constituted by 'acts.' Michael Sweet argues that identities at least based partially upon sexuality existed before the modern era.[34] The identity of the boy-lover did not preclude ongoing sexual involvement with women, whether inside or outside of marriage, and thus this identity differs from modern homosexuality. Carolyn Dinshaw argues that '[i]dentities may be constituted by acts,' and '"acts", as an analytical category, cannot in itself be regarded as sufficient and self-explanatory,' despite the centrality which many queer theorists have given to acts in analysis of pre-modern sexualities.[35] Because of the Muslim custom of not discussing homosexual acts, differentiation between boy and boy-lover was outwardly based on age and/or status than on an economy of acts, though such a dichotomy existed. Burton notes that a distinction was drawn amongst South Asians between the 'doer' and the 'done.'[36] A *ghazal* of Mazmoon indicates that sometimes position *was* mentioned: 'In the tavern what is done is totally indecent/But when I saw the school there too they talked only of the "active" and the "passive".'[37] Patriarchy, and the power invested in it, did not allow the South Asian adult male to identify (openly) as sexually passive, unless he lost the status associated with his masculinity (see below). According to Rahman, Mughal society did not create a socially acceptable place for egalitarian relationships between adult men.[38]

An egalitarian relationship with respect to age might have been socially acceptable only if two males were young. One such relationship may be depicted in a miniature from the 'Fitzwilliam album' (ca. 1555–60, see Fig. 2).[39] The text accompanying the illustration has not been analyzed to my knowledge. At this time it cannot be ruled out that one of the couple is a slave. However, a Persian miniature (ca. 1540), believed to be by the same artist, shows a very similar scene, in which two boys, courting, are attended by a third male, who is likely a servant (see Fig. 3).[40] Richard Burton indicates that the 'Persian vice' began in boyhood:

> It begins in boyhood and many Persians account for it by paternal severity. Youths arrived at puberty find none of the facilities with which Europe supplies fornication. Onanism is to a certain extant discouraged by circumcision, and meddling with the father's slave-girls and concubines would be risking cruel punishment if not death. Hence they use each other by turns, a 'puerile practice,' known as Alish-Takish the Lat. Facere vicibus or mutuum facere. Temperament, media, and atavism recommend the custom to the general; and after marrying and begetting heirs, Paterfamilias returns to the Ganymede. Hence all odes of Hafiz are addressed to youths ...[41]

Burton notes that the adult man continued to place his erotic attention on 'the Ganymede,' a Western term for a young male beloved. As the head of a household (*Paterfamilias*), he was expected to be the subject of sexual experience, but two youths (or two women), might have had an egalitarian or reciprocal relationship.

The 'Persian vice,' according to Burton, was widespread throughout Indo-Islamic societies (10:236). Burton writes:

> The cities of Afghanistan and Sind are thoroughly saturated with Persian vice. ... The Afghans are commercial travelers on a large scale and each caravan is accompanied by a number of boys and lads almost in women's attire with kohl'd eyes and rouged cheeks, long tresses and henna'd fingers and toes, riding luxuriously in Kajáwas or camel-panniers: they are called Kúch-I-safari, or traveling wives, and the husbands trudge patiently by their sides (10:236).

Mughal emperors ruled both Afghanistan and Sind. Afghani homoerotic relationships appear to be simultaneously age- and gender-differentiated. The youths are dressed 'almost' as women. The beloveds mentioned by Mir and Abru in Delhi wear turbans, and may have taken a more masculine tone than their Afghani counterparts. Both beloveds in Delhi and Afghanistan, however, wore henna on the hands and eye-liner. At the urban bazaars, according to Kidwai, 'men from different classes, castes, and communities mingled; here homoerotically inclined men met and established relations.'[42] Mughal poetry describes love affairs between Muslim and Hindu males (108).[43] One such poem describes a group of Hindu youths, dressed in women's clothing, catching the eye of a Muslim sufi, who joins them in their celebration of the Hindu Holi festival.[44]

According to Kugle, the most celebrated homoerotic love story, that of the Sultan Mahmud (d. 12th c. CE) and his slave Ayuz, acted as the 'archetype of perfect male' love.[45] Both Mahmud and Ayaz, according to Kugle, were 'adult men and some poets dwell on Ayaz's facial hair as a sign of his desirability' (35). Yet the poem of Mahmud Lahori (d. 1574), which Kugle translates, makes Ayaz seem like a young man, not a middle-aged or older adult. 'Faint whiskers emerge from the soft edge of your cheeks like wisps of perfume; Who could think that the luminous halo that circles the moon mars its beauty?' (35). This passage implies some societal anxiety over the growth of a beard (and hence loss of beloved status), even if the poet disagrees with society. In another poem written by Zulali (d. 1615), Ayaz is called a 'rose blooming' (34). The focus on his youth cannot be denied. It is possible that the relationship continued beyond Ayaz' youth, but this was not revealed, as an ideal, to society.

The word *launda*, according to Chatterjee, may have been used to represent slaves as well as boys.[46] Chatterjee suggests that scholars have misunderstood status-differentiated male homoeroticism (e.g. master/slave relations) as age-differentiated. Chatterjee argues that slavery has been overlooked as part of the identity of the beloveds of Urdu *ghazal* – and beloved slaves were, amongst others, 'deprived of their masculinity, agency, and adulthood in historical pasts' (73). Socially accepted or tolerated homoeroticism could have been *simultaneously* age- and status-differentiated, however. The idealized relationship of Mahmud and Ayaz is portrayed as both.

A letter of the poet Ghalib that reflects upon 'boy-love' in 1861 Delhi has not been used to date (that I am aware of) as evidence. It may help to resolve controversy surrounding the age-stratification of South Asian male homoeroticism:

> Listen to me, my friend. It's a rule with men who worship beauty that when they fall in love with a youngster they deceive themselves that he's three or four years younger than he really is. They know he's grown up, but they think of him as a child.[47]

The transgression of boy-love, according to Ghalib, occurs in a state of denial. Ghalib does not here comment on how long such a relationship might last, but he does imply that differentiation is drawn, with the lover thinking of the beloved as a 'child,' even if he is really a young man.

Hindus, *hijras*, and the forfeiture of masculinity

Hindu societies do not appear to have celebrated age-differentiated homoeroticism like their Muslim counterparts, though they appear to have tolerated it in some forms at least. According to the ancient *Kama Sutra* (2.6.49; 2.9) and its medieval commentary, oral homoeroticism was more accepted in pre-Muslim South Asia than anal intercourse. In the nineteenth century, Richard Burton noted that pederasty was permitted amongst Muslims and Sikhs in Northern India, and ignored in Southern India and the Himalayas.[48] He writes: 'Hindus, I repeat, hold pederasty in much abhorrence and are much scandalized by being called Gánd-márá (anus beater) or Gángú (anuser) as Englishmen would be' (237). Burton seems to equate pederasty with anal intercourse, but, unfortunately, does not discuss Hindu views towards oral homoeroticism.

Burton does relate, however, that a high-caste soldier in his regimen had taken up with a low-caste soldier. After some time, 'in an unhappy hour, the Pariah patient [lower-caste beloved] ventured to become the agent (237).' The higher-caste soldier then killed him, and was subsequently hung for murder (237–8). This defense of masculinity illustrates the fear of stigmatization that the higher-caste Hindu man held towards passivity. It also suggests that caste was another distinction on which homoerotic relationships could be differentiated, at least among Hindus.[49] Both men are described as young.

Chatterjee discusses an eighteenth-century document from the Hindu kingdom of Oriccha, in central India, in which the term *gandu* ('one who has his ass taken – a popular insult in north India even today') is used as a term of abuse (72). According to Pattanaik, '[a]nyone familiar with the traditional gay constructs in India will know that the penetrator/penetratee, active/passive, top/bottom, butch/femme divide dominates same-sex activity among men.'[50] The penetrating partner 'retains his 'masculine' even 'straight' identity' while the passive partner 'forfeits it' (15). Will Roscoe writes that in South Asia 'a third-gender pattern seems to be the locus for all homosexual expression from Vedic [ancient] times until the arrival of the Muslims ...'[51] There are references to age-stratified homoeroticism in pre-Islamic sources, however.[52]

Gender-variant men still practice prostitution in South Asia, as passive sexual partners, today. *Hijras* are a quasi-caste of homoerotically inclined, (usually) castrated males, intersexed persons, or others. They wear female clothing and are grouped together based on their inability to procreate. *Hijras* proclaim that they are 'neither man nor woman.'[53] Most are eunuchs. In addition to prostitution, *hijras* dance at Hindu birth ceremonies (a traditional religious function), as well as at both Hindu and Muslim weddings (1–12). *Jhankas* or *zenanas* are cross-dressed, uncastrated male prostitutes and/or dancers.[54] Due to the multiethnic populations of South Asia, other terms are used to describe figures similar to *hijras* and *jhankas*, but such a discussion is beyond the scope of this article.

A Portuguese priest, Sebastian Manrique, traveling through Mughal Sind in 1641, apparently encountered *hijras*, *jhankas*, and/or both.[55] When in a port city of Sind, which he calls 'a sink of iniquity', Manrique writes: 'the unmentionable vice is so common that catamites dressed and adorned like women parade the streets, soliciting others as abandoned as themselves. These men also take part in their barbarian festivals and weddings, instead of women dancers' (II:240). The account underscores the difference between Mughal integration of male gender variance into society and European tension over the relationship of gender fluidity to 'the unmentionable vice,' and 'barbarian' rituals, which would lead to increasing intolerance of *hijras* in colonial and postcolonial South Asia.

James Forbes, an English merchant traveling with a Maratha (Hindu) army (ca. 1780), described 'hermaphrodites,' as 'among the followers of an oriental camp.'[56] These 'hermaphrodites,' according to Forbes, all served in the capacity of cooks. The hermaphrodites 'were compelled, by way of distinguishing them from other castes, to wear the habit of a female and the turban of a man' (I:359). Forbes notes only that these persons were 'called hermaphrodites,' not that they were actually intersexed. Some or all may have been eunuchs. Forbes mentions only his disgust when examining the 'hermaphrodites' (I:359), indicating that perhaps they were eunuchs, but probably also underscoring his lack of comfort with sex/gender fluidity. This evidence suggests that a socially constructed in-between/third sex or gender did exist in Maratha society.

Preston argues that Forbes was wrong on several accounts. First, he states '[t]hat such people could have cooked for caste Hindus seems improbable.'[57] Forbes makes it clear that the Maratha army was made up of 'various nations and religions,' however, and he states that the 'third class' of soldiers were 'Mogul' (I:,344). Eunuchs also served Muslim kings, and cultural blending could have relaxed some orthodox Hindu standards – especially in the entourage of a Maratha king fighting Muslim princes. Furthermore, hijras are not necessarily from scheduled (untouchable) castes, nor are they relegated to such a position when they become *hijras*.[58] Second, Preston doubts that these persons would have worn the clothing of both men and women, as 'the peculiar clothing combination does not agree with later accounts' of *hijras*. Preston fails to see the possibility of diachronic change and/or regional variation.

Preston nevertheless proves that Hindu rulers had supported gender variant men, eunuchs, hermaphrodites, and/or others who belonged to the *Hijras* near Bombay and Poona, and that the British sought to end this aid in the nineteenth century.[59] The British undermined gender variance by revoking land grants and trying to stamp out gender-variant male prostitution (377–87). The British were aghast at having to support such 'abominations' and 'wretches' (386). In 1845, a British general, Napier, who conquered Sind, was informed that 'Karáchi, a townlet of some two thousand souls,' had 'no less than' three brothels, 'in which not women but boys and eunuchs, the former demanding nearly a double price, lay for hire ... The reason proved to be the scrotum of the unmutilated boy could be used as a kind of bridle for directing the movements of the animal.'[60] Napier put down 'the infamous beasts who, dressed as women, plied their trade in the Meers' time openly.'[61] Despite such colonial adversity, the *hijras* have survived, due to prostitution, their religious function, and their own perseverance.

Masculine behavior in Mughal women

South Asia today is strikingly devoid of any conspicuous social role for gender-variant women, however, despite the fact that 'masculine' women are described in both native and colonial texts. The social construction of precolonial masculinity is perhaps best demonstrated by the prescriptions of 'masculine' behavior to women. 'Virile Behavior in Women' (*Purushayita*) in women is both discussed and prescribed by the ca. third-century CE Sanskrit *Kama Sutra* (2.8, trans. Danielou), the *Jayamangala* commentary on the *Kama Sutra* (2.8, trans. Danielou), and the ca. third-century CE *Koka Shastra* (ch. 9, trans. Comfort). In the Mughal period, a seventeenth-century Persian translation of the Sanskrit *Koka Shastra* was illustrated with a painting of a woman poised to insert a dildo into another woman.[62] Unfortunately, this manuscript is now lost at the Biblioteque National de France, and the exact context of the illustration, photocopied years ago, is not known.

Saslow notes that '[t]his playful image, quoted almost exactly in multiple copies of the popular handbook, was already a late flower in an Indian tradition dating back to the renowned *Kamasutra*' (125). This scene may have illustrated the *Purushayita* ('Virile Behavior in Women') section of the Persian translation of the *Koka Shastra* – this would seem the most likely location for it. The earlier Sanskrit version of the *Koka Shastra* is extant and has been translated into English by Alex Comfort, who interprets *Purushayita* as the woman sitting on top of a man (in the same manner that Burton's Victorian English translation of the *Kama Sutra* explains this behavior).[63] According to Danielou, however, *Purushayita* in the *Kama Sutra* refers to the use of an artifical phallus, with a woman taking an active role in sex with both males and females. Ruth Vanita has argued convincingly that Danielou's translation is plausible.[64] Locating the Persian translation of the *Koka Shastra* and determining the exact context of the illustration might help to solve the controversy concerning the meaning(s) of *Purushayita*, and/or its Persian equivalent.

The illustration may attest Mughal tolerance of female homoeroticism. The *Quran* (4:15) discusses only vague female 'lewdness' as a punishable offense. Whether this applies to female homoeroticism is disputed. Most commentators have construed this 'lewdness' to mean adultery or fornication. In 1960, however, Yusuf Ali argued that this reference was to 'unnatural crime between women,' (a westernized statement influenced by sexology, no doubt).[65] Ali's argument is based on an ambiguous passage, however – we cannot be certain what it means, and Ali himself notes 'most commentators understand this to refer to adultery or fornication' (189 no. 523). In the *Shariah*, however, female–female voyeurism and sex are forbidden, as well as two women sleeping under one cover.[66] Such probibitions may have been relaxed in the homosocial world of the Mughal harem, as artwork suggests.

Gender-variant women appear to have held special positions within both Hindu and Muslim societies. South Asian kings and their harems were traditionally guarded by women. The hairstyle, clothing and other attributes of the penetrating partner (the bow, arrow, and dildo) may indicate that she was a female bodyguard assigned to the harem. The difference between these two women – one who is dressed and acts in a feminine manner, the other whose clothing, attributes, and behavior are more masculine – is illuminating. These two women participate in gender-differentiated sex. Women bodyguards, soldiers, and porters, dressed in typically male clothing, are vividly described by colonial travelers and ethnographers as masculine. William Knighton, for example, described women bodyguards in nineteenth-century Oudh as 'men-like women.'[67] Such ascription of warrior-like abilities to masculinity in women may not have originated with Westerners, however. Early Sanskrit medical texts assumed that masculinity in women was an essential characteristic, and terms were provided to describe such women, such as *narisandha*.[68] Masculinity in women was ascribed to the mother sitting on top of the father during intercourse, or to embryonic damage.

Women bodyguards are mentioned in descriptions of the seventeenth-century Mughal court. The traditions of using 'Tartar and Uzbek women' 'either to carry palanquins or to stand on sentry at night' in the harem, were noted by the Italian doctor Niccolao Manucci, who treated royal Mughal women.[69] Tartar and Uzbek female slaves, according to Manucci, were sold to the Mughal Emperor Aurangzeb by envoys because they were 'warlike, and skillful in the use of lance, arrow, and sword' (41). They guarded the king and his wives at night while they slept. Tartar and Kashmiri women are also mentioned by Francois Bernier, a French visitor to the court of Aurangzeb.[70] They rode, 'fantastically attired,' on horseback beside the royal women during a trip to Kashmir (372). The fantastic attire is not described, but may include weapons; the eunuchs are noted as carrying 'wands of state' (372). An anecdote about the warlike-ness of Tartar women is told by Bernier (122–3), however, and his account is certainly congruent with Manucci's, if not as explicative.

Chatterjee has written that such women in nineteenth-century courts were 'entertainers and dressed in warriors' clothes.'[71] They were called Amazons by Englishmen, which Chatterjee notes 'predisposed the reader (especially one trained in European classics) to imagine a community of armed, independent, men-spurning women' (70). While I agree with Chatterjee on this latter point, it is clear from William Knighton's account that female bodyguards in nineteenth-century Oudh actually fought.[72] These women were not independent of patriarchal structures, but some may have been independent of men sexually. The female guards of the royal family of Oudh were prohibited from getting pregnant, though some apparently did so anyway (131). Their gendered division of labor places them in a separate category from the women they guarded, who were secluded, did not handle weapons, and were expected by male relatives to concern themselves with childbearing and rearing. As Manucci discusses, the former were purchased for their ability to guard. They may have fulfilled a third, alternative, and/or 'masculinized' gender in South Asian societies.[73] Cross-dressed women apparently served as both entertainers and bodyguards. Manucci notes that both Mughal princesses and 'dancing-women,' wore jeweled turbans (typically male headdress) by permission of the king.[74]

William Osborne, who visited the court of the Punjabi Sikh ruler, Ranjit Singh, in the early nineteenth century, notes that Singh's women bodyguards held land grants from which they derived their income.[75] A passage from Osborne's diary indicates that, by the 1830s, the British had already begun revoking such land grants in the territories which they directly controlled: 'During our visit to Lahore, a considerable degree of excitement prevailed amongst the fairer portion of the Sihk army, owing to a report having arisen that the Maharajah intended to follow the example of the [British East India] Company, and resume all grants for which no formal title deeds could be produced; the report, however, proved to be premature, and I believe Runjeet would sooner face Dost Mohammed and his Afghans, than a single individual of his Amazonian bodyguard' (96–7). Osborne uses 'resume' here to mean 'take back.' Osborne illustrates the means by which the British ultimately undermined the 'masculine' women they found in South Asia – by destroying their sources of income and invalidating their posts.

Conclusion

Not only did colonialism change gender expectations of men and women, a determined effort was also made to rid British India of gender-variant persons. While British colonialism seriously challenged the role of the *hijra*, it virtually wiped out the economic framework that supported women perceived to be masculine by the British.[76] The flourish of male homoerotic poetry and artwork came to a grinding halt as the British annexed India for direct rule in the nineteenth century.[77] Sadly, independence did not stop this process, but only heightened it.[78]

I have refrained from using the term 'queer' throughout the Mughal portion of this essay because homoeroticism was often celebrated in text and art.[79] Though as today, *hijras* appear to have been marginalized from their families in precolonial India, they were not outcast from society in the same manner as the western Sodomite or even as untouchables in the Hindu caste system. The introduction of European norms of gender and sexuality, in many ways, 'queered' India, and in turn caused the celebration of male homoeroticism, the support of gender variance, and the toleration of both to be suppressed in a larger effort to eradicate the same lost practices which today we historians now try to reclaim by 'Queering India' to borrow Ruth Vanita's phrase.[80]

An article of this scope cannot begin to do justice to this issue, only to suggest that queer theory must embrace precolonial South Asia and bring it into a discourse from which it has often been excluded. For example, is there any resemblance to what we today deem 'queer' and precolonial 'queerness' in South Asia? The failed attempts of Akbar and Islamic fundamentalists to regulate Mughal sexuality complicate the picture. Sexual acts between Mughal males were technically considered sinful, but seem to have been largely tolerated and did not destabilize masculinity unless an adult male took the passive role. The stigmatization of anal passivity in precolonial South Asia may be said to have a history of queerness, perhaps more among Hindus than Muslims, more among adults than youths, but these distinctions are muddled. Historical *hijras* have lived, to use the terminology of Carolyn Dinshaw, in a 'queer community across time,' in the sense that they were marginalized from their families and forced into their own distinct quasi-caste.[81] Such a 'community' connection is not made via shared identities, but rather shared isolation. This interpration of 'queer' argues that aristocratic Mughal youth-lovers and their youths did not belong to queer categories, though *hijras* of the past did. Yet in traditional Hinduism *hijras* are sacredly 'neither man nor woman' and may issue the profane at either men or women. The marginalization and therefore queerness of the *hijras* has intensified with colonialism and now postcolonialism. Masculine behavior in women was deemed as essential – not chosen or socially created – in ancient South Asia. Europeans, however, deemed such behavior as queer and stamped it out to the best of their ability.

Islamic Mughal society tolerated male homoeroticism, as long as the adult male was outwardly the subject of such behavior. Nevertheless, Foucault states in *The History of Sexuality*, vol. 1: 'Power is not something that is acquired, seized, or shared, something that one holds on to or allows to slip away; power is exercised from innumerable points, in the interplay of non-egalitarian and mobile relations.'[82] The power of the patriarch made (outward, societal) differentiation in South Asian male–male relationships unavoidable, except perhaps where two young boys or two women were involved. Nevertheless, Abru describes a beloved youth, lying 'under' his lover and ruling Delhi. Didn't this youth exercise power even in the 'interplay of non-egalitarian' relations? (Where the youth is perceived, from the outside, as lesser, and where he may actually hold more power, through his ability to say no to or otherwise influence his lover.) Power differentiation is a factor that should neither be overestimated nor underestimated.

The evidence surveyed in this article reveals that socially tolerated South Asian male–male eroticism was complex and affected by religious, age, status, gender, and caste differences. In homoerotic relations between youths or between women, such differentiations appear to have been of less consequence. The celebration of age-differentiated male–male eroticism in the Perso-Urdu tradition must be juxtaposed to the relative silence of native Mughal texts regarding female–female eroticism and both male and female gender variance. Nevertheless, travel accounts, artwork, and other sources reveal that such forms of eroticism were tolerated if not celebrated. Colonialism halted native tolerance towards both homoeroticism and gender variance. Postcolonial South Asia, has, unfortunately, continued these trends. Perhaps knowledge of past tolerance can serve as one factor to rid South Asia of intolerance today.

Figure 2. *Two Youths*. From the Fitzwilliam Album, Mughal, ca. 1555–60. Courtesy of the Fitzwilliam Museum, Cambridge, UK (161.1948).

Figure 3. *A Couple with an Attendant.* Persian, ca. 1540. Courtesy of Harvard University Art Museums, The Arthur M. Sackler Museum (1958.69).

Notes

1 South Asia is used to refer to the modern countries of Bangladesh, India, Nepal, Pakistan, and Sri Lanka. Ruth Vanita also notes cultural continuity between Pakistan and Afghanistan. 'Preface', *Same-Sex Love in India: Readings from Literature and History*, ed. Ruth Vanita and Saleem Kidwai (New York: St. Martin's Press, 2000), xv. I would like to thank Randolph Trumbach, Michael O'Rourke, and Katherine O'Donnell for generous help with this article; Ruth Vanita for insights into South Asian history shared over coffee and by e-mail; Serena Nanda and Michael Sweet for generously sharing bibliographic information. None of these scholars is responsible for any inaccuracies in this article.

2 John F. Richards, *The New Cambridge History of India*, vol. 1 part 5, *The Mughal Empire* (Cambridge: Cambridge University Press, 1993), 5.

3 Richards, *The Mughal Empire*, 8. He was a descendant of Timur, who was said to be a descendant of Ghenghiz Khan, and hence the dynasty was called Mughal (Mongol). John Keay, *India: A History* (New York: Grove Press, 2000), 290.

4 At its height of expansion in 1707, The Mughal empire spread from modern-day Afghanistan through most of South Asia (see the map in Keay, *India*, 314).

5 James Saslow, *Pictures and Passions: A History of Homosexuality in the Visual Arts* (New York: Viking Press, 1999), 149.

6 Sweet and Zwilling disagree with historians who create a 'romantically affirmative view of a special spiritual or social role for third-gender people.' Leonard Zwilling and Michael J. Sweet, 'The Evolution of Third-Sex Constructs in Ancient India: A Study in Ambiguity', in *Inverted Identities: The Interplay of Gender, Religion, and Politics in India*, ed. Julia Leslie and Mary McGee (Delhi: Oxford University Press, 2000), 124.

7 On the growth of homophobia in colonial and postcolonial India see Ruth Vanita, 'Introduction', *Queering India: Same-Sex Love and Eroticism in Indian Culture and Society*, ed. Ruth Vanita (New York: Routledge, 2002), 3ff., with refs.

8 Keay, *India*, 392ff.

9 Kidwai, 'Introduction: Medieval Materials in the Perso-Urdu Tradition', in *Same-Sex Love*, 111.

10 Kidwai, 'Introduction: Medieval Materials', 110.

11 *Babur-Namah: The Memoirs*, trans. Annette Susannah Beveridge (London: Luzac & Co., 1921), I:120.

12 Kidwai, 'Introduction: Medieval Materials', 111.

13 See Louis Crompton, 'Male Love and Islamic Law in Arab Spain', in *Islamic Homosexualities: Culture, History, and Literature*, ed. Stephen O. Murray and Will Roscoe (New York: New York University Press, 1997), 142–57, esp. 144.

14 Kidwai, 'Introduction: Medieval Materials', 118–19.

15 Tariq Rahman, 'Boy-Love in the Urdu Ghazal', *Annual of Urdu Studies* 7 (1990): 4.

16 C.M. Naim, 'The Theme of Homosexual (Pederastic) Love in Pre-Modern Urdu Poetry', in *Studies in Urdu Gazal and Prose Fiction* , ed. Umar Memon (Madison: University of Wisconsin Press, 1979), 122–3.

17 Rahman, 'Boy-Love', 4–5.
18 Kidwai, 'Introduction: Medieval Materials', 120.
19 Scott Kugle, 'Sultan Mahmud's Makeover: Colonial Homophobia and the Persian-Urdu Literary Tradition', in *Queering India*, 35.
20 Rahman, 'Boy-Love', 8.
21 Lawrence Cohen, 'The Pleasures of Castration: The Postopesative Status of Hijras, Thankas and Academics,' in *Sexual Nature, Sexual Culture* (Chicago: The University of Chicago Press, 1995), 281.
22 Naim, 'The Theme', 125–6.
23 Kidwai, trans. and Vanita, versification, ' "Abru": *Advice to a Beloved* (Urdu)', in *Same-Sex Love*, 166.
24 See Naim, 'The Theme', 125–6.
25 Richard Burton, *Sindh, and The Races that Inhabit the Valley of the Indus, with Notices of Topography and History of the Province* (London: W.H. Allen &Co., 1851), 284.
26 Niccolao Manucci, *Memoirs of the Mogul Court*, ed. Michael Edwardes, trans. William Irvine (1907; reprint, London: Folio Society, 1957), 36.
27 Daniel J. Ehnbom, *Indian Miniatures: The Ehrenfeld Collection* (New York: Hudson Hills Press, 1985), 205 (no. 99), 207 (no.101), 209 (no. 102), and 236 (no. 117).
28 See Susan Stronge, *Painting for the Mughal Emperor* (London: V&A Publications, 2002), passim. For example, the sons of the Emperor Shah Jahan are depicted wearing pearls, 155 (no. 117).
29 Manucci, *Memoirs*, 57.
30 On hierarchical masculinities, see R.W. Connell, *Masculinities* (Cambridge: Polity Press, 1995), 76ff.
31 Vanita, 'Preface', *Same-Sex Love*, xx–xxi. Vanita, 'Introduction', *Queering India*, 1 ff.
32 Vanita, 'Preface', xx–xxi.
33 Homoerotic portraits of women of similar ages touching one another have been published in various works, including Daniel J. Ehnbom, *Indian Miniatures: The Ehrenfeld Collection* (New York: Hudson Hills Press, 1985); no. 33; Alex Comfort, trans., *The Illustrated Koka Shastra: Being the Ratirahasya of Kokkaka and other Medieval Writings on Love* (London: Mitchell Beazley, 1997), 41; Giti Thadani, *Sakhiyani: Lesbian Desire in Ancient and Modern India* (London: Cassell, 1996), plates betw. 52–3, esp. last plate.
34 Michael Sweet, 'Eunuchs, Lesbians, and Other Mythical Beasts, Queering and Dequeering the *Kama Sutra*', in *Queering India*, 78.
35 Carolyn Dinshaw, 'Getting Medieval: *Pulp Fiction*, Gawain, Foucault', in *The Book and the Body*, ed. Dolores Warwick Frese and Katherine O'Brien-O'Keeffe (Notre Dame, Ind.: University of Notre Dame Press, 1997), 153–4, with refs. See also Carolyn Dinshaw, *Getting Medieval: Sexualities and Communities, Pre- and Postmodern* (Durham, NC: Duke University Press, 1999), 192–205 esp. 204.
36 Richard Burton, 'Terminal Essay', in *A Plain and Literal Translation of the Arabian Nights, or The Book of the Thousand Nights and a Night*, (London: Printed by the Burton Club for Private Subscribers Only, 1886), 10:237.
37 Trans.: Rahman, 'Boy-Love', 15.
38 See Rahman, 'Boy-Love', 4.

39 Milo Cleveland Beach, *Early Mughal Painting* (Cambridge: Harvard University Press, 1987), 39, 44, 46 no. 30.
40 Beach, *Early Mughal Painting*, 45, 46 no. 31.
41 Burton, 'Terminal Essay', 10: 233.
42 Kidwai, 'Introduction: Medieval Materials', 108.
43 See Scott Kugle, trans. and comm., '*Haqiqat al-Fuqara*: Poetic Biography of "Madho Lal" Hussayn (Persian)', in *Same-Sex Love*, 145–56.
44 Scott Kugle, trans. and comm., 'The Mirror of Secrets: "Akhi" Jamshed Rajgiri (Persian)', in *Same-Sex Love*, 136–9.
45 Kugle, 'Sultan Mahmud's Makeover', 35.
46 Indrani Chatterjee, 'Alienation, Intimacy, and Gender: Problems for a History of Love in South Asia', in *Queering India*, 62, 72–3.
47 *Ghalib: 1797–1869*, trans. and ed. Ralph Russell and Khurshidul Islam (Cambridge: Harvard University Press, 1969), 254.
48 Burton, 'Terminal Essay', 10:236–7.
49 Chatterjee, 'Alienation', 72–3.
50 Devdutt Pattanaik, *The Man Who Was a Woman and Other Queer Tales* (New York: Harrington Park Press, 2002), 15.
51 Will Roscoe, 'Precursors of Islamic Male Homosexualities', in *Islamic Homosexualities*, 62.
52 On pre-Islamic texts which discuss boy prostitutes, see Vanita, 'Introduction: Ancient Indian Materials', in *Same-Sex Love*, 27–8. On mutual embracing/oral sex between male citizens mentioned in the *Kama Sutra*, see Michael Sweet, 'Eunuchs, Lesbians, and Other Mythical Beasts', 80.
53 Serena Nanda, *Neither Man nor Woman: The Hijras of India* 2nd edn (1990; Belmont, CA: Wadsworth Publishing Co., 1999), 13–23.
54 Cohen, 'The Pleasures of Castration', 276–77.
55 Sebastien Manrique, *Travels of Fray Sebastien Manrique 1629–1643*, trans. C. Eckford and H. Hosten (1927; reprint, Nendeln, Lictenstein: Kraus Reprint, 1967), II: 240.
56 James Forbes, *Oriental Memoirs: A Narrative of Seventeen Years Residence in India* (London: Richard Bentley, 1834), I: 359. The Marathas were Hindus who rebelled against the Mughal empire and were successful in creating independent Hindu states in central India prior to British absorption of their lands. Keay, *India*, 331ff.
57 Lawrence Preston, 'The Right to Exist: Eunuchs and the State in Nineteenth-Century India', *Modern Asian Studies* 21:2 (1987): 373.
58 While some modern-day *hijras* come from 'scheduled' (previously called untouchable) castes, those interviewed by Serena Nanda were from low or middle caste backgrounds. All renounce the caste system and it's rigidity regarding intercaste dining. See Nanda, *Neither Man nor Woman*, 42, with refs.
59 Preston, 'The Right to Exist', 371–87.
60 Burton, 'Terminal Essay', 10:205, 205 no. 2.
61 From the diary of Charles Napier, quoted by Fawn Brody, *The Devil Drives: A Life of Sir Richard Burton* (London: Eyre & Spottiswoode Ltd, 1967), 66.
62 Saslow, *Pictures and Passions*, 126 Fig 4.1.

63 Kokkoka, *The Illustrated Koka Shastra*: *being the Retirahasya of Kokkaka and other Medieval Writings on Love*, trans. by Alex Comfort, preface by W.G. Archer (2nd edn, London: Mitchell Beazley, 1997), 101.
64 Vanita, 'Vatsyayana's *Kamasutra*', in *Same-Sex Love*, 50. See 48–50 for further explanation. Vanita does note that Danielou incorrectly translates the term *svairini* as 'lesbian,' however, because the identity of the svairini is based upon a preference for taking an active role in sex.
65 *The Holy Qur'ān: Text Translation and Commentary*, trans. and ed. A.Yusuf Ali, rev. edn (Brentwood, MD: Amana, 1989), I:189 no. 523.
66 Kidwai, 'Introduction: Medieval Materials', 110.
67 For more on this subject, see Walter Penrose, 'Hidden in History: Female Homoeroticism and Women of a "Third Nature" in the South Asian Past', *Journal of the History of Sexuality* 10:1 (2001), 3–39, esp. 29.
68 Michael Sweet and Leonard Zwilling translate *narisandha* and similar terms as 'masculine lesbian female', 'The First Medicalization: The taxonomy and Etiology of Queerness in Classical Indian Medicine', *Journal of the History of Sexuality* 3:4 (April 1993), 593, 597. See also Thadani, *Sakhiyani*, 58–9.
69 Manucci, *Memoirs*, 41.
70 Francois Bernier, *Travels in the Mogul Empire AD 1656–1668*, trans. and annotated by Archibald Constable on the basis of Irving Brock's version (2nd edn, Delhi: Low Price Publications, 1989), 122–3; 372.
71 Chatterjee, in *Queering India*, 70.
72 Willam Knighton, *The Private Life of an Eastern King. Together with Elihu Jan's Story, or The Private Life of an Eastern Queen.* (1855; reprint, New York: Redfield 1921), 132. See Penrose, 'Hidden in History', 28–30, with refs and further discussion.
73 See Penrose, 'Hidden in History', passim.
74 Manucci, *Memoirs*, 37.
75 W. G. Osborne, *The Court and Camp of Runjeet Sing* (1840; reprint, Delhi: Heritage Publishers, 1973), 96.
76 See Penrose, 'Hidden in History', 30–6.
77 See *Same-Sex Love*, passim; and *Queering India*, passim.
78 On the appropriation of the ideology of the British by the Indian nationalist/post-colonial movement, see Thadani, *Sakhiyani*, 68ff; Vanita and Kidwai, 'Introduction: Modern Indian Materials', in *Same-Sex Love*, 191–217; *Queering India*, passim.
79 For further discussion of the problematic use of the category queer with Indian historical materials, see Vanita, 'Preface', *Same-Sex Love*, xxi.
80 *Queering India.*
81 Carolyn Dinshaw, 'Got Medieval', *Journal of the History of Sexuality* 10:2 (2001), 202–12, esp. 203–4. See further Dinshaw, *Getting Medieval*, 136–40.
82 Michel Foucault, *The History of Sexuality*, vol.1, *An Introduction*, trans. by Robert Hurley (1978; reprint, New York: Vintage Books, 1990), 94.

10
Colonial Latin America

Martin Austin Nesvig

In 1968 José Costa Pôrto completed *Nos tempos do Visitador,* an important social history of the earliest permanent Portuguese colony in Brazil in Pernambuco and Bahia, analyzing a broad range of political, cultural, religious, and administrative structures of this formative world. In addition to correspondence and governmental archival material, the study utilizes the archives of the Portuguese Inquisition that was established soon after the permanent settlement of Brazil. He argues that inquisitional material can elucidate cultural history found 'between the lines, on the fringes, in marginal aspects' of documentary material.[1] A great deal has changed since 1968, and for our purposes, the notion that one might write a history 'between the lines' and on the 'fringes' is especially important. After all, homosexuality in the early modern Hispanic world was always considered deviant and marginal. In the three decades since the appearance of Costa Pôrto's work, a nascent historiography of male friendship and homosexuality in early modern Latin America has emerged.

In 1968 there existed no scholarship on homosexuality in early modern Latin America. In the context of the late 1960s historians who might have been interested in the history of homosexuality might have considered a wide array of materials, but such study was considered unmentionable. In fact, the moniker 'the sin that could not be named' has its roots in Latin–Hispanic religious culture – the term used for homosexuality, the 'nefarious vice,' or *pecado nefando* (from the Latin, *peccatus nefandus*), literally means the sin that must not be mentioned. Eventually, the scholarship that appeared after 1970 erased this censure, and it is now fast becoming a standard part of the historiographic corpus of early modern Latin America.

The purpose of this chapter is to review this emergent scholarship. Thereafter, it will conclude with a reflection on the possibilities for future research on Latin American homosexuality. In due course certain central thematic and methodological questions will arise: What kinds of sources have been overlooked? How might new and previously unused sources be applied to a new scholarship? What theoretical frameworks might be useful in studying the history of homosexuality and male friendship in early modern Latin America?

The question of evidence and sources necessarily lies at the center of these considerations, precisely because the scarcity of extant sources renders the historical interpretation of male friendship complex with many logistical difficulties. Moreover, the nascent quality of the historiography elides many opportunities for syntheses and necessitates looking to European historiography for theoretical models. This often means looking to the debates on the 'new' cultural history and the anti-positivist postmodernist conception that blurs the distinction between 'what happened' and the manner in which the past is recorded. Indeed, many scholars of early modern Latin American homosexuality wrestle quite consciously over the dilemma of the realistic reconstruction of action as opposed to the study of collective representations. The lack of narratives by gay men, the issues of the 'filtration' of sources through those who wrote about the 'objects' of crime and sin, and the overall scarcity of material contribute to this dilemma. Consequently, theoretical models of gender and sexuality retain considerable allure in this field.

Two long-cherished assumptions about patriarchy and male-dominated sexuality inform a great deal of the overall historiography on homosexuality in Latin America. First, the honor–shame paradigm of Latin American and Mediterranean societies suggests that sexuality is a key component in its overall system. Julian Pitt-Rivers offers the classic formulation, arguing that penetration is the overriding metaphor for sexual and familial honor and as such women must remain virgins before marriage to save honor and men must never be sexually penetrated.[2] Numerous Latin American historians of women have shown that this framework inheres in domestic and marital culture; however, strategies for eluding or flummoxing social values abounded in early modern Latin America, even if the social values themselves were always ostensibly held in high regard.[3] The problem for the subject of homosexuality is that sexual metaphors and the honor–shame model do not always map neatly onto male–male sexual interaction. The result is that many have taken the male–female honor–shame paradigm as a strict corollary for the active-'male'-penetrator and passive-'female'-penetrated axis of male homosexual sexual encounters. Such a model assumes that only the passive partner incurs social stigma while the active partner is considered normal.

The Mexican poet and essayist Octavio Paz offered the second prototype on which scholars have drawn for theoretical guidance in his discussion of the 'hijos de la chingada' ('sons of the fucked bitch').[4] His propositions about the essential nature of Mexican sexual identity have cast a tremendous shadow over the historiography and ethnography of Mexican and Latin American sexuality.[5] In 'The Sons of la Malinche' he argues that the immutable characteristic both of Mexican sexuality and genealogical identity is bastardhood. According to Paz, Malinche, the Indian mistress of Cortés, forsook 'her people,' leaving the resultant Mexicans. Thus Malinche became *la chingada* who abandoned her offspring. According to this logic, to offer oneself passively (via intercourse) is akin to defeat and degradation, and to be the sexually active partner, correspondingly, is to be a victor. Extending the metaphor of sexual penetration for conquest and domination, Paz contends in the essay 'Mexican Masks' that homosexuality in Mexico operates according to a system in which the passive partners are denounced and the active partners are 'tolerated' insofar as they satisfy their male nature through penetration of a passive body.[6]

Anthropologists and sociologists describe such a 'system' of homosexual behavior as the 'Latino-Mediterranean' or 'gender-stratified' system.[7] The female in this construction is equated with passivity, disenfranchisement, receptivity, and helplessness. The male, likewise, is equated with agency, power, penetration, and dominance. Furthermore, because this system operates supposedly in cultures that place a premium on masculine honor, to take the passive role and 'become female' is to lose one's male honor.

With these theoretical models in mind, this essay will outline some of the important works that have been undertaken for the early modern period in Latin America. While disparate and embryonic, this scholarship analyzes the assumptions about the social and political structures flanking male–male sexuality. Additionally, the current scholarship offers potential foundations for a more robust field of study given the subject's acceptance among mainstream historians of Latin America. Indeed, in a recent volume of the leading journal of Latin American history, the *Hispanic American Historical Review*, editor Gilbert Joseph argues that the historical analysis of gender and sexuality represents a 'revolution in our time,' noting that homosexuality has been added to the standard Latin American historiographic corpus.[8]

Brazil

Two historians stand out as the most important scholars to have opened the doorway to studies of homosexuality in colonial Brazil. Indeed, before the subject was given serious scholarly attention in the Spanish Americas, Luiz Mott had begun an impressive and important body of investigation into sodomy, gay identity, and male friendship in colonial Brazil. Trained originally as an anthropologist, Mott turns his cultural attention to the questions elided by Costa Pôrto. In Mott's work questions about sodomy, religion, and morality can never be separated from questions of power, reflecting his reliance on the cultural philosophy of Michel Foucault. For Mott, as for Foucault, 'discourses of power' are intricately intertwined with both political mechanisms and cultural attitudes.[9] At his best in providing descriptive chronological history, Mott's essay 'Misadventures of a Portuguese Sodomite in Seventeenth-Century Brazil' is a tour-de-force narrative and accurately represents Mott's impressive body of work. Based on a large cache of Inquisition documents from Bahia, Rio, and Lisbon, Mott reconstructs the tale of Luiz Delgado, a libertine tobacco merchant, who was ultimately arrested in Brazil and sent to Lisbon to face the Holy Office. Authorities had questioned Delgado on several occasions, who was often given relatively light sentences for sodomy (at least compared with execution). In one case he was sentenced to exile for having committed the 'nefarious vice' with a young boy.[10]

The details provided by the Inquisition were often lurid, and Mott recapitulates the graphic and formulaic discourse of the Inquisition. Conviction hinged on a purely physical definition of sodomy. For example, intercourse without ejaculation was considered 'incomplete sodomy' and was less severely punished.[11] Contrary to Mott's claims, however, the Portuguese Inquisition, like its Spanish counterpart, made little inference about the inherent sexual orientation of the person accused of the 'crime against nature,' only to say that the man had violated nature and religion. Indeed, the legal–religious designation of sodomy included not only male–male encounters, but also any sexual activity outside of male–female missionary position intercourse, including, but not limited to, heterosexual anal and oral sex and female–female sex.[12] Consequently, the Inquisition did not distinguish between homosexuals or heterosexuals as a matter of law but of culture, since it was generally agreed that homosexual sodomy was worse than its heterosexual counterpart. As Emanuel Araújo shows, Portuguese law (applicable in colonial Brazil) construed sodomy, whether heterosexual or homosexual, as a violation of the order of procreation and called for equal penalties for both.[13]

Using the same documents as did Costa Pôrto, Mott provides distinctly different stories in 'Racial Relations between Homosexuals in Colonial Brazil,' compiling a registry of the sodomy cases brought before the Holy Office in Pernambuco, tabulating the race, sex-role preference (whether active or passive), and the racial combinations of sodomitical unions. The inclusion of sodomy in the historical analysis shows how things have changed since 1968: homosexuality has gained a certain respectability in scholarly circles in Brazil.

While Mott's work is important and perspicacious, it is not beyond criticism for its approach to Inquisition documents and as a methodology for a history of homosexuality in general. For example, in 'Racial Relations,' and another article, 'Captive Sex,' Mott spans a wide time frame in striving to prove the universal character of African homosexuality. Accordingly, he uses the twentieth-century anthropological scholarship along with travelers' reports from the eighteenth and nineteenth centuries to explain behaviors for sixteenth-century Brazil.[14] Nor are Mott's conclusions about the inter-ethnic nature of sodomy much more compelling. He uses a total of 46 cases from Pernambuco to talk about sodomy and concludes that white men were able to exploit their status in forcing themselves on non-white men. Mott thus resolves that white men would sexually penetrate the blacks to dominate them socially and politically. For example, he endeavors to prove this by showing that four *mulatos* were accused of being the active partner and that eight were accused of being the passive partner.[15] A difference of four cases for a 30-year period hardly proves that white men used anal penetration of non-whites to reinstate 'the hierarchic parameters of the white as dominator,' as Mott suggests.[16] Indeed, many white men had been accused of being the passive partner in sodomy with an active partner who was black.[17]

A frequent refrain of Mott is that men accused of sodomy in the sixteenth and seventeenth centuries were 'gay,' employing this term interchangeably with that of sodomite and 'fanchono.' Mott cites John Boswell for his authority on the use of the term gay as appropriate for this period and culture, arguing that Boswell had shown that the word gay was used in thirteenth-century Catalan, which spans centuries and cultures.[18] Even if one accepts the linguistic argument, Mott's insistence on the concept of gay men in colonial Brazil remains problematic. Did these men really conceive of themselves as gay? Boswell points out that the term gay properly refers to men who have an exclusive attraction for men.[19]

This 'essentialist' evaluation of homosexuality devolves not only from his data but also from Mott's highly political view of scholarship. In his work he invokes a debate well worth having: how people formerly reduced to 'object' status have now become academics in their own right. But for Mott, this means that 'blacks, women, homosexuals, Indians ... are the preferred spokespersons of their people.'[20] Therefore, ethnic property belongs to the 'oppressed,' and only to their particular form of oppression: blacks must own black history; gays must own gay history. The result is that Mott's vitriolic prose detracts from the force of his arguments, and he occasionally is merely chauvinistic and proprietary, claiming, in effect, that only gay men should be allowed to write the history of homosexuality.

In *Tropic of Sins*, Ronaldo Vainfas renders a more even-handed approach to the question of the Inquisition in Brazil. While he and Mott deal with many of the same stories, Vainfas is clearly less interested in using his historical examination for political purposes. Instead, Vainfas attempts to understand the relationship between law, ecclesiastical dogma, civil ordinances, and popular mentality and behavior.[21] Accordingly, he provides one of the best recent explorations of the tensions and the gaps between Church policy and everyday behavior, demonstrating that the expectations of the sixteenth and seventeenth-century Church for sexual mores were rarely met by the actions or even the beliefs of Brazilians.[22] Vainfas is similarly convincing in his assessment that the denunciation of sodomy was not always about the denunciation of a sodomite, but of the act.

Vainfas provides two important contributions to the history of homosexuality. He argues that the tremendous penalties for sodomy coupled with the effectiveness of rural Inquisitions predisposed most people to avoid sodomy for fear of the bonfire. Moreover, urban settings like Lisbon, Madrid, Venice, and Paris, as well as Mexico City, Lima, and Puebla, lent themselves to greater anonymity. Thus bathhouses and bars were places where sodomites could congregate. Using secret language and coded behaviors and dress, urban sodomites might more easily avoid denunciation, suggesting that the lack of sophisticated urban milieux and the dominance of rural, plantation society prevented the growth of an organized sodomite subculture in Brazil.[23]

The second important contribution of Vainfas' study is the suggestion that bisexuality was much more common than many scholars, like Mott and Boswell, have been willing to admit. Indeed, Vainfas seems to point out the obvious when he reminds the reader that many of the men accused of sodomy were married or engaged to women. This does not prove they were not exclusively interested in men while using marriage as a shield, but it does complicate the proposition of such men being 'gay.' This is fraught with complexity, for it hinges on the man's personal conception of himself, and as such may ultimately be inaccessible to the historian. Functionally, however, Vainfas is correct to call such men bisexual in the sense that they did not dedicate their entire lives to sodomy as an erotic expression.[24]

A third scholar who has touched on homosexuality in colonial Brazil, though to a lesser extent, is the above-mentioned Emanuel Araújo. Like Mott and Vainfas he depicts the nexus of moral and religious condemnation of homosexuality with its apparent frequency in colonial Brazil. His is a more legally oriented study and places emphasis on the ways that law overlapped with and drew upon the religious view of homosexuality. In his study *The Theater of Vices*, Araújo offers a succinct overview of the way that Portuguese law adopted a theological metaphysics and anthropology of sodomy. This understanding drew first on Paul's epistle to the Corinthians where he says that neither fornicators, adulterers nor sodomites will inherit the kingdom of heaven (I Corinthians 6) and was essentially codified by Aquinas in his *Summa Theologiae*. A religious exegesis may seem strange to a twenty-first-century reader, but in Iberian law there was never a division between religion and religious 'truths' and law since Iberian jurists always construed the latter as a redaction of divine truths.[25] Araújo offers a concise summary of this tradition and its relationship to the behavior and prosecution of homosexuality in colonial Brazil.

The work by Mott, Vainfas and Araújo suggests new avenues for both the history of mentality and homosexuality in other contexts, with their assiduous eye for detail and the difficulties in examining a topic usually left out of both the historical and historiographic record. Their ability to recount not only the aspects of inquisitional investigation but also their attention to the ways that such investigation reveal details germane to social history have given flower to Costa Pôrto's suggestion that 'between the lines' one might reconstruct the mental and social world of people otherwise accused of crimes.[26]

Likewise, Vainfas' discussions of sodomy demonstrate the difficulties encompassed in simple inversion of elite sources. Some people rejected

Church teachings while simultaneously accepting other aspects of them. For most people, the world was fraught with more inconsistency than the supposed elite-popular dichotomy suggests. As Vainfas argues, if Portuguese settlers engaged in fornication and concubinage on a wide scale, they did not do so without understanding that they violated Church teachings and morality.[27] Ultimately, the relationship between sexual behavior and Church injunctions was paradoxical and did not always amount to simple rejection of or adherence to the rules but revealed a fluid terrain where people struggled to understand their world as well as the teachings of the Church.

Spanish America

Like the scholarship on Brazil, that on the Spanish Americas continues to emerge. The overall historiography for Latin America witnessed an explosion of social history in the 1960s and 1970s; and, like the case of Brazil, no one wanted to discuss homosexuality at that time. For example, one of North America's leading practitioners of the social history of colonial Mexico, Richard Greenleaf, had nothing to say about homosexuality, even though the Inquisition archives he relied on contains cases of sodomy.[28]

One of the important issues for histories of homosexuality in the Spanish Americas is law and the boundaries of jurisdiction for prosecuting sodomy, since this is where the bulk of archival material on homosexuality can be found. Because Peru and New Spain (and later, New Granada and the River Plate) were viceroyalties with the same legal and administrative privilege and status as viceroyalties in Europe like Castile or Naples,[29] Spanish law applied to the Spanish Americas, even if often the theory missed the mark of the practice.[30] Unlike Brazil, however, the question of jurisdiction over the 'crime' of sodomy was more complicated in the Spanish Americas. A short case serves to highlight this. In October 1625, in Guadalajara, three men provided testimony to the representative of the Mexican Inquisition, condemning a 'known sodomite' who should therefore be prosecuted as such by the Holy Office. The sworn testimonies, along with a cover letter urging a formal arrest and trial, were then forwarded to the Inquisitor for his consideration. The response from the Inquisitor is quite astonishing. On December 16, 1625, in a tersely worded letter that amounts to a legislative fiat, the Inquisitor, Francisco Bazán de Albornoz, replied tersely that the Inquisition did not prosecute sodomy.[31] There ended the proceeding, and the case faded out of the historical record. On the other hand, in 1659, 14 young men were burned alive in a public spectacle in Mexico after having been convicted by civil authorities.[32] Yet we have no extant evidence of other similar civil proceedings against sodomites in colonial Latin America.

No one is quite sure where the boundaries of jurisdiction began and ended for the crime of sodomy. In Spain jurisdiction was locally determined and whereas some inquisitional tribunals were vigorous in prosecuting sodomy, like Valencia and Aragon, others, like Castile, virtually ignored it.[33] Lack of historical investigation into jurisdiction and a paucity of sources obscure the case of the Spanish Americas even more than that of the metropole. Nevertheless, numerous ambitious works have come to grapple with the questions of homosexuality, male friendship, and sodomitical 'culture' in colonial Spanish America from which we can draw some provisional conclusions. First, sodomy was far from acceptable. In fact, it was considered the most heinous offense to God, Crown, and society imaginable, at least if one trusts the elite and official sources. Likewise, there was a distinction between the active and passive partners. This seems to have been largely a functional distinction and in fact the active partner seems to have been considered even guiltier from the point of view of natural law and Aristotelian metaphysics. As in the case of Portuguese law, Spanish law relied on the religious view that any sexual activity that did not have procreation as its goal was a sin against nature and a violation of the Sixth Commandment.[34]

Despite the absence of a legal distinction between active and passive partners, some historians insist on the corollary of the honor–shame model that suggests that the passive partner is rendered female and the active partner escapes opprobrium. The most forceful proponent for an ideology of strict active–passive identities in the Spanish Americas is Richard Trexler, who published such a theory under the aptly titled book, *Sex and Conquest*.[35] Written in a polemic tone, Trexler ignores a vast body of early-modern theological and natural law scholarship, archival evidence, and important secondary material to conclude (dubiously) that all sex is rape. This is a somewhat clichéd rendering of the Andrea Dworkin dogma that assumes that given the opportunity all men would be rapists and that intercourse is necessarily a reflection of patriarchal values.[36] Thus Trexler attempts to prove the corollary of the Paz mythology with syllogism rather than with evidence. His logic can be summarized: if all intercourse is rape and conquest was fraught with sexual symbolism and actual rape, then conquest *is* rape and therefore to penetrate is to conquer; ergo, the penetrator is a conqueror and is free of all stigma regardless of the sex of the penetrated partner. Unfortunately, Trexler offers scant evidence for this conclusion.

The discussion of the active-passive issue was not absent from contemporaneous jurisprudential or theological discussions. The problem is that legal and religious writers of the early modern period never made any *moral* distinction between the active and passive partners. Both, in their view, were guilty of the sin against nature. Iberian law reflects some of the official attitudes common in the Spanish Americas concerning homosexuality. For example, the jurist Gregorio López furnished the authoritative gloss to the 1576 Salamanca edition of the *Siete Partidas*, a thirteenth-century law code promulgated by the king of Castile, Alfonso the Wise, which held considerable sway in civil proceedings.[37] Predictably, López considered homosexual sodomy to be the most heinous variety of this crime, and male sodomites were therefore to be executed. Another influential legal glossator to comment on sodomy was Antonio Gómez, who, in his gloss on the Laws of Toro, defined sodomy as being when 'someone realizes carnal access that is not oriented to natural coitus and procreation.'[38] Similarly, Gómez understood homosexual sodomy as the worst variety of the crime/sin against nature, recommending death and the confiscation of property for male sodomites. In a twist that many scholars overlook, Gómez reasoned that the penalty was as applicable for the 'agent' (or active, insertive partner) as for the 'patient' (or passive, receptive partner).[39] Furthermore, if the passive partner was significantly younger than the active partner, he might be considered a victim of rape and therefore less guilty of sodomy. In fact, the seventh *Partida* reasoned that a male under the age of fourteen who had been anally penetrated could not be guilty of sodomy as a matter of law.[40]

The debate over sex-role is not the only issue to engage scholars of early modern Latin American homosexuality. In the chronological sense, the first important work on homosexuality in the Spanish Americas came from Serge Gruzinski, who discussed the notorious 1658–59 case in Mexico City mentioned above. Gruzinski's use of the archival material is largely in a quantitative social history vein, noting that over 100 men were arrested, detained or questioned in this trial, conducted by the civil authorities. Gruzinski made some important conclusions in this essay.[41] First, like Vainfas, Gruzinski suggests that homosexuality and sodomitical cultures were urban, and not rural, phenomena in the Spanish American world. Second, Gruzinski shows that there was a clear preference for the 'age-stratified' system of homosexuality in which older men take the active role with younger passive partners, much as was seen in Renaissance Florence and ancient Greece.[42] Third, Gruzinski lends weight to the possibility that such interaction was often commercial and that many of the younger men taking the passive role were prostitutes.

In his unpublished dissertation, 'Criminal Sexuality in Central Mexico, 1750–1850,' Lee Penyak also addresses the question of a 'sodomitical culture' in Spanish America.[43] This important work outlines some basic archival sources and conclusions about male homosexuality for this time period. Penyak utilized the Mexican Inquisition records as well as some civil court cases to offer a provisory portrait of deviant sexual practices. One chapter specifically looks at the issue of sodomy, offering some caveats about the social history of homosexuality that seem to contradict the conclusions of Vainfas, Gruzinski, and others – or at least diverge from them in the late colonial Mexican context. For example, Penyak argues that there is no evidence that homosexual men 'established their own sub-culture.' Secondly, he shows that 'societal condemnation of homosexuality remained strong in Mexico' until 1850.[44] Third, he argues that priests were punished less severely than laymen, though the evidence for this conclusion does not appear especially strong, given the fact that Iberian and Mexican tribunals lessened penalties for sodomy across the board in this period. Finally, Penyak argues that homosexual men led furtive lives with little contact with a broader homosexual community. Penyak also adds important investigative clues for future research. He shows that one may in fact use archival materials to discuss this issue and scholars may find that civil and ecclesiastical court archives of other parts of Latin America may offer similar caches of documentation.

Because the scholarship for this period is sporadic, there is little thematic or chronological unity. Two essays on homosexuality among Native Americans merit attention. Geoffrey Kimball discusses the Aztec social 'construction' of homosexuality using some documents suggesting that the passive role in homosexual intercourse was reserved for special opprobrium for its abnegation of masculinity. Kimball uses such a small sample that his analysis does not necessarily provide a complete portrait of Aztec sexual values. Nonetheless, he mentions briefly the development concerning sexual passivity as the equivalent of losing male honor. This essay is an important beginning for some discussion of the earliest forms of homosexuality in Spanish America, but it is also so slight that we really only have a brief entrée.[45]

In an essay on the Maya, Pete Sigal evinces considerable sophistication in his treatment of the 'politicization of pederasty.' He examines

Mayan histories of their life in this time period to show how homosexual intercourse took on political, social, and ritual significance. Accordingly, Sigal is interested in how homosexually-charged dialogue in ritual persisted despite Spanish prohibitions to the contrary. Homosexual desire among the colonial Yucatecan Maya was politicized to the extent that older men employed intercourse with younger men as a way of demonstrating their status and prestige. This was seen as more or less acceptable, as long as it was understood that it held ritual and age-specific meaning. In due course older men penetrated younger men, assuming a teacher role and imparting a patron–client relationship between an older, active-partner man and a younger, passive-partner adolescent boy. This type of 'pederasty' also rested on the assumption that it was unacceptable for an older man to be penetrated. Sigal uses indigenous language sources to examine the question of pederasty (homosexuality) in Mexico, potentially opening an entirely new area of study that has been ignored by previous historians.[46]

A recent study has added further material to the historiography of Spanish America. *Vir: Conceptions of Manliness in Andalucía and México, 1561–1699* by Federico Garza-Carvajal is an important contribution to the growing field on Latin American homosexuality, adding to this increasingly sophisticated body of historiography in ambitious ways. Based largely on civil court cases against men for male–male sexual activity, this book traces both a social and legal history. Significantly, this is one of the first full-length monographs on homosexuality in colonial Latin America.[47]

The chapters are arranged thematically and each is organized around a vignette or theoretical sounding-point. First and foremost the book examines the prosecution and religious condemnation of homosexuality in the early modern Hispanic context. In the two introductory chapters the authors explains that understanding the Hispanic 'construction' of homosexuality requires more than a social or intellectual history but must encompass the overall goals of Spanish imperialism. Therefore, understanding homosexuality in early modern Spain and Mexico can only be done if one understands the overall context – of resurgent scholastic theology, Spanish imperialism, and anti-Semitism. The introductory chapters outline the author's thesis that negative attitudes toward homosexuality were a mixture of xenophobia and religious mentality. In short, sodomy was seen as a kind of cancer that infected the body politic.[48]

Chapter one of *Vir* provides a résumé of the problem of writing the history of homosexuality, rejecting a transhistorical 'gay identity' thesis in favor of a historicized identity of 'sodomites.' Chapter two offers a lucid summary of the arguments surrounding sodomy among moralists, theologians, and jurists. Heretofore such a summary has only been available in Spanish, and Garza Carvajal provides a valuable service to the academic community in this solid review. Chapters three and four are more prosaic, with narrative analysis of the bulk of his archival findings. These offer fascinating glimpses not only into the culture of homosexuality for this period but also into the collective mentality of legal and theological opponents of homosexuality. Finally, Garza Carvajal provides transcriptions of excerpts from many of his cases – civil court proceedings dispersed throughout the Spanish empire.[49]

The scope and ambition of *Vir* is impressive, not least because no one thus far has provided the extent of archival analysis of homosexuality for Spanish America that Garza Carvajal offers here, and this will be the enduring value of this study. The transcriptions alone offer a wealth of primary source material that can be used in classrooms. Moreover, this study is often audacious, and the author is unafraid to challenge some of the field's senior scholars in their assumptions about sexuality in early modern Latin America. For example, Garza Carvajal takes aim at the overly 'Creole' focus of many previous works on sexuality in Latin America insisting instead that a history of homosexuality for colonial Mexico can only be understood in the context of imperial endeavors.[50] This study is bound to generate debate and discussion which may be the best contribution such a study can make given the emerging strength of this field.

In concluding this brief summary of material on the Spanish Americas, the scandal of 1658–59 discussed by Gruzinski (and also by Garza Carvajal in *Vir*) demonstrates some of the difficulties of this research. The only apparent extant record of this sensational event are brief letters from the viceroy, the Duke of Albuquerque, and the prosecutor, Juan Manuel de Sotomayor, now located in the Archive of the Indies in Seville.[51] Both Gruzinski and Garza Carvajal draw on this correspondence in reconstructing the social world of these men, and both draw out the connections, intimate affairs, and partners of these men.[52] One of the complications of Gruzinski's and Garza's essays is typical of scholarship for this period. Since we do not have the original trial transcripts it is difficult to know exactly what transpired in this case. Nevertheless, these two essays show the civil authorities reviled sodomy for the same reasons as the theologians: homosexuality was a crime against nature, God, and the Crown. Furthermore, homosexuality was identified as effeminizing, regardless of the role on took in sexual intercourse. Interestingly, though, the case shows that the active partners identified their passive partners as their 'female' lovers.[53] In any case the trial and execution of the young men in 1659 remains shadowy. We lack the original trial material and have to rely on correspondence. Nevertheless, with the discussions by Gruzinski and Garza Carvajal we have some brief snapshots of the social history of homosexuality in colonial Spanish America that may be found in other archival and printed sources outside of Seville.

Theoretical questions

A variety of theoretical issues arise from this cursory review of the available scholarship on early modern Latin America. Many of these are addressed in the literature but, given the relatively narrow scope of this historiography when compared to that dealing with Europe, many of the theoretical questions were first developed in the latter context. Perhaps the most pressing from the point of view of historians and their craft is the issue surrounding sources. Can we trust sources when they discuss crime and stigmatized sexual behavior? Long a mainstay of the 'new' cultural history to emerge in the 1980s, as well as a frequent refrain of 'post-structuralist' analysis, the debate on truth in history as seen through sources is hardly new.[54] Yet for the question of homosexuality in early modern Latin America, this debate has only recently been examined. Recent work on the early inquisitions in Languedoc and Italy suggests that confession does not necessarily represent 'truth' and that we should be wary of criminal testimony.[55] Emmanuel LeRoy Ladurie offers the counterpoint to such a view in his study of the same region, attempting the reconstruction of a peasant village – from social and political structures, to food, sex, and folk religion – by relying almost exclusively on Inquisition testimony.[56] In addition to the question of truth from testimony in criminal trials, there is a correlative issue of power. Examined by a variety of Italian scholars in the journal *Quaderni Storici*, Guido Ruggiero and Edward Muir collected a volume under the title *History from Crime*.[57] Among these essays and the introduction, the suggestion that cultural values and behaviors can be determined from criminal testimony emerges. But whereas Given argues against any truth in testimony under duress, the *History from Crime* collection presents a shift in analysis, suggesting that historians look as well to the content of the questions being asked of witnesses.

The questions of truth, testimony, and power fall squarely into the milieu of a history of homosexuality in Latin America precisely because sodomy was considered such a heinous crime. Mott's work suggests that in Portuguese inquisitional testimony we may find narrative histories of unique men, therein unlocking an important clue to the overall personal history of male friendship in Latin America.[58] Others view such an assumption with skepticism – notably Garza Carvajal, who argues that criminal testimony shows us more about the mentality of the accusers than of the accused.[59] My own suggestion is that something of a middle path may be discerned between the two. While it is true that the prospect of execution was very real, we must also consider the fact that under Inquisitional law, confession was a means of escaping an execution. We must also distinguish between ecclesiastical tribunals and civil law courts, since the latter were notoriously more violent and meted out traditionally much more severe penalties, the stereotypes of the Black Legend of Spanish Cruelty notwithstanding.[60] Finally, in criminal case law we have the opportunity to mine very carefully the jurisprudential and religious framework of Latin American society. True, it may not tell us much about the sodomites themselves, but it reveals quite clearly the ideology of an imperial society bent on orthodoxy and sexual purity.

Guido Ruggiero proposed a second important theoretical dilemma for the Latin-Catholic world. In his essay on homosexuality in Renaissance Venice, he argued that one could discern a distinct sodomitical subculture in this city.[61] This theory has spawned a great deal of debate. Gruzinski and Mott suggest a theory along the lines of Ruggiero's sodomitical subculture.[62] Vainfas argues that in a rural culture like Brazil the opportunity for an organized sub- or parallel culture of homosexuality was virtually impossible.[63] Rather, he contends that only urban settings were capable of allowing such a social milieu to develop – in bathhouses, cantinas, plazas, streets, and brothels. Penyak, however, rejects almost entirely the notion that men in colonial Latin America would have organized a community or separate culture.[64] Unfortunately, as intriguing as these suggestions may be, there is to date simply too little information to provide a strong argument pro or contra. Rather, fine-grained analysis of both rural and urban milieux and the prevalence (or absence) of sodomitical communities are needed to demonstrate any conclusive evidence on this score.

Third, the debate on gay identity has always been in the forefront of the historical scholarship for Latin America. Mott is the most forceful proponent of the notion that men who had sex with men in colonial

Brazil can accurately be called gay. As I have noted above, I find his evidence for this conclusion weak. Nevertheless, the idea that men may have thought of themselves as unique, queer, or something along these lines, is not entirely impossible. Randolph Trumbach is the stalwart opponent of this view and has argued effectively against it for three decades in one of the literature's most impressive scholarly oeuvres, suggesting that the emergence of the homosexual as a unique cultural type and self-aware entity is a modern phenomenon occurring in the eighteenth century.[65] But we must ask ourselves whether Boswell's or Trumbach's views are themselves essentialized. After all, it may be possible that while in eighteenth-century London men who practiced sodomy did not consider themselves to be sodomites, in other contexts this may be different. Sigal's work on the Yucatecan Maya shows that there were age-specific identities in homosexual activity.[66] Nevertheless, the suggestion that men in colonial Latin America would have understood a modern political 'gay' identity, as Mott suggests, seems far-fetched and implausible. The question remains the extent to which such men understood or lacked a distinct identity.

The dilemma of 'gay' versus socially constructed sodomite leads us to a fourth theoretical issue. Did having sex with another man, or developing a romantic relationship with another man, mean the same thing as it might mean today? Vainfas has the most satisfying explanation to this by arguing that such men might be more accurately termed functionally bisexual.[67] Across the board men in colonial Latin America who register in the historical record as having practiced sodomy were married or involved with a woman. The secondary debate here is one of sex-role – whether passive or active. There can be no doubt that Hispanic society placed a heavy emphasis on the division of sex-roles and can be generally considered a 'machista' society.[68] However, no one has been able to prove that such a strict hierarchy of male–female, active–passive, dominant–submissive, was exactly transferred to male–male sexual and romantic encounters.

Finally, situational homosexuality may offer numerous explanations for male–male friendship and sexual activity in colonial Latin America. The elevation of the hymen as social (and indeed economic) capital was an important part of the calculus of colonial Latin American social life. An intact hymen in a bride was considered important and its importance rose concomitantly with social status. Accordingly, female prostitution was frequently tolerated and often officially codified.[69] But many men may have simply wished to get it cheaper. This is, after all, Trexler's thesis concerning the *berdache* – a boy-woman who fulfilled the role of community whore in order to protect the hymens and social purity of unwed girls.[70] Such a system may very well have been adopted in colonial Latin America. We know that situational homosexuality was practiced to a limited extent on the Spanish fleets that sailed between Spain and the Americas.[71] The problem with assumptions about the frequency of situational homosexuality occurs when we look at sexual patterns between men and women, marriage, and birth rates. Rates of illegitimacy in colonial Latin America were staggeringly high – at some places and times as high as 80 per cent. It seems more likely that the value of virginity before marriage was one quotient in an overall equation of social status that also placed a premium on lighter skin color, ancestry, money, and profession. For example, a white woman born in Mexico who had lost her hymen might actually have commanded a less impressive slot in the marriage market than a 'virtuous' *mestiza* with a substantial dowry.[72] In any case the importance of an intact hymen cannot be dismissed. This may therefore suggest that unmarried (or married) men sought out known passive sodomites to satisfy their sexual desires. Prostitution and keeping a lower-class mistress were other options, but the option of situational homosexuality may have been more appealing given its relatively smaller economic burden.

These areas of theoretical debate have thus far been sporadically mentioned in the scholarly literature on homosexuality in Latin America. In the future, when a more thorough body of historiography begins to develop and as more and more studies emerge, these issues will become inescapable. Importantly, a more thorough corpus of investigation will begin to answer the questions of whether or not European scholarly models can be effectively applied to Latin America.

Future avenues for research

A great deal remains to be known about homosexuality in colonial Latin America. I suspect that given a more complete scholarly community the gaps will be filled in. The question is less what is to be done and more how it might be approached. To some extent this is a question of theoretical issues discussed above, but the issue of sources can never be far from this speculation. After all only a minute portion of the available documentation has been covered and vast areas of archival documents, imprints, and manuscripts have yet to be approached. Given the generally nascent quality of this scholarship, a variety of potential research avenues await future historians. The seeming paucity of documentation has manifold explanations. There has simply not been a critical mass of historians who have located and catalogued the sources. In conclusion I suggest a few areas of investigation for future researchers.

Case law

Despite the potential for misinterpretation, case law remains an important source for the history of homosexuality in Latin America precisely because it was criminalized. Few archives have been mined or explored for potential data on both the jurisprudential and social history of homosexuality in Latin America. The Mexican Inquisition archives have been, thus far, the most extensively used.[73] Garza Carvajal also relied heavily on case law for his study, though he worked exclusively in Spanish archives where material relating to the Spanish seaborne empire is held. In any case a vast body of archival material lies untapped.

The obvious place to look would be civil court archives. These exist both on a global and local scale. To my knowledge no one has looked at either to determine the extent to which civil courts prosecuted sodomy. I have conducted research in the Judicial Archive of the State of Puebla, Mexico, only to find an astonishing absence of sodomy cases. This seems especially strange given the voluminous documentation of bigamy, cohabitation, and adultery cases that I found in this archive for the period between 1600 and 1800.[74] But Puebla is but one locality. No one has looked at other judicial archives for this material. I suspect that such cases must exist in a variety of archives, given the horror manifested in the correspondence in the 1658 case over the nature of sodomy.

A question of jurisdiction arises. It appears that at least in the Mexican case the Inquisition did not prosecute sodomy heavily. As noted above, in Spain prosecution was locally determined. Whereas the Inquisition in Valencia and Navarre heavily prosecuted sodomy, the Inquisition in Castile and Seville practically ignored it.[75] This may well be the case for the Spanish Americas, though in Brazil sodomy certainly fell under the jurisdiction of the Inquisition. Moreover, the exigencies of archival preservation also complicate this potential avenue. For example, in 1692 there was a massive riot in Mexico City, during which the viceregal palace was reduced to ashes. The archive of the *audiencia* (or high court) of Mexico was housed there and along with the fire went the civil court case files between the early sixteenth century and 1692.[76] Despite these restrictions, investigations in local civil archives, not to mention the huge *audiencia* court archives in other areas like Guatemala and Peru, may in time bear fruit.

In addition to civil courts, ecclesiastical courts were empowered to prosecute various sexual crimes, usually bigamy, adultery, and cohabitation, as well as adjudicate divorce hearings. Again, no thorough search has been made of these archives, which form a vast archipelago across Latin America, to look for sodomy cases. In sum, case law has been largely unexamined to my knowledge and for this reason could turn up a wealth of data for a history of homosexuality in Latin America.

Visitation records

An enterprising historian could look to records at the parish level and may also turn up intriguing clues. After the Council of Trent in 1563, an institutionalized duty of the Tridentine bishop was the visitation, in which he or his coterie went to each parish in a bishopric.[77] The result of these visits was extensive documentation on the spiritual and cultural life in individual parishes. Such records have been used by a variety of scholars to discuss popular religion and the sociology of religion. I suspect that a careful examination of this kind of documentation may turn up discussions of community mores or sexual habits. While such data may be scarce, without examining such records it is difficult to know what they contain. This kind of documentation is currently notoriously underutilized in the overall, general historiography of colonial Latin America. These archives have been left more or less to die on the vine for hundreds of years, partly as a result of poor preservation and partly as a result of complicated organization. In either case, diocesan archives exist broadly across Latin America and could be mined for data on sexual mores.

Imprints

While archival material is the meat and potatoes of historical research, printed material may also shed important light on the question of homosexuality for Latin America. Again, the problem here is that it is virtually impossible to glean first-hand discussion about homosexuality by men who profess male–male friendship or sexual behavior. Rather, we must look to sources like confession manuals and moral theology that discuss sodomy as a social and moral 'problem.' Nevertheless, the presence of discussions of homosexuality provides clues as to the orthodox views on the matter. Works of moral theology constituted one of the most popular genres of printed material in colonial Latin

America.[78] Within this genre even a cursory glance reveals a preoccupation with sexual mores and rectitude among some of the most influential writers of early modern Hispanic letters. For example, the first archbishop of Mexico, the Franciscan Juan de Zumárraga, printed what was considered to be a rather 'liberal' doctrine as a primer on the faith for the literate.[79] In this *Doctrina breve*, which first appeared in 1543, he discusses sexual morality. His conclusion concerning homosexuality is unsurprising, condemning it as the worst 'species' of the sin of lust.[80]

The view that all non-procreative sexual activity was a mortal sin remained virtually unchanged throughout the early modern period. One of the most influential moral theologians of his day, the Jesuit Tomás Sánchez, wrote a lengthy confessional manual and treaty on marriage at the beginning of the seventeenth century. One of his questions was whether or not sodomy precluded a woman from marrying a man who had committed this 'act against nature.' He concludes that sodomy is indeed grounds for divorce or refusing to marry given the 'enormity' of the crime. Moreover the metaphysical reasoning followed exactly along the Thomist line that sodomy was a grave sin precisely because nothing could be produced from it (*quia ex ea non potest sequi generatio*).[81]

These two works represent only a minute fraction of the avalanche of doctrinal material to flood into colonial Latin America from Europe, to say nothing of the material produced in the Spanish and Portuguese viceroyalties. While such discussions tell us little of how ordinary people responded to official teachings, they do inform us a great deal about the efforts being made to 'reform' the everyman. The teachings of the Catholic Church in the period after the conclusion of the Council of Trent, which ended in 1563, were notorious in their attempts to enforce strict sexual morality and marital stability, even if these same teachings met with significant resistance across all walks of life in both Europe and Latin America.[82] In addition to rampant concubinage that Vainfas shows occurred in colonial Brazil,[83] remarrying, cohabitation, and keeping mistresses seem to have been relatively common practices in colonial Mexico. For example, in the direct wake of Trent, the Mexican Inquisition prosecuted at least 113 cases for remarriage or bigamy between 1563 and 1579, an astonishingly high number considering the overall caseload of the Tribunal.[84] Furthermore, this says nothing of the virtual avalanche of trials for similar crimes at the diocesan levels. The abundance of case law and the prevalence of moral theology's obsession with sexual purity, such as Sánchez's inclusion of sodomy in his confession manual, suggests that violations of church norms of sexuality were not only widespread but of grave concern to the clergy and jurists.

Few historians have used printed material to discuss the formal religious and moral attitudes of the ruling class in colonial Latin America. This approach seems to be more favored among Spanish historians, and as yet there has not been much emphasis on the 'ideological' formation of anti-homosexual attitudes for early modern Latin America. In many cases I suspect this devolves from an innate distrust of religious sources and a general disregard for moral theology as noxious and 'homophobic.' Such attitudes are understandable, but by the same token vigorous historical investigation will, ultimately, need to address these issues. After all, when civil authorities or ecclesiastical courts prosecuted sodomy, the lawyers and theologians who ran the show had very clear and organized ideas about why homosexuality needed to be attacked. By examining jurisprudential and theological sources we bring ourselves much closer to a solid historical understanding of the roots of anti-homosexual attitudes and beliefs in Latin American society.

After having considered this brief and not always connected body of material, the overall perspective is one of dispersion or diaspora. Indeed, thus far there has not been a concentrated group of historians focusing on early modern Latin American homosexuality. Indeed, even the subject of sexuality in general as a focus of scholarly attention has only come of age recently in Latin American circles. Yet, it appears that the recent attention given to the subject of male friendship and homosexuality portends a greater attention to our abiding interests. Indeed, if the *Hispanic American Historical Review* were any bellwether, it would seem that the history of homosexuality for colonial Latin America is poised to become a serious and well-researched field unto itself. Precisely because so many questions remain unresolved, so many sources unread, and so many archives unplumbed, that makes this one of the more exciting areas of research today in Latin American history.

Notes

Parts of this chapter appeased previously in my essay 'The Complicated Terrain of Latin American Homosexuality,' *The Hispanic American Historical Review* vol. 81, nos 3/4 (2001): 689–729.

1 José Costa Pôrto, *Nos tempos do Visitador: Subsídio ao estudo da vida colonial Pernambucana, nos fins do século XVI* (Recife: Universidade Federal de Pernambuco, 1968).

2 Julian Pitt-Rivers, *The Fate of Shechem, or the Politics of Sex: Essays in the Anthropology of the Mediterranean* (London: Cambridge University, 1977).
3 Verena Martínez-Alier, *Marriage, Class, and Colour in Nineteenth-Century Cuba: A Study of Racial Attitudes and Sexual Values in a Slave Society* (Cambridge: Cambridge University, 1974); Asunción Lavrin, ed., *Sexuality and Marriage in Colonial Latin America* (Lincoln: University of Nebraska, 1989); Louise Schell Hoberman, *Mexico's Merchant Elite, 1590–1660: Silver, State, and Society* (Durham: Duke University, 1991); Muriel Nazzari, *Disappearance of the Dowry: Women, Families, and Social Changes in São Paulo, Brazil, 1600–1900* (Stanford: Stanford University, 1991); Patricia Seed, *To Love, Honor, and Obey in Colonial Mexico: Conflicts over Marriage Choice, 1574–1821* (Stanford: Stanford University, 1988); Solange Alberro, *Del gachupín al criollo* (Mexico: Colegio de México, 1992).
4 Octavio Paz, *El laberinto de la soledad* (Mexico: Fondo de Cultura Económica, 1972).
5 Martin Nesvig, 'The Complicated Terrain of Latin American Homosexuality', *Hispanic American Historical Review* 81 (2001).
6 Paz, *El laberinto de la soledad.*
7 Stephen O. Murray, 'Homosexuality in Cross-Cultural Context', *Latin American Male Homosexualities*, ed. Stephen O. Murray (Albuquerque: University of New Mexico, 1995).
8 Gilbert M. Joseph, 'Introduction to Special Gender Issue', *Hispanic American Historical Review* 81 (2001).
9 Michel Foucault, *The History of Sexuality: An Introduction*, trans. Robert Hurley (New York: Vintage, 1990).
10 Luiz Mott, 'Desventuras de um sodomita português no Brasil seiscentista', *O sexo proibido*: *Virgens, gays e escravos nas garras da Inquisição* (Campinas: Papirus, 1988).
11 José Antônio Gonsalves de Mello, ed., *Confissões de Pernambuco, 1594–1595: Primeira visitação do Santo Oficio às partes do Brasil* (Recife: Universidade Federal de Pernambuco, 1970), Mott, 'Desventuras de um sodomita'.
12 Luiz Mott, 'Relações raciais entre homossexuais no Brasil colonial,' *Escravidão, homossexualidade e demonologia* (São Paulo: Ícone, 1988); Bartolomé Bennassar, *L'Inquisition espagnole Xve–XIXe siècle* (Paris: Hachette, 1979); William Monter, *Frontiers of Heresy: The Spanish Inquisition from the Basque Lands to Sicily* (Cambridge: Cambridge University, 1990); Francisco Tomás y Valiente, 'El crimen y pecado contra natura', *Sexo barroco y otras transgresiones premodernas* (Madrid: Alianza, 1990).
13 Emanuel Araújo, *O teatro dos vícios: Transgressão e transigência na sociedade urbana colonial* (Rio de Janeiro: José Olympio Editorial, 1993).
14 Luiz Mott, 'O sexo cativo: Alternativas eróticas dos Africanos e seus descendentes no Brasil escravista', *O sexo proibido: Virgens, gays e escravos nas garras da Inquisição* (Campinas: Papirus, 1988).
15 Mott, 'Relações raciais entre homossexuais'.
16 Mott, 'Relações raciais entre homossexuais'.
17 Gonsalves de Mello, ed., *Confissões de Pernambuco.*
18 Mott, 'Relações raciais entre homossexuais', John Boswell, *Christianity, Social Tolerance, and Homosexuality: Gay People in Western Europe from the*

Beginning of the Christian Era to the Fourteenth Century (Chicago: University of Chicago, 1980).

19 Boswell, *Christianity, Social Tolerance, and Homosexuality*.

20 Mott, 'Desventuras de um sodomita'.

21 Ronaldo Vainfas, *Trópico dos pecados: Moral, sexualidade e Inquisição no Brasil* (Rio de Janeiro: Campus, 1989).

22 Vainfas, *Trópico dos pecados*.

23 Vainfas, *Trópico dos pecados*; Guido Ruggiero, 'Sodom and Venice', *The Boundaries of Eros: Sex Crime and Sexuality in Renaissance Venice* (Oxford: Oxford University, 1985).

24 Vainfas, *Trópico dos pecados*.

25 Marcelino Cabrero de Anta, Arturo Alonso Lobo and Sabino Alonso Morán, *Comentarios al derecho canónico* (Madrid: Biblioteca de Autores Cristianos, 1963).

26 Costa Pôrto, *Nos tempos do Visitador*.

27 Vainfas, *Trópico dos pecados*.

28 Richard Greenleaf, *Mexican Inquisition in the Sixteenth Century* (Albuquerque: University of New Mexico, 1969).

29 Anthony Pagden, *Spanish Imperialism and the Political Imagination* (New Haven: Yale University, 1990).

30 Gabriel Haslip-Vieira, *Crime and Punishment in Late Colonial Mexico City, 1692–1810* (Albuquerque: University of New Mexico, 1999); António Manuel Hespanha, *La Gracia del Derecho* (Madrid: Centro de Estudios Constitucionales, 1993).

31 Archivo General de la Nación, Mexico (hereafter, AGN), Inquisición, vol. 510, exp. 79.

32 Archivo General de las Indias, Seville (hereafter, AGI), México, vol. 38, num. 57.

33 Bennassar, *L'Inquisition espagnole*, Rafael Carrasco, *Inquisición y represión sexual en Valencia: Historia de los sodomitas, 1565–1785* (Barcelona: Laertes, 1985), Monter, *Frontiers of Heresy*.

34 Dennis Doherty, *The Sexual Doctrine of Cardinal Cajetan* (Regensburg: Friedrich Pustet, 1966); Tomás y Valiente, 'El crimen y pecado contra natura.'

35 Richard Trexler, *Sex and Conquest: Gendered Violence, Political Order and European Conquest of the Americas* (Ithaca: Cornell University, 1995).

36 Andrea Dworkin, *Letters from a War Zone: Writings 1976–1987* (London: Secker and Warburg, 1988).

37 *Siete Partidas del Sabio Rey don Alonso el nono, nueuamente Glosadas por el Licenciado Gregorio López del Consejo Real de Indias de su Magestad* (Salamanca: Domingo de Portonarijs, Impressor de la Real Magestad, 1576).

38 Antonio Gómez, *Ad Leges Tauri commentarium absolutissimum* (Madrid: n.p., 1780).

39 Gómez, *Ad Leges Tauri commentarium absolutissimum*.

40 *Siete Partidas*.

41 Serge Gruzinski, 'Las cenizas del deseo: Homosexuales novohispanos a mediados del siglo XVII', *De la santidad a la perversión: O de por qué no se cumplía la ley de Diós en la sociedad novohispana*, ed. Sergio Ortega (Mexico: Editorial Grijalbo, 1986).

42 Murray, 'Homosexuality in Cross-Cultural Context', Michael Rocke, *Forbidden Friendships: Homosexuality and Male Culture in Renaissance Florence* (Oxford: Oxford University, 1996).
43 Lee Michael Penyak, 'Criminal Sexuality in Central Mexico, 1750–1850', Ph.D. diss., University of Connecticut, 1993.
44 Penyak, 'Criminal Sexuality in Central Mexico, 1750–1850'.
45 Geoffrey Kimball, 'Aztec Homosexuality: The Textual Evidence', *Journal of Homosexuality* 26 (1993).
46 Pete Sigal, 'The Politicization of Pederasty among the Colonial Yucatecan Maya', *Journal of the History of Sexuality* 8 (1997).
47 Federico Garza Carvajal, *Vir: Conceptions of Manliness in Andalucía and México, 1561–1699* (Amsterdam: Amsterdamse Historische Reeks, 2000).
48 Garza Carvajal, *Vir.*
49 Garza Carvajal, *Vir.*
50 Garza Carvajal, *Vir.*
51 AGI, México, vol. 38, num. 57.
52 Gruzinski, 'Las cenizas del deseo', Garza Carvajal, *Vir.*
53 AGI, México, vol. 38, num. 57.
54 Roger Chartier, *Cultural History: Between Practices and Representations*, trans. Lydia G. Cochrane (Ithaca: Cornell University, 1988); Natalie Zemon Davis, *Fiction in the Archives: Pardon Tales and Their Tellers in Sixteenth-Century France* (Stanford: Stanford University, 1987); Robert Darnton, *The Great Cat Massacre, and Other Episodes of French Cultural History* (New York: Vintage, 1984); Lynn Hunt, ed., *The New Cultural History* (Berkeley: University of California, 1989); Joan Wallach Scott, *Gender and the Politics of History* (New York: Columbia University, 1988).
55 John H. Arnold, *Inquisition and Power: Catharism and the Confessing Subject in Medieval Languedoc* (Philadelphia: University of Pennsylvania, 2001); James B. Given, *Inquisition and Medieval Society: Power, Discipline, and Resistance in Languedoc* (Ithaca: Cornell University, 1997); R. Po-Chi Hsia, *Trent 1475: Stories of a Ritual Murder Trial* (New Haven: Yale University, 1992).
56 Emmanuel LeRoy Ladurie, *Montaillou: The Promised Land of Error*, trans. Barbara Bray (New York: Vintage, 1978).
57 Edward Muir and Guido Ruggiero, eds, *History from Crime* (Baltimore: Johns Hopkins University, 1994).
58 Mott, 'Desventuras de um sodomita', Mott, 'Relações raciais entre homossexuais', Mott, 'O sexo cativo'.
59 Garza Carvajal, *Vir.*
60 Ricardo García Cárcel, *La leyenda negra: Historia y opinión* (Madrid: Alianza, 1998); Francisco Tomás y Valiente, *El derecho penal en la monarquía absoluta* (Madrid: Tecnos, 1969).
61 Ruggiero, 'Sodom and Venice'.
62 Mott, 'Desventuras de um sodomita', Mott, 'O sexo cativo', Gruzinski, 'Las cenizas del deseo.'
63 Vainfas, *Trópico dos pecados.*
64 Penyak, 'Criminal Sexuality in Central Mexico, 1750–1850'.
65 Randolph Trumbach, *Sex and the Gender Revolution*, 2 vols (Chicago: University of Chicago, 1998–2000).
66 Sigal, 'The Politicization of Pederasty'.

67 Vainfas, *Trópico dos pecados.*
68 Pitt-Rivers, *Fate of Shechem.*
69 Stuart B. Schwartz, 'Pecar en las colonias. Mentalidades populares, Inquisición y actitudes hacia la fornicación simple en España, Portugal y las colonias americanas', *Cuadernos de Historia Moderna* 18 (1997).
70 Trexler, *Sex and Conquest.*
71 Garza Carvajal, *Vir*; Pablo Emilio Pérez Mallaína Bueno, *Los hombres del océano: Vida cotidiana de los tripulantes de las flotas de Indias, siglo XVI* (Seville: Sociedad Estatal para la Exposición Universal Sevilla, 1992).
72 Hoberman, *Mexico's Merchant Elite*; Lavrin, ed., *Sexuality and Marriage in Colonial Latin America*; Martínez-Alier, *Marriage, Class, and Colour*; Seed, *To Love, Honor, and Obey.*
73 Penyak, 'Criminal Sexuality in Central Mexico, 1750–1850'.
74 Archivo Judicial del Estado de Puebla, Puebla, Mexico.
75 Monter, *Frontiers of Heresy*; Carrasco, *Inquisición y represión sexual.*
76 R. Douglas Cope, *The Limits of Racial Domination: Plebeian Society in Colonial Mexico City, 1660–1720* (Madison: University of Wisconsin, 1994); Rosa Feijoo, 'El tumulto de 1692', *Historia mexicana* 14 (1964–65); Carlos de Sigüenza y Góngora, 'Alboroto y motín de México del 8 de junio de 1692', *Relaciones históricas*, ed. Manuel Romero de Terreros (Mexico: Universidad Nacional Autónoma de México, 1992 [1602]).
77 Jean Delumeau, *Catholicism between Luther and Voltaire: A New View of the Counter-Reformation* (London: Burns and Oates, 1977); R. Po-Chia Hsia, *The World of Catholic Renewal, 1540–1770* (Cambridge: Cambridge University, 1998).
78 'Memoria de libros de Paula de Benavides', 1660, AGN, Inquisición, vol. 581, exp. 3, fojas 368–444, Teodoro Hampe Martínez, *Bibliotecas privadas en el mundo colonial: La difusión de libros e ideas en el virreinato del Perú, siglos XVI–XVII* (Madrid: Iberoamericana, 1996); José Toribio Medina, *La imprenta en México (1539–1821)*, 8 vols (Santiago: Casa del Autor [Medina], 1908–12); Irving A. Leonard, *Books of the Brave: Being an Account of Books and of Men in the Spanish Conquest and Settlement of the Sixteenth-Century World* (Ann Arbor: University of Michigan, 1949).
79 Marcel Bataillon, *Erasmo y España: Estudios sobre la historia espiritual del siglo XVI* (Mexico: Fondo de Cultura Económica, 1966).
80 Juan de Zumárraga, *Doctrina breve muy provechoso* (Mexico: Cromberger, 1543).
81 Tomás Sánchez, *Disptutationum de sancto matrimonii sacramento* (Madrid: apud Ludouicum Sanctium, 1623).
82 Alberro, *Del gachupín al criollo*; Joanne Ferraro, *Marriage Wars in Late Renaissance Venice* (Oxford: Oxford University, 2001).
83 Vainfas, *Trópico dos pecados.*
84 AGN, Inquisición, vols 25–29, 91–108.

11

'Sodomitical Actings', 'Inward Disposition', and 'The Bonds of Brotherly Affection': Sexual and Emotional Intimacy Between Men in Colonial and Revolutionary America

Richard Godbeer

Jamestown, the first permanent British settlement in North America, was initially an all-male colony. Though women did migrate to the Chesapeake in subsequent years, they remained relatively few in number: male colonists outnumbered women by roughly six to one in the 1620s and by four to one in later decades. The Chesapeake's skewed sex ratio made it extremely difficult for men to find wives and establish conventional family households. It also meant that most colonists did not have access to sexual relations with English women during the initial period of settlement. There seems, furthermore, to have been little sexual contact with Indians during these years.[1] It is difficult to believe that a group of young and notoriously unbridled men remained celibate for an extended period of time. Early settlers often paired off to form all-male households, living and working together. As Mary Beth Norton has remarked, 'it would be truly remarkable if all the male-only partnerships lacked a sexual ingredient.'[2] Some men may have engaged in sexual relations with each other out of desperation; others may have taken advantage of an unusual situation to form relationships that would have been more controversial under normal circumstances. But whatever their motives, men who coupled sexually with other men are unlikely to have been anomalous in such an environment. It seems reasonable to assume that much of the sex that took place in the first few years of settlement in the south was sodomitical.

Early seventeenth-century southerners who had male servants working for them may well have sought to exploit their authority for purposes of sexual gratification.[3] One servant did formally accuse his master of raping him. As a result of that servant's testimony, Captain Richard Cornish was convicted of sodomy and hanged in 1625. This is the only trial for sodomy known to have taken place in the early Chesapeake. Cornish's execution and the merits of the case aroused heated controversy among the colonists. The death sentence was certainly open to question, given the lack of corroborative testimony: no one had witnessed the captain's assault of his servant. Edward Nevell declared that the captain had been hanged 'for a rascally boy wrongfully.' Nevell was arrested for his criticism of the court and sentenced 'to stand on the pillory with a paper on his head showing the cause of his offense in the market place, and to lose both his ears, and to serve the colony for a year.' Thomas Hatch, who also denounced the court's decision, was whipped, made to stand on the pillory, lost one of his ears, and had his period of service extended by seven years.[4]

The government was clearly determined to silence those who criticized its handling of the case. As women arrived in greater numbers, enabling the formation of more conventional households and marriages, the authorities may have wanted to make an example of Cornish. Critics of the court may have been anxious about the vulnerability of other men, perhaps including themselves, especially if incidents of sexual aggression were to become capital offences on the basis of an accusation without corroborative evidence. It is striking that none of the reported conversations suggested any revulsion toward sodomy itself. Some Virginians may have felt that a veil of silence regarding sexual activity between men in the fledgling colony was being ripped away, much to their consternation.

That veil of silence was soon back in place and would remain there. In sharp contrast, sodomy would figure as a regular topic of public discourse further north in seventeenth-century New England, where Puritan leaders were eager to protect their New Israel from pollution, sexual or otherwise, through vehement denunciation of sin in all its manifestations. Most surviving information about sexual intimacy between male colonists comes from New England and so it is not surprising that almost all scholarship on early American same-sex relations has focused on the northern colonies. Pioneering work in the 1970s and early 1980s chronicled the colonial laws against sodomy and judicial prosecutions for that offense, pondering the significance of that evidence for our understanding of same-sex intimacy in particular and early American culture in general.[5] More recent essays have built upon that foundation, examining sodomy both as a sexual category and as a social issue in early New England.[6] The study of same-sex intimacy in early America is now reaching forward into the eighteenth century and the revolutionary period.[7] Yet largely missing from the scholarship to date is an examination of emotional and romantic ties between men, a topic with profound implications for our understanding of manhood and social identity in early America.

A recent history of sexuality in North America declares that Puritan leaders in early New England condemned sodomy because it 'so clearly defied the norm of reproductive sexuality.'[8] This was certainly one of the reasons for official disapproval of same-sex intimacy, but Puritan theologians did not see reproduction as the sole or even primary goal of sex. They taught that marriage was intended first and foremost to foster spiritual endeavor and obedience to God's law through loving support and mutual stewardship. Marital sex was ordained by God as an expression of love and fellowship between husband and wife; all other sex was sinful and disorderly. Official condemnation of non-marital sex in general and sodomy in particular was bound up with a clear conception of the body's role in the drama of redemption. The physical body, ministers taught, could serve both virtuous and sinful purposes. Sermons often referred to the body as a temple for the soul that should be consecrated to God and kept safe from the pollution of sin.When Puritans referred to illicit sex as 'unclean,' 'filthy,' 'defiling,' and 'polluting,' they framed the subject in terms of their duty to protect their bodies from contamination for the sake of their souls.[9]

That incorporation of sex and the body into a larger moral drama conditioned the ways in which New England ministers explained sexual urges. They evoked neither sexuality as an independent force that gave rise to erotic desire nor sexual orientation as a determinant of who was attracted to whom. They explained masturbation, sex between an unmarried couple, adultery, sodomy, and bestiality just as they did any other sin, such as drunkenness or falling asleep during a sermon: they were all driven by the innate corruption of fallen humanity and all embodied disobedience to God's will. Official teaching did not, then, conceive of sodomy as fundamentally distinct from any other manifestation of human sin. Nor did it see particular men or women as constitutionally inclined or limited to any one form of sexual offense. The basic issue at stake was moral rather than sexual orientation. Sexual sins could be traced to a particular frame of mind, but that mental state was not specific to any one category of offense, nor was it even specifically sexual.

Ministers reminded their congregations of the fate suffered by the citizens of Sodom in order to warn against all of the sins in which the Sodomites had engaged, not only their sexual offenses. Michael Warner has shown that Sodom's principal significance for Puritan writers lay not in the specific sins committed by that city's inhabitants but in the collective and public judgment passed upon them for their individual and private offenses. New Englanders had committed themselves in their personal and national covenants with God to regulate themselves and each other according to divine law. If they failed to do so, providential punishment would rain down upon them. 'The fable of Sodom' constituted 'an argument not for what we would call heterosexuality but for public regulation.' The biblical city 'represented a people held responsible for its disposition as a people': if New England became another Sodom, it should expect to suffer the fate of Sodom.[10]

Yet although pastors taught that sexual sin should be understood in tandem with, not in isolation from, other forms of sin, their condemnation of illicit sex was far from indiscriminate. Pastors addressing their flocks on the subject distinguished carefully between different kinds and degrees of offense. Samuel Danforth argued that 'uncleanness' could be 'expressed by and comprehended under these two terms, *fornication*, and *going after strange flesh*.' He explained that '*fornication*' was to be 'taken in a large sense' to include four offenses: sex between two unmarried persons, adultery, incest, and masturbation. The second category, '*going after strange flesh*,' incorporated sodomy ('filthiness committed by parties of the same sex') and bestiality ('when any prostitute themselves to a beast'). Samuel Willard used different terminology to make a similar distinction. He told his congregation that 'unlawful and prohibited mixtures' could be 'ranked under two heads': 'natural' and 'unnatural.' Bestiality and sodomy, he claimed, were 'unnatural' because of 'the species and sexes' involved, whereas sex 'between persons who are single,' adultery, polygamy, and incest were '(in some sense) more natural' because they came 'within the compass of the species and sexes.'[11]

For New England clergymen, sodomy was far from being the 'confused category' to which Michel Foucault and others have alluded in discussing premodern sexuality. Danforth and Willard classified sexual acts in terms of those involved and their relationships to each other: their marital status, sex, and species. They and other commentators made a clear distinction between illicit sex performed by a man and woman and that between either two persons of the same sex or a human being and an animal. According to New England's spiritual teachers, sodomy and bestiality disrupted the natural order and crossed scripturally ordained boundaries between sexes and species. They were thus more egregiously sinful and disorderly than was 'uncleanness' between a man and a woman. New England, wrote Charles Chauncy, was 'defiled by such sins.' They should be punished, declared Cotton Mather, 'with death, without mercy.'[12]

Two recent studies have linked denunciations of sodomy in seventeenth-century New England to an allegedly intense fear of femininity and effeminization. According to Roger Thompson, the virulence of Puritan 'homophobia' was due in large part to 'the presence of gender role confusion and sexual insecurity within an aggressively masculine environment.' Male New Englanders were, he claims, 'emasculated' by the depiction of men and women as utterly dependent upon God's will; they also faced 'effemination' through the frequent use of bridal imagery to characterize the relationship between the redeemed and their savior. In addition to 'the psychic toll' which these facets of Puritan theology inflicted upon its male adherents, a significant number of 'threatening Amazons' in seventeenth-century New England, women who usurped men's roles and challenged their authority, created a parallel 'source of insecurity.' Colin Talley also points to 'a profound fear of femininity in its various constellations, which resulted in an inherently anxious hypermasculine gender identity,' expressed in part through vehement condemnation of sodomy.[13]

This approach is based upon a fundamental misconception of Puritan gender ideology. Early modern notions of gender were in some respects remarkably fluid and capacious. Puritans, in common with other members of seventeenth-century Anglo-American society, had a clear sense of masculinity and femininity as distinct constellations of qualities, the former associated with authority and the latter with subordination. Yet roles and attributes labeled as masculine or feminine were not attached inflexibly to male or female bodies: women could assume male-identified roles in particular contexts and be treated in those contexts as functionally male; men were likewise expected to adopt feminine roles in certain circumstances and did so without qualm. Social, political, and spiritual order rested just as firmly on male as on female submission to those placed above them; men made sense of situations in which they performed a subordinate and deferential role by assuming in those contexts a female persona. John Winthrop, for example, equated a citizen's 'subjection to authority' with a wife's 'subjection to her husband's authority': male subjects should defer to magistrates as if wives deferring to their husbands. The godly also embraced biblical language that depicted Christ as a bridegroom and the redeemed, whether male or female, as his bride. Puritans, in other words, thought of themselves as embodying a variety of gendered roles rather than a single gender identity.[14]

Early modern conceptions of gender were, of course, far from unconditionally fluid. Context was crucial, so that a woman who asserted male prerogatives in a situation seen by others as inappropriate or who seemed to claim authority in her own right as a woman rather than as an occasion-specific and male-identified role was vulnerable to attack. But femininity was not intrinsically undesirable or threatening in Puritan eyes: indeed, feminine attributes were virtuous and laudable in appropriate contexts, whether embodied by men or women. Puritan men developed a range of gendered social capacities, relating to Christ as brides as well as emulating him in the role of bridegroom. The notion that seventeenth-century male New Englanders would necessarily have been disturbed by adopting a feminine role is thus unfounded.[15]

There is another problem with Thompson's argument, which assumes a connection between effeminacy and sodomy that did not exist in seventeenth-century New England. It is assuredly true that such a connection would become an important, even crucial, component of the homoerotic subculture that emerged in London by the early eighteenth century; the inhabitants of late colonial North America would read accounts of English 'sodomites' who assumed a feminine persona and also of foppish men who, it was implied, might engage in sodomy. But it is striking that colonial court cases and controversies involving cross-dressing did not include allegations or even insinuations of same-sex intimacy; nor were any defendants in sodomy cases during the colonial period accused of cross-dressing. Fear of disorder and of spiritual pollution, not of femininity or effeminization, drove official condemnation of sodomy.

Puritan ministers included in their definitions of 'unnatural' sex not only the coupling of 'men with men' but also that of 'woman with woman.'[16]Yet New England's laws against sodomy focused much more specifically on male sex. That was due in large part to the legal system's conception of sex as an act of phallic intercourse. Because lawmakers and magistrates understood sex in terms of penetration, they found it difficult to conceive of a sexual scenario that did not involve a penis along with a male to which it was attached. As a result, there was little room for the recognition or prosecution of sex between women. On only two known occasions did women appear before New England courts on charges of 'unclean' behavior with each other.[17]

Magistrates were sometimes willing to consider broadening their conception of sodomy, especially during the first few decades of settlement, which were avowedly experimental. In 1642, the Massachusetts General Court discussed the possibility of treating sex between a man and a prepubescent girl as sodomy on the grounds that both were non-reproductive, but it decided against doing so. During the course of that trial, the court sought advice from ministers and magistrates throughout the northern colonies as to whether actual intercourse was necessary for conviction and execution in cases of sodomy. The stakes were high since a number of recent cases had involved sexual dalliance between men that apparently did not culminate in penetration. Depending on the advice now given, offenses such as these might become punishable by death. According to Winthrop's account, 'most' of those consulted took the cautious view that 'there must be such an act as must make the parties one flesh.' This rigorous interpretation became the fundamental criterion used by New England courts in handling sodomy cases and other capital sex crimes.[18]

Subsequent trials for sodomy hinged on the crucial issue of whether penetration had occurred. Magistrates took care to distinguish between sodomy, attempted sodomy, and suspicious behavior that might be leading to sodomy. In practice, most courts had only circumstantial evidence on which to base their deliberations: deponents may have seen the accused in compromising circumstances, but they rarely claimed to have witnessed penetration itself. When dealing with capital offenses, New England courts generally insisted that the allegation be substantiated either by a confession or by at least two independent witnesses. The two-witness rule combined with the legal system's narrow definition of sex as an act of intercourse to make conviction extremely difficult.[19] As a result, those accused of sodomy in seventeenth-century New England rarely suffered the death penalty: defendants were much more likely to be whipped or fined for either suspicious behavior or an attempted crime. Only two individuals, William Plaine and John Knight, are known to have been executed for this crime in the northern colonies. In neither case was the route to conviction straightforward.[20]

Not only were executions for sodomy rare in seventeenth-century New England, but prosecutions were also remarkably few in number. Roger Thompson concludes from the paucity of cases that 'homosexual behaviour was virtually unknown in everyday life.' He explains this in terms of a roughly even sex ratio that enabled most New Englanders to marry, official hostility to sodomy, vigilance against its practice, and the apparent rarity of sodomy in seventeenth-century England, 'the culture from which almost all New Englanders drew their basic moral values.' Thompson rejects the argument made by Alan Bray, for early modern England, and by Robert Oaks, for seventeenth-century New England, that there was 'undoubtedly much more homosexual activity than the court records indicate.'[21] Thompson is doubtless right to argue that New England's sex ratio would have militated against the kind of situational same-sex intimacy that probably occurred in the early south. But his assumption that official 'homophobia' was reflected in popular attitudes is much less compelling. 'It does not seem to occur to Thompson,' writes Warner, 'that the scarcity of court evidence might indicate non-reporting from any of a number of causes.'[22]

Throughout the colonial period, New England communities preferred to handle problematic behavior through informal channels; they resorted to ecclesiastical discipline or the legal system only when private exhortation or local and informal measures failed to resolve the situation. In several cases of sodomy that came before courts or church congregations, it emerged during the proceedings that the accused had long been notorious for their sexual interest in men and that it had taken extraordinary circumstances to bring about a formal charge. Any number of local incidents and controversies involving sodomy may have escaped record because of this preference for non-institutional forms of social control. Though most of the surviving information about illicit sex comes from court records, colonists did not see such behavior primarily as a legal problem. The rigorous demands of the legal system may also have deterred some New Englanders from initiating formal action against offenders. Addressing the situation through non-juridical channels was, moreover, less dire than invoking capital law and so would have appealed to those who disapproved of sodomy but did not want the accused to hang. Many sexual offenses came to light because pregnancy resulted; in this respect there was less risk for those engaging in sodomy.

Some New Englanders may have neglected to act against sodomitical behavior in their communities because they were slow to recognize or label it as such. Both Colin Talley and I have argued that sex occurring in the context of a recognized hierarchical relationship, such as between a master and his male servant, would not necessarily have been defined specifically as sodomy by contemporaries. Just as sexually predatory behavior toward a female servant might not always be perceived as a distinct issue because it could be understood in terms of a master's prerogative, so too there was no compelling need to treat sexual advances made by a master toward a male servant as distinct from the broader relationship or to label it explicitly as sodomy. Some townsfolk may have been disturbed by what they saw but understood such behavior in terms of a householder's abusing his authority since the master's overtures were bound up with the expression of conventional social power.[23]

We cannot assume that even those who did identify such behavior as sodomy always reacted with the unequivocal hostility expressed in legal and theological pronouncements. Some colonists clearly did condemn such behavior and Warner is doubtless on firm ground in suggesting that a considerable proportion of incidents may not have come to light because fear of social stigma and retribution ensured that sodomy was clandestine. Yet it is striking that locals were often extremely slow in taking any kind of action, formal or informal, against even notorious offenders. Much of the time, colonists appear to have found nonsexual aspects of a person's behavior more significant in determining his or her social worth. If the individual was otherwise popular as a neighbor, if he was valued for his role in the local community, and as long as his sexual behavior did not outweigh his more positive attributes, then risking the loss of a good neighbor along with the disruption of social and economic relationships in the local community may have struck the practical-minded as too high a price to pay for moral cleansing. In the case of prominent householders, their local status may also have shielded them to some degree unless or until their behavior became so disruptive as to override their social authority and value as employers. Difficult though it was to secure a conviction for sodomy in a New England court, the greater challenge for those who favored legal action was persuading their neighbors to join them in pressing charges, even against notorious individuals. The weight of unofficial opinion does not appear to have rested with those actively hostile toward sodomy.[24]

Fragmentary evidence suggests that the ways in which some New Englanders interpreted sexual impulses and behavior also departed from official doctrine. Puritan theologians conceived of sex as an act that embodied universal depravity: the modern notion of sexuality as a distinct and pivotal aspect of human identity that impels each man and woman toward members of the same or opposite sex had no place in their ideological framework; any individual had the potential to commit any sin. Yet some New Englanders apparently recognized in particular individuals an ongoing preference for specific kinds of sexual partner. Sensing that official ideology was of limited use in making intelligible their actual experiences and observations, they created what seemed to them more appropriate categories and frameworks of meaning. These colonists did not go so far as to posit sexual identity as such, but they did perceive in certain individuals a persistent inclination toward sodomy that transcended the sexual acts themselves.[25]

When Nicholas Sension of Windsor, Connecticut, was tried for sodomy in 1677, witnesses recounted his 'sodomitical actings' over a period of several decades. They identified in him a life-long predilection for members of the same sex. One young man whom Sension had propositioned declared, 'You'll never leave this Devilish sin till you are hanged.'[26] Sension himself apparently characterized his persistent sexual overtures toward other males as a distinct realm of activity. When neighbor William Phelps berated Sension for attempting to seduce various men in the vicinity, Sension purportedly admitted that he had 'long' practiced 'this trade,' which he 'took up at the school where he was educated.' It is not clear from Phelps's deposition whether he or Sension introduced the word 'trade' into their conversation; indeed, Phelps may have used it retroactively. But the application of the term to Sension's 'sodomitical actings,' by whomever, is significant in that 'trade' implied a specific calling or way of life. Use of that word to describe Sension's behavior indicates a sense of its significance, distinctiveness, and permanence in his life. The designation 'trade' went well beyond the act-oriented view of sodomy propounded in official statements. Indeed, it fitted Sension's own experience much better than did authorized categories. Phelps's deposition, then, provides a rare glimpse of ordinary people creating their own sexual taxonomy.[27]

The gap between official and popular attitudes on this issue should not be overdrawn. The remark about Sension's 'Devilish sin' was, after all, framed in religious terms and another man overheard Sension himself 'pray God to turn him from this sin he had so long lived in.'[28] To argue that New England townspeople and villagers identified distinct sexualities would be to stretch the evidence far beyond the bounds of credibility. But observation of men like Nicholas Sension does seem to have led neighbors and acquaintances to treat sodomy as a specific and consistent impulse; it became in their minds a habitual course of action that characterized some men throughout their lives.

When the inhabitants of Windsor told court officials about Nicholas Sension's long history of attraction toward young men, their remarks were of little use in proving a legal charge of sodomy unless they had seen penetration occur (only one witness made this claim and so Sension could not be executed). Nor did their perspective fit with the theological paradigm that emphasized a sinner's inclination toward all manner of depravity. Yet relating Sension's male-oriented sexual appetite made sense to them.

During the years between Nicholas Sension's trial in 1677 and the outbreak of the American Revolution, representations of sex between men in English print culture underwent a dramatic transformation. The emergence of the 'sodomite' as a social category – referring to a specific cadre of men with a consistent, though not necessarily exclusive, sexual interest in other men – represented a significant shift away from earlier typologies. Sodomy was now perceived as a crucial part of specific personality types; male Londoners attracted to members of the same-sex could find partners and social camaraderie in recognized gathering places such as the so-called 'molly houses' scattered across the city. Surviving evidence from colonial cities in North America gives no signs of a subculture such as London offered. But recent studies by Thomas Foster and Clare Lyons have begun the task of examining perceptions of same-sex intimacy in eighteenth-century America and the degree to which new metropolitan conceptions influenced colonial attitudes.

Foster's work on early eighteenth-century New England reveals 'complex discourses of sodomy' that combined older conventions with new conceptions and concerns. Readers of eighteenth-century Massachusetts newspapers encountered items describing police raids on 'molly houses' in London and the prosecution of those who participated in that city's sodomitical subculture. References to such men as 'sodomites' (a term hardly ever used in seventeenth-century New England to describe those who engaged in same-sex intimacy) amounted to the depiction of sodomy as 'a feature of character' or 'personhood.' Yet such representations were by no means equivalent to 'the modern medicalized and psychologized homosexual subject.' Older religious frameworks that understood sodomy in terms of moral corruption inviting divine retribution still exerted a powerful influence in eighteenth-century Massachusetts. One newspaper likened London to Sodom and Gomorrah, declaring that 'sodomitical clubs' in the metropolis invited the same 'just judgments' that had rained upon the biblical cities.[29]

That blend of conventional religious polemic with a newer conception of sodomy as a specific 'feature of character' was more compatible with popular responses to men such as Nicholas Sension than had been official Puritan ideology. The mid-eighteenth-century case of Stephen Gorton highlights this blend of perceptions. Gorton, minister at the Baptist church in New London, Connecticut, was suspended from his pastorate in 1756 for 'unchaste behavior with his fellow men.' Gorton had apparently exhibited an attraction to men 'in many instances through a number of years.' In 1757 the General Meeting of Baptist Churches judged that his behavior indicated 'an inward disposition ... towards the actual commission of a sin of so black and dark a dye.' The meeting did not explain what it meant by 'inward disposition,' but went on to recommend that Gorton absent himself from the Lord's Supper for 'several months at least' and give 'effectual evidence' of his repentance and reformation.[30]

The assumption that Gorton could overcome his proclivities suggests that the meeting viewed his 'sin' in terms consistent with earlier religious formulations, as a expression of inner corruption that sinners could defeat with Christ's support. Yet although the phrase 'inward disposition' was not being used to denote a permanent sexual orientation, it did depict Gorton's depravity as expressing itself in a particular and consistent form. The plain facts of Gorton's sexual history prompted the meeting to recognize attraction to men as an ongoing facet of his life. The official judgment against him was a diplomatic and subtle response to the situation: it pushed religious categories to their very limits in accommodating local impressions of Gorton's behavior and also printed representations of sodomy as a persistent, specific impulse; yet it used language in ways that did not actually breach the parameters of theological discourse.

Gorton managed to survive more or less unscathed, despite his sexual reputation. Though 'many' members left the church 'on that account,'the remaining members voted by a two-thirds majority to restore him to the pastorate, once he acknowledged and confessed his sins. This case suggests a remarkable forbearance toward individuals attracted to members of the same sex. Indeed there were even fewer prosecutions for sodomy in the eighteenth than in the seventeenth century.[31] In addition to the factors that had worked against formal censure of even those notorious for sodomy in seventeenth-century New England, three additional developments in the late colonial period militated against prosecution. First, the courts paid less and less attention to moral regulation in general as their caseloads became dominated by financial and commercial issues. That redirection of legal energies did not mean that local communities had lost interest in addressing problematic behavior informally, but it did represent a significant change in the tone of public life. At the same time a growing preoccupation with privacy and increased aversion to the public exposure of malefactors made New Englanders eager to avoid formal proceedings. It is striking that Gorton's congregation took formal action against him only after his activities became public knowledge. Most of the correspondence relating to the case addressed not Gorton's exploits but the fact that gossip about them had reached other communities. The pastor's flock resorted to disciplinary proceedings against him only once the spread of scandal made action imperative.[32]

A third development involved the linkage of sodomy to commercial corruption, urban development, and foreign vice. Foster shows that printed descriptions of English sodomy cases in eighteenth-century Massachusetts often linked perpetrators of the crime to the seamier aspects of commercial enterprise. Concern about the potentially corrupting impact of economic development had been a staple of seventeenth-century Puritan writing, but anxiety relating to the moral ramifications of commercial and specificially urban life took on new significance in the late colonial and revolutionary periods as Americans sought to distance themselves from what they depicted as a decadent metropolitan culture across the Atlantic. Foster points out that attempts by satirists to associate early Freemasons with sodomy went hand-in-hand with their mockery of the brotherhood for its aristocratic pretension: both enabled critics to equate Freemasonry with a corrupt imperial culture that Americans increasingly sought to contrast with their own more straightforward and allegedly wholesome way of life.[33]

Clare Lyons has also argued compellingly that the portrayal of sodomy as a foreign problem served as 'a way of keeping distance from British vice.' Lyons considers the stark contrast between a clear interest on the part of eighteenth-century Philadelphians in sodomy across the Atlantic and their 'lack of interest in prosecuting homoerotic practice' in their own city. Through a painstaking examination of printed matter that circulated in Philadelphia, lending lists that survive from circulating libraries, booksellers' inventories, and the advertisements that these tradesmen placed in local newspapers, Lyons demonstrates that a wide social spectrum of city-dwellers were exposed to imported images of the homoerotic through accounts of police raids and prosecutions in London as well as through fictional works. Philadelphians who participated in this 'shared print culture' and the many seafarers who spent time in the metropolis were well aware of the new models for understanding same-sex intimacy that had emerged across the Atlantic.[34]

Yet there is no sign of these new models being incorporated into Philadelphian society or of any efforts to police same-sex relations in the city. Indeed, the local historical record is almost completely silent on the subject of sex between men. The lack of prosecutions is not in itself surprising, Lyons argues, given the general disinterest of Philadelphia's city government in regulating nonmarital behavior, but that still leaves the resounding silence of other sources on the subject of sodomy in the city. One promising explanation for this silence, as Lyons points out, is that Philadelphians were making a choice not to acknowledge or police such behavior in their midst as 'a way of not integrating the social type of the sodomite *into* colonial and early national society.' Because sodomy served as a handy measure of British corruption, Americans were loathe to acknowledge its presence in their own communities. The silence of the eighteenth-century historical record thus points not to the absence of sodomy but to its implication in the project of American separation and the assertion of cultural as well as political independence.[35]

Lyons' work underscores the challenges involved in recovering the social history of same-sex intimacy in early America and yet the rich possibilities for a reconstruction of the homoerotic as a cultural motif. We need to know much more about representations of and responses to same-sex relations in the colonies south of New England so as to uncover regional distinctions, commonalities, and changes over time. Anne Myles has pointed out that such studies would do well to avoid treating sex as distinct from broader conceptions of 'deviance' and 'desire.' Early American condemnations of illicit sex were usually framed as part of a larger attack on behaviors that were seen as socially and spiritually pernicious. Meanwhile, same-sex friendships in this period often included expressions of romantic and physical affection that suggest a broad spectrum of possibilities for intimacy between men.[36]

Early American scholars writing about same-sex relations have thus far focused almost exclusively on physical intimacy between men, paying scant attention to same-sex friendship, love, and romance. Yet it was not unusual for correspondence between men in the seventeenth and eighteenth centuries to include effusive expressions of love and affection, sometimes framed in explicitly romantic terms. Michael Warner has alerted us to 'the language of seduction, possession, and marriage' used by John Winthrop in public addresses and private correspondence to characterize 'the bonds of brotherly affection.' Winthrop drew on an ardent reading of the biblical relationship between David and Jonathan as well as the passionate language of Canticles. Such language does not, of course, mean that Winthrop had or wanted to have sexual relations with men, but it does suggest a wide range of possibilities within early modern male friendship that emerges also from other letters written by men to men in colonial and early national America.[37]

Scholars of early modern and eighteenth-century England have explored with great subtlety the contours of male friendship, love, and romance. They have noted that a society in which sodomy was condemned and criminalized found ways to idealize male friendships that incorporated the expression of intense and romantic endearment. These studies refuse to ignore the passionate nature of many male friendships and yet insist that we not imbue such relationships with a modern subjectivity; they seek to understand how male romance was fashioned so as to become not only acceptable but even honorable within English society.[38] Nineteenth-century Americanists have also written insightfully about male friendship and love during that period. Donald Yacovone, writing about 'the language of fraternal love' in Victorian America, notes that nineteenth-century Romanticism intensified but 'did not create' such language and quotes from several eighteenth-century letters that express fervent love between men.[39]

There is as yet hardly any scholarship focused on same-sex love in eighteenth-century America. The striking exception is Caleb Crain's essay on the 1780s romance between James Gibson, an undergraduate at Princeton, and John Mifflin, a young Philadelphian lawyer. The loving friendship that developed between Gibson and Mifflin was emotionally intense and effusive. Crain sees their romance as 'a story of affection between American men at a crucial moment: at the acme of the culture of sentiment and sensibility, when individuals first considered following the unruly impulse of sympathy as far as it would go.' Crain's principal point, that Gibson and Mifflin used the language of sensibility, a fashionable and even conventional idiom, to express their feelings for one another, is assuredly an important step toward understanding the articulation of male love in the late eighteenth century. What we now need is a careful analysis of the language used in other diaries and correspondence expressing love between men so as to reconstruct a range of linquistic and cultural performances through which men gave voice to their love for each other, paying close attention to the spectrum of feelings that could be involved.[40]

In the eyes of early Americans, male intimacy could nurture and reinforce or corrupt and undermine authorized cultural endeavors, depending upon the mode of its expression. In 1630 John Winthrop celebrated 'brotherly affection' in his famous sermon aboard the *Arbella*, yet the year before 'five beastly sodomitical boys' were exposed on the *Talbot* and subsequently sent back to England for punishment, so 'foul' was their offence. As Michael Warner points out, Winthrop's glorification of male love 'was thus delivered in the very space of the repudiation of sodomy, en route to the New Canaan.' Warner suggests that Winthrop and others may have feared sodomy as a warped version of the 'brotherly affection' that, in Winthrop's words, should unite New England's citizens as 'members of the same body.' The 'bonds of brotherly affection' would provide the sinews of a godly commonwealth, yet the distortion of that affinity could pollute and destroy it.[41]

Over a century later, male love had equally profound implications for early republican society, in a period when conceptions of sexuality and gender identity were under fundamental renegotiation. During the eighteenth century a transformation had taken place in the gendering of moral virtue: in sharp contrast to earlier representations of women as morally corrupt and untrustworthy, American writers now portrayed women as the guardians of virtue; negative characteristics previously associated with women were now transposed onto men. As republican ideology sought to nurture civic virtue as the social and political cement that would replace loyalty to the crown and inspire citizens to disinterested public engagement, political writers placed increasing emphasis upon the role to be played by republican wives and mothers in fostering a moral rectitude and altruistic spirit of which men were often incapable if left to their own instincts. Though post-revolutionary political discourse claimed that the ties of social affection could hold men together in civic fraternity, the nature of those ties had to be negotiated with great care, given a male propensity toward personal vice and political corruption.[42]

Late eighteenth-century Americans worried that male rakes and profligates might corrupt other young men who kept company with them, yet contemporaries also believed that men could influence each other in more positive directions, quelling each other's corrupt tendencies and appealing to each other's potential for virtue. The families and friends of men who engaged in loving, even romantic, relationships with other men often saw such relationships as morally, socially, and politically desirable. Loving friendship and virtue would nurture each other: both were personal and private in their origins; both had public, political, and constructive implications. Fraternal love, in conjunction with the ministrations of mothers and wives, could redeem American manhood and so sustain the republic, just so long as it did not include sexual intimacy. The ways in which such intimacies were framed, culturally and linguistically, would have been crucial in making them appear not only harmless but also beneficial. Examining those frameworks will help us not only to understand how eighteenth-century Americans legitimized same-sex love but also the ways in which a morally endangered and endangering masculinity, potentially so deadly to the republican body politic, could be redeemed through certain forms of intense male friendship.[43]

Early studies of gender, as Jane Kamensky has remarked, 'tended to cast women as the only gendered beings in the human drama.' But now the history of masculinity as a cultural artefact is now finally being written: 'gender has come to be understood as an analytical category that covers more than simply women's experiences.' Manhood, 'once the invisible backdrop to almost all traditional studies,' is now being treated as 'a "marked" entity, worthy of exploration in itself.'[44] That reconceived history should include men's sense of themselves, their relationships with women, and their relationships with other men. The latter included a wide range of emotional and physical intimacies with profound social, political, and cultural ramifications. We have already embarked upon a history of sexual relations between men in early America. We now need to explore in all of its variations and implications love between men in the colonial and early national eras. We need, in other words, an anatomy of male friendship and love in early America.

Notes

1 See Richard Godbeer, *Sexual Revolution in Early America* (Baltimore: Johns Hopkins University Press, 2002), chap. 5.

2 Mary Beth Norton, *Founding Mothers and Fathers: Gendered Power and the Forming of American Society* (New York: Knopf, 1996), 354.

3 See John M. Murrin, ' "Things Fearful to Name": Bestiality in Colonial America', *Pennsylvania History* 65 (1998, supplemental issue): 12.

4 *Minutes of the Council and General Court of Colonial Virginia, 1622–1632, 1670–1676*, ed. H.R. McIlwaine (Richmond: Virginia State Library, 1924), 78, 81, 83, 85, 93.

5 Louis Crompton, 'Homosexuals and the Death Penalty in Colonial America', *Journal of Homosexuality* 1 (1976): 277–93; Jonathan Ned Katz, *Gay American History: Lesbians and Gay Men in the U.S.A.* (New York: Avon Books,

1976); Jonathan Ned Katz, *Gay/Lesbian Almanac: A New Documentary* (New York: Harper and Row, 1983); Robert F. Oaks, 'Perceptions of Homosexuality by Justices of the Peace in Colonial Virginia', *Journal of Homosexuality* 5 (1979–80): 35–41; Robert F. Oaks, ' "Things Fearful to Name": Sodomy and Buggery in Seventeenth-Century New England', *Journal of Social History* 12 (1978): 268–81; Robert F. Oaks, 'Defining Sodomy in Seventeenth-Century Massachusetts', *Journal of Homosexuality* 6 (1981): 79–83.

6 Alan Bray, 'To Be A Man in Early Modern Society: The Curious Case of Michael Wigglesworth', *History Workshop Journal* 41 (1996): 155–65; Richard Godbeer, ' "The Cry of Sodom": Discourse, Intercourse, and Desire in Colonial New England', *William and Mary Quarterly* 52 (1995): 259–86; Anne G. Myles, 'Queering the Study of Early American Sexuality', *William and Mary Quarterly* 60 (2003): 199–202; Nicholas F. Radel, 'A Sodom Within: Historicizing Puritan Homoerotics in the Diary of Michael Wigglesworth', in Tracy Fessenden, Nicholas F. Radel, and Magdalena J. Zaborowska, eds, *The Puritan Origins of American Sex: Religion, Sexuality, and National Identity in American Literature* (New York: Routledge, 2001), 41–55; Colin L. Talley, 'Gender and Male Same-Sex Erotic Behavior in British North America in the Seventeenth Century', *Journal of the History of Sexuality* 6 (1996): 385–408; Roger Thompson, 'Attitudes towards Homosexuality in the Seventeenth-Century New England Colonies', *Journal of American Studies* 23 (1989): 27–40; and Michael Warner, 'New English Sodom', in Jonathan Goldberg, ed., *Queering the Renaissance* (Durham, N.C.: Duke University Press, 1994), 330–58.

7 Thomas A. Foster, 'Antimasonic Satire, Sodomy, and Eighteenth-Century Masculinity in the *Boston Evening Post*', *William and Mary Quarterly* 60 (2003): 171–84; idem, 'Sex and the Eighteenth-Century Man: Anglo-American Discourses of Sex and Manliness in Massachusetts, 1690–1765' (unpublished Ph.D. diss., Johns Hopkins University, 2002); and Clare A. Lyons, 'Mapping an Atlantic Sexual Culture: Homoeroticism in Eighteenth-Century Philadelphia', *William and Mary Quarterly* 60 (2003): 119–54.

8 John D'Emilio and Estelle B. Freedman, *Intimate Matters: A History of Sexuality in America* (New York: Harper and Row, 1988), 30.

9 For a more detailed discussion of Puritan sexual ideology, see Godbeer, *Sexual Revolution*, chap. 2.

10 Warner, 'New English Sodom', 331, 348.

11 Samuel Danforth, *The Cry of Sodom Enquired Into* (Cambridge, 1674), 3–5; Samuel Willard, *A Complete Body of Divinity* (Boston, 1726), 681–2.

12 Michel Foucault, *The History of Sexuality*, vol. 1: *An Introduction*, trans. Robert Hurley (New York: Vintage, 1978), 101; 'Opinions of Three Ministers on Unnatural Vice' (1642), in William Bradford, *of Plymouth Plantation, 1620–1647*, ed. Samuel Eliot Morison (New York, 1952), 410; Cotton Mather, *The Sailor's Companion and Counsellor* (Boston, 1709), viii.

13 Talley, 'Gender and Male Same-Sex Erotic Behavior', 404; Thompson, 'Attitudes Toward Homosexuality', 34, 39.

14 John Winthrop, *History of New England from 1630 to 1649*, ed. James Savage, 2 vols (Boston: Phelps and Farnham, 1825–26), 2: 281.

15 For a much fuller discussion of these issues, see Godbeer, 'Performing Patriarchy: Gendered Roles and Hierarchies in Early Modern England and Seventeenth-Century New England', in *The Worlds of John Winthrop*, ed. Francis J. Bremer and Lynn A. Botelho (Boston: Massachusetts Historical Society, forthcoming).
16 See Godbeer, *Sexual Revolution*, 105.
17 For more detailed discussion of New England's sodomy laws, see *ibid*, 105–7.
18 Winthrop, *History of New England*, 2: 47; see also Oaks, 'Defining Sodomy' 79–83, and Godbeer, *Sexual Revolution*, 107–9.
19 Katz, *Gay/Lesbian Almanac*, 54–8; Oaks, 'Defining Sodomy', 82; and Godbeer, *Sexual Revolution*, 102–12.
20 See Godbeer, *Sexual Revolution*, 110–11.
21 Thompson, 'Attitudes Toward Homosexuality', 30–1, 34; Alan Bray, *Homosexuality in Renaissance England* (London: Gay Men's Press, 1982), esp. chap. 2; Oaks, ' "Things Fearful To Name"', 271; see also Peter Laslett, *The World We Have Lost: England Before The Industrial Age* (New York, 1984), 157.
22 Warner, 'New English Sodom', 353 n.12.
23 Talley, 'Gender and Male Same-Sex Erotic Behavior', 406–7. See also Bray, *Homosexuality*, 49–51, 56, 76, and Bruce R. Smith, *Homosexual Desire in Shakespeare's England: A Cultural Poetics* (Chicago: University of Chicago Press, 1991), 193.
24 For a case study in support of this argument, see Godbeer, *Sexual Revolution*, 45–50.
25 This distinction between acts and identity was developed by Foucault in *The History of Sexuality*, vol. 1: *An Introduction.*
26 'Crimes and Misdemeanours', 1st ser. (1662–63 to 1789, Connecticut State Library, Hartford), 1: 87a (see also 93, 95).
27 'Crimes and Misdemeanours', 1st ser., 1: 98b.
28 'Crimes and Misdemeanours', 1st ser., 1: 96.
29 Foster, 'Sex and the Eighteenth-Century Man', 166, 174, 197.
30 The surviving documentation for this case can be found in the Backus Papers (Andover-Newton Theological School, Newton Center, Mass.), box 7. For further discussion of the case, see Susan Juster, *Disorderly Women: Sexual Politics and Evangelicalism in Revolutionary New England* (Ithaca: Cornell University Press, 1994), 90–2, and Godbeer, 'Cry of Sodom,' 277–9.
31 Foster, 'Sex and the Eighteenth-Century Man', 155 n.9.
32 See Cornelia Hughes Dayton, 'Turning Points and the Relevance of Colonial Legal History', *William and Mary Quarterly* 50 (1993), 12–13, and Godbeer, *Sexual Revolution*, chap. 8.
33 Foster, 'Sex and the Eighteenth-Century Man', 175–96, and idem, 'Antimasonic Satire,' 171–84.
34 Lyons, 'Mapping an Atlantic Sexual Culture', 121, 137, 152.
35 Lyons, 'Mapping an Atlantic Sexual Culture', 137–8, 152.
36 Myles, 'Queering the Study of Early American Sexuality', 201–2.
37 Warner, 'New English Sodom', 339–44 (quotations 343).
38 For discussion of this literature see *Love, Sex, Intimacy, and Friendship Between Men, 1550–1800*, ed. Katherine O'Donnell and Michael O'Rourke (Basingstoke: Palgrave, 2003).

39 Donald Yacovone, ' "Surpassing the Love of Women": Victorian Manhood and the Language of Fraternal Love', in *A Shared Experience: Men, Women, and the History of Gender* ed. Laura McCall and Donald Yacovone (New York: New York University Press, 1998), 198.
40 Caleb Crain, 'Leander, Lorenzo, and Castalio: An Early American Romance', *Early American Literature* 33 (1998): 6–38 (quotation 6) and *American Sympathy: Men, Friendship, and Literature in the New Nation* (New Haven: Yale University Press, 2001), chap. 1.
41 Warner, 'New English Sodom', 339, 345.
42 See Godbeer, *Sexual Revolution*, chap. 8.
43 I hope to contribute toward this goal in a forthcoming book, *'The Overflowing of Friendship': Love Between Men in Early America.*
44 Jane Kamensky, 'Talk Like a Man: Speech, Power, and Masculinity in Early New England', in *A Shared Experience*, 21.

12
Homosexuality in Early Modern France

Michael Sibalis

A historical dictionary of early modern France published in 1996 has entries for 'Love' (courtship and marriage), 'Sexuality' (premarital and extra-conjugal sex, masturbation and rape), and 'Sexual Deviancies' (prostitution and homosexuality).[1] This classification of homosexuality as deviant in a work of scholarship testifies to the negative attitude toward non-conventional sexuality prevalent among French academics, who remain by and large indifferent or even hostile to gay studies. Professional historians in France have been reluctant to work in gay history and have left the field to independent (and poorly funded) scholars in their own country and to professional historians elsewhere. Some professional historians may be homophobic, like Emmanuel Le Roy Ladurie, a leading historian of early modern France, who has written newspaper attacks on Gay Pride marches and homosexual partnerships as 'contrary to the Judeo-Christian heritage.'[2] Others object to gay history on purportedly scholarly grounds. They may argue, for example, that homosexuality is an aspect of private life unworthy of historical study (an objection that has lost much of its force as historians bring more and more of past private life under scrutiny). Or they may protest that there is insufficient source material for analysis of homosexual behavior in the past, although the apparent lack of such material results only from their own failure to look for it. As Jeffrey Merrick and Bryant T. Ragan Jr.'s recent collection (in English translation) demonstrates, there in fact exists a wide variety of primary sources for the study of gay and lesbian history in early modern France: theological, medical, philosophical and literary texts, but especially documents generated by the state's repression of sodomy.[3]

Records of repression

In strict legal terms, sodomy was any sexual act not leading to procreation, including fellation, anal intercourse and even bestiality. In common usage, however, sodomy meant sexual relations between two persons of the same sex (usually male). Men who engaged in sodomy were 'sodomites' or (more rarely) 'buggers'. By the latter half of the eighteenth century, 'pederasts' (with no connotation of cross-generational sex) had become the more usual term. People also used euphemisms like 'vile creatures' (*infâmes*) or (more humourously) 'men of the cuff' (*gens de la manchette*) or 'knights of the cuff' (*chevaliers de la manchette*), possibly an allusion to the fancy cuffs worn by effeminate aristocrats. Homosexuality (the word dates only from 1869) was then called sodomy, buggery, pederasty or even 'the philosophical sin', because of either the alleged practices of ancient Greek philosophers or the supposedly lax morality of Enlightenment thinkers who rejected Church teachings. Homosexual acts were 'anti-physical', which is to say outside the natural order; by extension this made homosexuals 'anti-physicals'.[4]

French jurists considered sodomy a heinous a crime that deserved the severest punishment. According to one legal text from 1715, 'The penalty for sodomy could not be strong enough to expiate a crime that makes nature blush, to put the active one and the passive one to death by fire that consumes them and have the ashes thrown to the wind.'[5] In practice, however, French law courts tried sodomites infrequently and rarely imposed the death sentence. Claude Courouve has counted only 53 sodomy trials in France between 1317 and 1783 and only 39 executions for sodomy (of 66 men charged). His figures are undoubtedly incomplete, but harsh repression was the exception rather than the rule.[6]

Prosecutions of sodomites produced trial records, but few survive. Some records may have been burned along with the condemned – apparently a customary practice – and others simply thrown out over the centuries. In the eighteenth century, somebody put together two manuscript volumes comprising the recopied records of 'trials of diverse sodomites judged before the parlement of Paris', which was the highest law court for half the country. The first transcribes the records of ten cases of sodomy (in addition to cases of incest, bestiality, etc.) tried between 1540 and 1692; the second deals entirely with the celebrated sodomite Benjamin Deschauffours, burned in 1726 for abducting, selling and sometimes murdering boys.[7] Historians have often consulted these volumes, but in 1984 Alfred Soman questioned the authenticity of their contents. Soman argued that the cases themselves are genuine, but judged the reproduced documents to be fabrications, which he labelled 'pornographic literature' and 'fantasies probably drafted for private delectation.'[8] Given the abundant factual detail in the documents (names, dates, addresses, circumstances), Soman's conclusion seems dubious. Soman also claimed to have found the original records of several previously unknown sodomy trials, but has never published them. There may well be more such records still undiscovered in the judicial archives of provincial France, where a dozen different parlements exercised jurisdiction.

Hundreds of police reports document the arrest, interrogation and incarceration of sodomites in eighteenth-century Paris, but no similar reports have turned up for the capital before the 1690s or for the rest of the country for any time in the early modern period. Although police reports have obvious limitations – they deal with men who solicited sex or committed indecencies in public places and say little about those who conducted their sexual lives more discreetly – they do reveal a great deal about Parisian sodomites and historians have exploited them many times over the last century.[9] On the other hand, the lack of police reports from before 1700 means that historians have to write about French homosexuality very differently for the sixteenth and seventeenth centuries than for the eighteenth century. Sources from the earlier period – like memoirs, diplomatic dispatches, private correspondence, libels or songs – focus on the elites and, apart from a few enticing references to men in the army, aboard ship or in prison, barely mention the commoners who appear frequently in eighteenth-century police reports.

Famous personalities

For the period before 1700, then, the history of French (male) homosexuality is largely the history of great men: kings, statesmen, military leaders and intellectuals. This has often led to heated debate between those who seek to 'out' figures from the past – i.e. reveal their homosexuality – and those who believe that by denying the homosexuality of their subject they are defending him against a smear. But as Didier Godard has observed, 'When a traditional historian believes that he must solemnly affirm that there is no proof of a personage's "homosexual tendencies", it generally means that there is even less proof of his heterosexual tendencies.'[10]

The debate over Henry III (1551–89, reigned 1574–89) is a good example of the problem. Henry's contemporaries and generations of historians were scandalized by the king's conduct, especially his occasional transvestism and his excessive affection for his 'minions' (the term actually meant nothing more than 'favorites'), a band of youthful courtiers rumored to be his lovers. Certainly, as Godard has shown, homophobia lurks behind attempts by such eminent historians as Pierre Chevallier or Emmanuel Le Roy Ladurie to 'rehabilitate' Henry by dismissing any and all evidence of his homosexual activities.[11] But, in fact, the truth remains elusive and the evidence for Henry's homosexuality is indirect and biased: court gossip and polemical attacks on the king and his minions by Catholic fanatics, who wanted Henry to take a harder line against Protestantism, and by powerful nobles, who resented the influence of favorites from lesser families. Henry consequently became victim of 'the most intensive and successful propaganda campaign ever mounted. For perhaps the first time in modern Western history the printed word was used as a means of waging a relentless cold war against an unsatisfactory ruler.'[12] Of course, none of this means that accusations against Henry were false, and Godard asks rhetorically, 'if the assertion of the king's homosexuality was unfounded, dictated by malice, why did [this malice] harp solely, constantly, obsessionally on a single theme? ... In reality, propaganda uses the arms at its disposal.'[13] But Godard has overstated his case. David Teasely has pointed out that sodomy was not the only accusation levelled against the king, but was 'associated with a host of other sins: irreligion, atheism, sorcery, treason, rape, tyranny, monstrous animalistic behaviour, and the killing of children.'[14] A dictionary of gay biographies has concluded that the king 'probably never in his life laid hands on anyone but his Queen' and that ' "Henry III the Queer" is, in sum, a cultural fabrication that evinces the enduring power of xenophobic and religious paradigms' used by his enemies.[15]

Perhaps the (ultimately unknowable) truth about the king's reputed homosexuality is less important than the implications raised by the accusation itself. A recent study of Henry III's minions, adroitly sidestepping the whole question of whether or not the king had sex with them, has argued that 'Henry III's sexuality does not constitute an historiographical issue. ... It is less the supposed or real sexual practices of the king and those close to him that interests the historian than the image of illegitimacy conveyed by the discussion of sex.' Henry's alleged sodomy became 'the privileged metaphor for social disorder' in France and an indication that public opinion misunderstand and disapproved of the king's obvious affection for his favorites.[16] The libels (known as *mazarinades*) directed against the Italian-born Cardinal Jules Mazarin (1602–61), who governed France between 1643 and 1661, should be understood in the same way. It seems unlikely that Mazarin, possibly the Queen-Regent's lover or even her secret husband, was a sodomite and highly improbable that he sexually abused the boy-king Louis XIV (as one enemy claimed), but the charge of sodomy, as metaphor for corruption and civil disorder, stigmatized the 'unnatural' political dominance of a foreign prelate and sapped the legitimacy of his authority.[17]

On the other hand, there can be little doubt about the 'homosexual tendencies' of Louis XIII (1601–43, reigned 1610–43), although these most likely remained latent.[18] And there can be no doubt at all in the case of this king's second son (and Louis XIV's younger brother), Philippe, Duke d'Orleans (1640–1701), known as Monsieur. 'Not only did his sexual preference develop into a cardinal aspect of his character,' Nancy Barker has written, 'but ... in great measure it defined his reputation for posterity.'[19] The letters of Monsieur's wife, Elisabeth-Charlotte, Duchess d'Orleans (1652–1722), are a major source for homosexuality at the court of the Sun King. Perplexed and amused by her husband's tastes, but ultimately accepting of them, she explained in one of her letters (12 October 1712): 'In France I have become so knowledgeable on this subject that I could write books about it.' She claimed (23 June 1699) that 'the horrible vice' of sodomy 'is so in fashion here [at court] that no one hides it any more' or rather (13 December 1701) that aristocratic sodomites 'hide it as much as they can so as not to offend the common people, but among people of quality they speak openly about it.' 'There are [sodomites] of all kinds', she told her sister (3 December 1705). 'There are those who hate women and can love only [adult] men. Others love both men and women. ... Others love only children of ten or eleven, others youths of seventeen to twenty-five, and the last are the most numerous.' Many sodomites also slept with women, like the Marquis d'Effiat, one of Monsieur's lovers. 'There is surely no greater sodomite than he in all of France', the princess wrote (26 August 1689), and yet she also complained that 'without the least respect ... for me, he made one of my chambermaids pregnant.'[20]

Monsieur was by no means the only sodomite at Louis XIV's court. In the 1670s–80s (if one can believe the scandal-mongering of Roger de Bussy-Rabutin), there was even an 'Italian Confraternity' with formal statutes and four grand masters. It reportedly provoked the king's wrath by recruiting one of his illegitimate sons, then 18 years old.[21] A study of such circles of court sodomites is of more than anecdotal interest. With the Duke d'Orleans and his friends in mind, Robert Orsko has advocated using memoirs and notarial records to reconstitute networks of sex and friendship among homosexuals belonging to national elites in order to understand better the distribution of patronage and preferment in early modern courts.[22] Homosexual networks also played a role in the cultural and intellectual history of early modern France. If the love between the great essayist Michel de Montaigne (1533–92) and his friend Étienne de la Boétie (1530–63) was almost certainly not sexual, Montaigne's famous lines in his essay 'Of Friendship' – 'If I should be pressed to say why I loved him, I feel that it cannot be expressed, except by answering: "Because it was he, because it was I." ' – have caused historians to speculate on the nature and limits of male friendship in the French Renaissance.[23] There are other more pertinent cultural examples. David Parris has remarked that 'It would only be slight exaggeration to say that classical French prose and poetry stemmed from a single pair of [homosexual] lovers', Théophile de Viau (1590–1626) and Louis Guez de Balzac (1597–1654). Belonging to a circle of heterosexual and homosexual 'libertines' in early seventeenth-century France, these two lovers helped create a new literary style. Both faced the very real threat of death at the stake for their nonconformism in religion (atheism) and sexuality (sodomy).[24]

A century later, the great Voltaire (1694–1778) dominated French intellectual life. David Wootten has advanced the thesis that as a schoolboy Voltaire was sexually abused by his Jesuit schoolmasters and that as an adult he manifested bisexual tendencies. The philosopher surrounded himself with homosexual friends, not the least of them Prussia's Frederick the Great (1712–86, reigned 1740–86), and died in the Paris mansion of the Marquis de la Villette (1734–93), the most notorious sodomite of his day.[25] Olivier Blanc has studied the homoerotic and homosexual ties that reinforced certain aristocratic and intellectual circles (including Voltaire's) in late eighteenth-century France. To take but one significant case: Blanc has demonstrated that in the 1780s and 1790s, friends with a common interest in freemasonry and homosexuality promoted the career of Jean-Jacques-Régis de Cambacérès (1753–1824), who became the second most important man in France as Napoleon's second consul in 1799 and his arch-chancellor in 1804.[26]

In an otherwise rigidly hierarchical society, sodomy often linked men across class boundaries, which is why many saw it as subversive of the social order. Although some historians have dismissed eighteenth-century gossip about homosexual relations between masters and servants as unreliable – Cissie Fairchilds has written of 'tales with only a slight foundation in fact'[27] – Blanc has used notarial archives to show that many upper-class homosexuals recruited their lovers from below stairs and often rewarded them with life annuities. Police records also confirm the role played by domestic servants in the eighteenth-century sodomitical subculture, both as lovers of and pimps for their homosexual masters.

The eighteenth-century homosexual subculture in Paris

Indeed, almost everything that we know about the sodomitical subculture of eighteenth-century Paris comes from police reports. (Louis XIV created the first effective police force in the city only in 1667.) Police inspectors carried out regular evening and night-time 'pederasty patrols' in hopes of catching sodomites engaged in the act or at least behaving suspiciously. Their reports, which cover most of the period from the late 1690s to 1789, are missing (or were never made) for the years 1749–80. Until mid-century, the police regularly resorted to entrapment by special agents provocateurs, commonly known as *mouches* (literally: 'flies'). The *mouche* was an attractive young man, often himself a sodomite bribed, blackmailed or otherwise pressured into acting as bait. He hung around well-known cruising grounds to draw out his prey and chatted up men who approached him. He later reported any information collected this way about venues, networks of friendship or other details of interest to the police. Finally, once a sodomite made an explicit sexual advance, the *mouche* signalled a policeman waiting nearby to make an arrest.[28]

Michel Rey has argued that in the course of the eighteenth century the police replaced the Church as buttress of the social order and that the repression of sodomy took on new meaning: 'Sodomy no longer appeared as a sin, but as contrary to public order, due to furtive encounters [and] the unstable social relations [*glissements sociaux*], at least imaginary, that it seemed to permit; due as well to a desire to raise the prestige of the family, and therefore to eliminate or contain all forms of nonproductive sexuality that threatened it.'[29] The police, who knew full well that they could never eradicate sodomy, concentrated on limiting its manifestations (solicitation and copulation) in public spaces and preventing confirmed sodomites from 'corrupting' adolescents and other men. According to Jeffrey Merrick, Marc-René de Voyer d'Argenson, Paris's lieutenant-general of police from 1697 to 1718, 'assumed that the best, indeed the only, way to stop the multiplication and start the rehabilitation of sodomites was to confine them, encourage them to confess and renounce their depravity, and relegate them to the provinces, where they presumably would be safe from the temptations of the capital.'[30]

Policing undoubtedly interfered with the sodomite's search for sex – one Parisian remarked on returning from Normandy and Brittany in 1728 'that one could amuse oneself boldly there because there were no *mouches*'[31] – but there was still plenty to be found in the capital, despite the dissuasive threat of arrest and trial and even execution. An assistant tailor arrested in 1728 for homosexual activity in the Tuileries Gardens remarked 'that he had not come to the gardens since they burned a man of rank [Deschauffours in 1726] for these sorts of things', but went on to say that 'it was useless to try to prevent these kinds of pleasure, that they would never succeed.'[32] And in 1784, while trying to pick up a young man, Claude-François Lemaire 'showed him his private parts while saying that one had to be wary because people are arrested here every day.' Lemaire himself was not careful enough: the young man turned out to be working for the police.[33]

Modern homosexuals obviously did not originate the practice of frequent, furtive and usually anonymous sex in public or semi-public places. Already in the eighteenth century (and undoubtedly well before), Parisian sodomites hunted for sexual partners in the city's streets and especially its parks and gardens, where they copulated under the trees, behind the hedges and even on the benches. It was not unusual at the time for Parisians of all sexual orientations to have sex out of doors. Paris was a city where, as Arlette Farge has observed, 'lodgings offered so little privacy that from time to time the street in which people lived gave the illusion of calm that home did not. ... People sometimes made love outside ... paradoxically protected by the tumult of always bustling [urban] space.'[34] Pederasts favored the Tuileries Gardens, although they had to be respectably dressed for admittance to this royal park. The abbé Boisrenaud accosted a stranger there one evening in 1724: 'You probably want to find some company to have fun with? I well know that one is not in these places at this time for any other purpose.'[35] The Palais-Royal was much frequented by female prostitutes, especially in the 1780s, but pederasts as well haunted its alleys and crowded its cafés and gambling dens.[36] Then there was the Champs-Élysées: not the broad avenue itself, but the 'Elysian Fields' between the Place Louis XV (Place de la Concorde) and the Rond-Point.[37] The banks of the Seine (as yet unpaved) drew sodomites not only after dark, but also during the day when they ogled and picked up the men who swam naked there in defiance of police ordonnances. An official complained in 1724, 'It's a horrible scandal that a large number of libertine men swim in the nude in Paris in sight of so many people, principally of the opposite sex. ... They also commit abominations with those of their own sex.'[38]

Men habitually urinated and even defecated outdoors, which offered them frequent occasions to expose themselves and gauge reactions. In May 1784 in the Champs-Élysées, for instance, a policeman arrested a 40-year-old postilion 'whom he saw prowling about in a suspicious manner for a long time, then going from tree to tree pretending to make water.' A man might fondle himself while pretending to urinate or make some inviting comment, like 43-year-old Jean-Baptiste Lefevre, arrested on the Quai des Orfèvres in January 1785, because 'he told an individual who passed by while he was in a posture to make water that he couldn't [urinate] because he was too hard, which was true.'[39] Another sodomite showed more wit than discretion in 1723 when he saw a young man (who was in fact a *mouche*) urinating and asked him 'what time it was by [his] cock, and [said] that by his [own] it was noon.'[40]

Then there were the more subtle ways that sodomites indicated a mutual interest. One informant reported in 1737 that Bernard Girardot 'stared at me rudely [*sous le nez*], giving me the usual signal of the vile creatures.'[41] A report about a patrol in the Champs-Élysées in 1780 explained that 'Mr. Noël and his men ... know the signals of these debauchees, consisting of the placement of the hat, spitting, two successive blows of the cane against a tree, etc.'[42] Verbal contact could begin with a claim of prior acquaintanceship. In May 1788, the police arrested Pierre Corby, a 50-year-old upholsterer, after he approached an inspector on the northern boulevards, 'telling me that he thought we knew each other, a means used by pederasts to make a pick up.'[43] Or a sodomite could strike up a seemingly innocent conversation by asking the time, commenting on the weather or requesting tobacco. In 1723, one sodomite, asked by another if he had any tobacco, responded with a gesture toward his genitals: 'I'm sure that you prefer this to a pinch of tobacco.'[44]

Once they had made contact, two men might have sexual relations on the spot (in the parks or along the riverbank) or go elsewhere for privacy. Cabarets and taverns provided rooms to customers who wished to eat and drink in private, but some owners were leery of accommodating just anybody. The abbé de Boisrenaud commented in 1724 that 'since half of Paris was of that [sodomitical] inclination, none of the tavern keepers was ignorant of it, and all were, in this respect, on the lookout.'[45] In truth, however, some tavern keepers catered profitably to the city's sodomites. In May 1748, the sodomite Nicolas Harault told police 'that this summer he found himself seven or eight times in the gatherings held in different cabarets at la Courtille [a northeastern suburb] and notably three or four times in the Horseshoe Cabaret.'[46] Another sodomitical hangout in the 1780s was the Bright Moon in suburban Vaugirard to the south-west of the city, described as a 'very suspect place' where 'orgies are held.'[47] A contemporary print depicts the Café Alexandre on the boulevard du Temple as an elegant venue, but it had a bad reputation in the 1780s:

> here one finds only street-walkers, buggers and bardashes [youthful passive sodomites]. In this café infamous acts and horrors take place that it is pointless to name. ... The police keep watch there, but people know how to fool their vigilant eye; the wisest and safest course of action would be to shut down this receptacle of tribades [lesbians] and sodomites.'[48]

At some of their gatherings, the sodomites wore extravagant clothing, powdered their face, put on artificial beauty spots, took female nicknames and even referred to each other as 'sisters.' One informant told police in 1748:

> This past summer, he attended several gatherings of the Men of the Cuff, at la Courtille [a Parisian suburb] or at the Sign of the Six Sparrows on the Rue aux Juifs [within the city]. There were some [men] who put handkerchiefs on their heads, imitating women, mincing like them. When there was some new young man there, they called him the Bride, and in this case, he becomes the object of everybody. They choose each other in these gatherings for mutual fondling and to commit infamies.[49]

Not everyone liked this behavior. One sodomite remarked in 1748 that 'he withdrew from these gatherings because they were too scandalous. Several men imitated women ..., that often he chided several of them saying: "Can't you behave like men rather than women?"' Another upbraided his fellow sodomites: 'What! You're men and you give yourself women's names?'[50]

Despite the tone of disgust evident in their reporting and in spite of the formal harshness of the law, policemen almost never turned sodomites over to the courts, except in the most unusual circumstances involving abduction, rape or murder. The one (unexplained) exception is the case of Jean Diot and Bruno Lenoir, two hapless wretches (both working-class) burned by way of example in July 1750 after the night watch caught them one evening having sex in the street.[51] Although the police had the authority to deport to the colonies (a clergyman, intervening for the release of his servant, arrested for sodomy in 1723, suggested: 'If he does it again, either burn him or ship him to the Mississippi'[52]), they applied even this punishment rarely. They ordinarily detained an arrested pederast for a period ranging from a week to several months, while releasing others (generally nobles or those socially well connected) with no more than a warning. In 1725, an inspector tried to arrest the Marquis de Bressey in the Tuileries Gardens. The nobleman threatened to kill himself because of the shame, invoked his social relations and generally made such a fuss that the inspector let him off 'so as not to be compelled to [use] violence against a man of rank.'[53] More ordinary men could win release by giving up the names of other sodomites or by getting family, friends, neighbors or employers to petition on their behalf. Foreigners risked expulsion from France, clergymen might be reported to their superiors, who often then transferred them to a distant parish, and repeat offenders might be forcibly enrolled in the army or expelled from Paris (which did not keep them from returning without authorization).

The sodomitical identity

The eighteenth-century sodomites tracked by the police undoubtedly participated in a semi-clandestine subculture centred on the satisfaction of their shared sexual inclinations. Whether or not they also shared a distinct *identity* that set them apart from 'normal' men is more problematic.

In his memoirs of Louis XIV's court, Primi Visconti, Count de Saint-Mayol (1648–1713), recounted how, in the mid-1670s, his friend, the Marquis de la Vallière (1642–76), made a pass at him:

> He approached me saying: 'Monsieur, in Spain the monks [do it]; in France, the grandees; in Italy, everybody.' I pulled back, and I replied jokingly that I was far from any such thought, that I was 25-years-old and had a beard. He replied that Frenchmen of good taste paid no attention either to age or to body hair; in short, it was not

> easy for me to extricate myself; I told the story to the abbé del Carretto. He replied that one should show compassion, because men of such an inclination were born with it, like poets with rhyme.[54]

The anecdote presents two contrasting visions of sodomy and sodomites. Visconti, who presumably engaged in sex only with women, thought of sodomy as something committed by adult men with hairless youths. This may have been the pattern in Renaissance Italy and Visconti was in fact from Northern Italy.[55] In contrast, la Vallière, an admitted sodomite (and a Frenchman), conceived of sodomy as something that occurred between adult men. It is also worth noting that some worldly men (in this instance the abbé del Carretto) believed that certain individuals were born with sodomitical tendencies and that it was unkind to condemn them out of hand.

Two centuries later, historians are more likely to see early modern homosexuality through Visconti's eyes rather than la Vallière's. Randolph Trumbach, for instance, has contrasted the pre-1700 sodomite (any man who commits an act of sodomy) to the post-1700 one (an effeminate man with a specific identity). Until the eighteenth century, he has argued, the typical European sodomite was an adult male (the rake or libertine) who took the 'active' (or 'insertive') role in sexual relations with both women and 'passive' adolescent boys. This changed in northwestern Europe (England, France and the Netherlands) in the period 1690–1725. People came to assume 'that all men who engage[d] in sexual relations with other men [were] effeminate members of a third or intermediate gender, who surrender[ed] their rights to be treated as dominant males, and [were] exposed instead to a merited contempt as a species of male whore.'[56] The even more influential Michel Foucault has claimed that the new homosexual identity crystallized much later, in the years around 1870, when medical science began classifying men and women according to their sexual behavior. Until then, people conceived of the sodomite as any man who gave way to the universal temptation to have sex with another male; the sodomite himself did not imagine that he belonged to a separate category of men, nor did others view him as fundamentally different from the rank and file of mortals. That is what Foucault meant by his famous and oft-quoted sentence: 'The sodomite had been a temporary aberration; the homosexual was now a species.'[57]

Not all historians agree with this interpretive framework. Gert Hekma, for one, has cautioned that 'different models [of homosexuality] can be operative at the same time,' and the French case suggests that he is probably right.[58] There is little hard evidence that the sexual interest in both women and boys manifested by some nobles and intellectuals in the sixteenth and seventeenth centuries was anything more than a cultural trope. It may have borne no closer relationship to reality in their own time than the scenarios and images of gay pornography bear to the real lives of today's homosexuals. Joseph Cady's analysis of sixteenth- and seventeenth-century texts has shown the existence well before 1700 of 'authors and audiences who were quite aware of what we would now call a "homosexual orientation" – that is, of the fact that some people are predominantly or exclusively attracted to their own sex and are identifiable by that desire.'[59]

On the other hand, the line between men inclined to sex with women and those who preferred men was certainly drawn less sharply in early modern Europe than in today's 'gay ghettoes.' Many sodomites were married men – about one-third of those arrested in the 1720s and 1730s.[60] (Even the Duke d'Orléans was married twice and fulfilled his dynastic duty by fathering several children.) Some men saw sodomy as a variant pleasure or an escapade. In his youth, the Count de Sade (1702–67), father of the more famous Marquis de Sade, enjoyed sex with both men and women. The police arrested him for cruising in the Tuileries Gardens in 1724 and the Count even boasted in verse of his sexual versatility:

> Like an inhabitant of Sodom
> I play the woman's role with a man,
> That's what infuriates you.
> But why get angry, ladies?
> You alone make me happy:
> I am very much a man with the women.

According to his son's biographer, 'as for many young lords the "philosophical sin" was nothing more [for the Count] than an aristocratic caprice, a sort of game made more exciting by being forbidden. ... What was the risk when one possessed a great name and powerful patrons?'[61]

But commoners, too, might enjoy an occasional same-sex adventure, like the master glazier Jacques-Louis Ménétra (born 1738) whose memoirs, written in the late 1700s, appeared in print only two centuries later. Their editor has described Ménétra's sexual experiences as 'hopelessly normal' because the memoirs do not refer to either 'childhood masturbation' or 'homosexual temptations.' They do mention that one morning on the Boulevard du Temple in Paris a nobleman propositioned Ménétra, who turned him down flat: 'I hear you [,] I run after women but nothing else [,] goodbye.'[62] They say nothing, however, about another incident late one Friday evening in April 1786, when the police questioned Ménétra after observing him accost men on the Boulevard Montmartre. Ménétra denied any wrongdoing – he claimed that 'feeling drunk and not wanting to go home in that condition, he took a walk' – but his equivocal behavior in a place notorious for homosexual pickups left little room for doubt. The police let him go with a warning.[63] It seems likely that Ménétra, especially with a few drinks under his belt, had an occasional interest in sex with other men, perhaps developed during his days as an unmarried journeymen living in all-male lodging houses.

Sodomy was no more than incidental in the lives of de Sade and Ménétra. In no way did it define them (in their own minds or in anybody else's) as fundamentally different from most men. In contrast, remarks made by some sodomites stopped by the police suggest that many others did have a sense of being set apart by what they described as a 'taste' for male sexual partners (and a distaste for womankind). For example, in 1724 a lawyer remarked 'that he had a wife, but rarely used her ... that he had no taste for women, that he preferred a cock to a cunt.'[64] A 50-year-old nobleman said in 1725 'that as for him, he did not like women, that he had never liked another sex but his own, ... that the miser loved money, the drunkard drink, that as for him he was not prey to those passions, that his was to love his own sex.'[65] In 1786 a 36-year-old merchant told a 19-year-old whom he was trying to seduce and who insisted that he loved women, 'that his [own] taste was not to love women ... that his taste was to enjoy himself with men.'[66] Given the lack of police sources from before 1700, it is impossible to know whether such attitudes were prevalent in the earlier period.

Comparing sodomites arrested in the early decades of the eighteenth century to those arrested in the 1780s, Jeffrey Merrick has concluded that the latter were less often married, more likely to seek out partners of their own age, less obviously effeminate, but more likely to wear clothing made them stand out from the multitude. By the 1780s:

> [the police] did not seem to think that all men were likely to have sex with other men. They thought that some men, many of whom evidently had no interest in women, performed certain kinds of sexual acts and displayed certain kinds of sexual inclinations that could be acquired much more easily than they could be abandoned. ... [The police] arrested such men not only because of their individ-

> ual acts but also because of the shared tastes that distinguished them from other men, not only because of what they had already done but also because of what they might still do.[67]

Moreover, in their reports, the police began referring to pederasts as 'men of this species' (*gens de cette espèce*) and 'men of their clique' (*gens de leur clique*).[68] And they claimed, in at least some instances, to be able to distinguish 'the appearance and the tone of pederasts.'[69] Thus, they questioned a 37-year-old servant in November 1783, because he 'appeared to us to be wearing the dress, [and] to have the manners and the jargon adopted by these kinds of debauchees,' and a 21-year-old servant in June 1784, because he was 'wearing the pederast's dress, and [was] heavily perfumed with musk and amber.'[70] But what exactly made these men so obvious? No single item of clothing stands out in police reports, but generally speaking suspected sodomites wore clothing too elegant for their social class, like a long frock coat, rosettes (instead of buckles) on their shoes, a wide necktie, a gold earing, or a fancy hat. For instance, the police stopped 26-year-old Hyacinthe Le Leu, a stock-raiser, as he came out of the Tuileries Gardens one evening in April 1786 when they noticed that he had replaced his shoe buckles with ribbons and sported a black feather in his hat, 'although he is not a gentlemen' (they noted). They let Le Leu go after warning him 'not to spend evenings in suspect places,' but they first ordered him to take off the offending feather![71]

Attitudes: toward a sodomitical liberation?

Religious strictures and legal precepts expressed a consistent hostility to sodomy throughout the early modern period, although in practice, attitudes were less inflexible, as the abbé del Carretto's comments to Visconti or the failure of the police to enforce the letter of the law would indicate. Even so, understanding was not tolerance and the common people in particular showed an extreme hostility to sodomites. In Paris in April 1781, for example, two young men, aged 18 and 20 and recognizable as sodomites because of their clothes, were 'stopped by the public hue and cry and pursued by the populace that called them fags [*rivettes*].'[72] The French have regularly deemed sodomy not only 'unnatural,' but also 'un-French' and have often attributed homosexuality to foreign influences: English and German in the nineteenth and twentieth centuries, but Italian in the early modern period, when they called sodomy the 'Italian taste'. When the Renaissance first entered France from Italy in the sixteenth century, it provoked a rejection of the Italian style in culture and politics as foreign and 'unnatural.' At the same time, 'French popular opinion drew a strong connection between Italians in France and homosexual behaviour', such that one historian describes the anti-Italian rhetoric of the period as 'xeno-homophobic'.[73] These negative connotations of 'Italian taste' may have faded by the late eighteenth century; indeed, Olivier Blanc argues that by then the phrase was 'straightforwardly positive' because the educated looked on Italy as 'a cradle of civilization.'[74]

The eighteenth-century Enlightenment, with its emphasis on Reason and human rights, helped to modify attitudes toward sodomy, at least among the elites. Enlightenment writers and philosophers never endorsed homosexuality and frequently charged their enemies with practising it – even Voltaire ridiculed his clerical enemies, particularly the Jesuits, as prone to sodomy – but they did engage in serious philosophical and scientific discussions of it. As Bryant T. Ragan, Jr., has explained: 'At a time when a distinct sodomitical subculture was becoming increasingly visible in Paris, philosophes and pornographers started to set out the kinds of arguments that could be made to defend same-sex sexuality. Without always realizing the radical implications of their projects, they undermined the church's condemnation of sodomy, and they decried the cruel penalties the law prescribed for sodomites. As part of their more general efforts to study culture and nature, they also found same-sex sexuality throughout history and around the globe.'[75]

Was this why, on the eve of the French Revolution, some pederasts were becoming more defiant of authority and more willing to stand on their rights? In February 1781, when police suggested to one suspected sodomite, a 26-year-old unemployed clerk, that he was wasting his time in the disreputable taverns of the Porcherons district, he replied 'that everyone takes his pleasure where he finds it.' Ten months later, when the police reproached a 19-year-old for frequenting the public promenades 'at suspect times,' he replied 'that it was to take walks there and that everybody is free.' Arrested as a pederast in May 1785, a 28-year-old assistant tailor declared 'that he was not the only one, that he was harming nobody but himself, that he had given himself over to it very young, and that it was in his blood.'[76]

At the beginning of the French Revolution, a number of satirical pamphlets purported to call for recognition of the rights of sodomites. In *The Little Buggers of the Riding School* (1790), for example, 'M. de. V.' (the Marquis de la Villette) declared that, according to the principles of 'individual liberty, decreed by our most august and most respectable representatives,' his sexual practices ought not to be subject to legal restraint: 'I can dispose of my property, whatever it is, according to my taste and whims. Now my cock and balls belong to me and whether ... I put them in a cunt or an ass, no one has the right to complain.'[77] But it would be naive to believe (as the editors of one anthology do) that pamphlets like this one represent 'the first time lesbians and gay men organized as such to address a national government' and to claim their rights.[78] Such pamphlets were satirical, pornographic and, if anything, politically counter-revolutionary. They implied that the French Revolution and its principles had subverted the natural order. Even so, they were premonitory. In the autumn of 1791, the National Constituent Assembly passed a new penal code that decriminalized sodomy, along with other 'phoney offenses, created by superstition' (meaning religion) like blasphemy, heresy, sacrilege, witchcraft, bestiality and incest.[79] The Revolution opened the modern era in which, whatever social opprobrium French homosexuals might still encounter in their daily lives, they need no longer fear legal penalties.

Notes

1 *Dictionnaire de l'Ancien Régime: Royaume de France XVIe–XVIIIe siècle*, ed. Lucien Bély (Paris: PUF, 1996).

2 Emmanuel Le Roy Ladurie, 'Pourquoi le Pacs contredit l'héritage judéo-chrétien', *Le Figaro*, 19 Oct. 1998.

3 *Homosexuality in Early Modern France: A Documentary Collection*, ed. Jeffrey Merrick and Bryant T. Ragan, Jr. (NY and Oxford: Oxford University Press, 2001).

4 Claude Courouve, *Vocabulaire de l'homosexualité masculine* (Paris: Payot, 1985).

5 Antoine Bruneau, *Observations et maximes sur les matières criminelles* (Paris: Guillaume Cavelier, 1715), 403, translated in Merrick and Ragan, *Homosexuality in Early Modern France*, 18–19.

6 Claude Courouve, 'Sodomy Trials in France', *Gay Books Bulletin* 1 (1979):22–3, 26. According to Alfred Soman, 'The Parlement of Paris and the Great Witch Hunt', *Sixteenth-Century Journal* 9/2 (1978):36, n. 7, the Paris *parlement*, whose jurisdiction covered half of France, heard 176 appeals in cases of sodomy between 1565 and 1640 alone, and confirmed 77 of 121 death sentences imposed by lower courts.

7 Bibliothèque nationale, Ms. fr. 10969–10970, 'Procès faits à divers sodomites jugés au Parlement de Paris.' See excerpts in Ludovico Hernandez, *Les procès de sodomie au XVIe, XVIIe et XVIIIe siècles* (Paris: Bibliothèque des curieux, 1920).

8 Alfred Soman, 'Pathologie historique: le témoignage des procès de bestialité aux XVIe–XVIIe siècles,' in his *Sorcellerie et Justice Criminelle (16e–18e siècles)* (Brookfield, Vermont: Variorum, 1992), 160–1.

9 G. Dubois-Desaulle, *Les infâmes: Prêtres et moines non conformistes en amour* (Paris: Éditions de la Raison, 1902); Paul d'Estrée, *Les infâmes sous l'ancien régime* (Paris: Gougy, 1902); Claude Courouve, *Les gens de la manchette* (Paris: Claude Courouve, 1981); idem, *Les assemblées de la manchette: Documents sur l'amour masculin au XVIIIe siècle* (Paris: Claude Courouve, 1987); Maurice Lever, *Les bûchers de Sodome: Histoire des 'infâmes'* (Paris: Fayard, 1985); Michel Rey, 'Les sodomites parisiens au XVIIIe siècle' (Unpublished Mémoire de Maîtrise, Université de Paris-VIII, 1980); idem, 'Police et sodomie à Paris au XVIIIe siècle: du péché au désordre', *Revue d'histoire moderne et contemporaine* 29 (1982):113–24; idem, 'L'art de "raccrocher" au XVIIIe siècle', *Masques* 24 (Winter 1984/85):92–9; idem, 'Justice et sodomie à Paris au XVIIIe siècle', in *Droit, histoire et sexualité*, ed. J. Poumarède and J.-P. Royer (Lille: Espace Juridique, 1987), 175–84; idem, 'Police and Sodomy in Eighteenth-Century Paris: From Sin to Disorder', in *The Pursuit of Sodomy in Renaissance and Enlightenment Europe*, ed. Kent Gerard and Gert Hekma (NY: Haworth Press, 1989), 129–46; idem, 'Naissance d'une minorité', in *Amour et sexualité en Occident*, ed. Georges Duby (Paris: Seuil, 1991):309–14; idem, '1700–1750, les sodomites parisiens créent un mode de vie,' in *Cahiers Gai Kitsch Camp* 24 (Lille: Cahiers GKC, 1994), xi–xxxiii, revised version of 'Parisian Homosexuals Create a Lifestyle, 1700–1750s', in *'Tis Nature's Fault: Unauthorized Sexuality During the Enlightenment*, ed. R.P. Maccubbin (New York: Cambridge University Press, 1987), 179–91; Jeffrey Merrick, 'Sodomitical Inclinations in Early Eighteenth-Century Paris', *Eighteenth-Century Studies* 30 (1997):289–95; idem, 'Commissioner Foucault, Inspector Noël and the "Pederasts" of Paris, 1780–83', in *Journal of Social History* 32 (1998):287–307; idem, 'Sodomitical Scandals and Subcultures in the 1720's', *Men and Masculinities* 1 (1999):373–92; idem, ' "Brutal Passions" and "Depraved Taste": The Case of Jacques-François Pascal', in *Homosexuality in French History and Culture*, ed. Jeffrey Merrick and Michael Sibalis (Binghamton, NY: Harrington Park Press, 2001), 85–103; idem, 'Sodomites and Police in Paris, 1715', *Journal of Homosexuality* 42 (2002):103–28; idem, ' "Nocturnal Birds" in the Champs-Élysées: Police and Pederasty in Prerevolutionary Paris', *GLQ: A Journal of Lesbian and Gay Studies* 8 (2002):425–31.

10 Didier Godard, *L'autre Faust: L'homosexualité masculine pendant la Renaissance* (Montblanc: H & O Éditions, 2002), 30.

11 Godard, *L'autre Faust*, 113–59. See Pierre Chevallier, *Henri III: roi shakespearien* (Paris: Fayard, 1985) and Emmanuel Le Roy Ladurie, *The Royal French State 1460–1610*, trans. Juliet Vale (Oxford and Cambridge, MA: Blackwell, 1994), 192–3.

12 Keith Cameron, 'Henry III – the Antichristian King', *Journal of European Studies* 4 (1974):152–63.

13 Godard, *L'autre Faust*, 134.

14 David Teasley, 'The Charge of Sodomy as a Political Weapon in Early Modern France: The Case of Henry III in Catholic League Polemic, 1585–1589', *The Maryland Historian* 18 (1987):26.

15 Philip-Joseph Salazar, 'Henry III de Valois', in *Who's Who in Gay & Lesbian History*, ed. Robert Aldrich and Garry Wotherspoon (London and NY: Routledge, 2001), 205–7.

16 Nicolas Le Roux, *La faveur du roi: Mignons et courtisans au temps des derniers Valois (vers 1647–vers 1589)* (Paris: Champ Vallon, 2001), 653–5.
17 Jeffrey Merrick, 'The Cardinal and the Queen: Sexual and Political Disorders in the Mazarinades', *French Historical Studies* 18 (1994):667–99; Lewis C. Seifert, 'Eroticizing the Fronde: Sexual Deviance and Political Disorder in the Mazarinades', *L'Esprit Créateur* 35 (1995):22–36.
18 Pierre Chevallier, *Louis XIII, roi cornélien* (Paris: Fayard, 1979), 453–5.
19 Nancy Nichols Barker, *Brother to the Sun King: Philippe, Duke of Orléans* (Baltimore and London: Johns Hopkins University Press, 1989), 57. See also Didier Godard, *Le goût de Monsieur* (Montblanc: H & O Éditions, 2002).
20 There are several editions of Madame's letters, including *Letters from Liselotte*, ed. Maria Kroll (London: Allison & Busby, 1998). See Dirk Van der Cruysse, *Madame Palatine, Princesse européenne* (Paris: Fayard, 1988), esp. chapter 5: 'Entre Saint-Cloud et Sodome: Monsieur, prince gay'.
21 See Lever, *Les bûchers*, 156–67; the original source is 'La France devenue italienne,' in Roger de Rabutin, comte de Bussy, *Histoire amoureuse des Gaules*, ed. Paul Boiteau and C.L. Livet, 4 vols (Paris: Jannet et Daffis, 1856–76), 3:345–60. See also Marc Daniel [Michel Duchein], *Hommes du grand siècle: Études sur l'homosexualité sous les règnes de Louis XIII et Louis XIV* (Paris: Arcadie, [1957]).
22 Robert Oresko, 'Homosexuality and Court Elites of Early Modern France: Some Problems, Suggestions, and an Example', in Gerard and Hekma, *Pursuit of Sodomy*, 105–28.
23 Philippe-Joseph Salazar, 'Herculean Lovers: Toward a History of Men's Friendship in the 17th Century', *Thamyris* 4 (1997):249–66; Marc D. Schachter, ' "That Friendship Which Possesses the Soul": Montaigne Loves La Boétie', in Merrick and Sibalis, *Homosexuality in French History and Culture*, 5–21. For quotation, *The Essays of Michel de Montaigne*, ed. Jacob Zeitlin, 3 vols (NY: Knopf, 1934–36), 1:166.
24 David Parris, 'Viau, Théophile de', and 'Guez de Balzac, Louis', in Aldrich and Wotherspoon, *Who's Who*, 194, 461–2.
25 David Wootten, 'Unhappy Voltaire, or "I Shall Never Get Over It As Long as I Live" ', *History Workshop Journal* 50 (Autumn 2000):137–55.
26 Olivier Blanc, *L'amour à Paris au temps de Louis XVI* (Paris: Perrin, 2002); for Cambacérès, see 67–71.
27 Cissie Fairchilds, *Domestic Enemies: Servants and their Masters in Old Regime France* (Baltimore and London: The Johns Hopkins University Press, 1983), 187.
28 On the *mouches*, their reports and their changing tactics, see especially the works by Lever and Rey, cited in note 9.
29 Rey, 'Les sodomites', 43.
30 Merrick, 'Sodomitical inclinations', 291–2.
31 Quoted in Rey, 'Les sodomites', 11.
32 Quoted in Rey, 'Les sodomites', 26.
33 Archives nationales [henceforth AN], Y 11724, 17 Sept. 1784.
34 Arlette Farge, *Vivre dans le rue à Paris au XVIIIe siècle* (Paris: Gallimard/Julliard, 1979), 38.
35 Quoted in Lever, *Les bûchers*, 300.

36 Michael Sibalis, 'The Palais-Royal and the Homosexual Subculture of Nineteenth-Century Paris', in Merrick and Sibalis, *Homosexuality in French History and Culture*, 117–29.
37 Merrick, ' "Nocturnal Birds" '.
38 Quoted in Augustin Cabanès, *La vie aux bains*, 2nd edn (Paris: Albin-Michel, n.d.), 329–30.
39 AN, Y 11723, 25 May 1784; Y 11725, 27 Jan. 1785.
40 Quoted in Rey, '1700–1750', xv.
41 Quoted in Lever, *Les bûchers*, 269.
42 AN, O 1589, 12 Nov. 1780.
43 AN, Y 11731, 31 May 1788.
44 Quoted in Rey, '1700–1750', xiv.
45 Quoted in Rey, '1700–1750', xiii.
46 Quoted in Courouve, *Les assemblées*, 27–9.
47 AN, Y 13408, 16 Aug. and 15 Oct. 1781; Y 13409, 19 July 1781.
48 [François-Marie Mayeur de Saint-Paul], *Le désoeuvré, ou l'espion du boulevard du Temple* (London: N.p., 1781), 38–9. For a contemporary print of the café, see Jean Chagnot, *Nouvelle histoire de Paris: Paris au XVIIIe siècle* (Paris: Hachette, 1988), 65.
49 Quoted in Rey, '1700–1750', xxvi.
50 Quoted in Rey, '1700–1750', xxix.
51 For relevant documents, see Merrick and Ragan, *Homosexuality in Early Modern France*, 77–9; Claude Courouve, *L'affaire Lenoir-Diot* (Paris: Claude Courouve, 1980).
52 Quoted in Rey, 'Les sodomites', 30.
53 Quoted in Lever, *Les bûchers*, 259.
54 *Mémoires de Primi Visconti sur la cour de Louis XIV, 1673–1681*, ed. Jean-François Solnon (Paris: Perrin, 1988), 81.
55 Michael Rocke, *Forbidden Friendships: Homosexuality and Male Culture in Renaissance Florence* (New York and Oxford: Oxford University Press, 1996).
56 Randolph Trumbach, 'Gender and the Homosexual Role in Modern Western Culture: The 18th and 19th Centuries Compared', in *Homosexuality, Which Homosexuality? International Conference on Gay and Lesbian Studies*, ed. Dennis Altman *et al.* (London: GMP, [1989]), 149–69; see also idem, 'The Birth of the Queen: Sodomy and the Emergence of Gender Equality in Modern Culture, 1660–1750', in *Hidden from History: Reclaiming the Gay and Lesbian Past*, ed. Martin Duberman, Martha Vicinus and George Chauncey, Jr. (New York: Meridian, 1989), 129–40; and idem, 'Homosexuality', in *A Dictionary of Eighteenth-Century World History*, ed. Jeremy Black and Roy Porter (Oxford and Cambridge, MA: Blackwell, 1994), 381–2.
57 Michel Foucault, *The History of Sexuality*, vol. I: *An Introduction*, trans. Robert Hurley (New York: Pantheon, 1978), 43.
58 Gert Hekma, 'Same-sex relations among men in Europe, 1700–1990', in *Sexual Cultures in Europe*, ed. Franz X. Eder, Lesley A. Hall, and G. Hekma (Manchester and NY: Manchester University Press, 1999), 80.
59 Joseph Cady, 'The "Masculine Love" of the "Princes of Sodom" "Practising the Art of Ganymede" at Henri III's Court: The Homosexuality of Henri III and His *Mignons* in Pierre de L'Estoile's *Mémoires-Journaux*', in *Desire and*

Discipline: Sex and Sexuality in the Premodern West, ed. Jaccqueline Murray and Konrad Eisenbichler (Toronto, Buffalo, London: University of Toronto Press, 1996):123.

60 Rey, 'Les sodomites', 74.

61 Maurice Lever, *Sade: A Biography*, trans. Arthur Goldhammer (San Diego, NY, London: Harcourt Brace, 1994), 24–7 (my translation of poem).

62 Jacques-Louis Ménétra, *Journal of My Life*, ed. Daniel Roche, trans. Arthur Goldhammer (NY: Columbia University Press, 1986), 162–3, 275.

63 AN, Y 11721, 21 April 1786.

64 Quoted in Rey, '1700–1750', xxii.

65 Document reproduced in Rey, 'Les sodomites', Appendix # XXIX.

66 AN, Y 11727, 9 Feb. 1786.

67 Merrick, 'Commissioner Foucault', 302.

68 For example, AN, Y 13407, 30 Oct. and 10 Dec. 1780.

69 AN, Y 11725, 13 May 1785.

70 AN, Y 11722, 7 Nov. 1783; Y 11723, 19 June 1784.

71 AN, Y 11727, 20 April 1786.

72 AN, Y 13408, 11 April 1781.

73 Rebecca E. Zorach, 'The Matter of Italy: Sodomy and the Scandal of Style in Sixteenth-Century France', *Journal of Medieval and Early Modern Studies* 28 (1998):581–609 (quotations 583–4).

74 Olivier Blanc, 'The "Italian Taste" in the Time of Louis XVI, 1774–92', in Merrick and Sibalis, *Homosexuality in French History and Culture*, 69–84.

75 Bryant T. Ragan, Jr., 'The Enlightenment Confronts Homosexuality', in *Homosexuality in Modern France*, ed. Jeffrey Merrick and Bryant T. Ragan, Jr. (Oxford and NY: Oxford University Press, 1996), 25. See also D.A. Coward, 'Attitudes Toward Homosexuality in Eighteenth-Century France', *Journal of European Studies* 10 (1980):231–55; Pierrre Peyronnet, 'Le péché philosophique', in *Aimer en France 1760–1860*, ed. Paul Viallaneix and Jean Erhard, 2 vols (Clermont-Ferrand: Association des Publications de la Faculté des Lettres et Sciences Humaines de Clermont-Ferrand, 1980), 2:421–7; Michel Delon, 'The Priest, the Philosopher and Homosexuality in Enlightenment France', in Maccubbin, *'Tis Nature's Fault*, 122–31; Jacob Stockinger, 'Homosexuality and the French Enlightenment', in *Homosexualities and French Literature*, ed. George Stambolian and Elaine Marks (Ithaca, NY: Cornell University Press, 1979), 161–85.

76 AN, Y 13408, 12 Feb., 1 Dec. 1781; Y 11725, 25 May 1785.

77 *Les Petits Bougres au Manège* [N.p.: Paris, 1790]. I have used the translation in Merrick and Ragan, *Homosexuality in Early Modern France*, 192–8.

78 *We Are Everywhere: A Historical Sourcebook of Gay and Lesbian Politics*, ed. Mark Blasius and Shane Phelan (NY and London: Routledge, 1997), 35.

79 Michael Sibalis, 'The Regulation of Male Homosexuality in Revolutionary and Napoleonic France, 1789–1815', in Merrick and Ragan, *Homosexuality in Modern France*, 80–101.

13
Between Men in Early Modern England

Goran V. Stanivukovic

> *Homosexuality shocks less, but continues to be interesting; it provokes…feats of discourse.*[1]

The life of a man, however modern he may be, is always a public event.[2] For some time the historiography of early modern masculinity has explored masculinity in spaces that produce it as normative, ranging from the battlefield to the court, from parliament to pulpit, from travel to conquest. In early modern England (and Europe), these are spaces that enable masculine self-identification as powerful and central to the foundation of the early modern state, for in them man is constructed as hero, prince, preacher, lawyer, overseas explorer, master of the household. Yet once we start exploring both the center and the periphery of those very same spaces and institutions within which masculinity is constructed, and start looking at male sexuality outside the sphere of marriage and procreation, the historiography of early modern masculinity enters a zone of pleasure and horror. In the realm of male sexuality outside the boundaries of what Michel Foucault calls 'the most intense focus of constraints'[3] – of the body assured by marriage, early modern male sexuality is inherently transgressive. Many conduct books in early modern England, for example, did not even refer to *ero[-]s*, the term closest to 'sexuality' in early modern England, outside the context of procreation. In a rare instance when they mention *ero[-]s*, those conduct books condemn the useless spilling of seed through masturbation, as Robert Cleaver does in *A godly form of hovseholde gouernment.*[4] Simply put, human sexuality did not matter as such unless in the context of procreation. Male sexuality, and masculinity in general, thus were conceptualized in early modern culture within the parameters of the public sphere. It is because of this dependence of masculinity on publicity that difficulties with, as well as ambiguous complexities of its representations, occur once that masculinity transgresses the boundaries of normativity.

Introducing recently a volume of essays on sodomy in early modern Europe, Tom Betteridge asks questions that have both inspired and plagued writing on early modern homoerotic sexualities over the past two decades: 'Were there homosexuals in early modern Europe? Did men who had sex with each other in this period regard their behaviour as determining their identity.'[5] What has been central to the critical writing about early modern sexualities in England, between 1550 and 1800 are arguments about *whether*, in the complex pre-enlightenment history of (homo)sexuality, we should be talking about sexual acts or erotic identities, history or heritage.

In his book that created the study of early modern homoeroticism in England, Alan Bray investigates the problem of how to identify homosexual behavior in the English Renaissance, asking a similar question from a different, more empirically- inflected angle:

> Have we ... so easily found what we are looking for, an eyewitness account of how homosexuality appeared in the society of Elizabethan and Jacobean London? The answer is a clear and unequivocal no. One obvious objection is that these [Renaissance homosexuals] are stock figures not identifiable individuals.[6]

The issue that Bray raises – what makes an individual 'identifiable' – is also one that makes his dichotomy of 'stock figures' and 'identifiable individuals' somewhat problematic. Is there not a real possibility that stock figures, in this case homosexuals in Renaissance England, have something in common with identifiable individuals? Whether a sexual act occurred between friends, neighbors, nobleman and servant, master and apprentice, teacher and pupil, prince and an aristocrat, the act itself was still not necessarily a sign of self-identification. Practised between familiars, not strangers, as Bray suggests,[7] homosexuality in early modern England was to some extent even devoid of the pitfalls of dangerous adventures. This idea of early modern English homosexuality is significant because it positions homosexuality at the heart of the public man. Thus what defines the 'public' are relationships among strangers. The molly houses of the eighteenth century suggest a more or less organized homosexual behavior of London at the point of its transformation from an early modern to a modern city. Molly houses are not yet sites of self-identification; they are more spaces that signify consciousness of a sort of institutionalization of male intimacy that falls outside the public realm of marriage that attempts to preserve and control sexual behavior and, hence, social morality.

Yet Benjamin Carrier, a Catholic priest, reports that, allegedly, in 1632, there was in London:

> a company of *Sodomieticall Persons*; (whereof some are apprehe[*n*]ded but diuers fled,) in number about fourty, or more; in state competent, and some of very good meanes; in Religion *all Puritanes*; and in entercourse among themselues (a thing wonderfull to be reported) so linked, as that they made a peculiar Society or *Body*, hauing common designed place for their publike meeting ... Now seeing these prodigous Monsters ... are *all Puritans* in faith, & hould themselues far more illuminated in the Lord, then the more moderáte and learned Protestants; of which nu[*m*]ber of learned Protestants, most do wholly abandone & disclaime from the other *Puritanical Doctrines*; And further seeing, that they may make show to warrant this *their Sodomiticall State* fro[*m*] their owne *Principles*, admitting them for true.[8]

This passage, on the one hand, reflects a common way of employing sodomy to slander the religious opponent. It would not be uncommon for a Catholic priest to present this as an imagined libelous scenario, not a record of a historical situation; for the scenario only reverses the strategy often employed by the Puritans in associating Catholicism with sodomy. On the other hand, what is curious about this passage is the concrete manner in which this early version of a space designated for urban sodomites and an early modern raid on them is imagined. It suggests, first, that the author possesses a consciousness of what such an organization might look like. Second, the incident implies that the members belonging to such a society might identify themselves according to the sexual act they practice ('their Sodomiticall State'). Discursive as it is, this scenario is founded nevertheless on the idea, even a possibility, that self-identification is a separate and secretive form of masculinist culture in early modern London. Although this urban society does not yet show signs of an organized homoerotic male culture of the kind that, for example, existed in Renaissance Florence it nevertheless gestures towards imagining what that organization (and its social policing) might have looked like. Whether the described raid happened, it is still not enough evidence of either a more prolifically organized 'gay' culture in early modern England, or of the state's policing of it. It is perhaps the relative silence of authorities on the issue of public sodomy, if it ever was public enough to cause panic that enabled the discourse and representations of sodomy to continue. Thus in the absence of substantial evidence for anything like homosexual identity in the Renaissance, homoerotic masculinity of early modern England was mostly reconstructed as what we would define as queer, as relating to desire, not gender, and forms of the non-normative sexual behavior (non-normative at least from the historical perspective of our times).

Current gay historiography of early modern England shies away from the concepts of identification and identities, and privileges queer methodologies of gaps and overlaps, performances of sexual and gender behavior, and a circulation of flexible and often ambiguous desire in order to capture what might have been the male–male sexual culture of early modern England. Queer theory has done so not only because identity smacks of determinism but also because, as predominantly a theory of discursive and epistemological phenomena, queer theory depends on rhetorical constructions, and social and textual representations. Thus to read for signs of homoerotic desire and acts in early modern England means to 'read relationally', to look at 'texts as sites of self-identification', and to analyse 'the syntax of desire not readily named.'[9] Yet the question of inquiry into early modern English homoerotic masculinity arises precisely in the problem of self-identification; there are no early modern English texts where self-representation is affirmatively established. Because of the lack of affirmative self-identification, the early modern queer archive is, in a sense, 'a satire on the object of its knowledge.'[10] That even at the point at which, one could argue, early modern queer criticism has reached its peak and exhausted its archives (and, it seems, much of its arguments as well), the homoeroticism of even the most queer of early modern English writers, Christopher Marlowe, continues to be seen as a puzzle of identification, is best illustrated by two recent studies on this writer. Thus, in her biography of Marlowe, Constance Brown Kuriyama does not even mention once, let alone entertain the thought that Marlowe might have had homosexual leanings. Kuriyama's Marlowe, in fact, has no sexuality. Rather, she argues that what 'we know of Marlowe himself', including that he was 'an openly gay man', 'was tweaked to fit new iconic models and political agendas.'[11] Leaving aside the quibble that 'openness' is historically specific and that may not necessarily manifest itself in behavior but, in Marlowe's case, in dramatic and non-dramatic poetry that is exclusively masculinist and almost entirely devoid of women, Kuriyama's point implies that the image of Marlowe as a transgressor and rebel is a construction of later history, not of his own period. In that sense, her view is similar to Stephen Orgel's, who argues that 'the transgressive Marlowe is largely a posthumous phenomenon.'[12] However, Orgel's point is that, rather than being subversive, the licentious, daring, ironic, and racy Marlowe in fact explores humanity and desire within the limits of a period already known for its restless ambition, individual aspiration, and 'a higher tolerance for obscurity than we have.'[13] Thus after over a decade of criticism about queer Marlowe we have come to the point at which Marlowe's queerness has been rendered ahistorical and, hence, nonexistent or, at best, ambiguous. If Marlowe has been a metonymy for early modern English queer masculinity, even homoeroticism, what do views like Kuriyama's and Orgel's leave us with? The question is not whether Marlowe was or was not homosexual, but what constitutes queerness in early modern England. Expanding on Orgel's argument about our modern, not early modern, construction of Marlowe (and Renaissance England) as a subversive homosexual, Mario DiGangi challenges 'the kind of evidence we possess regarding the presence of male same-sex relations in early modern England' and he questions 'the methodologies used to interpret that evidence.'[14] For DiGangi, like for Orgel, Renaissance England, was a world without many inhibitions 'about public discussion of illicit sexuality.'[15]

One of the central tasks of queer theory's investigations of early modern sexuality, then, is to 'call into question the historiographical status of concepts of alterity and sameness.'[16] This is undoubtedly true, but the question still remains to what extent the distinction between alterity and sameness produces knowledge about kinds of masculinity, including homoerotic masculinity, in a culture that conceptualized sexuality only in terms of gender and specifically around matrimony and procreation. The queer approach to early modern homoeroticism, rendered as sodomy, is too broad a term for any kind of sexual transgression or sexual act that is socially disruptive. Claude J. Summers, for instance, has criticized Jonathan Goldberg's approach to Renaissance queerness, helping us to see male–male sexuality through a series of historically contingent signifying practices.[17] Similarly speaking about homosexuality from the position of material historicism, Mario DiGangi argues:

> whatever claims modern science might make for homosexuality as a 'materiality' pertaining to the body will still tell us nothing about the materiality of sexual practices and discourses ... in early modern

England. What can tell us something about how bodies were used and understood in early modern England is the language through which homoerotic relations were defined and described.'[18]

The place of sodomy in early modern culture, as it has been well documented by now, is not to define identity but the role or position of the alleged practitioner in the society. Sodomy is typically tacked on to a more specific sin that lies outside the realm of sexuality, such as bribery, usury, Catholicism, foreignness (Italians and Spaniards) and race and religion (Turks, Moors, Saracens, and Jews). Although in Foucault's theory of the history of sexuality, the repressive hypothesis is a fiction – that is, repression actually produces more discourse about sexuality – cultural materialism and new historicism in the historiography of the early modern queer masculinities has taken up as its task to uncover and bring out not only repressed desires discursively coded in the normative narratives, typically of combat and courtship, but also attitudes towards specific social phenomena and institutions (law, for example) in which sodomy was inscribed. Most of the writing about early modern queer masculinities in England has taken up Bray's premise that speaking about homosexual identity is not possible in the context of the homophobic English Renaissance not only because there was neither the language to describe it nor a specific male culture to warrant self-identification. In spite of this, there have been attempts to consider Renaissance homoeroticism as a form of identity, as Ian McAdam shows in his study of identity in the plays of Christopher Marlowe. Where queer critics see homoerotic identity discursively constructed in the literature of the English Renaissance, McAdam sees attempts at self-identified homoerotic selves emerging at the point at which the enlightenment of the Christian humanism of the Renaissance challenges the medieval culture of sin and guilt. This is the point at which a desire for personal achievement conflicts with the sense of spiritual integrity, or wholeness, inherited from the medieval period. Where we see best the pleasures and perils of this emerging self is at the point of a conflicting and often contradictory but a 'surprisingly unmoralistic approach to homosexuality'[19] in *Edward II* where it is the threat to social order and the integrity of monarchy, not the inherent abomination of a sexual act, that triggers ire among the barons. The rich genealogy of early modern representations and interpretations of gender dependent sexual practices that influenced contemporary approaches to early modern queer masculinities can be set, Alan Bray suggests, between two poles: 'of ubiquity on the one hand

and identity on the other.'[20] Bray's succinct synthesis of two only seemingly disparate approaches to early modern male homoeroticism encourages us to explore where in the archives of early modern historiography of queer masculinity can we look for our subject, in cultural, specifically literary, allegories or practices.

I will start my search, using an episode from a travel writing, in which a traveller comes to a library of a stranger and is shown the library's book holdings. The example illustrates the fact that, when it does not use sodomy sweepingly to slander an individual, early modern culture tends to relegate sodomy to the past and to imagine it as an archaic sin. Thomas Coryate tells us a story how, allegedly, upon visiting Zurich he met Henry Bullinger, 'the nephew of that famous preacher and writer of godly memory *Henry Burrlinger*, the successor of Zuinglius.'[21] When the two men met, the Swiss host led the narrator:

> into his studie, which is exceedingly well furnished with diuinitie bookes, and much augmented with many of his grandfathers ... he shewed me most execrable booke written by an Italian, one *Ionnes Casa*, Bishop of Beneuentum in Italy, in praise of that vnnatural sinne of Sodomy. This booke is written in the Italian tongue, and printed in Venice. It came first to the hands of this mans grandfather aforesaid, who kept it as a monument of the abhominable impurity of a papistical Bishop, to which end this mans also that received it from his grandfather, keepeth it to this day.[22]

What is curious in this allegory is not the usual association of Catholicism with sodomy, but how queer texts and discourses circulate among Protestants readers and scholars. The emphasis in Coryate's text is not on the abomination of sodomy but on the fact that several Protestant book collectors in one family obviously cherished Casa's filthy book, passing it from one generation to another. 'The abhominable impurity' that fills the pages of Casa's book circulates both between the narrator and his Swiss host, as well as between generations of Coryate's English readers to thumb through his own book of 'crudities'. The queer library in Coryate's story becomes a hiding place for queer desire, not a gap, but a space of desire inherent to the fabric of the narrative of travel. Queer desire takes a detour in Coryate's narrative, for what the narrative presents as a libel of a specific sexual practice in one, Catholic, community becomes a textual source of pleasure in another, Protestant, community of humanist men.

In a narrative that presents a reverse situation, the Catholic priest Benjamin Carrier, imagines a similar scenario involving books and sodomy, though this time the agent is a reformed Swiss theologian Theodore Beza. In his anti-Puritan tract, Carrier refers to some epigrammatic verses by Beza in which he writes about his sins such that he:

> practices the most execrable Sinne of *Sodomy*, and therein led the way to other *Sodomiticall* persons. ... [he also had] a boy called *Andebertus* (which Beza kept as his *Adonis*, or *Ganimede*, by abusing the boys body) and his whore *Candida*. In which verses he co[*m*]pareth the pleasure of the one with the other *Sinne*; and in the end preferreth the sinne with his boy, before the *Sinne* of fornication with his woman. This *Epigramme* of *Beza* touching his *Ganimede Andebertus*, and his whore *Candida*, is extant among others of his Epigrammes, printed at Paris in the yeare 1548. by *Robertus Stephanus*.[23]

Textual inscription of male–male desire in the space of reading is assured through the transmission of texts among readers from the time when Stephanus is supposed to have printed the text, and the moment when Carrier is sharing it again with his readers. Both fornication and sodomy are at the same time slanderously employed and used to remind the readers of the queer charges in their own humanist education of the classics in which Adonis, god of love, and Ganimede, Jupiter's cup bearer, are frequently implicated with homoerotic desire. By referring to Beza's text almost a century after it had been printed, Carrier's own text assures the continuation of the discourse of sodomy within a morally strict culture of seventeenth century counter-reformation. What the above two examples of sodomy that circulates through texts and in scholars' studies also suggest is that sodomy is hidden in private spaces, buried in old texts and shelved in scholars' studies, and that the 'close readers'[24] of those texts are the ones who recognize it. Both Coryate's and Carrier's scenarios, of two men perusing a book on sodomy published in the past, is not too distant from any scene of two men reading together, or studying together, which Alan Stewart identifies as private situations within which transactions between humanist men conflate studying with homoerotic pleasure.[25] Thus the study in the above examples features as a form of closet, not the one the men come out of, but one they get into, in order to share pleasure. What Coryate's and Carrier's book owners do when they open a book to a relevant page and show it to their guest is use earlier models to construct an environment for the continuation of homoerotic desire. This practice of sharing texts to inscribe desire in a meeting of two scholars is thus similar to the Renaissance practice of the imitation of the classics whereby 'many Renaissance writers used classical models to construct their own homoerotic discourses.'[26] One might call this form of circulation of homoerotic desire and sodomy through texts a form of 'textual intercourse' among early modern English writers, where the intercourse is not exactly what Jeffrey Masten thought of it, that is the exchange of desire through male collaboration, but, in this case, through a symbolic circulation and possession of texts from the past. In the examples in which sodomy circulates textually between men who inherit books of the past and show them to strangers, the language of sodomy becomes a medium that brings both strangers and familiars together and assures their power and pleasure. As both Coryate's and Carrier's narratives show, it is, in fact, the queer stories about familiars that enable queer connections to be established among strangers.

Textual representations of queer masculinities, those that transgress socially normative masculinity, in early modern England frequently serve a number of roles, roles that depended upon the specific social, historical, or political contexts in which such representations occurred. It is often the case within the representations of sodomy in early modern literature and culture that the rhetoric of sodomy performs a double function: it inscribes pleasure in the text and mounts criticism of an ideology or a social more. Note, for example, the following two quotations from an early seventeenth-century travel account, the verisimilitude of which is violated by a heavy dose of fantasy, characteristic of prose romances. In his travels in the eastern Mediterranean and its hinterland, Anthony Sherley, an English knight, finds himself in Persia and desires to see the King, which turns out to be possible only with the help of an Augustine friar (he makes his living by procuring women for men), who stays with Anthony while helping him reach the King of Persia. The friar:

> who the first night ... lodged in sir Anthonies house, found the means to haue a Persian curtezan to lie with him, and so had night by night during his continuance there; which if he wanted, hee would hyre a boy sodomitically to vse. And that he was a sodomiticall wretch, it dooth appear thereby: sir Anthony at his first commiting, bought twoo Christians boies in the market, which afterwards he bestowed on this Frier, whose name was Nicolao de Melo. He no

> sooner had them, but he was in hand with them concerning his sodomiticall villany. The boyes finding whereso hee was inclined (being incessantly importuned to him that solde them, hee likewise to the office, the Officer to the King, by means whereof the king espied his villany). Whereuppon the king sent for the boyes from him, and send him worde, that were it not for sir Anthonies sake, he should loose his head.[27]

This passage constructs sodomy in one of its most common forms of representation, as an abominable sin that occurs among those of unequal social and material status (the friar and the boys). In a context removed from Protestant England (Persia and Catholicism), this example represents less a privileging of homoeroticism and more Protestant English anxiety concerning anti-Catholic threat and the stereotyping of pre-Reformation monastic culture believed to have sunken into sodomy and debauchery of other kinds. Anti-catholic sentiments that imbue this episode are voiced not only in the discourse of sodomy, but also in the narrative of the friar's seedy lifestyle (the narrator also says that the friar sexually abuses women during confessions and indulges in sex with whores). The relegation of Catholicism outside English boundaries into the East, often deplored for sybaritic luxuriousness in early modern times, is yet another sign of a fiction steeped in the rhetoric of Protestant nationalism to marginalize Catholicism and render it morally corrupt. Yet again, it is the fiction of homoerotic desire exchanged among strangers, desire that circulates outside the public sphere in England that enables that desire among the familiars in England.

Very similar anti-catholic reactions transcribed in a discourse of sodomy are found in early modern English drama, most explicitly in Barnabe Barnes' play *The Devil's Charter* (1607), in which 'profane and monstrous sodomy' (1.1.1) is referred to by one of the gentlemen at the very beginning of the play. This reference locates the world of the play in transgression, a world dominated by Pope Alexander VI who at one point in the play draws his Italian captive-youth, Astor Manfredi, to his desire in the following manner:

> [Astor] My delight, my joy,
> My star, my triumph, my sweet fantasy,
> My more than son, my love, my concubine,
> Let me behold those bright stars, my joy's treasure,
> Those glorious well attemper'd tender cheeks;

> That specious forehead like a lane of lilies;
> That seemly nose, Love's chariot triumphant,
> Breathing Panchaean odours to my senses;
> That gracious mouth, betwixt whose crimson pillow
> Venus and Cupid sleeping kiss together;
> That chin, the ball vow'd to the Queen of Beauty,
> Now budding ready to bring forth love-blossoms.
> Astor Manfredi, turn thee to my love. (3.2.1–13)[28]

This is one of the most explicit examples of homoerotic seduction in early modern English drama, which surprisingly has been overlooked in all critical accounts of early modern homoeroticism and sodomy. Alexander's tragic end – he is dragged screaming to hell – is punishment for his cumulative sins, involving murders and sodomy. His death represents the early modern Protestant culture's punishment for Catholic transgressions. What emerges out of these fictions which mix horror and titillation is an early modern historiography of male pleasure that is at the same time about private pleasures and about the public realm (state, court, church), nationalism, and male power.

In this historiography, that comes out of homophobic early modern culture, sodomy becomes not only a metonymy for other sins but also for other non-sexual discourses, of state, empire, and religion. What is interesting about sodomites in sixteenth- and early seventeenth-century texts is that they tend to be associated either with religion or the court. It is towards the end of the seventeenth century that the figure of a 'secularized sodomite' emerges, 'signaling a radical break with the past.'[29] What is common to all the examples of homoerotic culture that I have described thus far is their focus on sexual behavior and the maligned practice of sodomy. In all these examples, the heinous figure of the sodomite destabilizes the notion of masculinity in early modern culture and threatens the foundation of aristocratic hierarchy or a Christian state. Writing about sodomy in English humanist culture, Alan Stewart has argued that despite numerous representations of sodomy within the sphere of public representation, sodomy often occurred in very private spaces and homosexuality was an 'intensely personal concern',[30] regardless of the type that is involved in it, 'the beating schoolmaster, the cloistered monk, the humanist bedfellow, the closeted secretary.'[31] If classroom, church, household, and the court are institutions of normative culture than the presence of a sodomite within those spaces exposes 'the weak links in normative regimes, expose the regimes' arbitrariness.'[32]

One of the best examples of the regime's arbitrariness in appearing to be at the same time disturbed by and blind at implications of sodomy can be seen in the selective legal treatment of sodomy in the case of the 1631 trial of Mervin Touchet, Lord Audley, the secoud Earl of Castlehaven, which was 'the earliest secular English prosecution for sodomy for which we have extensive documentation.'[33] Castlehaven was tried (and ultimately beheaded) for aiding the rape of his own wife and for committing sodomy with two of his male servants, Laurence Fitz Patrick and Thomas Broadway. Castlehaven's trial was 'an uncharted challenge'[34] to the order, even though its threat appeared huge only when a charge of sodomy was connected with treason, but not as much when it was linked to property and rape. As in Marlowe's *Edward II*, sodomy in Castlehaven's case appears to be a problem primarily because it threatens the (hetero)masculine order, not because it runs counter to normative – heteroerotic – sexuality. What Castlehaven's case suggests is that as a sin sodomy appears to be considered dauntingly hazardous only if it has public consequences for masculine order, while its effects on household, on women and property, is less threatening, at least outside the boundaries of the domestic, where it affects children, property, servants and, of course, the wife.[35] In early modern England sodomy was linked with monstrosity, as Thomas Beard does following the Biblical denunciation of that carnal sin. For Beard, sodomy is directly linked to 'violence ... without all shame and measure.'[36] At the same time, however, Castlehaven's household becomes a space in which transgressive desire, specifically sodomy, disrupts relationships among the familiars within the private sphere, within, that is, the cultural trope of normativity.

The examples I have quoted above all deal with sodomy, with a specific, maligned and outlawed, sexual practice associated either with Protestant England anti-Catholic sentiments, foreignness, or non-Christianity. Although the early moderns clearly understood sodomy to be a carnal sin, 'they were far less certain about the distinction between hetero- and homosexuality and often had sexual relations with both sexes without regarding their behaviour as contradictory or strange.'[37] Since sodomy is a libelous term connoting wide range of not necessarily sexual practices, and a slanderous term that does not necessarily refer to an actual erotic experience, it is uncertain whether it can be used as a sign of homosexual masculinity. And since it is difficult to speak about homosexuality as identity because evidence for such self-identification is tenuous and sparse, the question, then, is what is there for queer historiography to turn to in continuing and expanding its arguments about early modern homoeroticism? Examples get duplicated and episodes multiplied even in a literary and cultural corpus that has yet to be fully explored. For example, the recurrent trope of queer masculinity in early modern English prose fiction and travel writing is the one of a sodomite Eastern king, sultan, or a warrior. But this narrative trope in fact only replicates the cultural stereotype of deprecating oriental masculinity by linking it to sodomy. It seems, then, that we have exhausted archives for new examples of sodomitical behavior or for different cultural scenarios in which homosexuality appears in new forms.

In the realm of cultural history one of the most profitable corpuses of texts for queer evidence is the history of humanist pedagogy. As Alan Stewart has recently shown, the humanist classroom and education (and disciplining) of boys are profitable areas for redefining the social history of early modern sodomy and the culture of male transactions. In literature, however, there are opportunities that we have not yet tackled. Among topics worth exploring are kinship relationships, especially the socially marginalized figure of the younger brother, lewd aristocrats and idle citizens of Caroline drama, the middling sorts' pastime pleasures in popular literature, heroic friends and traveling knights in popular fiction, and Englishmen in Moslem captivity in the eastern Mediterranean.

In the absence of any objective knowledge of how early modern homoeroticism manifested itself, at least beyond the issue of sexual behavior and sodomy, we may want to look for passions among men that are separate from desire (or power) and that do not depend on the possibility of homoeroticism. In his recent book on sodomy and the sublime in the post-Pauline tradition, Richard Halpern argues 'The very possibility of the beautiful as something that excites a passion distinct from desire therefore depends on the non-existence of male homoerotic desire.'[38] If representations of early modern homosexuality are ambiguous and unstable, then we might want to start thinking about it not as a possibility for male–male erotic desire arranged around the axis of power and between socially unequal men, but as any sort of passion between equal men outside the realm of *erōs*.

I want to turn now to literature as a constitutive and unavoidable factor in the historiography of early modern homoerotic masculinity not only because in literature some of the stereotypes in the representation of homosexuality break down, but also because literature imagines other male bonds, based not on behavior but on emotions. Thomas Wyatt's elegy CXCVII ('In mourning wise since daily I increase'), composed 'after May 1536'[39] and the dramatization of the relationship between Caesar and Anthony in Shakespeare's *Anthony and Cleopatra*, performed in 1607, are what interest me here. Both Wyatt's elegy on the death of friends and Shakespeare's Roman tragedy turn friendship, specifically feelings among absent friends, into a site of passion. What interests me about this odd literary pair is how the rhetoric of mourning enables ambiguous emotions (of love, longing, despair, loss – queer emotions) that bind friends, even dead friends.

Wyatt's elegy for dead friends may appear an unlikely poem for a discussion of male passions, especially since the cause is the execution of four men (Sir Henry Norris, Sir Francis Weston, Sir William Brereton, and Mark Smeaton) charged with adultery because they were implicated in a sexual involvement with Anne Boleyn. Yet it is precisely in the realm of heterosexual desire, as Eve Kosofsky Sedgwick has shown through the example of Shakespeare's sonnets, that one looks for love between men in early modern English literature.[40] The lyrical subject, the mourning friend, in Wyatt's elegy dismisses a collective claim that the deaths are justified because they are seen as treason ('... some perchance would say will say, of cruel heart, / "A traitor's death why should we thus bemoan?" / But I, alas, set this offence apart, / Must needs bewail the death of some be gone'). The poem privileges the sense of loss of friends, and the friends' worth, over the collective injustice because of the offence ('Alas, thou [Norris] are far overseen / By thine offences to be thus dead and gone.'). With every stanza the speaker's solitude for the loss of friends intensifies, as he remembers his dead friends for faculties and pleasures that exceeded the world around him. Thus Weston is missed because 'he was pleasant ... and young' and incomparable in 'active things.' Because 'Great was [Brereton's] love with diverse', his friends mourn his death and 'other hear their piteous cry and moan.' Mark is lamented most, and the speaker's rhetorical question about the nature of his own lament for the dead friend:

> Ah, Mark, what moan should I for thee make more
> Since that thy death thou hast deserved best,
> Save only that mine eye is forced sore
> With piteous plaint to moan thee with the rest?

suggests the magnitude of his loss. In the final stanza, the poet contrasts the gruesomeness of the friend's death ('... farewell, each one in hearty wise. / The axe is home, your heads be in the street.') to swelling emotions that cause creative paralysis and bring out tears that stop writing ('The trickling tears doth fall so from my eyes, / I scarce may write, my paper is so wet.'). The cumulative effect of mourning intensifies the speaker's solitude and enables Wyatt to construct the relational terms between the speaker and the friends in the language of intimacy and grief for its interruption. Thinking of friends in emotional terms is not uncommon for Wyatt. Wyatt resorts to an 'affective plea' for friends 'by using an intimate and embodied register' in some other poems, too.[41] What is at stake in this poem is not homoerotic desire. Rather, at the emotional center of this poem about mourning and loss is a passion for men. The figure imagined here is what Alan Bray calls 'the masculine friend', a type that stands 'in stark contrast to the forbidden intimacy of homosexuality.'[42] The masculine friend is the figure that shares the all-male space of courtly culture with other men. Both Wyatt, his historical friends and their poetic characters belong to it – and their loss is thus both personal and collective.

Lament for the lost friend intensifies the ambiguous passion that binds men in *Anthony and Cleopatra*. It is a play characterized by many levels of emotion and yearning. Among those levels one that stands out in particular is the heroic friendship between Anthony and Caesar. This is how Caesar reacts at the news of Anthony's death:

> O Anthony,
> I have followed thee to this; but we do lance
> Diseases in our bodies. I must perforce
> Have shown to thee such a declining day,
> Or look on thine: we could not stall together
> In the whole world. But yet let me lament
> With tears as sovereign as the blood of hearts
> That thou, my brother, my competitor
> In top of all design, my mate in empire,
> Friend and companion in the front of war,
> The arm of mine own body, and the heart
> Where mine his thoughts did kindle – that our stars
> Unreconciliable should divide
> Our equalness to this. (5.1.35–48)[43]

This is the only moment in the play at which Caesar relinquishes his sense of duty and ambition and allows emotion to speak out. Beginning by imagining a kinship relationship with Anthony ('my brother'), Caesar's memorial lament for a heroic friendship ('my competitor / In top of all design, my mate in empire, / Friend and companion in the front of war') turns into his fantasy of Anthony as part of his own body ('The arm of mine own body'), and ends up with a suggestion, 'contrary to all that we have seen of their relationship in the play' that imagines their hearts, 'like those of friends and lovers'[44] linked as one ('the heart / Where mine his thoughts did kindle'). The rhetorical structure of this speech is based on transactions between Anthony and Caesar ('I have followed thee to this, but we do lance / Diseases in our bodies.'; 'we could not stall together'). Throughout the play, Caesar goes back and forth between his loyalty to his friendship with Anthony and his own ambition. Despite acknowledging differences in they way they act, Caesar remains loyal to his friendship with Anthony ('We shall remain in friendship, our conditions / So diff'ring in their acts.' [2.2.118–19]). And in a climax of loyalty to his friend, Caesar gives Anthony his sister Octavia as a wife in an attempt to 'To join our kingdoms and our hearts; and never / Fly off our loves again' (2.2.158–9). In Caesar's love scenario, a woman is here a conduit for one man's affection for another, an enabler of love meant permanently to bind kingdoms and hearts of men. This is an example of how the discourse of *amicitia*, of friendship and love, subordinates office and political agency to the private self of longing and passion. In both his lament for Anthony and his arranged marriage contract, Caesar's absorption of office into the private discourse of love and longing, shows the power of friendship over the power of sovereignty. Thus instead of a ruler 'holding sovereign sway over others, friendship proposes a sovereign self holding title to itself.'[45] The larger dramatic context for Caesar's fantasy of Anthony as two selves in one body, which is how early modern England imagined equal friends, and for his love for Anthony, lies in his own predicament. As an unmarried ruler whose only emotional tie is to his sister, Caesar's only other emotional link outside the realm of kinship is, as we have seen, to Anthony. The association of friend with an object of affection (or with kin) within the heroic context is not exclusive to the early modern period. David Halperin has shown that in the ancient cultures of the eastern Mediterranean and in the *Gilgamesh*, 'the erotics of male comradeship ... and representations of heroic friendship'[46] circulated freely and interchangeably. In both Wyatt and Shakespeare, death of a friend becomes an occasion for an intense articulation of tenderness and 'the climax of the friendship',[47] to which the living, hence unsatisfied, friend displaces his unspent passion. Thus in both Wyatt's elegy and in *Anthony and Cleopatra*, the condition of possibility for expressing male homoeroticism is death and absence. Looking at death and absence as evidence that enable the discourse of male–male passion, I would argue, helps us resolve the complex and ambiguous dichotomy between the familiar and the stranger as symbolical agents of homoerotic desire within different communities of men, and within the material history of early modern homosexuality in England.

This essay started with an example of what appears to have been – if it indeed existed – a community of men who loved other men, with, in other words, an example of a loosely self-identified male community. In the aggressively masculine culture of early modern England, however, such a community would have been only marginally different from any other homosocial societies of men formed in early modern England, such as, for example, the Inns of Court, monasteries, or courts. I have finished the essay by giving two examples of how death, friendship, and mourning bring out of men, more or less ambiguous, emotions. Emotions, including love, especially if they are articulated outside marriage, are not easily distinguishable in the early modern period. As Catherine Belsey has shown in her example of Shakespeare's play *The Merchant of Venice*, one never quite knows what love means in early modern Venice.[48] The historiography of queer masculinities has so far grappled with the question of whether when we speak of those masculinities we speak of history or heritage, practices or feelings, fantasies or records of cultural phenomena. In any of these cases, and regardless of approach, this historiography has asked the question of what is at stake in the constructions of early modern queer masculinity. There were many answers, but one seems to have prevailed, that whatever stance on the issue of early modern queer masculinity we take, the normative order seems to be subverted. Yet despite this argument, the early modern English state continued to thrive, even under King James I whose passions lay with men, and expand its empire, augment its power, wage wars, and colonize new lands and trading routes. It may not, then, be profitable to continue to argue about how the order was destabilized, even when it did police (and it did it rather lamely) transgressive desire. If we separate outlawed sodomy from homoerotic desire, for the two were exclusive in early modern England, it may not even be helpful for the historiography to continue to speak about transgression of the sort of desire that was not systematically and rigorously recognized as transgressive. From various literary and non-literary documents available in early modern England, it appears that once procreation was assured, sexuality and desire, except for acts of rape and buggery, did not matter much to the outside world. It might, then, be better to talk about the kind of desire between men that we now call homoerotic, or even queer, not within the context of power, violence, and domination, but within the context of emotions, love, and friendship where desire and passion are not clearly demarcated or reduced to one meaning. Looking at passions between men in this way, we may come closer to what the elusive early modern queer sexuality, and queer masculinity, against which every other subjectivity was measured, might have meant to early modern England.

Notes

1 Roland Barthes, *The Rustle of Language*, trans. Richard Howard (Berkeley and Los Angeles: U of California P, 1986) 291.

2 I am grateful to Natasha Hurley, Ian McAdam, and Alan Stewart for their advice while I was at work on this essay. I thank Michael O'Rourke for his generous comments on an earlier draft of this essay. The research for this essay was funded by The Social Sciences and Humanities Research Council of Canada, and by Saint Mary's University through a Faculty of Graduate Studies Research Grant.

3 Michel Foucault, *The History of Sexuality*, vol.1, trans. Robert Hurley (New York: Vintage Books, 1990) 37.

4 Robert Cleaver, *A godly form of hovseholde gournment: for the ordering of private families according to the directions of God* (London: by Thomas Creede, 1598) E7^{v}.

5 Tom Betteridge, ed., *Sodomy in Early Modern Europe* (Manchester and New York: Manchester UP, 2002) 1.

6 Alan Bray, *Homosexuality in Renaissance England* (New York: Columbia UP, 1995) 34.

7 Bray, *Homosexuality* 43.

8 B[enjamin] C[arrier], *PVRITANISME The Mother, SINNE THE DAUGHTER, or A Treatise, wherein is demonstrated from Twenty seuerall Doctrines, and Positions of Puritanisme; that the Fayth and Religion of the Puritans, doth forcibly induce its Professours to the perpetrating of Sinne, and doth warrant the committing of the same* (St. Omer: English College P, 1633) 4^{v}–5^{v}.

9 Jonathan Goldberg, *Sodometries: Renaissance Texts, Modern Sexualities* (Stanford: Stanford UP, 1992) 22–3.

10 Ian McCormick, ed., *Secret Sexualities: A Sourcebook of 17th and 18th Century Writing* (London and New York: Routledge, 1997) 10.

11 Constance Brown Kuriyama, *Christopher Marlowe: A Renaissance Life* (Ithaca and London: Cornell UP, 2002) 170.

12 Stephen Orgel, *The Authentic Shakespeare and Other Problems of the Early Modern Stage* (New York and London: Routledge, 2002) 211.

13 Orgel 219.

14 Mario DiGangi, 'How Queer Was the Renaissance?', *Love, Sex, Intimacy and Friendship between Men, 1550–1800*, eds Katherine O'Donnell and Michael O'Rourke (Houndsmills and New York: Palgrave Macmillan, 2003) 129.

15 DiGangi, 'How Queer Was the Renaissance?' 129.

16 Louise Fradenburg and Carla Freccero, ed. *Premodern Sexualities* (New York and London: Routledge, 1996) xviii.
17 Claude J. Summers, rev. of *Sodometries*, by Jonathan Goldberg, *Journal of Homosexuality* 29.1 (1995): 119–23.
18 Mario DiGangi, 'Marlowe, Queer Studies and Renaissance Homoeroticism', *Marlowe, History, and Sexuality: New Critical Essays on Christopher Marlowe*, ed. Paul Whitfield White (New York: AMS P, 1998) 196–7.
19 Ian McAdam, *The Irony of Identity: Self and Imagination in the Drama of Christopher Marlowe* (Newark: U of Delaware P and London: Associated UP, 1999) 202.
20 Alan Bray, 'Epilogue', Betteridge 165.
21 Thomas Coryate, *Coryats Crudities* (London: by W.S., 1611) Ff7^{v}–8^{r}.
22 Coryate Ff8^{r}.
23 Carrier E4^{v}.
24 Alan Stewart, *Close Readers: Humanism and Sodomy in Early Modern England* (Princeton: Princeton UP, 1997) xlv.
25 Stewart, *Close Readers* 149.
26 Stephen Guy-Bray, *Homoerotic Space: The Politics of Loss in Renaissance Literature* (Toronto, Buffalo, London: University of Toronto Press, 2002) 5.
27 Anon., *A new and large discourse of the Trauels of Sir Anthony Sherley Knight, by Sea, and ouer Land, to the Persian Empire* (London: by Valentine Simmes for Felix Norton, 1601) C1^{r}.
28 Barnabe Barnes, *The Devil's Charter*, ed. Nick de Somogyi (New York: Globe Education and Theatre Arts Books/Routledge, 1999).
29 Cameron McFarlane, *The Sodomite in Fiction and Satire, 1660–1750* (New York: Columbia UP, 1997) 27.
30 Stewart, *Close Readers* 3.
31 Stewart, *Close Readers* xlv.
32 Bruce Smith 'Premodern Sexualities', *PMLA* 115: 3 (2000): 318–29.
33 Cynthia B. Herrup, A House in Gross Disorder: Sex, Law, and the 2nd Earl of Castlehaven (New York and Oxford: Oxford UP, 1999) 2.
34 Herrup 58.
35 My take on Castlehaven's trial for a 'crime' that signifies political and social disorder contrasts Nicholas F. Radel's reading of the same case as being about 'the *discursive production* of certain kinds of same-sex desire and proscriptions that surround them' (myitalics). See Nicholas F. Radel, 'Can the Sodomite Speak? Sodomy, Satire, Desire, and the Castlehaven Case', *Love, Sex, Intimacy and Friendship Between Men*, ed. O'Donnell and O'Rourke, 151.
36 Thomas Beard, *The Theatre of Gods Iudgements. Tr. ovt of French, and argumented by more than three hundred Examples* (London: Adam Islip, 1597) S7^{v}.
37 Andrew Hadfield, *The English Renaissance, 1500–1620* (Oxford: Blackwell, 2001) 255.
38 Richard Halpern, *Shakespeare's Perfume: Sodomy and Sublimity in the Sonnets, Wilde, Freud, and Lacan* (Philadelphia: U of Pennsylvania P, 2002) 5.
39 R. A. Rebholz, ed. Sir Thomas Wyatt, *The Complete Poems* (Harmondsworth: Penguin, 1978) 11.
40 Eve Kosofsky Sedgwick, *Between Men: English Literature and Male Homosocial Desire* (New York: Columbia UP, 1985).

41 Laurie Shannon, *Sovereign Amity: Figures of Friendship in Shakespearean Contexts*. (Chicago and London: The University of Chicago Press, 2002) 224.
42 Alan Bray, 'Homosexuality and the Signs of Male Friendship in Elizabethan England', *History Workshop Journal* 29 (1990): 3.
43 Michael Neill, ed., William Shakespeare, *Anthony and Cleopatra* (Oxford and New York: Oxford UP, 1994) 300. I have adopted Michael Neill's spelling of Anthony with an 'h'.
44 Neill 300.
45 Shannon 235.
46 David M. Halperin, *One Hundred Years of Homosexuality: and Other Essays on Greek Love* (New York and London: Routledge, 1990) 85.
47 Halperin 79.
48 Catherine Belsey, 'Love in Venice', *Shakespeare and Sexuality*, ed. Catherine M. S. Alexander and Stanley Wells (Cambridge: Cambridge UP, 2001) 72–91.

Index